ASK YOURSELF sections prompt students to put themselves in situations discussed in the text. Questions from this feature can be used for journal writing or class discussions.

ASK YOURSELF

Can infants really learn at this age, or are they merely being cared for? Does it really make a difference how I interact with these children? Do I want to teach in an infant program? Why or why not?

In the creepe[...]
about who to tr[...]
dent in that ar[...]
taken a step ye[...]

Florine Fu[...]

I had two d[...]
cried all th[...]
with them[...]
beginnin[...]
other w[...]
wonde[...]
wonde[...]
them[...]

ASK YOURSELF

What would I do if I suspected that:
• A young child was locked in a closed car on a ninety-degree day?
• A mother refused to seek necessary medical treatment for a child?
• A parent failed to send a child to school regularly?
• A young child in your care had numerous bruises on his body?
• A parent slapped and spanked a child in the grocery store?

As you may recall from Chapter 5, child abuse has been an issue throughout history. Our ideas about what defines child abuse have also changed. Even today, there is not complete agreement among parents on what child abuse is. For example, cultural differences in child-rearing practices lead to different conclusions about spanking. Some parents advocate spanking children while others view it as abusive. When children are harmed, early childhood professionals are in a critical position to recognize and report suspected abuse. It is important to know that children have a great deal of potential for resilience. Between one-half and two-thirds of children from abusive families grow up to lead productive lives. One reason for their success is having caring relationships with adults. The most important help to a child who is suffering the effects of violence, including abuse, is an adult who cares. Having a caring adult in his life tells the child that he is worthwhile and valued. This *unconditional positive regard* is critical as it enables the child to overcome the effects of abuse. An early childhood teacher can be the caring adult who makes an important difference for an abused child. As a teacher, you cannot solve the child's problems, but you can help the child learn to cope.

Healing begins with relationships. Early childhood teachers are in a key position to have healing relationships with children. Teachers with an ethic

Ideal for assessing student performance and promoting problem solving, **CONSTRUCTIONS** features may ask students to interview a human service worker, go to a children's museum to gather information, or conduct a Piagetian task and reflect on the results.

CONSTRUCTIONS

1. Research

Invite a classmate to join you as you both observe the same two children for fifteen minutes. Make sure the children are engaged in an activity or experience rather than interacting with you. These children can be relatives or friends who are visiting or children in your care. Use the tips for observing that we have offered.

2. Analysis

Once you have completed the actual observations, write them up. Compare your observations with your classmate's. Compare them with your experience with children.

3. Research

Invite that same classmate to join you in observing a classroom of children for twenty minutes. Just as with the other observation, make sure the children are engaged in an activity or experience rather than interacting with you. Use the tips for observing that we have offered.

4. Writing

Once you have completed the actual observation, write it up. Compare your observation with your classmate's.

EARLY CHILDHOOD EDUCATION
A CONSTRUCTIVIST PERSPECTIVE

N. Amanda Branscombe
University of Wisconsin–Stout

Kathryn Castle
Oklahoma State University

Anne G. Dorsey
University of Cincinnati

Elaine Surbeck
Arizona State University

Janet B. Taylor
Auburn University

ATHENS

Houghton Mifflin Company   Boston   ·   New York

Senior Sponsoring Editor: Loretta Wolozin
Associate Editor: Lisa Mafrici
Senior Project Editor: Kathryn Dinovo
Senior Manufacturing Coordinator: Sally Culler
Senior Marketing Manager: Pamela J. Laskey

Cover design: Nina Wishnok/Dynamo Design
Cover images: Everard Williams Jr. (yellow blocks); Ted Horowitz/
The Stock Market (boys)

This book is dedicated to
Douglas B. Aichele
Gaines and George McMillan
Alex and Ally Grey Pendergraph
Camilla and Marion Surbeck
Seth and Ben Taylor and
Bob

Part opening photo credits: Page 1, © Frank Siteman/Stock Boston; page 89, © Elizabeth Crews; page 271, © Bob Daemmrich, Stock Boston; page 341, © Elizabeth Crews

Acknowledgments: Credits appear on page 492, which constitutes an extension of the copyright page.

Printed in the U.S.A.
Library of Congress Catalog Card Number: 99-72039
ISBN: 0-395-73308-1
123456789-QF-03 02 01 00 99

CONTENTS

PART 2   *CHILDREN*

CHAPTER 3   OBSERVING CHILDREN'S DEVELOPMENT IN EARLY CHILDHOOD EDUCATION   91

CHAPTER 10 MEETING TODAY'S EARLY
CHILDHOOD PROFESSIONALS   387

Early Childhood Education: A Constructivist Perspective is written for those considering early childhood education as a career and for those already preparing to work with young children, birth through age eight. The book's content is based on constructivist explanations of early childhood education and reflects a constructivist approach that actively engages the reader in dialogue about what it means to be an early childhood professional.

We, the authors, designed the book from a constructivist perspective to help *readers* answer key questions such as: How do we define the field of early childhood education? Who works with young children? Why become an early childhood professional? Why become a teacher who takes a constructivist approach?

AUDIENCE

The book is written for preservice students in early childhood education programs. It has potential for use in two-year as well as four-/five-year teacher education programs. It is a versatile book providing an overview of the field for use as a standalone text in an introductory course in early childhood education. In addition, it contains content and devices that would help connect it with other texts and courses in a program with more expanded course work. The text will give students sufficient background information to interact with children and teachers in early childhood programs in appropriate ways. It also provides a solid foundation upon which other courses in early childhood teacher preparation programs can build, such as subsequent courses in early childhood curriculum and program planning.

AUTHORS' BACKGROUND AND IDEAS ABOUT THE BOOK

The five authors of this book came together as professional colleagues having similar interests and beliefs about how children construct knowledge and experience in using a constructivist approach in working with college students as well as with children. Our professional relationships led us to collaborate on presentations on constructivist education and to write this book. We describe ourselves and how we came to write this book in our "Letter from the Authors" in Chapter 1. All of us thought that the book should be more than a book about constructivist early childhood education. It should be a constructivist book that would actively engage the reader in constructing knowledge of the early childhood field. We believe the book invites the reader into the text to become an active learner. The book uses several student character portraits to represent a variety of student types we have encountered in our own teaching. We think you may recognize parts of yourself or people you know in our student simulations.

All five of us entered this field at different stages in our lives and at various points including teaching and administering early childhood education programs. We also write from perspectives as classroom teachers, relatives, parents, and grandparents adding a dimension of thoughtfulness and experience not found in all texts. The five of us work at different universities throughout the country. Making time to get together to work on the book was a challenge. But we feel the effort was worth the result of a text that is balanced by our experiences working in five very different early childhood education programs. We feel our diverse experiences in the field help enrich the text by addressing numerous possibilities of career perspectives within the field. Our collaborative interactions in creating the book, including discussions and debates over content and processes, have strengthened the book far beyond what a single authored text might provide. The labor of the text represents numerous years of collaborative "scrambled eggs" writing, in which we would meet for extended periods of time at central locations, because we knew that face-to-face collaboration would strengthen our work and result in a high-quality text. We have shared equally in creating this book, from conception to completion, as represented by the alphabetical, nonhierarchical listing of authors.

UNIQUENESS OF THE BOOK

The book has unique features that make it interactive and interesting. We begin the book by introducing five students who are together in an introductory early childhood education course. The students appear in each chapter and express their own questions and ideas as they struggle to make sense of the early childhood field. Readers will readily identify with the students and their concerns and become co-learners along with the students as they move from university classroom to various early childhood settings. In every chapter, we prompt the reader's thinking about early childhood issues. We've included thought-provoking questions for readers to explore by gathering additional information to share with others, interviewing professionals in the field, reflecting on professional goals, and considering what's next for them in their own professional development. The final chapter helps readers chart their future in early childhood education.

The book provides a range of content one might expect in an introductory text, along with challenging "constructions" to help the reader make sense of the field, and very basic information, such as commonly endorsed safety and health practices necessary in early childhood education settings. The "Multiple Perspectives," explained below, present authentic voices from professionals in the field. All of this has been done within a constructivist framework. The content in the text is current and reflects our goals of providing a text sensitive to cultural diversity and issues impacting children, families, and early childhood education professionals today such as the issue of technology. We believe the text provides substantial resources for exploring possibilities in the early childhood education field.

CONTENT AND ORGANIZATION

The book is organized into four parts: in Part 1, _Community,_ readers become acquainted with other early childhood students and with information about the early childhood professional community and acquire strategies to begin to construct an understanding of the field; in Part 2, _Children,_ readers explore the world of children and families; in Part 3, _Settings,_ readers examine the variety of programs for children; and in Part 4, _Professionalism,_ readers meet today's early childhood professionals and are invited to consider their own development as professionals.

Throughout the text are guidelines coming from professional associations, such as the National Association for the Education of Young Children, representing best practices arrived at through consensus among early childhood professionals. In addition, we have introduced the idea of autonomy in both teaching and learning, as a means of considering multiple perspectives and making reasoned, professional decisions. The theme of autonomy and promoting autonomy in children threads through every chapter in the book.

Part 1, _Community,_ consists of two chapters. In Chapter 1, _Joining a Community of Learners,_ readers meet students Danielle, Amy, Eric, Tillie, and Zenah, who are taking an introductory class in early childhood education.

Readers journey with these students through the text as they learn about working with young children. Chapter 1 provides readers with a set of strategies for studying children and the field: questioning, interviewing, observing, analyzing and synthesizing through discussing, researching, reflecting, writing, and documenting through portfolios. Chapter 1 encourages readers to keep a journal and apply the set of strategies to their learning about working with young children. Chapter 2, *Getting Information and Support,* encourages students to explore multiple sources for getting information and presents current information about professional organizations, print materials, Web sites for children and professionals, and human resources that can be used to learn about the field and develop professionally. Readers who complete the activities in Chapter 2 will begin to develop a professional resource file and personal library that will support their inquiry throughout their early childhood education program.

Part 2, *Children,* has four chapters focused on the children found in early childhood programs, how they think and learn, how society's views of them and their early years have changed over time, and issues currently making an impact on children and families. Chapter 3, *Observing Children's Development in Early Childhood Education,* provides readers with examples of a variety of children in early childhood settings: infants, toddlers, preschoolers, kindergartners, and primary school students. The children are diverse in all aspects of development, culture, individual and special needs, and socioeconomic backgrounds. Readers will see how each early childhood education setting is adapted to meet the physical, social, cognitive, and individual needs of the children it serves. Chapter 4, *Children as Sense Makers,* introduces the readers to Piaget's explanation of the three kinds of knowledge and explores how children construct knowledge as they make sense of the world. Chapter 5, *Views of Children Over Time,* presents a historical perspective of the concept of childhood, how the concept developed over time, and how this knowledge is necessary to how we view childhood today. Chapter 6, *Exploring the Lives of Young Children and Families,* presents major issues facing children and families today, including violence and technology, and suggests ways early childhood professionals can help address these issues.

Part 3, *Settings,* consists of two chapters that focus on the world of early childhood professionals and programs. Chapter 7, *Professionals in Early Childhood Settings,* introduces readers to the many types of programs for young children, ways in which programs differ including how they are funded and administered, and presents the variety of career options open to early childhood professionals. Chapter 8, *Creating Curriculum in Field Experiences,* takes readers into the field sites of early childhood education students and focuses on how constructivist curriculum is created by children and teachers.

This chapter identifies the elements that are crucial to any quality constructivist curriculum.

In Part 4, *Professionalism,* readers meet past and present early childhood professionals and get an overview of the roles they have played or currently play in shaping the field. Readers are invited to enter the profession by engaging in reflection on personal and professional goals. Chapter 9, *Views of Professionals Over Time,* explores the historical ideas and figures impacting the field, including Vico, Jean Piaget, and Hermina Sinclair. Chapter 10, *Meeting Today's Early Childhood Professionals,* introduces readers to a variety of individuals in the field commenting on their lives working with young children and families. This chapter helps readers consider for themselves various careers available in the field. Chapter 11, *Personal Development as a Professional,* helps readers think through all the different possibilities for entering the early childhood education field. A variety of perspectives that exist about the field and the importance of autonomy in making decisions are highlighted. Also presented are the role of constructivist teachers and multiple views on what is good teaching. Readers are asked to take stock by reflecting on how far they have come since beginning the book, and then to look forward to the paths they might set in entering this multifaceted field of early childhood education.

USING CONSTRUCTIVIST LEARNING FEATURES TO CREATE KNOWLEDGE

We have included a variety of constructivist devices to encourage active involvement of readers in learning about early childhood education as well as reflecting on their own professional development. These constructivist learning features ask readers to observe, question, reflect, research, analyze, and make decisions. They are interspersed throughout each chapter, encouraging an inner, reflective dialogue as well as a dialogue with the authors, with others reading the book, and with those in the field. In writing the book, we feel we have maintained an active conversation with readers. Every constructivist feature has been developed with the reader's understanding in mind. We hope that these features will be used as tools by readers to make sense of early childhood education.

STUDENT DIALOGUE Our student characters, Danielle, Amy, Eric, Tillie, and Zenah, represent typical and diverse student concerns within the context of the early childhood education preparation program. They appear in every chapter so that readers will identify with them and enter into their dialogues. They wonder about children, curriculum, the roles of professionals, and their own roles as novices in the field. They are situated within contexts that might occur in programs such as yours. They are unabashedly honest and fresh in their questioning of the field and each other. They also represent a collaborative support group we hope students will find as they progress through their programs. Dr. K. is their guiding mentor who creates a safe, secure setting in which they can expose their ideas, question each other and their teacher, and develop deeper understandings of what it means to be an early childhood education professional.

ASK YOURSELF Each chapter includes several "Ask Yourself" prompts. Readers are asked to reflect on issues in the text in relation to their own experiences. The questions in this feature can prompt journal writing or class discussions whose purpose is to reflect on issues in early childhood education. The questions ask readers to put themselves in the situations being discussed in the text.

MULTIPLE PERSPECTIVES FROM THE FIELD AND COMMUNITY Voices from the community of real individuals working in the field such as teachers, child-care directors, and principals present an array of career options. These interviews were designed and conducted specifically for this book. The interview segments give honest opinions of early childhood education professionals and those who work with children in other ways as well. We have provided a diverse range of individuals and early childhood education career options in these perspectives from teachers to human service personnel to police officers. It is an opportunity for those in the community to speak directly to the readers and an opportunity for the readers to consider the diversity that exists in the field and community today.

CONSTRUCTIONS These features ask readers to apply what they are learning to various situations. Examples of constructions include **Analysis/Synthesis, Reflections, Interviews, Research, Collaboration,** and **Writing**. Readers may be asked to interview a human services worker, go into the field such as to a children's museum to gather information, or conduct a Piagetian task and reflect on the results. Constructions can be used by the instructor as a means of performance assessment. We think this form of assessment is preferable to testing because it represents the students' thinking expressed in real work.

END-OF-CHAPTER SUMMARIES Each chapter offers an end-of-chapter summary, which highlights the major concepts introduced in the chapter.

END-OF-CHAPTER CONSTRUCTIONS Constructions appear throughout each chapter and also at the end of each chapter. The end-of-chapter constructions help students consolidate their learning and form new connections between what they already know and what has been introduced in the chapter. They require application of what students have learned.

MARGIN NOTES Major points from the text are highlighted in the margin notes to encourage reader reflection on the key ideas.

RESOURCES An annotated list of resources, books, articles, children's literature, materials, Web sites, etc., is provided for each chapter. These resources have been carefully selected for students wanting to do additional reading or gathering of information for the development of their own resource files.

GLOSSARY Key terms that may not be familiar to readers are printed in boldface the first time they appear in the text, and presented in the glossary with concise definitions at the end of the book.

Instructor's Resource Manual

The Instructor's Resource Manual is designed with activities and materials useful to an instructor using the text. Materials include a sample syllabus, sample lesson plans, discussion prompts, ideas for using technology, and additional resources and information that will supplement each chapter of the text. Suggestions will be given for using the Constructions presented in the text as a means of assessing student knowledge.

Teacher Education Station Web Site

The Teacher Education Station Web site (go to **http://www.hmco.com/ college**, and then select "Education") provides additional pedagogic support and resources for beginning and experienced professionals in education, including the unique "Project-Based Learning Space." For more details on all that this Web site offers, see the site map on the back inside cover of this book.

ACKNOWLEDGMENTS

There are so many we would like to thank who have helped us in various ways on the completion of this book. We would first like to acknowledge the valued and respected mentors who stimulated our thinking about constructivism. Rheta DeVries, Eleanor Duckworth, George Forman, Catherine Twomey Fosnot, Constance Kamii, and Hermina Sinclair have been role models to us and have inspired us to rethink our ideas of constructivism along Piagetian lines, especially in their application to teacher education.

We would like to thank all those who interviewed with us and provided the diverse, authentic, and profound voices found throughout the text. Additionally, we would like to acknowledge interviewers Kathryn McNaughton and Angela Carr, and the assistance of Anna Henson, and Ashley Harvard for many arduous tasks. We appreciate the suggestions and feedback from the following text reviewers: Ginny Ann Buckner, Montgomery College; Susan B. Cruikshank, Fordham University; Cheryl Foster, Central Arizona College; Barbara Fredette, University of Pittsburgh; Carol Sue Marshall, University of Texas at Arlington; Peggy Tampkins, Oklahoma City Community College; and Toni Ungaretti, Johns Hopkins University. We would like to thank Pam Brown for preparing the Instructor's Resource Manual and Loretta Wolozin for her help and encouragement.

PART 1

Community

*T*HE TWO CHAPTERS *in Part 1 offer important strategies and resources for beginning your study of early childhood education from a constructivist viewpoint. Constructivist theory specifies that interaction with individuals who make up the community can play a unique role in your development as a teacher. These two chapters provide the tools to begin the process of interaction in the early childhood community. Chapter 1 will help you devise the strategies you need to know and study young children. Questioning, interviewing, observing, analyzing and synthesizing through discussing, researching, reflecting, writing, and documenting through portfolios are basic strategies that will help you elaborate, compare, adapt, and perhaps transform your current theories.*

Chapter 2 introduces different sources you can use to obtain information and support as a student and as a professional. It acquaints you with early childhood professional organizations, models, and sites so you can begin to connect with professionals in the field. Finally, the chapter discusses the importance of human sources of interaction and support, as you chart your unique route to becoming a professional.

1

Joining a Community
of Learners

We trust that you are reading this text because you are interested in becoming a teacher of young children and are eager to learn about this field. We are enthusiastic about your beginning, but before you start, you need preparation for the journey. This first how-to chapter is written to help you devise the strategies you need to know to study children and the early childhood education field. We selected the following strategies as processes that will help you elaborate, compare, adapt, and perhaps transform your current theories about the field of early childhood education. We also hope that as you use these strategies, you will have a better understanding of your teaching practices with young children. After reading this chapter, you should be able to discuss and use each of these strategies:

▶ Questioning
▶ Interviewing
▶ Observing
▶ Analyzing and synthesizing through discussing
▶ Researching
▶ Reflecting
▶ Writing
▶ Documenting through portfolios

People become interested in teaching young children through baby-sitting, coaching, lifeguarding, volunteering at schools and hospitals, as well as helping in school settings. *(© Bob Daemmrich/Stock Boston)*

INTRODUCTION

Danielle, Amy, Eric, Tillie, and Zenah are students who are taking their introductory class in early childhood education. We will follow them, some of their classmates, and their instructor, Dr. K., throughout this book. When they enter Dr. K.'s classroom for the first time, they find that the tables are filled with construction materials (Legos and Lazys).

DR. K.: Come on in. Join a group and begin working with the materials. You can talk, ask questions, and experiment with the materials—in other words, play! When you finish, I want you to have several questions formulated.

(Several students move to the building materials table and begin to pick up the materials.)

ERIC: This is a different way to start class. Isn't this course titled "Early Childhood Education"?

ZENAH: Yeah, that's what my schedule said! What do you think the teacher expects us to do with these things? I hope we don't have to do a paper in this class.

ERIC: Just think! She could make us write a paper on using these materials.

TILLIE: That's a sick joke. If we're just going to play around, I don't want to be in here. I don't know why we have to have a class on how to play with Legos. Everyone knows how to do that. I thought we were going to learn the important stuff, like how to teach children.

Through social interaction and questioning, we find out information and form communities of learners.

AMY: Well, I think playing is important. This looks like a great class to me. Is this your first class here? Have you worked in a school or child-care center before?

TILLIE: Yes! I've been a teacher's assistant for ten years. I do all the work, and the teacher gets all the pay. Everyone says so.

ERIC: I've worked with kids in summer camps, coached baseball a couple of years, and am a Big Brother.

AMY: Yeah! I'm a Big Sister. I've been doing that for about three years and just love it! In fact, I thought I'd seen you somewhere before. I bet it was at the last cookout.

ERIC: Probably was.

DANIELLE: My social club wants to do that as a project. I just don't know whether I have time to volunteer with all this schoolwork. Do you know anything about this instructor's grading? Did she say how many questions she wanted? Does she want us to write them down?

AMY: Look! I built a house. I wonder how I could add more windows.

ERIC: I made a space station. But how could I make it fly?

TILLIE: You call that a house? My son knows how to use Legos. I got him the largest set I could buy at the mall.

ZENAH: Looks as good as your tower.

AMY: Thanks, Zenah. You've been pretty quiet. Have you worked in the Big Brothers Big Sisters program or with children?

ZENAH: You could say that. I have two of my own. Right now, I'm working as a waitress to pay for my schooling, so I don't get to see them very much. One, my boy, is in Head Start, and my girl is in third grade. Dr. K., how many questions do you want us to have when we finish?

DR. K.: *(Moves to their table to observe their work.)* Looks as if you're busy working with the materials. What questions have come up as you've worked? Do you have questions about each other's constructions? What have you learned?

The students puzzled over the reasons that their instructor, Dr. K., avoided opening class with a lecture like most of their other instructors. They even questioned her knowledge and their need to work with materials. As they reflected on their conversation, they realized that through social interaction and questioning, they found out information about one another and formed the foundations for a community of learners. They reconsidered their views of Dr. K. and her choice of an opening for class.

You have already used most of the strategies (questioning, interviewing, observing, analyzing and synthesizing through discussing, researching, reflecting, writing, and documenting through portfolios). Now we are going to ask that you learn even more about them. As you read, be sure to remember that we are offering you our personal ways of defining and using these

ASK YOURSELF

How do you think a teacher should begin a class? Why?

Before you begin learning about each of the strategies, think about the following questions:

• What do I know about questioning, interviewing, researching, observing, reflecting, writing in journals, and documenting through portfolios?

• How have I used these strategies in the past?

• Where did I learn about them?

• How will these strategies help me with my career in early childhood?

• How will they help me get a job?

strategies. If you came to our classes, you'd find that each of us defines and uses the strategies for her own purposes and encourages her students to do the same. As you think about each strategy, don't be afraid to expand on what we say, as well as try other strategies so that they can become supports for your constructions and needs.

LETTER FROM THE AUTHORS

Hello, Readers,

We designed this book with you in mind. We know how excited you are about becoming early childhood educators. Each of us remembers when we entered our early childhood education courses. We weren't thinking about a textbook or a specific course; we just wanted to work with young children. At that time, we didn't realize that our careers in early childhood education would include many different jobs and take us all over the country.

One of us began her career by working with children in hospital settings before directing a child development center at a university, teaching at the university level, directing graduate programs, and working in a professional development school. Another of us directed a child-care center, worked in a campus child development center, and taught the Tohono O'odham tribal children, later returning to university teaching and administration. One of us taught in primary school and then began teaching at the university level. Another of us taught her first public school kindergarten class before she finished her four-year college degree and then taught kindergarten and first, second, and third grades in public schools in Colorado and South Carolina. One of us began her teaching career as a high school English teacher. At one time in her career, she taught in a psychiatric center. After many years of teaching, she began her career in early childhood education by teaching public school kindergarten and directing a university child development center. All of us have done postdoctoral study. All of us have used the inclusion model when working with special needs children. All of us have worked with children who have English as their second language. We thought about totaling the number of years of early childhood education experience we have had but decided you might be too shocked to continue reading the book!

Because we are from Alabama, Arizona, Ohio, Oklahoma, and Wisconsin, you might wonder how we formed our writing community. Our friendship really exemplifies the kinds of friendships that

---

Our teaching experiences are broad and varied.

A basic premise of constructivism is that each of us constructs our own knowledge through observing, questioning, documenting, and reflecting.

Autonomy means that a person has the ability to know what is morally just and intellectually true. That knowledge comes when you consider others' perspectives, coordinate your own views with theirs, and then make a reasoned and informed decision based on that coordination.

can occur when you join the early childhood community. First, we are all members and four of us are past presidents of the National Association of Early Childhood Teacher Educators (NAECTE). Our involvement in that organization allowed us to get to know each other through committee meetings, presenting together at professional meetings, and visiting during social events.

The second reason we formed this community is that we are all constructivists. **Constructivism** is a scientifically researched theory that explains learning as a physically and mentally active process. The theory takes into account experience, growth, and development over time (maturation), social interaction with peers, being puzzled about things that don't fit with what is already known (disequilibration), and autonomy (moral and intellectual). A basic premise of constructivism is that each of us constructs our own knowledge through observing, questioning, documenting, and reflecting. Much of what we learn is the result of the relationships we create among objects, experiences, and ideas over time. Another basic premise is that autonomy is an aim of education. To a constructivist, **autonomy** means that a person has the ability to know what is morally just and intellectually true. Autonomy is evident when you consider others' perspectives, coordinate your own views with theirs, and then make a reasoned and informed decision based on that coordination. This definition may surprise you, as you may have thought autonomy was independence. As you read Chapters 3, 4, and 11, you'll have the opportunity to continue to shape your definition of autonomy.

Most of your past experiences with teaching and learning have focused on acquiring information from an expert source, memorizing it, and then offering it to others. You are probably wondering how constructivism fits into this model. It doesn't! We now know that each person *constructs knowledge* rather than merely accepting information that someone else has transferred to him or her. At this point, you may be totally confused. Don't worry; as you read, reflect, talk, write, and even represent your ideas graphically, you'll begin to understand how to interact with ideas about knowing rather than memorizing facts.

Each of us became a constructivist at a different point in her career. Three of us graduated from educational programs that advocated behaviorism. Over time and through experience, we began to question that theory. As we questioned, we began to read about Jean Piaget's work. One of us was an intuitive constructivist who came to the theory through Lev Vygotsky's theory and John Dewey's work. Another one's schooling supported Dewey's approach. All of us agree that the more we worked with children and studied Piaget, the more what we knew from intuition and experience matched what he was finding in his research.

You're probably thinking, who is this Piaget? He was a Swiss researcher and epistemologist who studied about knowledge by studying his own children. He got so interested in what his children did and thought that he expanded his work to include hundreds of children. Many researchers, psychologists, and linguists became interested in Piaget's work and went to Geneva, Switzerland, to study with him. You'll read more about Piaget's work in other chapters in the text.

As you read, you may think we are biased about our ways of thinking about early childhood education. We are. We have dealt with and continue to deal with hard issues within our experiences with children. Those experiences have caused us to shape our thinking so that we feel that we know some things about young children and the field of early childhood education that cause our bias. We are very sensitive to the issues that you may encounter as students. Because of this, we wanted to write a book that might give you some tools for knowing about young children for yourselves.

We hope this book will be different from others you have read. You will have conversations with us like the one we are having now, opportunities to interact with others in the field, and opportunities to construct information that you need as an early childhood educator. Because of the technology explosion that has allowed all of us to have so much knowledge at our fingertips, we hope to offer you tools for knowing, rather than the usual information you find in a textbook.

Enough about us! Now let's focus on you and your role in joining a community of early childhood students. We want you to enter into a contract with us. As authors, our contract with you is to provide you with relevant information about the early childhood profession and to stimulate your thinking about children. We hope to encourage you to examine your own beliefs and knowledge and that of others whose work will impact your current and future thinking and behavior. As you challenge yourself and one another, your thinking will change. We want you to challenge, question, and have doubts. Healthy skepticism, within limits, leads to evaluation of information rather than blind acceptance. Yes, it's a lot of work. But as you begin that work, you are beginning your goal of becoming a professional early childhood educator.

Now we want to invite you to join us in a class very much like your class. The students in this class are composites of students we have taught. Their attitudes may be similar to yours. You may feel the same way as you read this book's chapters and try to make sense of the field of early childhood education. You may wonder how you will construct your own answers regarding your contribution to early childhood education.

The goal of this chapter is to explain some of the procedures you might find helpful as you begin to construct theories about who you are and hope to become as an early childhood professional.

—*The Authors*

QUESTIONING AS A STRATEGY

Questioning is a spontaneous search for information that allows us a way to build understandings and figure out causes, origins, or rules.

Danielle, Amy, Eric, Tillie, and Zenah's instructor asked them to begin their study of early childhood education by acting on materials and questioning. Dr. K. views **questioning** as a spontaneous search for information (Gruber & Voneche, 1995, p. 80), a way to build understanding and figure out causes, origins, or rules. She knows that questions can be both social and introspective. The students' conversations had both kinds of questions. For example, when Eric asked how he could make his object fly, his question was introspective, while Amy's question about Zenah's experience was more social in nature. Also, this vignette demonstrates how people ask questions and then either carefully listen to others' answers or ignore those answers because they think they already know more than the person they asked.

As you read this textbook, we hope that you will create your own questions about the textbook's information that require explanations or justifications. For example, you may want to know how Eric built his space station so that it balanced on a stand. In addition, you may learn a new way to use questions to learn about certain rules that govern your work with children or to evaluate others' work with children. You may even find yourself asking questions about the origin of an issue in early childhood or a teaching approach. Questioning will help you gather information, construct knowledge, and build theories about your own learning and your own teaching approaches, as well as help you to study children. The **simultaneity** of learning to ask questions of your own knowing and of children's knowing is the most exciting part of the questioning process. How and why

Simultaneity is part of the questioning process.

Questioning helps construct knowledge about how young children make sense of their worlds.
(© Ellen Senisi/The Image Works)

ASK YOURSELF

Now that I have thought about using questions to examine my own thinking, how can I use questions to learn about children? Will I ever ask the children questions about subject matter? Did my favorite teachers use questions to help them find out what they knew about the teaching/learning process and how I learned?

· ·

you choose your questions and where you choose to focus those questions (for example, your knowing or the children's knowing) will relate to how they can function for you.

Questioning is most important in learning about young children and how they learn. It helps teachers focus their attention on classroom management, room arrangement, and discipline, as well as instructional objectives and the students' learning. This kind of questioning helps you to construct theories about children's learning and about what knowledge is.

When you question children to understand their thinking, try to tease as much information out of a question as you can. Don't ignore questions such as "How high up does the sky go?" Rather get as much information as possible from such questions. Don't get frightened by the children's "mistakes" and feel a need to correct them. Don't get caught up in the scientific answers you learned in school. Recognize that such questions from young children deal with the physical world and the human species—both of which you are studying. Use follow-up probing questions when you get such questions from children.

Follow-up questions clarify and extend the information you get from your initial question. Follow-up questions come after the children's responses to the interviewer's question or explanation of a task. They are designed to test or check the learners' answers with how logical their explanations and thinking are and how those explanations fit with their theories. The very nature of a follow-up question provokes learners to revisit the reasoning behind their explanations. Follow-up questions also are designed to see whether learners change when questioned or hold to their reasoning and original theories.

CONSTRUCTIONS

1. Questions

We want you to try your hand at questions. As you listen to your classmates talk about their ideas and experiences, write down questions they might ask. Then think of questions you might ask. Think about using a difficult question. How would it be different from a simple question—a yes or no question? Think about using questions to find out what children know. Notice that as you engage in this "thinking about" process, you are constantly asking questions.

2. Analysis

Jot down the questions as you think about doing this construction. Try classifying them. Did you ask more questions related to explanation and information or more related to causes and origins? How might your questions change as you actually interview a child?

3. Journal Entry

As you reflect on your written questions, begin a dialogue with your questions and yourself (see Chapter 2 for a more complete discussion of dialogue with self). This dialogue may take you to an even deeper level of knowing than you had earlier. It may generate a new set of questions.

4. Practice

Now that you have thought about questions and questioning children, try using them with classmates and their awareness of your knowing or their own knowing. Don't forget those follow-up questions. You may even have a series of questions. The questions may take the form of an interview.

INTERVIEWING AS A STRATEGY

One purpose of an interview is to gather information about someone's thinking, beliefs, and preferences on a specific topic.

Although we may not realize it, when we read newspaper and magazine articles, watch television talk shows and newscasts, or use the Internet, we are reading or hearing information from interviews. An **interview** is a series of questions. Interviews can be formal, like the ones Piaget and his colleagues used to probe children's ways of thinking, or informal, like the ones you've used in other courses. The primary purpose of an interview is for you to gather information about someone's thinking, beliefs, ideas, and preferences on a specific topic. It is not a time or place for you to express your views, to gossip, or to argue with the other person.

Let's join Dr. K. and her students as they try one of Dr. K.'s interview assignments. The assignment is to learn what experiences the class members have had in early childhood education.

DANIELLE: What does the instructor want us to do?

TILLIE: Interview each other. I guess we just talk to each other.

ZENAH: No, I think there's more to an interview than that. Remember she said that interviews aren't just times to gossip, argue, or express opinions. She also mentioned that Piaget used formal interviews to learn about children's reasoning. I studied some of his ideas in my CDA [Child Development Associate] training.

AMY: I was on my high school newspaper staff and did lots of interviews. Do you think she wants us to write the questions and answers? We also had to have forms signed that gave us permission to print the interview. It protected the person's right to privacy and reminded us of our responsibility to be truthful, accurate, and fair.

ERIC: Maybe. I think she wants us to decide what we need to ask and to do to gather information about each of our experiences with early childhood education.

TILLIE: I just don't understand her. We need to learn about doing bulletin boards and making materials for our classrooms. What good does it do us to spend all of this time getting to know each other?

DANIELLE: Yeah! We'll be together in this course, and that's it.

ERIC: I don't think the purpose of learning how to interview is having us become "buds."

ZENAH: I agree with Eric. She just wants us to use each other as we think about interviews and the interviewing process.

AMY: Yeah! First we'll practice, and then we'll interview children or early childhood professionals. Back to the questions—do we want to decide on a set of questions or just have each pair ask whatever?

ERIC: I say we brainstorm a group of questions.

TILLIE: Well, we don't have time to brainstorm, 'cause I have to be at my son's ball game at five. Let's just do this as a group. It'll be faster.
(The students continue their discussion for a few more minutes before agreeing to Tillie's idea of the entire group interviewing each member. Let's listen to parts of their interviews.)

TILLIE: I'll go first.

ERIC: No, I'd like to ask Zenah to be first. *(Zenah gives an affirmative nod of her head. Eric continues.)* Tell me about your experiences in the field of early childhood education.

ASK YOURSELF

As you think about interviewing, ask yourself how well you question others. Do you know how to ask probing questions? Do you know how to use culturally sensitive questions? How have you used questions in an interview?

ZENAH: You all know I'm a single mother. When my little girl, Erika, started going to Head Start, the teacher asked me to volunteer to help at the center. At first I said no. Then I missed Erika so much that I told the teacher I'd help once a week. One day the director observed me working with the children during activity centers' time and told me I should consider becoming a teacher.

AMY: What did you think of her comment?

ZENAH: She had no way of knowing it, but that was my dream. When I was a little girl, I went to first grade and had Ms. Smith for my teacher. She wore the prettiest clothes I'd ever seen and smelled like orange blossoms. Each day she'd read to us. My favorite book was *A Snowy Day*. I wanted to be just like her. I'd stay after school to help her get ready for the next day. I even went back and helped her after I finished first grade. She called me her teacher's helper! When the director said what she did to me, I decided it was time to make my dream a reality. I started working with the Head Start center every spare minute I had.

AMY: I thought you had a younger child. How did you work and take care of him?

ZENAH: When I had my little boy, Cory, I stopped working for a few months. When I went back, I asked the director if I could start working as a teacher. She told me about CDA and helped me get started. When I finished the CDA program, I decided to get a college degree. I started working as a waitress and saved enough money to enroll in my classes.

DANIELLE: Wow, Zenah, that's quite a story. Who goes next?

ERIC: Wait! Don't we want to have follow-up questions?

DANIELLE: Yeah.

TILLIE: No we don't. Not today. *(Looks at her watch.)* Let's ask each person one question and then ask more later if the instructor makes us.

DANIELLE: But I just have one tiny question to ask Zenah!

ZENAH: Okay, but make it short, because I have to be at work at five to set up tables for tonight.

DANIELLE: What's a CDA program?

ZENAH: Glad you asked. I'm really proud of my CDA certificate. It's the Child Development Associate program, which offers an educational course of study that leads to a competency-based early childhood credential. Now, why don't we interview you, Danielle?

ERIC: That was a "get to work by five o'clock" answer if I ever heard one. Let's hope you tell her a little more about the CDA credential when you aren't in a hurry or Dr. K. explains it when she talks about professionalism.

DANIELLE: I'd rather tell you about my life than learn all about CDA. I just wanted to know what those letters meant. Now, what do you want to know about me?

ZENAH: Tell us how you became interested in early childhood education.

DANIELLE: Daddy wanted me to go into business, so at first I majored in public relations. You see, he has a public relations firm and wants me to come work with him. After I failed economics and chemistry the second time, he got mad. He told me that if I failed another course, he wouldn't pay for my clothes or that new CD player I wanted. So I told him I hated business.

TILLIE: What did you do then?

DANIELLE: I transferred to early childhood education. I love little kids. I used to work with the four-year-olds in Bible camp every summer. Mama was glad I changed to education because she used to be a teacher before Daddy got rich. She says once you have that certificate, you can always teach. So here I am. Any questions?

TILLIE: Next?

ERIC: Okay, Tillie. Tell us about yourself. We all know you've been a teacher's assistant and have a family. How did you get interested in early childhood education?

TILLIE: Well, you might as well know. The social workers took me and my brothers and sisters away from my mama and daddy when I was two 'cause they'd beat me if I cried. My oldest brother blamed me. He said the neighbors reported Mama and Daddy one night 'cause they were both drunk and yelling. They scared me, so I started screaming and wouldn't stop. The police came about two in the morning and took us to a foster home for the night. Then the social workers investigated and decided we would be better off living in foster care.

At first we'd live in foster care and then back with Mama and Daddy, and then in another foster home and then back with Mama. Like, my first foster home, the woman beat me and tied me in the bed to make me quit talking so much. *(Several students snicker, and Tillie blushes. Eric realizes she's hurt and responds.)*

ERIC: Tillie, we aren't snickering at your story. We're just thinking about the fact that you're still very talkative!

TILLIE: That's true! Couldn't even shut me up when they tied me in the bed. Back to my story. My oldest sister kept trying to get us all together in one home. She finally made it happen when I was in third grade.

AMY: Says something about how effective corporal punishment is, doesn't it?

TILLIE: I lived with that family until I was fifteen, when I dropped out of school. For about two years I ran around, drank beer, went from one job to another. Got myself pregnant. When the baby came, I didn't have anywhere to go. My oldest sister took me and the baby in. She started raising it just like it was her own. She made sure I got my GED [general equivalency diploma] and helped me get a job at the mall. That's when I met my husband, Ray. We got married, bought a double-wide trailer, had another baby, and settled down for what I thought was the rest of our lives. But Ray's a skirt chaser. He comes around some. He don't help me, but he does pay for the children's school clothes.

My sister was a school bus driver and knew the person in charge of personnel at the school board office. She told me to apply for a teaching assistant's job because I'd have more time with the children. I did, and I got the job. It's an okay job. Like I told you. I do all the work, so I decided to come over here and get a degree so I can get paid for what I do. I've said all I'm going to say about me! I don't care what that instructor tells us to do!

ZENAH: This must have been hard for you to tell us.

TILLIE: Well, life ain't easy!

DANIELLE: Let's change the question. Amy, tell us what you plan to do when you finish this program.

ERIC: Danielle, we agreed we would ask everyone the same question. Why change now?

DANIELLE: I just wanted to change the subject.

ZENAH: Eric, we agreed this would be one of the questions, so we can ask it now and use the other later in the interviews.

AMY: That's okay with me if you agree. *(Everyone agrees.)* Like I said the other day, I've been a Big Sister for the last three years. Before that I baby-sat, taught junior lifesaving and swimming at the recreation center pool, taught ballet, and even worked as a live-in baby sitter last summer at the beach.

DANIELLE: Oh, you were an au pair!

AMY: Yes, and I loved it.

TILLIE: You can come live with me and help raise my kids.

AMY: Well, it doesn't work exactly like that. But back to what I want to do in early childhood education. I haven't worked in a child-care setting, so I hope to do that this summer. I've contacted a director of a corporate child-care center. She needs a person who can cover for her employees when they take their vacations.

After I finish the program, I plan to apply for a yearlong internship so I can teach in New Zealand. I've always wanted to live in another country and can't afford to do it on my own. If I had some financial assistance, I could have more education and an experience outside the United States. Once I finish that year, I plan to teach kindergarten for a couple of years and then begin working on my master's degree.

TILLIE: You got it all figured out. But it ain't that simple, is it Zenah?

ZENAH: Amy's different. We're all different, so I just hope it works out for you. Okay, Eric! You're next. Tell us what you plan to do with your career in early childhood education.

TILLIE: And make it short!

ERIC: Teach and then become a principal.

DANIELLE: That's short!

As you listened to the students' interviews, you no doubt noted that they used questions. They tried to ask open-ended questions that prompted the interviewee to answer in depth. They also used follow-up questions to prompt the interviewee to provide more information.

In this textbook, we are including many interviews from professionals in the field of early childhood—people who work with children and children themselves. In the accompanying box, a student interviews an instructor in the field of early childhood education. Not only does it serve as a model for interviewing, but it also introduces us to what teaching means to one person.

MULTIPLE PERSPECTIVES

From the Field

Interview with Willie Mae Parks, instructor, at the Alabama A&M Child Development Resource Center in Huntsville, Alabama.

INTERVIEWER: What age children do you work with?

WILLIE MAE: Four-year-olds

INTERVIEWER: How did you get into this field?

WILLIE MAE: My B.S. degree was in home economics, and from there my first job was working with fifth-graders—and from fifth grade, I applied for kindergarten. At the time, there was a federally funded early intervention program (EIP) working with kindergarten, so I started working with kindergarten. I worked with kindergarten down to four-year-olds up to this present time.

INTERVIEWER: What is your day like?

WILLIE MAE: Well, it is a busy day. Well, once I get to school, I prepare for the day. Then the children start coming in, and they get involved with activities they would like to work with at the time. We have all kinds of activities planned for the children, fun activities. We are just busy and working all day until time to go home.

INTERVIEWER: What do you look forward to in your work?

WILLIE MAE: Well, working with the children, seeing how I can make a child smile or feel good about himself or make a child just look so happy.

INTERVIEWER: What is the hard part? What do you dread?

WILLIE MAE: I dread not having enough time to do what I need to do. I work from the time I get here to the time I leave. Yet I feel like I haven't done all of the things I need to do. Every day, every week, every month I get to thinking of things—ooooh if I had more time—things I could do with the children.

INTERVIEWER: Have you ever thought of getting out of teaching?

WILLIE MAE: No, I've been working at A&M twenty-two years. When I see parents of children that I have had, they say, "You cannot retire until you get my grandchild." But I really enjoy working with children. I plan on retiring in seven years. But after retiring, I yet plan on doing volunteer service work with children, because I really enjoy working with children.

INTERVIEWER: Of the children you've worked with, who was the most perplexing and why?

WILLIE MAE: I can recall this little boy. He was from another country, and when he came to me, he could not talk, and he had other problems with resting and really following through other activities. But as the year progressed and with me working with him, giving him all of this loving and caring and confidence that he can do things and just individual attention, he started talking and he started resting, but I had to be right there with him. Once he started taking a nap, after that time then I gradually moved from him during naptime. He was able to rest on his cot by himself without Mrs. Parks being there near him. So, to me, it made him feel comfortable being in the center by himself—resting on the cot, not having a teacher near him. He was just my shadow. He could not stand for me to be out of his sight. He was such a sweet little boy. I am just so proud of the child. . . . I just had to give them that individual attention, that loving and hugging. I just had to be a mom—a school mom. It is amazing to see how they just mature and just blossom out and how they learn to just—I don't know what other words to say. It's amazing really. And sometimes I wonder, What did I do? I use so many techniques when working with children, and a lot of times I go home and pray about it, you know? Because it's just like when working with children and if a child had a problem, they are just like my child. That is the way I feel. They are like my child, and I want to do all I can to help that child—so when that child grows up, he can face life without all these problems, you know? . . . And so I pray about it, and then I just use all kinds of techniques. And so I don't know what works because I use so many techniques. But, anyway, something worked, and that's my reward really. When I see them just learn and do so well and be so happy and smiling.

INTERVIEWER: That was the next question. I think you answered it. Describe the greatest success you've experienced! Your success is in seeing them grow up?

Teachers' understanding of children's affective needs are used each day. (© *Elizabeth Crews*)

WILLIE MAE: That's right. Grow up and mature and develop and feel good about themselves.

INTERVIEWER: What was the most challenging day?

WILLIE MAE: Really I guess when I had the fifth grade. I had more boys, and I had *some* boys in this class. . . . This was my first experience with teaching. And I had these boys, and I was very young at the time, and every day I went home my head would be killing me. I said, "I'm not sure this is what I want to do!" They really gave me a hard time, and the more I stayed on and talked with different ones, things got better. And once I got to the younger group, it really got better. I said, "This is where I need to be, with the young!" I've been working with the young group twenty-five years.

INTERVIEWER: If you could change your job, what would you do?

WILLIE MAE: Well, I don't know really. I really don't know, unless I could find some way of doing the things I would like to do that I don't have time at school to do—some way to fit it into my day schedule.

INTERVIEWER: What would you suggest to a beginner in the field?

WILLIE MAE: First, if you are going to work with children, you are going to have to have that love. You have to have patience. You have to have understanding. And also, working with children, you have to look at that child as an individual, because all children are different. So you have to be able to adjust to the attitude and the personality of each child. You have to adjust your personality, your way of working with children, by looking at each individual child. Because where with one child you might need to give more love, you are going to have to do that. Whereas another child might not need as much love but something else. . . . So you are going to just have to adjust your schedule so you can give each child what they might need. And really sometimes you can give a child what he might need in a group. Because I have had a child with the need of more attention, and the way I do this is in a group situation. When that child is sitting nicely, I will praise that child. I'll reward that child by a hug or "I'm so proud of you" or "I like the way you are doing so and so; you can be my helper." And see they like that, and that will really help change their behavior. A lot of time people give tangible rewards, I give *intangible* ones. And even if they . . . also too I use my tone of voice. When I talk to the boys and girls, even when they do something that I don't like, I use a low tone and get their attention. Because the whole class just be jumping up and down. I can just talk very quietly. And I'll keep my voice down real low. And even if they are all being loud at something and I see one child, I say, "Oh, boys and girls, I like the way so-and-so is using their voice." Right then, I don't reward the children. I give them time to get themselves in control, and then I'll say, "Oh, so-and-so is doing whatever.". . . Sometimes I give them tangible words, and then sometimes I just give them a hug. And I will go over. Like now I have a child. She is hyper! And whenever I see her sitting or paying attention doing her work, I just go over and whisper in her ear, "I'm proud of you." She'll look at me and smile. "Are you going to tell my mama I been good?" . . . And I say, "Yes!" Just things like that, you know.

● ●

> Interviews serve as a form of written conversation that helps construct knowledge.

Interviews are talk written down—instant wording without an instant replay. They don't have the person's inflections, emphases, gestures, or facial expressions to help the reader have a clear understanding of what the interviewee meant. However, they serve as a form of written conversation or social interaction with you and the interviewer that helps you construct knowledge. You may feel that you know Willie Mae Parks because you read an interview another student had with her. You learned about her work, her successes, and her philosophy of teaching.

Interviewing is not easy. Many times people think they know how to interview but find themselves in trouble because of the kinds of questions they are asking, their lack of awareness that interviews are interactive, or their lack of preparation for the interview. They also ignore the kinds of words, the lengths of sentences, the transitions, the dialect, and the repetition of words that the interviewee uses to help the listener make meaning. The guidelines in the accompanying box should help you when you conduct your interviews.

TIPS FOR INTERVIEWING

▸ Decide on the kinds of information you need from the interview.

▸ Read so that you have some content knowledge about the information you hope to discuss in an interview. For example, if you plan to interview a family court judge, read about the role and responsibilities of such a judge in relation to early childhood professionals.

▸ Decide on the major questions you can use to guide you to that information and how you'll record that information. For example, you might use a note pad along with either an audio or video recorder.

▸ Decide on people (both in the field of early childhood education and in other fields) who could help you obtain information.

▸ Practice doing an audiotaped or videotaped interview with a classmate or friend.

▸ Revise your questions.

▸ Set up an interview with someone. Be sure to have an agreed-upon time and place for the interview.

▸ Obtain or design a form that serves as an agreement between you and the interviewee that gives you permission to tape, write, print, and/or publish the interview.

▸ When you set up the interview, explain how you plan to use the information, why you are asking for a signed agreement giving you permission to write up the interview, and approximately how much time you will need.

▸ Be on time for the interview and have all the necessary equipment (extra batteries for the tape recorder) and forms (a release form).

▸ During the interview, be sure that you are polite and to the point. Don't waste time!

▸ Avoid questions that can be answered with a yes or no.

▸ Use follow-up questions as well as those you planned to ask.

▸ Once you have finished the interview, thank the person for his or her time. Before you leave the person, make sure you have the agreement that gives you permission to print the interview and protects the interviewee. Follow up with a written thank-you note.

▸ As quickly as possible, transcribe the tape so that your notes, your memory, and the taped conversation are fresh.

CONSTRUCTIONS

1. Journal Entry

Now that you have read about Willie Mae Parks, write what you think her philosophy of teaching is. Reflect on ways her philosophy differs from yours. Have you had any experiences with young children? Write how those are similar to or different from Mrs. Parks's experiences.

2. Interview

Try to interview a classmate or family member about his or her early schooling. Design your questions and select the equipment you'll use to record the interview. Set a date, time, and location for the interview. After you complete the interview, write a thank-you note and transcribe the interview. Once you have completed the interview, talk with a classmate about the process.

OBSERVING AS A STRATEGY

As we observe, we must think about what we are seeing and raise questions.

Observing may be one of the most important strategies for constructing knowledge. Chaille and Britain (1997) point out that **observation** is the basis for everything the teacher does. Mere looking is not enough. Unless you think about what you are seeing (reflect on it) and raise questions about what you saw, you will make erroneous hypotheses based only on perception. Does this sound a little paradoxical? Well, it is. However, Piaget warned us that perception, or just looking, is unreliable by itself. He noted that direct observation is not how we learn about children's knowing. To him, we learn through our own internal, mental operations that we "carry out on our observations, and these operations themselves develop into a life history" (Gruber & Voneche, 1995, p. 80).

We recognize the importance of observations but ask you to consider Piaget's point about perception. What we want you to do when you observe is more than just looking. We hope that you will coordinate your own perspective with what you are seeing. This process may result in a reorganization of your thoughts.

Dr. K. gave her class an assignment requiring that they observe in a classroom for twenty minutes. Let's join two of them as they begin their observations.

TILLIE: Where should we stand?

ERIC: The teacher didn't say. He just said stand so that we're not in the way.

TILLIE: I wonder what the others are doing.

ERIC: We're supposed to observe, not talk. Let's pick a center and observe the children who come to that one activity center.

TILLIE: What if they don't come to that center?

ERIC: Do you have a better idea?

TILLIE: No, let's stand here, where this rope and ball are hanging from the ceiling.

ERIC: Look, here comes a little girl.

(Eric and Tillie prepare to observe and take notes. Because the classroom teacher has prepared the children for visitors, the little girl, whose name is Shirley, ignores Eric and Tillie. She reaches for the rope and begins to swing the ball at a stack of blocks. The ball hits the blocks and swings back toward her, and she catches it. She then restacks the blocks, steps back to the same spot, grabs the rope, moves her hand to a different place on the rope, and releases it. Eric and Tillie watch. Finally another child joins her and watches her game.)

SHIRLEY: Scott, you want to swing my rope at the blocks?

SCOTT: Sure. *(Reaches for the rope and pulls it back, ready for the release.)*

SHIRLEY: You gotta watch out for that rope. It's got a curve in it.

SCOTT: No it hasn't!

SHIRLEY: Yes it do.

SCOTT: *(Looks at the rope he has pulled taut.)* No it don't!

SHIRLEY: Yes, it do! Turn it loose and you'll see.

(Scott releases the rope. Because of his location in relation to the blocks, the rope and ball appear to curve toward the blocks. Scott stares.)

SHIRLEY: Told you so. You see'd it curve, didn't you?

SCOTT: *(Inspects the rope and nods his head in agreement.)* That doesn't make sense. The rope is straight.

SHIRLEY: It's magic. The rope's magic. See, it won't do it every time. It's just when I put the spell on it. *(Moves to a different location and releases the rope, which swings in what appears to be a straight line.)*

SCOTT: Look at that.

(They continue swinging the rope and restacking the blocks.)

(Tillie leans over to Eric and whispers.)

TILLIE: Our twenty minutes are up. Let's go.

ERIC: Okay. *(Reluctantly leaves as he is studying the events.)*

TILLIE: That rope did look like it had a curve in it.

ERIC: Sure it curved, but there was no curve in the actual rope.

TILLIE: I know that! When's the teacher going to correct them?

ERIC: I doubt he is.

TILLIE: Well, that's wrong! Those kids are learning the wrong information. Besides, they didn't say much. What were we supposed to write down?

ERIC: I wrote down what I saw and heard.

TILLIE: Okay. Here's mine.

ERIC: A little short!

TILLIE: Well, Dr. K. told me to write what I saw. I know you wrote a book. Showoff!

ERIC: Let's meet tomorrow before class and study each other's written observations.

(Eric and Tillie meet for the discussion of their written observations. Tillie looks at his.)

TILLIE: Let's see. You dated your observation and gave the time. You told what center we were using for the observation and how it looked.

ERIC: So did you. I like this notebook you are using for your observations.

TILLIE: Got it at the mall.

ERIC: I didn't notice that the teacher came over.

TILLIE: Sure. He came right after Shirley knocked down the first block structure and asked her to move around, shorten the rope, change the way she stacked the blocks.

ERIC: Good job! Better go on into class. It's time.

(The instructor begins class. She looks at the papers and begins inviting the students to analyze and synthesize their observations.)

Myriad formal and informal methods or approaches can be used for observations. To get as many different perspectives from your observations as possible, you may use checklists, videotapes, audiotapes, time-sampling, and anecdotal notes, to name only a few methods. Before you choose the kinds of observational instruments you might use, you will need to think about what you want to learn from your observation and when and how to record the information that you see and hear. After you decide that, you will want to think about the ways you'll organize the information in your observations. Finally, you'll want to follow Piaget's recommendation and go beyond the mere observation. You have to connect it to something, combine it with something. Remember, an observation in isolation is mere perception and can cause you to have erroneous thinking.

TIPS FOR OBSERVING

- Decide on the purpose of your observation.
- Decide on what you will observe.
- Decide whether you will try to do cycles of observations of individuals or one observation of either a group or an individual.
- Decide what times each day or week you plan to observe. Select ways to record your observations (checklists, photographs, field notes, audiotapes, videotapes, mailing labels, clipboard, sample of children's work, and so on).
- Date (day of week, month and specific date, and time of day) and label each observation in a notebook (often called a field note notebook).
- On a regular basis, such as every fifteen minutes, record exactly what you see and hear. You must decide how often your observations will occur. This decision should be based on your needs and purposes of the observations. If you have several observations, you may want to organize those observations and store them in file folders, on computer disks (with backup floppy disks), or in plastic crates.
- Read and reread the observations. Jot down your first impressions each time you read.
- Look for patterns within your observations and make notes or color-code those patterns. Write summary statements about those patterns.
- Consider your personal beliefs and theories and how they are shaping your interpretation of the observations.
- Make sound conclusions from your study of the observations. As you draw your conclusions, remember to avoid those based on perception and perception alone.

CONSTRUCTIONS

1. Research

Invite a classmate to join you as you both observe the same two children for fifteen minutes. Make sure the children are engaged in an activity or experience rather than interacting with you. These children can be relatives or friends who are visiting or children in your care. Use the tips for observing that we have offered.

2. Analysis

Once you have completed the actual observations, write them up. Compare your observations with your classmate's. Compare them with your experience with children.

3. Research

Invite that same classmate to join you in observing a classroom of children for twenty minutes. Just as with the other observation, make sure the children are engaged in an activity or experience rather than interacting with you. Use the tips for observing that we have offered.

4. Writing

Once you have completed the actual observation, write it up. Compare your observation with your classmate's.

ANALYZING AND SYNTHESIZING AS STRATEGIES

ASK YOURSELF

Have you done analyses in other classes? Have you read analyses in the newspaper? Have you observed the teacher doing an analysis of some problem or issue? What did you focus on as you attempted to analyze an issue? How did you synthesize the information?

The hardest and most necessary components of the process of constructing knowledge are analyzing and synthesizing. These components cause you to use and understand the patterns in your information as you manipulate, organize, and categorize them. These are the steps that help you advance your thinking.

Analyzing means that you find patterns in your information that help you identify motives or causes, find evidence, and draw conclusions. The information may come from a book or from a real experience. We call that information *data*. When you analyze your data, you study and identify the parts of a situation, event, interview, or experience that caused the outcome or led to the reasoning of a person. When you analyze, you might ask questions such as these: What activity centers did the children select? How long did they stay in each center? What characteristics seem to contribute to the children selecting the art center over the block center?

When we analyze and synthesize, we use patterns to advance our thinking.

We offer the following suggestions as beginning guides to help you with analyzing. You don't have to use all of our suggestions, and you don't have to use them in any particular order. Some of you will choose one method, others will choose another, and some will try all of them. You may come up with your own additional ideas. Remember, think of what you need and do that.

TIPS FOR ANALYZING

- Read, read, and reread your data.
- On the third or fourth reading of the data, use a highlighter or marker to highlight parts of the data that puzzle you, repeat information, or have elements of a pattern or various aspects of a situation.
- Try using a *semantic map* (see Figure 1.1). A semantic map is a device you use to organize your data. Put what you consider the topic or most meaningful point of the data in the center of the page, and then draw lines to circles or squares that contain the various subparts, substeps, or meaningful subcategories.
- If you decided to highlight your data, write down the highlighted sections. Read them to see what meaning you can make from them.
- Ask a series of questions about your data, then try to answer those questions.
- Make connections. Think about other readings, interviews, experiences, and situations that the data cause you to recall.
- Make categories by grouping what you think is important.

Synthesizing occurs after you analyze your data. It is another step in constructing knowledge. When you synthesize, you put what you learned about the data and from the data into a whole. In other words, you put the pieces of the analysis together to make predictions, to solve problems, or to create new hypotheses. You coordinate and combine your ideas or categories so that you have some main ideas about what you have observed. One strategy that might help you with your synthesis is to formulate questions about each aspect of that synthesis. An example of a synthesis question might be to consider how to change a center so that it attracts more children. The questions function in an interactive fashion so that you "converse" with the data. Such social interaction might offer you new perspectives.

Let's join Eric and Tillie as they attempt to analyze and synthesize their observations in the classroom.

Figure 1.1
Semantic Map
See semantic feature analysis (pp. 252–256) in J. David Cooper, *Literacy: Helping Children Construct Meaning* **(3rd edition), Houghton Mifflin, 1997.**

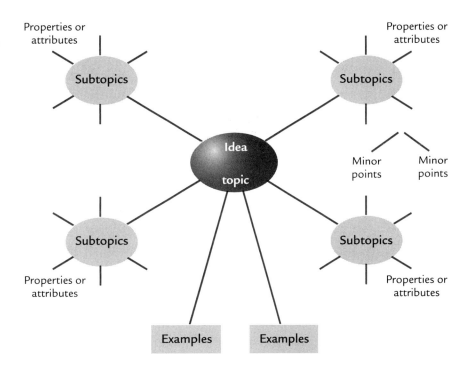

TILLIE: Did Dr. K. tell us how to do this analysis?

ERIC: She gave us some guidelines, but she told us to decide what we need to use to make sense of our observations. So I think we need to decide how we want to study what we observed.

TILLIE: Okay. So what do we do?

ERIC: Let's exchange observations and read them. Then let's read them aloud. Like, I'll read yours and you read mine.

TILLIE: What good is that going to do?

ERIC: Well, I don't know exactly, but it might give us a different perspective on our own observations. As you read mine to me, I'll jot down questions or notes. Then when I read yours to you, you do the same.

TILLIE: Okay, let's get on with it.

(They read each other's observations and make notes.)

TILLIE: Wait a minute. I've got notes on the instructor's lecture on this. She said to make categories. Categories of what?

ERIC: Well, I think we should try to look at the data in terms of what we saw first, second, and so on, then do categories. Like, first we saw Shirley hold the rope so that the ball was about twelve inches from her hand. Then she released the rope, knocked down four blocks, and watched the ball swing until it stopped.

TILLIE: I get it. Next, we both wrote that we saw Shirley take two steps to the left, grasp the rope about twenty-four inches from the ball, and release it. *(Eric and Tillie continue to work on the data.)*

ERIC: Now we're ready for categories. One category I see is the location of the child's body in relation to the blocks.

TILLIE: Yeah! Another is the location of the child's hand on the rope.

ERIC: Yes! Another is the trajectory of the rope.

TILLIE: What?

ERIC: Flight pattern!

TILLIE: Flight pattern? Whatever!
(They continue to analyze the data, complete that, and then begin to synthesize.)

TILLIE: Okay, next we have to synthesize this.

ERIC: Right! Let's revisit the assignment and think about what it means now that we have done the observation and analysis.

TILLIE: Busywork!

ERIC: No, it really isn't.
(They begin to read and talk about the assignment.)

TILLIE: Okay, let's try this representing the data in a different way. Let's make a poster.

ERIC: Poster? Okay.

TIPS FOR SYNTHESIZING

▸ Revisit and reflect on your purposes for gathering your data. In other words, review your assignment or hypotheses (questions that you were studying).

▸ Revisit and reflect on your actual data.

▸ Revisit and reflect on your analysis of the data.

▸ Create another way of representing your analysis of the data that focuses on the whole rather than the parts. For example, if you wrote your analysis in paragraphs, try representing it with charts and graphs.

▸ Prepare a new set of questions.

▸ Create a text that represents your coordination and understanding of your data and your analysis.

CONSTRUCTIONS

Research

Use one of the dialogues in this chapter, one of your own constructions, or collect new data. Analyze that data and then attempt to synthesize it.

Share your synthesis with a classmate and compare the process you used, the actual written documents that you produced, and the strategies you used to synthesize your data.

RESEARCHING AS A STRATEGY

Danielle, Eric, Tillie, Amy, and Zenah became researchers the minute they decided to ask their first questions and do their first interviews. You did the same when you began questioning—especially if you used your own questions. When you moved into interviews and observations, you simply moved into a more formalized and detailed aspect of **research**. Needless to say, when you wrote anything down, you also were engaged in research. Finally, when you began analyzing and synthesizing your data, you were studying it to construct new knowledge.

When we engage in the research process, we become inquirers and collaborators with knowing.

Ann Berthoff, a Vygotskian philosopher and advocate of naturalistic research, defines research as re-searching, or looking and looking again (Berthoff, 1978). To her, research is the way to get to the very core of knowing. When you think of research from Berthoff's perspective, you avoid the fears of writing a research paper that you experienced in other courses. What you find instead is a dynamic process that allows you to become an inquirer and even a collaborator within the research process. Just this process of formalizing, making explicit, and thinking about how we come to know changes your perspective of and theories about the classroom. You begin to question, generate hypotheses, negotiate, read, analyze, study, and write about how ideas come into being.

As a result of the research process, you will find yourself focusing on designing checklists, creating interview questions and follow-up questions, examining classroom approaches to determine whether those approaches hinder or help you, and checking places for a videotape or audiotape player so that it records what the learners are saying and doing but does not interfere too much. Your goal will be to study what learners are doing with their ideas and their knowledge, rather than focusing on drill and practice worksheets and extension activities that provide grades for an accountability-seeking public. As a result of your research, you will find, as we have, that you know more about what learners need, how they learn, and how their needs fit into the curriculum. You will find that this research is how your theories about learning and teaching come into being.

When you engage in classroom research, you are the scientist who is attempting to be objective, so that any observer would see what you are seeing.

TIPS FOR CLASSROOM RESEARCH

- Observe learners as they explore materials, a situation, or a task. Jot down your observations.
- Formulate and jot down some questions that arise from your observations.
- Reflect on those questions and classify, categorize, or group them to see if a pattern emerges.
- Identify the pattern and formulate a question regarding that pattern. If no pattern emerges, pick one or two questions that really intrigue or bother you.
- Read to find out whether others have raised questions like yours.
- Look at some of Piaget's work and decide whether any of his tasks or apparatus might address your questions.
- Decide on your question and on an apparatus and method for addressing that question.
- Write and request permission from everyone who might be involved in your research (principal, teacher, child, and parents of child).
- Begin your research by administering the task and gathering the data.
- Analyze your data.
- Write about what you learned.
- Share what you learned through your writing.

You want your procedures to be clear enough for another person to be able to duplicate those procedures. You want to note your limitations and concerns rather than trying to hide them. Your plan should allow others to take your work and go beyond it. As you research, you have a responsibility to enable others to use your work to advance their own thinking. Discuss your findings with a classmate.

CONSTRUCTIONS

1. Research

Read several articles or chapters written by teachers who view themselves as researchers in their classrooms. Outline their approaches to research.

2. Journal Entry

Write a reflection about the processes teacher/researchers used as they researched various aspects of their classrooms. Discuss your findings with a classmate.

REFLECTING AS A STRATEGY

Many people think of reflection as having a mystique or enlightened quality. In reality, reflection is like a mirror. It gives back a likeness or image. This process of giving back involves both distance and time. The distance gives learners a sharper perspective of the situation (a step back). That perspective may offer learners a chance to see the parts of the whole or may allow them to see the connections between those parts. The time allows learners to ponder or meditate. It also frees learners so that they can think back to the past as well as project into the future. **Reflection,** the ability to think about the past and future as well as the present, allows you to construct theories. The theories may be limited at first, but over time and through reflection, you will develop your ability to make theories, test them, and evaluate them.

> When we think back into the past and project into the future, we are engaged in the reflective process.

What do you do when you reflect? You ask yourself questions. You link previous ideas, experiences, and observations to present ones. If you are reflecting as a critical thinker, you examine, clarify, organize, analyze, hypothesize, predict, assess, and so on. If you are thinking creatively, you generate new ideas, create alternatives, challenge assumptions, and explore options. If you are using information as you reflect, you make decisions, choose strategies, and even set goals or assess your abilities to use goals.

TIPS FOR REFLECTING

▸ Pick an area of interest in early childhood education or a passage you have written about early childhood.

▸ Look at the area or passage as if you were looking in a mirror. Look first at one part and then at another until you have examined the whole.

▸ Use "why" and "how" questions to help you look into the imagined mirror.

▸ Consider a different way of representing your thoughts. For example, create a semantic map, or web. Draw the situation.

▸ Look at the representation. Does it offer new thoughts?

▸ Jot down those thoughts.

▸ Go back to step one and look at the area of interest or passage.

▸ Follow this cycle again until you have further insights.

▸ Once you have used the above cycle several times, formulate the problem or situation in terms of definition, cause, and location (internal experience or external experience).

> ▸ Revisit the causes and add the effects of the problem or situation.
> ▸ Propose possible results or solutions.
> ▸ Evaluate.
> ▸ Consider various actions or ways of reacting to a given situation.

CONSTRUCTIONS

Journal Entry

Try reflecting on your values and how they fit a career in early childhood education. Be sure to include values related to finances, contributions to the community, and contributions to the field of early childhood education. For example, reflect on your salary needs and expectations. Reflect on what contribution you hope to make to early childhood education. How do you plan to change the field? Follow that reflection to see if it leads you into other areas of the field.

WRITING AS A STRATEGY

A journal is a repository for all those fragmentary ideas and odd scraps of information that might be lost and which someday might lead to more "harmonious" compositions. (Thoreau, 1854, p. 67)

Thoreau's quote offers us a place to begin to think about using journal writing as a constructivist strategy. Journal writing is a way and a place to be reflective about yourself, your experiences, the ideas you are exploring, and your observations. It fits on a continuum between diaries and class notebooks (Fulwiler, 1987). Like a diary, a journal can be highly personal and private, or it can chronicle your learning or constructing ideas. You can use free-writing journals, dialogue journals, project journals, class logs, writer's notebooks, response journals, class journals, computerized class journals, and personal reaction journals (Fulwiler).

The process of writing in journals allows us to take on different perspectives and experience simultaneity.

Constructivists like journals because, by their very nature, they cause the student to take on different perspectives and experience simultaneity. On the one hand, the student is the writer of the journal entry. She can explore and interact with the entry's topic. On the other hand, the student can be the only audience for that entry. Because she is the audience as well as the writer, the interaction between writing and thinking becomes a powerful strategy. The student can look back over several entries and read how her views, attitudes, or ideas have changed.

KINDS OF JOURNALS

- **Dialogue Journals**   Students carry on a dialogue with the teacher, the text, an idea, or other students.
- **Project Journals**   Individual students or groups of students record their ongoing work on a project. A group of students also may record the processes they are using to work together to solve problems, and so on.
- **Writer's Notebooks**   Writers use these to record their observations, metaphors they like, images, and interpretations of what they see.
- **Class Logs**   Someone keeps notes and records of what happens in class. The students and teacher decide who will write the class log. They can refer to the log to see what happened when they were absent, what assignments have been made, and what will happen.
- **Response Journals**   Students usually respond to their readings in a response journal. It is not designed for note taking but for personal responses regarding whether the readings make sense to them. Their writing focuses on the content of the readings, not on personal reactions or digressions.
- **Class Journals**   Students keep notes about class lectures and notes on their readings. These notes are factual and summative.
- **Personal Reaction Journals**   Students react in a personal way to the readings and class lectures. They may also react to the discipline as a whole. For example, a student might draw a cartoon in a personal reaction journal as he writes about attitudes toward math.
- **Reflective Journals**   In some respects, all journals are reflective. All require introspection. However, some students use a form of journal that has reflection as its primary purpose. You may want to use some strategies for reflecting. For example, you may want to read and re-read earlier entries, then begin to write. You may want to use a phrase from an earlier entry as a starting point. However you engage in writing a reflective journal, its focus is on your interpretations, attitudes, ideas, and feelings rather than on content. It is like a personal reaction journal, only more open-ended.

DOCUMENTING THROUGH PORTFOLIOS AS A STRATEGY

ASK YOURSELF

Rather than write a journal entry or some other piece, revisit several of the writings you've done thus far. Read the pieces as if someone else wrote them. Ask yourself how the writer's thinking has changed over time. Ask yourself if you are surprised at the changes. Think about your views of writing as a tool for learning when you began this chapter and now.

....

We use the portfolio process to document professional growth over time.

As you read other chapters in this book, you'll encounter several references to your portfolio. Perhaps you have studied art and have created a portfolio of your work. You selected your best work to illustrate a variety of your talents and skills. Some of you may have created portfolios in high school or elementary school. Together you and your teachers chose samples of your writing, photographs of completed projects, and maybe even audiotapes or videotapes of presentations.

Portfolios, in the physical sense, are folders or cases for holding documentation of your work. Today they may be electronic, in that they are kept on a computer or Web page. They may be a leather or synthetic container used to hold papers, photos, and various other kinds of documentation. They may be interactive, reflective, or a showcase of work. When educators speak of creating a **portfolio,** they use the term to mean the contents of the folder, much as a diplomat presents her portfolio of credentials to demonstrate her credibility. They also mean that you are to give a sample or glimpse of yourself as an early childhood educator over a specific time.

As you prepare for your career, begin to create your portfolio so that you can see your professional growth over time. Be sure to save items on a regular basis. Weed them out when your collection becomes too large, but always retain some of your early work to document your growth and development. Initially, you may consider only those items that relate to your education classes. But as you analyze what you are learning in your liberal arts classes, such as history or biology, you may recognize vital connections to your study of teaching. Your instructors may require that you prepare a portfolio as a method of assessment. Some interviewers value not only the evidence available from the portfolio contents but also your demonstration of farsightedness as you plan. Even after you begin teaching, your portfolio may help you focus on the changes you continue to make in your thinking and planning. An important aspect of constructivism is continual learning. A portfolio is a tangible picture of your knowledge and skills.

Because of the complexity of the portfolio process, summarizing it in a table is difficult. The following is a discussion of the portfolio process, as well as suggestions for beginning one.

▶ As you collect materials for your portfolio, you will want to include photocopies of your students' work samples.

▶ You will want a commentary section and a reflection section for each entry in your portfolio.

The *commentary section* should include relevant background information, such as goals, rationale for goals, topic or subject, relevant information about the context, and reasons for including this in your portfolio. This section also may include a discussion and assessment of family and community issues (for example, how you involved or included parents).

The *reflection section* should include reflections about your work, the child's work, theory, research, and/or the interconnectedness of the different aspects of the portfolio entry. Remember, reflection usually occurs after the event and focuses on the self. It addresses the "why" and "how" aspects of your actions rather than the "what" aspect. You want to look at why something happened the way it did rather than what happened. What happened is a description of the event. Why it happened addresses motives, attitudes, reasons, and interpretations.

▶ You may want to include videotape clips.

If you decide to include videotapes, you will want to edit the tapes so that you show clips, not long samples that confuse the audience. Besides editing the tapes, you will want to make sure the clips show children interacting with others, relate to your goals and purposes for including the clips, are of good quality, and include necessary permission slips. The tapes should have a key for the viewer's use. The key should be an annotation and reflection.

▶ You may want to include a section on classroom curriculum and practices.

This section should include your views on classroom environment, working with parents, working with children who have special needs, and working with children who speak English as a second language. It should include your ideas about methods or approaches for various content areas of the curriculum. For example, if you decide to have a section on classroom arrangement, address issues such as how you organized space, selected materials, and used existing structures such as built-in bookcases, electrical outlets, and windows. You may also want to show how your ideas changed over time or in different settings. How did the children help you with your decisions? If you decide to include classroom rules and routines, you might want to address how you established the rules and routines, what role the children had in establishing them, and how the rules and routines helped you with your theories about how children come to know.

▶ You may want to include a section that documents your accomplishments.

You might include letters of support, documentation of your community work, documentation of your work in clubs or professional organizations, and evaluations of your work with children.

▶ You will want to consider the presentation of your portfolio.

Two important aspects of presentation are *ease of handling* and *page layout*. A portfolio must be easy to handle and to open. Pages must be securely attached to the folder, easy to turn, and easy on the eye. If pockets are used for additional material, they shouldn't be stuffed so full that materials fall out when the portfolio is opened. If you include videotape clips or use an electronic portfolio, you should make sure viewing equipment is necessary and available.

Page layout is an important consideration. It will influence the reader's view of you as a professional. For example, you should use a typeface (Garamond, Times New Roman) and type size that is clear (not under 10 point), creates the maximum space for your text, and appeals to the reader's eye. Avoid an italic or script typeface. You will also want to consider the color of borders on your pages and of the pages themselves. Don't forget to consider eye appeal, clarity, and professional look. For example, you could use one color for all the pages and one for the borders. Avoid multiple colors, cute or faddish clip art, cute kinds of paint, and glitter.

▶ Have others react to your portfolio.

Remember that the portfolio is not only a presentation of your work but also an example of your interaction with the field of early childhood education and the learning process you used to study that field. Because it serves at least two functions, you want it to make a statement to the reader.

The strategies we have mentioned in this chapter have helped us construct our theories about what it means to be a professional in early childhood education. In no way is our selection all-inclusive or magical. As you look at the selection, you'll probably think, "How can I observe without asking questions and reflecting?" or "How can I do an interview without using questions?" You are correct. We have separated these strategies and their processes only to discuss them. They really can't be separated when you are actually using them. In addition, we hope that you will add to the list as you develop your own investigative strategies and theories.

Our goal for this chapter was to provide you with some explanations for the strategies we have picked for you to use as you explore the field of early childhood education and formulate theories. We realize that some of you will prefer to write down your own theories and plans. For you, writing, reflecting, and observing may be your favorite means of addressing theory building and a life plan. Others of you will prefer a more scientific approach in which questioning, classroom research, observing, analyzing, and interviews will be helpful. Still others will prefer to use visual representations to shape your theories; you may find the portfolio the most meaningful approach.

We are not as concerned about your means of constructing theories and plans as we are about what happens to you as you go through the process. We hope that as you develop theories, you will link and test them out with classmates, researchers, teacher/educators, readings, and early childhood professionals, both in the classroom and in other child-care delivery systems. As you test the theories, we anticipate that you will discard some, revitalize others, save some, and create new ones. Don't be afraid to do this. It's all part of the process. Look back at your past and into your future to see what may be possible for you in the field of early childhood education.

SUMMARY

▶ Questioning is a spontaneous search for information, a way to build understandings and to figure out causes, origins, or rules. Questions can be both social and introspective.

▶ The primary purpose of an interview is to gather information about someone's thinking, beliefs, ideas, and preferences on a specific topic.

▶ Observing is an essential process in studying young children and the teaching/learning process. It allows you to differentiate between perception and seeing.

▶ Researching requires that you coordinate several strategies in an effort to find an answer or raise questions. The process of researching requires questioning, observing, analyzing and synthesizing, reflecting, writing, and documenting.

▶ Documenting through portfolios provides a record of your learning process over time.

CONSTRUCTIONS

1. Research

Begin to plan your portfolio. Check prices for binders and acid-free paper. Buy or borrow a camera, film, tape recorder, and tapes. Make sure they work and you know how to use them. Decide what to put in your portfolio from your first classes.

2. Research

Find students who have completed their portfolios and ask to see the finished products. Talk with the students about the process of compiling a portfolio and what they learned from it.

3. Journal Entry

Write a brainstorming entry about what you want to know about and do in the field of early childhood education. Your journal entry may consist of narrative writing, a series of questions, a drawing, or brief phrases.

RESOURCES

Bredekamp, S., & Copple, C. (Eds.). (1997). ***Developmentally appropriate practice in early childhood programs*** (Rev. ed.). Washington, DC: NAEYC.

This book provides readers with the NAEYC position on developmentally appropriate practice for children ages birth through eight.

Clay, M. M. (1993). *An observation survey of early literacy achievement.* Portsmouth, NH: Heinemann.

This book is an excellent example of an observational survey that students could use in their study of young children.

Cooper, J. D. (2000). *Literacy: Helping children construct meaning* (4th ed.). Boston: Houghton Mifflin.

This resource provides an excellent discussion of semantic maps and step-by-step directions for ways to develop them.

Edwards, C., Gandini, L., & Forman, G. (Eds.). (1993). *The hundred languages of children.* Norwood, NJ: Ablex.

This book describes the Reggio Emilia approach, which could be considered a model for students and teachers who want to use close observation and documentation of young children.

Forman, G. E., & Kuschner, D. S. (1983). *The child's construction of knowledge: Piaget for teaching children.* Washington, DC: NAEYC.

This resource is invaluable in that it helps readers begin to think more about close observation of children, behaviorism, constructivism, and teaching young children.

Heimlich, J. E., & Pittleman, S.D. (1986). *Semantic mapping: Classroom applications.* Newark, DE: International Reading Association.

If you become interested in using semantic mapping as a strategy for planning and organizing, this resource will provide you with ideas for your teaching.

Power, B. M., & Hubbard, R. (Eds.). (1991). *Literacy in process.* Portsmouth, NH: Heinemann.

This is an edited collection that offers readers an accessible look at journal writing, reflective writing, and teachers who are researchers. In addition, the section on further resources provides additional titles for students who are interested in the "teacher as researcher" movement, journal writing, and literacy.

Wilson, J., & WingJan, L. (1993). *Thinking for themselves.* Portsmouth, NH: Heinemann.

This book is an excellent resource for teachers and learners. It will give you ideas for strategies to help you know about your own thinking. It will also provide you with strategies and examples of these strategies for teaching children.

2

Getting Information and Support

• •

This chapter invites you to investigate the many sources of information about the early childhood field that will be most helpful to you personally. Through your own investigations, through reading, and through listening to the voices of others, you will begin to build on the knowledge of resources related to the field.

The resources we share are both personal and professional and include those offered by individuals, community and national organizations, and professional associations, as well as books, other printed materials, and computer-related resources. We encourage you to consider resources you encounter in your local community as well as the professional community. After reading this chapter, you should have knowledge of the following topics:

- ▶ What you can do individually and collectively to find information
- ▶ Human sources of support and information
- ▶ Professional organizations, models, and sites to connect with other professionals
- ▶ Print materials that are helpful to children and to you as a teacher
- ▶ Technology that can assist you as a developing professional

Finding helpful resources and materials is important for children and for you as a developing professional. *(© Elizabeth Crews)*

INTRODUCTION

The class has gone on a field trip to a local resource site for teachers, the Center for Establishing Dialogue (CED). After an orientation to the center, Amy goes directly to the section on children's literature and begins to thumb through *Two Bad Ants* by Chris Van Allsburg (1988). She settles into a comfortable chair. Eric goes into the area that contains announcements of upcoming teacher workshops and local conferences and begins to read various fliers. In dismay, Danielle looks around the reference room at all the books on early childhood available to check out or buy. The amount of material seems overwhelming, and she wonders where she can get the help she needs. She tentatively approaches the center director and asks, "Do you have a book that starts with the first day of school and tells a teacher everything to do?"

HOW CAN YOU FIND INFORMATION AND RESOURCES?

Danielle's feeling is similar to that of the Velveteen Rabbit (M. Williams, 1922/1969) as he questions the Skin Horse about what it means to become real. He wishes it didn't have to take so long and be so difficult to be authentic. You probably recognize the intellectual dependence, or *heteronomy,* that both the rabbit and Danielle seem to display. It is natural to feel this way when you are entering a new professional field, but there is a more au-

ASK YOURSELF
What do I already know about finding the resources I need? What information do I want to find? What possible sources or resources have I not considered previously? How do I use the resources and sources I find to move forward on a career path?
• • • • • • • • • • • • • • • •

tonomous way to to create your own answers so they are meaningful to you. Recognizing the power of your role in this process, we want to help you find the resources and support that will assist you in becoming a "real" teacher.

Did you notice that most of the "Ask Yourself" questions are those that only you can answer? We hope that you will use this chapter to look over some of the sources of information and support that we suggest, but remember that your best resource is your own thinking about what you find as you actively investigate and move beyond our initial suggestions. Each reader will be at a different point in this process depending on past experiences and knowledge. Your store of information will not be completed by the time you finish this chapter, or even the entire course. Our intention in this chapter, which we have deliberately placed at the beginning of the book, is to encourage you to develop the foundation on which you will build as you move through levels of understanding about the field of early childhood education.

Organizing and Developing a Plan of Action

An action plan provides focus and guidance in finding information.

Begin by designating a resource notebook or creating some other system for recording information about resources (for example, a card or computer file). Using this notebook or system, list the sources of support and information you already have. Then use this list to determine what else you want to find out. How could you begin this process? Look back at the list of topics on the first page of this chapter. Consider those about which you have the least information. Start there and think about how you might begin to acquire more.

One way to approach this task is to jot down a question. Below the question, list any ideas you already have about finding answers to it. Narrowing the focus of your question is important, because you will undoubtedly encounter many more questions as you pursue the first one. Be as precise as you can. This process is exemplified by a brainstorming session in class.

Before class begins, Eric approaches Dr. K. for a reference to help him understand more than he already knows about how young children develop and learn.

ERIC: Hi, Dr. K. I was thinking over the weekend that what I'd like to know more about is how children learn. That seems really important to me. Where should I start?

DR. K.: This is an important topic for any prospective teacher, Eric. I think that the other students might have some suggestions, and they might also benefit by talking with you about how to get this kind of information.

ASK YOURSELF
What do I think of the suggestions Eric's class-mates made? Are there other places or resources I think he should investi-gate? What have I found helpful in finding infor-mation? How would Dr. K. help Eric most: by telling him or by *not* telling him?

(Right after the class announcements and sharing, Dr. K. poses the question to the whole class, and they make the following suggestions to Eric.)

DANIELLE: Well, first you should go to the library to look for the most recent books on child development. But, you know, I really hate to go to that big library. Maybe you could call Carol at CED! Will you tell me what she says?

ZENAH: Why not call a friend who's ahead of you in the program for suggestions?

TILLIE: Yeah, or ask a really good teacher which book was especially helpful to her when she started teaching.

AMY: I'd look in the campus bookstore at texts ordered for child develop-ment classes—maybe one at a level just beyond the last class I took in child development. Or I'd look at texts on cognition or constructivism, since you want information on how children think.

ERIC: These are good suggestions. I'm going to list them in the resource notebook I'm starting.

DANIELLE: Why don't you just ask Dr. K.? She knows which books are the best ones for us. Dr. K., why don't you just tell Eric?

The list begun in class could easily be made into an **action plan,** which is a formalized plan aimed at answering a question or moving forward on an agenda. Eric might have used these and other ideas as part of his action plan. The important thing is to get started.

CONSTRUCTIONS

1. Organizing

Organize a notebook or some other system for keeping resource information.

2. Research

Is there a question you can develop to help you find specific types of resources? Try writing down your question and begin to develop an ac-tion plan.

3. Analysis

After you have determined a plan of action or developed another strategy to find resources, ask the next question of yourself or a friend: How else could I get this information? See if you can come up with a couple of ideas that are a little unusual or creative. Are there new sources to investigate?

The tasks presented in these constructions are one way that you might begin to add to and reflect on your knowledge about children. This text also will assist you in examining the information you already have about children, and hopefully it will challenge some of your beliefs and assumptions about how children learn and teachers teach. You may find that a constructivist perspective about children's learning is different from what you expected.

Developing Your Ideas

As you begin this process, you will find that you have many ideas that will help you to develop other strategies for finding answers. By now you no doubt realize that this creative process of finding answers adds to your existing knowledge of the sources and resources available to you in your local community. Keeping resource information on cards organized in an index box or listing the information in a file on your computer to put in a separate notebook will prove useful when you look for information later. Over time you can develop a comprehensive and helpful resource file. After you consider resources available to you in your area, read the following pages for examples of other categories you might explore.

EXPLORING SOURCES AND RESOURCES

Human Sources and Resources

An individual's own thinking and experience can enhance professional growth.

Yourself.   One resource that you may tend to overlook is the one that resides inside yourself. As you will read in Chapter 4 on the child as sense maker, Piaget believed that individuals construct new knowledge—in this case, knowledge about sources and resources—from what they already know. New ideas and resources will emerge as you investigate your sources of information further. This ongoing process is facilitated by an inner dialogue that often occurs as you write journal entries. Or you may just converse with yourself.

Try dialoguing with yourself. What other ways can you think of to deepen what you already know about sources of support or resources in your community? If there are individuals or locations in your community

---

THE IMPORTANCE OF INNER DIALOGUE

"A purpose of dialogue is to bring you into some . . . private ruminations about a topic. Dialogue is a way to get you, the learner, actively involved in making your own meaning of the world. Out of the interplay between your prior knowledge and your current learning experience, you are creating something new—a fresh understanding of something, a new or improved skill, a different way to solve a problem" (Ryan & Cooper, 1995, p. xxvi).

that you are aware of but have never taken the time to visit or explore, take the initiative and do so now.

Peers make valuable contributions to professional development.

Peers. In addition to your inner dialoguing and your own thinking, interaction with your peers is an important means by which you can learn about community and professional resources. As the class discussion about child development information suggested earlier, collective thinking can add both breadth and depth to your information and understanding. Working with a group of people is not always easy. Sometimes it results in disagreements. It is especially important that you recognize the power that a disagreement with a friend can have. When you disagree, it makes you think more deeply to prove a point. Through such interaction, you think more carefully and fully, and as a result you learn more about the topic at hand. In one sense, a peer is a better learning resource than a university teacher, because it is more comfortable to question and disagree with a friend than with your professor. Piaget has written about the unequal power between learners and teachers and the more equal status that exists between peers (Piaget, 1954/1981).

ASK YOURSELF

Have I ever had the experience of not really understanding an assignment until I talked to friends in class? What are my thoughts about the ways that peers can help me learn?

Your friends and classmates will know different resources than you do. When you take the opportunity to engage in this kind of an experience, you have participated in Piaget's description of cooperation, which you could literally translate as "thinking with another," since for Piaget the term *operate* means "to think." The following construction on collaboration is intended to exemplify how the social context of groups and how peers can also assist each other in developing professional resources.

CONSTRUCTIONS

Collaboration

To demonstrate the peer sharing process, consider the following activity that each member of a group or an entire class could do on a voluntary basis on a designated day. As a group, agree to work together. Following your own interests, look in the telephone book, newspaper, or other resources and generate a list of informational sites (museums, aquarium, zoo, libraries) relevant to children in your area. Arrange for each individual or pair to visit a different site and participate in children's learning activities there. If all the members of a group or class share the information they gleaned from their visits, your resource collection will grow quickly. The strategies listed in Chapter 1 will help you organize your information and answer questions. As suggested in the box "The Children's Museum," key questions about each site will provide information that will be useful now and in the future.

Peers are important resources who help us think more deeply about issues of education. *(© Bob Daemmrich/Stock Boston)*

THE CHILDREN'S MUSEUM

Data Gathering Through Observation and Questioning

1. What are the hours of operation and the cost of admission? Is there a rate for children or groups of children?
2. What is the address, how do you get there, and whom can you contact for additional information and to make arrangements for future visits?
3. Does the museum have additional resources available? Would any future events there be beneficial?
4. Does the museum have a Web site?

Analysis Through Reflecting and Discussing

1. What are the benefits of visiting this site? How could it fit into a project or experience of interest to young learners?
2. In what ways do the activities and displays "teach" information? Are they well done, or would they be confusing for young learners?
3. What ideas could you use in a classroom setting, and what else would you need to make the experience appropriate?

Teaching Tip. For any field trip you plan to undertake with children, you should personally visit that site prior to taking the children. Although another person's suggestion may be informative, only your own experience will provide you with specific details about the planning necessary for visiting that particular site.

A mentor will share information and resources and also encourage your autonomy.
(© Bob Daemmrich/The Image Works)

ASK YOURSELF

Whom might I consider as a mentor? What are important criteria for selecting a mentor? (Jot your criteria down now to compare with others as you continue to read.)
....

Mentors. Another wonderful source of support and information can be a mentor. A mentor is a trusted person who serves as a personal counselor or coach. Do you have someone who provides this service for you in your personal life? If so, you know how valuable a mentor can be for your growth. Although it is early in your journey to becoming a professional, you may want to think about finding a professional mentor now.

Selecting a mentor is not always an easy process. You should consider a whole array of individuals, not just the first person you think about. Although the term *mentor* means someone who takes a guidance role, you should be prepared to take an active role in the relationship as well. It is important to consider what benefit you can offer to your mentor. After considering your options carefully, ask someone you feel is the most knowledgeable, willing, and appropriate person to serve in this role. Be aware that the person you ask may not be willing or able to serve as your mentor. Don't be upset if that happens; the mentor-student relationship is one that both people must commit to, or it won't work. You might also think about choosing different mentors for different purposes.

A good mentor provides choices, gives suggestions, and honors autonomy.

Typically, a good choice for a mentor is someone who has displayed a particular interest in your growth within the teaching profession and who has recognized professional expertise. Good mentors have been described as advisers, supporters, tutors, sponsors, and models. An interesting feature of mentoring is that it provides both freedom and guidance. A mentor should assist you in ways that encourage your autonomy rather than simply telling you what to do. Naturally, a mentor will share helpful facts and information, but if she asks *you* questions and suggests several possibilities for you to choose among, she will be encouraging your thinking rather than promoting heteronomy. When that occurs, the role the individual takes on is that of a coach and mentor rather than a director or dictator. Such an individual may not be easy to find but will be truly valuable. A mentor may be a teacher you know or have worked with previously, a teacher who taught you in school, or someone who has lived in the community for a long time and has knowledge of community resources. See if the criteria you jotted down fit with our suggestions to lead you to a short list of individuals you can ask to be your mentor. If it does, take the risk to ask your top candidate. If that person refuses, work your way down the list.

Professionals. What other human sources besides mentors and peers might you find helpful? Within the field of education, many individuals can provide you with assistance without taking on the more intense mentor role. Such individuals may be other teachers, special education teachers, child-care center directors, CDA advisers or assessors, child-care licensing agents, school counselors, school social workers, principals, parent-school liaisons, curriculum specialists, or child advocates who work within the state system for the well-being of families and children. Meeting and interviewing an education professional can provide you, as a teacher-to-be, with a wealth of information. Typically, these individuals are very busy but more than willing to set up a time to assist you. As you learned in Chapter 1, it is important to be organized, with prepared questions, when you conduct an interview.

In a similar manner, other professionals outside the field but within the community may provide valuable information and support. These individuals may not be teachers, but they can offer important perspectives on the teacher's role and the needs of children and families. For example, a school nurse can give you valuable information on young children's health needs. A social worker can tell you where to direct parents who need community services.

Consider a wide variety of professionals in the human services professions: speech and hearing specialists, community nurses, social workers, child psychologists, occupational and physical therapists, physicians, and child assessment specialists, to name only a few. In addition, of course, are those individuals in your community who have expertise in particular topics you might study with children. These individuals might include the director of a nursing home, the person who manages the landfill, a museum docent, the botanist who works at the local arboretum, or individuals who own or manage businesses or services of interest to young learners.

Interacting with early childhood professionals deepens understanding of the field.

Specialists in related professions and fields can broaden your knowledge about children, families, content, and the community.

ASK YOURSELF

Who are other community members I could turn to? (In your resource notebook, list those individuals and where you can contact them, including Web sites or home pages if they are available.)

ASK YOURSELF

What other ways can I think of to engage families? Which would be the most interesting to parents and families in my community?
....

Parents.   A very special group of people who are vital resources for any classroom teacher are parents. Parents and other family members can not only provide all sorts of information about their children but also have talents, skills, and the motivation to share them with children. They know the community and have a great deal of insight about places, events, and activities of interest to children. Because parents are often eager to share their perspectives with other parents and people within a particular program, school, or community, they can be your most ardent supporters or your most difficult critics.

Developing ideas for how to build relationships with families on more than a superficial level should be a priority of any prospective teacher. Think beyond just parent open house!

MULTIPLE PERSPECTIVES

From the Field

Read and Reflect

Kathy Mason is a teacher in a first-through-third-grade classroom in Gilbert, Arizona. She sets up informal Saturday morning meetings once a month for children and parents at a large, well-known bookstore. She and the families share stories, have discussions about literature, and find new books to read. Not only has she developed a friendly rapport with the children and their families, but her focus on children's literature also supports an important educational goal. The bookstore also benefits by seeing literacy, and its business interests, promoted.

● ●

Although we have all heard stories about parents who don't seem to care about their children's school experiences, most parents want to be involved and will participate in events that seem meaningful and doable in regard to their schedules. Parents are particularly interested in the earliest years and are likely to participate in their young children's programs or schools. This gives early childhood educators both the responsibility and the opportunity to make that exchange meaningful and important. It has been well documented that parental involvement in their children's early schooling experiences has educational benefits for the child (Powell, 1998).

Parents and families are important educational partners with teachers.

Individuals in a Diverse Society.   Increasingly, teachers are asked to be responsive to the rich diversity brought to the classroom by individual

Ethnic diversity in communities provides many resources for teachers in early childhood education. *(© Hazel Hankin/Stock Boston)*

ASK YOURSELF

Who among my friends offers me the opportunity to develop awareness of diversity? In addition to understanding something about members of other cultures, what do I know about other aspects of diversity? What is my attitude and knowledge about community members who have religious beliefs and practices different from my own? How do I respond to individuals who have different abilities and physical or mental health challenges?

children, families, and groups in their communities. To respond appropriately, it is important both to obtain more knowledge about diversity in your teacher preparation program and to draw on all facets of your community, including people with handicaps and those who have different beliefs and backgrounds from your own. Thus people who reside in the community are important resources. They must not be thought of as artifacts or stereotypes of particular religious, ability, or ethnic groups. Rather, they are individuals who can help you develop and deepen your information base about values, beliefs, practices, and heritages that exist in your community. For example, having personal friends from different cultures can help you understand yourself and members of other cultures. It is almost certain that children of different ability, religious, and cultural groups will be present in your classroom. You have the responsibility to understand their perspectives so that you can function in a competent and sensitive manner.

In your professional preparation, you will certainly be required to broaden your understanding of all these issues and to know what your legal and professional responsibilities are in your interactions with children and families. Exploring resources and information about groups now can help you to become a competent pre-professional who is aware of personal biases and who has a plan for being sensitive to all children and families. Piaget recognized the importance of *awareness* as the first step in coming to

Friendships with individuals who have languages, cultures, capabilities, and perspectives different from your own promote awareness and sensitivity.

understand something. By taking this step, you will begin the process of developing a deeper, more complete understanding of your own perspective as well as the perspectives of others.

As you can see, the human sources of information and support are infinite and varied. You will have only begun to delve into these sources by considering the categories of people listed above. Can you think of other groups or individuals? Add them to your resource list as we rejoin the class to consider other sources of professional development.

CONSTRUCTIONS

1. Reflection

Think about the knowledge and dispositions you have that will assist you in responding to children and families who are different from you. What do you need to know more about or to examine further?

2. Analysis

As you move through the rest of this chapter, think about how diversity can be taken into account in each of the topics. What resources can you develop or collect to help you teach in a manner that focuses on the similarities and honors the differences among people in your community? Are there Web sites that can assist you in extending your knowledge and awareness?

Professional Organizations

Dr. K. has assigned a class research project on early childhood resources. The class has broken up into small groups to organize for their tasks. Danielle, Tillie, and Zenah have chosen to investigate and describe professional organizations.

ZENAH: I'm glad we chose this topic first, because there probably aren't very many professional organizations for early childhood. I do know that there's one that focuses on teaching African-American kids.

DANIELLE: Really? I don't know of even one.

TILLIE: Well, I do—and it's just alphabet soup out there!

ZENAH AND DANIELLE: *What?*

TILLIE: Yeah, it is—you know—NEYC-CDA, blah-blah-blah. I can't keep all the letters straight or what they stand for, but there's a bunch.

DANIELLE: How can we start if we don't know how to spell 'em? Why do you think we should know this?

Like Danielle, you may wonder why knowing about professional associations is important. As you may recall from Chapter 1, Piaget (1973) identified interaction with the social environment as one of four factors that affect cognitive development. He described social experience as critical to identification with and introduction into the social world. In a sense, this same function is mirrored for adults in professions. The experience of meeting and interacting with other professionals concerned about professional problems and issues allows for entrance into the culture of professionalism in teaching.

Membership in professional organizations admits a person into what has been termed the "invisible university." What do you think this term means? Think about that as you investigate the information on associations.

As you will see in both this and other chapters, a variety of professional organizations have historically focused on young children and their learning. As an individual new to the field, you should be aware of the most prominent groups and their functions. If you are committed to becoming an early childhood teacher, it would be useful for you to join at least one professional organization and to receive its journal and the other benefits of the "invisible university." Joining an organization will encourage you to begin to use existing resources and to find new ones. To decide which organization to join, after you read this information, skim the journals mentioned and attend a local affiliate group meeting. By doing this, you will begin to develop your knowledge of current practice and meet members of the early childhood community in your city, region, and state.

As Danielle, Tillie, and Zenah are about to find out, many professional organizations focus on either children in early childhood or on content and how to help young children learn it. In this chapter, we present three organizations that we think you'll find the most helpful initially: National Association for the Education of Young Children (NAEYC), Association for Childhood Education International (ACEI), and Association for Constructivist Teaching (ACT). A brief sketch of each of these organizations follows. Your own investigations of other organizations will be important expansions.

> Joining a national organization provides admission into the early childhood community of professionals.

QUESTIONS ABOUT PROFESSIONAL ORGANIZATIONS

The following questions provided the framework for our research:

What is the purpose of the organization?
What benefits does it offer its members?
What could I expect if I went to the national conference?
How can I contact the organization?

National Association for the Education of Young Children.

We will start with the largest group, which is the National Association for the Education of Young Children, or NAEYC. Although some pronounce this as Nay-C, the leadership prefers that you say all the letters.

Purpose of the Organization. This group began as the National Association for Nursery Educators, a nonprofit organization founded in 1926. Its purpose is to ensure quality services for young children through the improvement of early childhood professional practice. The organization provides professional development opportunities and promotes standards for professional practice. It promotes public policy and advocacy for families and their children and works to enhance public understanding of the importance of high-quality early childhood services. NAEYC defines the early childhood phase as ranging in age from birth through age eight. It has the largest membership of all the early childhood organizations, with more than 100,000 members. Diversity characterizes the membership, which includes persons who serve children and families who possess no formal preparation, as well as those with doctorates in the field. It therefore encompasses a wide variety of programs and services.

NAEYC is the largest early childhood professional organization.

Benefits of Membership. There are at least five personal and professional benefits of belonging to NAEYC: opportunities for members to receive the journal *Young Children* and other publications, to attend conferences and workshops, to join in advocacy activities, to participate in the public education event called Week of the Young Child, and to join a local or regional AEYC affiliate group. All of these benefits connect you to the profession and to other professionals who are actively working to improve their own practice and to advocate for better conditions for children and families.

The Annual Conference. NAEYC's annual conference is always exciting because of its size. It is not unusual for twenty thousand or more people to attend the vast array of workshops, meetings, seminars, and events. The annual conference is held in a different large city each year so that members in different regions of the country have access to it. At the annual conference, well-known practitioners and authorities on children discuss practices, policies, and new ideas. As a student, you pay a reduced rate to attend, and you can attend sessions designed especially for students. Special student accommodations also may be available. In addition to visiting the exhibits of educational resources at the conference, you can go on tours of outstanding local programs. Perhaps best of all is the opportunity to network with other early childhood students, professionals, and authorities from all over the United States and from other countries as well.

> ### CONTACTING NAEYC
>
> *Mailing address:* NAEYC, 1509 Sixteenth Street NW, Washington, DC 20036-1426. *Telephone*: (202) 232-8777 or (800) 424-2460. *Fax*: (202) 328-1846. *E-mail*: naeyc@naeyc.org. *World Wide Web home page* **http://www.naeyc.org/naeyc.**
>
> At the Web site, you will find E-mail addresses for information about membership, affiliate services, the conference, and other organizational features.

Contact Information. This information is always available on the inside cover of the journal *Young Children*. The current officers are listed there, along with the organization's address and telephone numbers. Current contact information is included in the accompanying box.

Association for Childhood Education International. A second group with a long history of involvement with young children is the Association for Childhood Education International, or ACEI. ACEI is one of the oldest early childhood organizations, founded in 1892 as the International Kindergarten Union by a group of kindergarten teachers and other professionals. Although the initial focus was on kindergarten-age children in the United States, the association now addresses worldwide issues related to children who range in age from infancy through adolescence. Though not as large as NAEYC, ACEI has branches in thirty countries and in every U.S. state.

Purpose of the Organization. The purpose of the association is as follows:

▹ To promote the inherent rights, education, and well-being of all children in their home, school, and community.
▹ To work for desirable conditions, programs, and practices for children from infancy through early adolescence.
▹ To bring into active cooperation all individuals and groups concerned with children.
▹ To raise the standard of preparation for those actively involved with the care and development of children.
▹ To encourage continuous professional growth of educators.
▹ To focus the public's attention on the rights and needs of children and the ways various programs must be adjusted to fit those rights and needs. (ACEI, 1996)

ACEI has a strong international perspective, with branches in many countries worldwide.

Benefits of Membership. A student membership rate is available at approximately one-half the cost to professional members. Members receive seven issues of the journal *Childhood Education* each year. In addition, for a small fee members can join a division and receive a newsletter aimed specifically at working with children in a particular developmental period (for example, early childhood, infancy, or middle grades). The cost to attend the annual study conference is less for members than for nonmembers. One membership benefit of particular importance is the availability of low-cost liability insurance for those who student teach or work with young children. ACEI also sponsors several grants and awards, one specifically directed at students who demonstrate leadership in their local ACEI student branch.

The Annual Study Conference. About one thousand people attend ACEI's annual study conference. Some students find this a more comfortable beginning than NAEYC conference, as the sessions tend to be smaller. Students are encouraged to be involved, and leadership opportunities exist for those who wish to pursue more interaction within the organization itself. Student housing is available at a reduced rate. Tours of local programs and cultural and environmental opportunities also are available. Most years, a nationally recognized teacher of the year is one of the featured speakers, along with a host of well-known authorities in educational and related fields. Generally, an author of an outstanding children's book is featured and available for conversation. Rich opportunities abound for meeting professional peers and authorities from around the world. ACEI study conferences are held in major cities around the country.

CONTACTING ACEI

Mailing address: ACEI, Olney Professional Building, 17904 Georgia Avenue, Suite 215, Olney, MD 20832. *Telephone:* (301) 942-2443 or (800) 423-3563. *Fax:* (301) 942-3012. *E-mail:* ACEIED@aol.com. *World Wide Web home page:* **http://www.udel.edu/bateman/acei.**

Contact Information. The ACEI officers and members of the headquarters staff are listed on the inside front cover of the journal *Childhood Education.* Current contact information is listed in the accompanying box.

Association for Constructivist Teaching.

The Association for Constructivist Teaching, or ACT, is a relatively new group, established in 1985. It has the smallest membership (about seven hundred) of the organizations featured here. Members are classroom teachers, administrators, supervisors, consultants, college and university personnel, students, and retired educators. The organization has grown from a group of committed educators in

New England to a national association with two regional groups, one on the West Coast and one on the East Coast.

Purpose of the Organization. As stated in the magazine *The Constructivist*, the mission of ACT is "to enhance the growth of all educators and students through identification and dissemination of effective constructivist practices in both the professional cultures of teachers and the learning environments of children." Its goals include the following:

- To provide increased and varied resources to an expanding membership.
- To increase attendance at and participation in the annual conference.
- To publish effective and practical strategies for applying constuctivism in the classroom through the magazine.
- To provide a network through which teachers, researchers, speakers, and other professionals can support and extend each other's efforts to integrate a constructivist theory of learning into the classroom and within the context of federal, state, or local mandates.
- To encourage members to contribute actively to the association's development and engage others in expanding the network of those who are willing to support each other's growth as constructivists. (Association for Constructivist Teaching, 1995)

ACT focuses specifically on encouraging constructivist approaches in early childhood education.

Benefits of Membership. Members of ACT receive a quarterly magazine, *The Constructivist,* designed for preschool, elementary, secondary, and post-secondary educators who are striving to apply constructivism to the teaching process. For many reasons, it is a good time to join ACT, as opportunities for leadership within the organization will grow as the membership increases in size and the publication increases in recognition. ACT sponsors an annual conference, whose location alternates between the East Coast and the West Coast. The most beneficial aspect of membership is the exposure to ideas of other teachers and professors as they strive to implement a constructivist approach in a variety of settings. One of the benefits of membership is to receive information and news of other seminars, institutes, events, and conferences that focus on Piagetian theory and constructivist practice.

The Annual Conference. The two-day event features keynote addresses, panel discussions, and a series of workshops. There is also a business meeting that all members are invited to attend. Full-time students qualify for a reduced registration fee. The small size of the workshops typically allows for active interaction and participation. One feature that has made the annual conference especially attractive is co-sponsorship with other groups, such as the Jean Piaget Society and the Constructivist Math Conference. This cooperation between groups allows an even greater opportunity for networking with other individuals who are implementing constructivist practice.

CONTACTING ACT

For information about ACT or to submit articles, contact Catherine Fosnot, NAC Room 3/209A, City College, 138th Street & Convent Avenue, New York, NY 10031. To subscribe to the magazine, contact Sharon Ford Schattgen at the Project Construct National Center, University of Missouri–Columbia, 27 South Tenth Street, Suite 202, Columbia, MO 65211-8010. *Telephone*: (800) 335-PCNC. *World Wide Web home page:* **http://www.projectconstruct.org.**

Contact Information. See the accompanying box.

Of course, there are several other organizations for teachers and prospective teachers. Most of these organizations are described in the *Encyclopedia of Early Childhood Education* (Williams & Fromberg, 1992). This is a particularly valuable reference book to explore.

CONSTRUCTIONS

Research

Investigate more of the early childhood organizations listed in the *Encyclopedia of Early Childhood Education* or investigate the Internet to become aware of the many professional groups that serve teachers of young children in your area.

As the information about NAEYC and ACEI indicated, there are local branches of these associations. Membership in a branch is the best way to begin developing an understanding of the teaching profession. The accompanying box offers the perspective of one student, Alison Rae Toaspern.

MULTIPLE PERSPECTIVES

From an Early Childhood Student

Read and Reflect

Alison Rae Toaspern, age twenty-three, has just completed her A.A. degree at Scottsdale (Arizona) Community College (SCC), works at the campus Child Enrichment Center, and has enjoyed working with preschool-age children for the past three years. Alison was recently awarded the Valley of the Sun Association for the Education of Young Children (VSAEYC) Community College/University Student Scholarship and plans to continue teaching while taking classes at Arizona State University.

I first heard about NAEYC when I worked in a child-care center in Flagstaff, Arizona, when the program was seeking NAEYC accreditation. I was involved in the Child Development Associate (CDA) classes at the same time, and my CDA instructor suggested that I join the regional AEYC branch. I joined in Flagstaff and was a member there for a year before I moved to the valley (Phoenix) and began school at SCC. I joined the organization because I wanted to get involved and to meet other teachers in early childhood programs. I feel that I learn new things from other teachers. The benefits I have experienced have included winning the scholarship award, of course, but membership in the organizations has also helped me a lot in networking with others and in finding job opportunities. I feel it is a good experience to meet with others who do the same thing that you do. It will also look good on my résumé when I seek the kindergarten position I ultimately hope to have!

I think participating in the Week of the Young Child and attending VSAEYC workshops has given me a professional edge. I would recommend that other students join a professional organization, because it encourages you to continue your own education and career. I plan to stay in early childhood for a long time, because at the end of the day, even though I am really tired, it is a "positive" tired. I go home feeling good about the children, and I bring home amusing stories. Their feelings stay with me, especially when I think about a particular child's accomplishment that day. That is so different from the other job I have in sales. I know that I always want to work with young children.

ASK YOURSELF

Earlier I was asked to think about what was implied by membership in an "invisible university." What did I determine? What elements of the invisible university emerge from the narrative shared by Alison?

Professional collaboration connects individuals who share a common vision and mission for families and children.

As you probably discovered, the defining essence of an invisible university is that individuals (like Alison and other professionals at different levels) have a common focus and mission. They meet regularly to talk about ideas and new information. Through this process, they form a community of learners who operate without the walls of an institution. Many professional exchanges occur informally, during social events that evolve from the academic meetings held during workshops, conferences, and institutes. In fact, the agenda for the next meeting and future directions for an organization are often determined during such social exchanges. For this reason alone, it is important to attend local events, as well as national ones when it is feasible for you to do so. As suggested by Alison, you are invited to join an invisible university when you begin to attend and take an active role in becoming a professional.

MODELS OF PROFESSIONAL COLLABORATION

Let's return to the students in the class. As with Zenah, Tillie, and Danielle, the other students were also involved in the class research project on resources. Eric, Amy, and Jeff, another student in the class, had chosen models of professional collaboration as their subtopic.

JEFF: I'm not certain what Dr. K. means by "model of professional collaboration." What do you guys think that means?

ERIC: Does she mean a national or local level of people working together? Maybe it's both.

AMY: I think so. I saw something in the newspaper about some big statewide organization in Missouri where they worked together through the public school.

ERIC: If we use "professionals working together" to focus on young children, it could be lots of things. Should we ask Dr. K.?

AMY: Nah—let's try first and see what we can find out. I think she wants us to do our own thinking. I'll see what I can dig up about Missouri. Jeff, what will you do?

JEFF: I'm going to talk to a teacher at the school where I volunteer. I heard him talking about team meetings for focusing on some kids he was concerned about.

ERIC: I'm going back to the CED. That center might qualify as a model.

Working Cooperatively for Children and Families

In a general sense, Eric is right: Collaborative models have features in common, whether they are local, state, or national. In addition to the large national professional associations and their branch chapters that we described earlier, there are other models and types of professional collaboration that are growing in popularity. Following are descriptions of three levels of professional collaboration that Eric, Amy, and Jeff might have encountered as a result of their investigations. We will describe several examples: one that began at the state level, one at the local level, and one that is implemented in various ways via individual programs or school sites. These models are only three of the many programs that exist throughout the country. Undoubtedly, your community and state have other examples.

State-Level Collaboration

Project Construct is a good example of individuals at the state level working across agencies and fields to develop better policies and educational approaches for children. The project grew out of a desire on the part of many people who began working together to determine what an excellent education for three- to seven-year-olds could be. The project began in 1986 in the Missouri Department of Elementary and Secondary Education. The University of Missouri–Columbia (MU) became a partner the following year, when the Center for Educational Assessment at MU began developing assessment and curriculum materials to enhance the vision that was developed. As you can see from the title, the project is based on constructivist theory. It is a process-oriented curriculum and assessment framework for teachers who work with children.

> Project Construct is based on the belief that the teacher is a professional whose day-to-day decisions in the classroom influence the child's development. Within the framework for curriculum and assessment, the teacher has considerable autonomy in choosing or designing experiences that will actively involve children and best promote learning. Project Construct is based on four basic principles of child development and related teaching practices. (Project Construct National Center, n.d., pp. 1–3.)

An example of these principles and related practices follows to give you a flavor of how the educators involved in the project approached the theory and practices encouraged in the classroom.

> *Principle.* Children have an intrinsic desire to make sense of the world. What they genuinely need to know and are genuinely interested in knowing helps them learn.

> *Practices for teachers.* Create learning activities that are meaningful and interesting to young children; create conditions in which children need to construct, develop, and apply additional knowledge or skills; provide activities that offer children choices and opportunities to function as planners, decision makers, and creators; allow sufficient time for children to pursue their ideas. (Project Construct National Center, p. 2)

Another interesting feature of the project is how it incorporates assessment. In contrast to traditional education, where testing is used to measure student achievement, Project Construct has organized program outcomes according to four interrelated developmental domains: sociomoral, cognitive, representational, and physical development. In this way, the project seeks to ensure that learning and development are closely linked.

> ### CONTACTING PROJECT CONSTRUCT
>
> Information about this project is available from the Project Construct National Center, University of Missouri–Columbia, 27 South Tenth Street, Suite 202, Columbia, MO 65211-8010. *Telephone:* (573) 882-1610 or (800) 335-PCNC. *Fax:* (573) 884-5580. *World Wide Web home page:* **http://www.projectconstruct.org.**

Since 1986, many teachers of young children in the state of Missouri have been trained in this approach, and Project Construct, a national project, now offers institutes and workshops to teachers from anywhere in the United States. Although Project Construct has an ambitious agenda and vision, such a successful state initiative is possible when leaders collaborate to find creative ways to work within existing agencies or to create new partnerships.

Local-Level Collaboration

A second collaborative model begins at the local level in a grassroots fashion. This model emanates from teachers, parents, and others who collaborate across school districts and educational institutions. Remember the class field trip to CED at the beginning of the chapter? If a student had picked up a brochure the day of the visit, she would have read the following:

> The Center for Establishing Dialogue is a non-profit organization comprised of educators, parents, and interested individuals who share common beliefs about how children develop and learn. The emphasis is on establishing dialogue among teachers, parents, children, schools and the community at-large; preserving the dignity and rights of children; valuing diversity; and working towards equity and justice for children and families in each individual school community. It is our purpose to promote innovation and reform in education practices that keep children at the center of teaching and learning. (Center for Establishing Dialogue in Teaching and Learning, n.d., Membership Application, p.1.)

Following is the story of CED, as shared by Carol Christine (Christine, 1991, p. 410).

MULTIPLE PERSPECTIVES

The Development of a Local Resource Center

Read and Reflect

In January of 1979 a small group of classroom and university teachers representing four different school districts (in the metropolitan Phoenix area) and Arizona

State University met for breakfast in Tempe, Arizona. We were interested in language experience and whole language, and we were aware of how the school curriculum and our teaching was influenced by our peers, as well as the general public and our district administration. In this first meeting we identified the following mutual needs: (1) communicating with other teachers, (2) identifying research to support what we do, (3) informing elementary principals, (4) communicating with our State Department, (5) watching legislation and (6) identifying teachers and classrooms to visit. By the end of the morning we had created our acronym, SMILE (Support and Maintenance for Implementing Language Expression) and we were making plans for our first workshop—less than two months away.

We selected a school where we knew the administrator would support our work, and the first SMILE workshop was held in March with 50 teachers in attendance. During the morning there were two workshop sessions: teachers selected from presentations on children's literature, bookbinding, puppetry, language experience resources for teachers, and learning center ideas. In later years, attendance grew at successive conferences to more than one thousand.

Word spread quickly from our support group to other groups as teachers began to cluster to protect and to develop their work. In 1982 SMILE began selling professional literature at workshops. We saw this as a way to raise money and as another opportunity to involve teachers in their professional growth. In December 1985, CED was created to sell books and provide workshops on a more frequent basis. The center is a direct result of the professional activities of classroom and university teachers working together.

The center has continued to promote dialogue through workshops and study groups. During the 1987–88 year, a group sponsored by CED was successful in changing legislation in Arizona on standardized testing, mandatory testing of students in first and twelfth grades was made optional. In 1989–90, we examined evaluation with Pat Carini from Vermont. Teachers from four different school districts met three times during the year to explore ways to observe, document, and evaluate classroom settings and children's growth and learning. At the final meeting the participating teachers shared their work with other teachers and with administrators from their school districts.

A continuing function of the center is a monthly writing support group. In our first two years, Shelley Harwayne and Mary Ellen Giacobbe [recognized authorities in literacy development] worked with children writing in classrooms, while a small group of teachers observed.

Looking back it is possible to see that in the networks that have developed, more and more teachers and administrators are working together for children. Our opportunities for learning and collaborating have spread beyond our local boundaries, and I like to think of our groups as one thread of many, gently but persistently weaving change in and out of our classrooms throughout our nation's schools.

· ·

ASK YOURSELF

CED is an example of teachers who are child advocates. What does that mean? What do I see as the benefits of starting a community grassroots organization? How would that enhance the development of information, support, and resources in ways that a state-level organization might not?

· · · · · · · · · · · · · · · · ·

CONTACTING CED

Information about CED can be obtained by writing to Director, 325 East Southern Avenue, Suite 107–108, Tempe, AZ 85282. *Telephone:* (602) 894-1333. *Fax:* (602) 894-9547.

Classroom-Level Collaboration

The education of young children today demands broadened roles of teachers (Surbeck, 1998). Working with very young children requires teachers to be in close contact with parents, and in some ways to be particularly vigilant about the well-being of children and families. The final model of collaboration is that which focuses on individual children (and families) in program or school settings. Working together at the classroom level may take different forms, but the central concept is that professionals work in partnership to solve problems and accomplish positive outcomes for children and families. In each case, there are teachers, school-related professionals, parents, and others who share a commitment to a vision or outcome for children. This collaboration can occur within a school or within a classroom, whether the classrooms are at the preschool or elementary level.

Three models that use teamwork or partnerships are described in this section. They include early intervention/inclusion, child study, and neighborhood schools.

Models using a team concept occur at different levels: state, community, school, and classroom.

Early Intervention/Inclusion.

One model, termed early intervention, provides collaborative services for children with special needs who are between the ages of birth and three years. Another type of classroom where you will find an emphasis on teamwork is in inclusive (or mainstreamed) classrooms, where teams provided through the public schools serve children older than age three. Inclusive classrooms have children who are developing in a typical manner, as well as children who have atypical development or physical or intellectual challenges. For children with special needs, a team is designated, as required by law. (The laws and inclusive classrooms are explained more in Chapters 5 and 10.)

Most teams include the regular classroom teacher, a special education teacher, and the parents. It may also include other service providers needed by a particular child, such as a social worker or family advocate, a speech and language pathologist, or an occupational therapist. The team meets together regularly to plan ways to assist the child in attaining individualized educational goals. This model is formally in place for children with special needs, but taking a team approach is used for other children as well.

Child Study.   A collaborative approach also occurs when teachers, parents, and other adults voluntarily choose to focus on a particular child. This approach is one that teachers and parents have used when they repeatedly watch a child over time and discuss the meaning of the child's behavior and thinking. On a continuum of least to highest intensity, the process has been variously termed child observation, child study, descriptive review, and, in medical cases, child staffing. The process also has been used by child development researchers in a scientific, formal way to study the behavior of children in early childhood. As you learned in Chapter 1, systematic observation is an important strategy. This approach makes extensive use of both observation and analysis as described in Chapter 1. Although teachers can and should conduct ongoing observations of all the children in their groups, child study goes further.

The purpose of child study is to advance understanding of why a child acts in a particular way or to determine how to adapt the curriculum and interaction for a specific child. To begin, several teachers agree to systematically study children in their own classrooms. Each teacher in the study group selects a child to study. The children are discussed on a rotating basis, so that each teacher presents his child (or children) during the course of the year.

Who participates on the team besides the teachers? Teachers may involve other people who have insight into a particular child's life. If other professionals (such as a social worker) are involved with the child and family, they may attend the session when the teacher is discussing the child, adding insights and expertise. Parents and family members are invaluable team members, and their inclusion is critical. Their insight and perspective are helpful in understanding the child and in agreeing on a consistent way of interpreting and responding to the child's behavior.

How are children chosen for study? Teachers might want to choose a child whose parents have expressed concern or perplexity about the child's behavior. A teacher also may identify a child in need of additional assistance, which may call for the expertise of other professionals. Because child study involves an intense look into a child's life, it is critical that such studies are handled in a professional and ethical manner. Teachers on child study teams do not label children, and all information and discussion about the child and family are confidential. The child is given a fictional name to protect the child's identity and that of the family.

Child study team members usually meet on a regular basis, perhaps once a week or every two weeks, during the school year. Having chosen a child of particular interest or concern, the teacher observes and gathers anecdotal information about the child. The child's behavior also can be recorded with a video camera and viewed again and again for greater comprehension of her behavior and language. Written field notes—anecdotal records jotted down in the child's natural environment—also are important. When the teacher feels that enough documentation has been collected, information about the child is presented to the team for discussion.

Typically, the presentation begins with a description of the child's physical characteristics, written in such a way that other individuals can easily picture the child. The child's height, weight, age, and demeanor are described, as well as the intellectual and language characteristics, activity level, movement, and emotional tone the child displays. A form for recording and summarizing this data might resemble Figure 2.1.

Any information about the child's development and history that is available through program or school records or obtained from an interview of the parents is also reported. Once participants have this background information, the team addresses the teacher's concern or question about the child. The study of that child continues until the teacher has a better understanding of how to interact with the child, what motivates him, and how he adapts. In addition, the teacher and family agree on strategies for interaction with the child.

This may sound simple, but if you consider what is involved in studying children in order to help them learn, you will recognize the complexity of the task. When you study a child this way, you will be operating as Piaget did as he studied his own (and other) children to develop his theory of how humans learn. If you read any of Vivian Paley's books, particularly *Wally's Stories* (Paley, 1981), you will understand the wealth and depth of information gleaned from the careful study of just one child.

The study of one child provides a great deal of information about children.

Neighborhood Schools. A third example of how collaboration and teamwork occur is evident at the school level. Neighborhood schools are schools that seek to offer specific experiences and services that families in that neighborhood need or want. Sometimes neighborhood schools provide a health clinic or a food bank on the school grounds. Other social, educational, or economic services may be part of a school campus, so that the school is seen as a hub in the community. Neighborhood schools are created when a community and school agree that the school is the best site for providing multiple services to children and families. Usually neighborhood

Figure 2.1 **Child Study Summary Sheet**

Child's Name: Age:

Physical Description:

Height: Weight:

Behavorial Characteristics:

Intellectual and Language Characteristics:

Activity Level:

Movement and Emotional Tone Displayed:

schools have a solid partnership with parents and families, so parents share in the responsibilities of developing and maintaining school policies and direction.

The advantages of neighborhood schools are that parents are actively engaged and the needs of families are met at a location where children naturally gather. Teams in these schools typically include school administrators, teachers, parents, and representatives from other agencies that implement or provide services at the school site.

SAN MARCOS NEIGHBORHOOD SCHOOL

An example of a neighborhood school is San Marcos School in Chandler, Arizona. The school is located in a neighborhood where both low- and middle-income families reside. Since the low-income families have difficulty with transportation, it was decided that a health clinic on the school site would facilitate the healthy development of children. A local businessman provides funding for the clinic. The school also provides Sunset Preschool for young children. This begins once classroom space is available at the end of the regular school day. Similarly, the library is open for extended hours, and literacy events engaging whole families are provided. The school also works in partnership with students from a nearby university who are preparing to be family counselors. Under supervision, the students counsel families and children in need of such a service.

The models of collaboration described here require flexible and community-oriented individuals. With increasing frequency, teacher preparation programs are striving to meet training needs for the expanded roles of teachers. Preparation for working in these kinds of programs and classrooms is based on a solid understanding of child development and behavior as well as commitment to families. Some college or university courses embed the concept of child observation and study in their child development courses; some offer credit for child study as an independent course. Increasingly, early childhood classes are blended with special education courses to provide prospective teachers with skills and knowledge about cross-professional functioning. Foremost among these skills are collaboration, communication, and conflict negotiation, all needed to work with other human services professionals and families.

CONSTRUCTIONS

1. Research

Locate a school or an early childhood program in your city where teams operate. Arrange to observe the program, classroom, or school and a team meeting. Write down your observations about how the collaboration or teamwork occurred.

2. Analysis

What teamwork is in evidence? What benefits and challenges does teamwork present to teachers? To families? Would you be interested in working in a collaborative setting? Why or why not?

This section has delineated the benefits of finding and creating resources while working with others. Let's return to Danielle's concern about where to find professional literature that she can access on her own to help her become a teacher. As you will see, it isn't contained in one book.

PROFESSIONAL LITERATURE

A collection of textbooks, journals, journal articles, and other printed documents provides a foundation for best practice in the classroom.

One of the most obvious sources of information about the career you are contemplating is found in the literature that abounds on early childhood education. Textbooks, journal articles, and professional literature form the repository of the most up-to-date knowledge and best practice in the field. As part of your preparation program, you are required to buy textbooks, collections of readings, and other written information. Consider the benefit of keeping those resources and using them to form the core of your own professional library. Naturally, a beginning personal library will not be as big as the library on your campus, so you must select carefully.

Most professors choose a text or readings because they consider them to be the best ones currently available. The professional literature you will acquire for class work has both an immediate value in its contribution to your understanding of the course and a long-term value in its contribution to your career development. As you have seen in the constructions, our suggestion is that you begin your collection now, selecting a manageable number of books, journals, journal articles, and other written documents that are of enduring value to you as a prospective teacher. We also suggest that you begin a collection of high-quality children's literature. Suggested strategies for selection of these resources follow, although you may find a different way to build a collection of resources that is more meaningful to you. Your

> ### BASIC COMPONENTS OF A PERSONAL LIBRARY
>
> Books
> Journals and journal articles
> Monographs and other documents
> Children's literature

decisions, motivation, creativity, and financial resources will determine the collection you create, but it is important to choose carefully.

Books

Being a teacher of young children means that you must have a wide knowledge base. Since children are new to the world, they have many things to learn, and most of their questions do not fit neatly into specific categories. That means you need to have general knowledge of many things that children experience as "content." This is part of the rationale for prospective teachers having a broad general education as well as specific information about children and families. As you progress through your general education courses, you should be asking questions about how the content of a general education course, such as a biology, could be useful to you as a teacher of young children.

Since we are focusing here on collecting professional literature specific to early childhood and constructivism, however, we suggest that you strive to own at least one high-quality book that covers each of the topics listed in the box "Categories for Professional Library Development" by the time you complete your program. The books should be written by people who are considered leaders in early childhood education and in the constructivist approach. By the time you finish this book, you will able to identify those authors by the approach they advocate for children.

CONSTRUCTIONS

Organizing

Begin preparing for the professional literature section of your resource collection by organizing the categories. Think of the categories listed in the accompanying box as suggestions and remember that the list is purposely minimal. You should alter and add to our suggested framework in ways that seem necessary and logical to you and that fit with your own knowledge about the categories. The categories are placed in a sequence that is a rough indication of a suggested order of acquisition.

> ### CATEGORIES FOR PROFESSIONAL LIBRARY DEVELOPMENT
>
> ▸ Child growth and development
> ▸ Best practice in early education
> ▸ Overview of or introduction to early childhood education
> ▸ Family interaction/empowerment/involvement
> ▸ Child guidance
> ▸ Teaching/learning in a diverse world
> ▸ Constructivist theory
> ▸ Constructivist approaches to teaching/learning with young children
>   –Math/logico-mathematical knowledge
>   –Science/physical knowledge
>   –Literacy/social conventional knowledge
>   –Assessment of children's thinking/learning
> ▸ Approaches to integrated curricula (health, creative activities, expressive arts, and other content areas)
> ▸ Legal responsibilities and ethics
> ▸ Teacher resources and references
>
> This collection of eight to ten books (in some cases, two or more categories may be contained within one resource) should be enough to give you a good start on a professional library. Your challenge is to choose the best book or text for the category, given our suggested guidelines or the development of your own criteria. The strategies presented for the selection of a good resource on how young children learn, found on page 41, may give you a start on your task.

Journals and Journal Articles

As we stated earlier in this chapter, one of the benefits of student membership in a professional organization is the regular receipt of a journal. Staying current on issues and topics central to the profession is easier if you regularly read journals; getting your own journal in the mail or accessing on-line journals can help you develop that habit. If you follow our recommendation and join at least one professional organization, you will begin to acquire journals. But for assignments, questions, and projects, you will want to search other journals as well. To facilitate this process, we have listed several, though certainly not all, of the early childhood journals you should find in your library (see the box "Early Childhood Journals"). Be aware that *journals,* written for professionals, are different from *magazines,*

> **EARLY CHILDHOOD JOURNALS**

▸ Journals written primarily for practitioners in classrooms and programs:
Child Care Information Exchange
Childhood Education
The Constructivist
Dimensions of Early Childhood
Early Childhood Education Journal
Young Children

▸ Journals that focus on child development and research:
Child Development
Child Study Journal
Early Childhood Research and Practice (**http://ecrp.uicu.edu./**)
Early Childhood Research Quarterly
Human Development
Journal of Exceptional Children
Journal of Research in Childhood Education

▸ Journals that focus on content areas:
Art Education
Language Arts
The Reading Teacher
Science and Children
Social Studies and the Young Child
Teaching Children Mathematics

Journals provide current information and supplement information in textbooks.

which are written for the general public. Although magazine articles are good sources of information and serve the important function of educating the general public, journal articles are reviewed by other professionals to ensure that practices advocated within them are educationally sound and in the best interests of children and families. (An exception to this is *The Constructivist*, which is reviewed by professional peers but called a magazine.)

In addition to being familiar with the early childhood journals on-line or located in your library, you also will benefit by keeping journal articles that are of particular interest to you or that you may want to share with parents. Articles you keep can deepen your understanding of content, especially when they overlap, extend, contradict, or update information contained in the books you read.

> The journal articles you keep should include complete source information and have print that is dark enough to copy clearly. Review the references for journal articles at the end of this book for examples of source information.

Monographs and Other Documents

Besides journal articles, a variety of other documents add to a professional library. Chief among these are publications such as the NAEYC's Code of Ethical Conduct (NAEYC, 1989) and a wide array of position papers containing professional points of view or advocacy statements related to young children and their families. These resources are often particularly helpful for parents of children in programs and for other individuals who need a short professional overview of a topic. Both the NAEYC and the ACEI list these documents in their resource catalogs, which are mailed to members twice a year. Your classes in early childhood education will undoubtedly provide you with such documents. In addition, several of these documents are listed in the "Resources" sections of this book.

CONSTRUCTIONS

1. Collecting

Using an organizational scheme similar to that for the construction on page 68 or of your own design, create a journal and document resource file.

2. Reflection

Which articles or other documents do you already have that you think should be placed in the file to keep? What makes them important or helpful?

Children's Literature

Let's return to the college classroom again. The students are waiting as the previous class begins to leave. Dr. K. is busy setting up materials for her next class. As Amy enters the classroom, she spies the children's story *Roxaboxen* by Alice McLerran (1991).

AMY: *(To Danielle.)* I know that story; it's a book for children! I wonder why Dr. K. has it up on her table today. Do you think she is going to read it to *us?*

ASK YOURSELF

Why would a professor take time to read children's literature in a college class? What benefits could I gain by having children's literature integrated into early childhood course work?

....

Children's literature provides teachers with a pathway to building community among children, as well as a valuable source of content information.

ASK YOURSELF

What are other guidelines for selecting children's books? (Write them in your resource notebook.)

....

Why should you need to have knowledge of children's books? For one thing, high-quality literature provides adults with a sure way to enter into the hearts and minds of children. If you have read good books to children, you are intuitively aware of the response that a good story elicits: quiet listening, stillness, and, usually, requests of "Read it again, teacher, read it again!" Stories capture all humans in a way that other media do not, and we seem to pay attention to them. As teachers, we all need ways to gain the attention of others. But there are more educationally oriented reasons for integrating children's literature.

A literature-based curriculum fits well with programs for young children that advocate an integrated content method and constructivist orientation. Why? Not only are thinking and the use of language critical to the process of learning and the development of literacy, but, more specifically, *stories* enhance and extend multiple levels of meanings about a wide variety of topics. In addition, *factual books* allow children to become researchers as they search for answers to their questions. Books of *jokes and riddles* can tickle the absurd possibilities of our thinking, and *poetry* invites reflection about feelings and ideas in a unique way. Literature also can serve as a key element in creating a sense of community that binds a group of children together with a shared understanding as they talk about Max and his wild rumpus in *Where the Wild Things Are* (Sendak, 1963) or create new adventures and perspectives for *Two Bad Ants* (Van Allsburg, 1988). Finally, many experts in content areas such as math and science encourage teachers to develop ways to use good literature to encourage and extend children's awareness and understanding of a subject. For example, *Counting On Frank* (Clement, 1991) encourages children to estimate quantities of all sorts of things found in their own environments. Although using literature is a good idea, we do not suggest that you begin collecting just *any* books, but rather those that are of high quality, interesting to children, and of enduring value.

Because children's literature is so useful to teachers of young children, we suggest that you be sure to take a class on this topic. Perhaps you have already done so. If so, you have access to guidelines for the selection of books. If not, the accompanying box provides guidelines to consider when beginning your collection.

A collection builds over time. Your finances will determine how many books you can acquire, but remember that even a few books are a start. You can always request children's books as gifts for any occasion. As a student working with children, you may have the opportunity to subscribe to children's book clubs. These clubs offer good literature in paperback form at low prices. Other suggestions for reasonable acquisition of books and other materials helpful to teachers can be found in the next section.

> ### GUIDELINES FOR CREATING A COLLECTION OF CHILDREN'S LITERATURE
>
> 1. Look for books that have won the Newbery or Caldecott Medal for outstanding children's literature or illustration.
> 2. Purchase books that children request over and over, but do look through the book yourself to determine whether you agree with their judgment and like the book, too.
> 3. Select books that depict people who represent a variety of cultures, capabilities, and ethnic groups.
> 4. Choose books that were favorites of yours as a child.
> 5. Ask your mentor, the local librarian, and several classroom teachers for suggestions of books that they believe are particularly good.
> 6. Skim the many resources that list content area–related literature, such as *Read Any Good Math Lately?* (Whitin & Wilde, 1992).
> 7. Build a collection of books written by one author or about one topic that you or the children especially enjoy.
> 8. Select books that feature good rhythm, rhyme, and predictable text through repetition.
> 9. Select books from many categories: fiction, fact, picture, poetry, humor, big books.

CONSTRUCTIONS

Organizing and Collecting

Using your own organizational scheme, provide the structure for beginning your collection of children's books.

COMMUNITY RESOURCES

The students have had a class session about the importance of linking the community to the classroom. Let's see what they are thinking as they prepare to leave class.

ZENAH: I really liked the African proverb that Dr. K. used today—"It takes a whole village to raise a child."

TILLIE: I thought she said "to educate a child." Which was it?

DANIELLE: Does it matter?

TILLIE: Well, I'd like the village to help me with both, but we don't live in any village! People in this village aren't racing to my door. In fact, I think government does what it can to make it difficult to—

ERIC: You guys are missing the point, going off on a tangent! What that quote was about has to do with collective responsibility to provide for the healthy development of children as future citizens. That should include community attention to educating the youngest citizens.

TILLIE: Okay, but the community isn't coming to me, saying "I want to help you teach"!

AMY: I think the point is that learning happens in locations other than just an early childhood program or a school. There are lots of places in the community that teachers can utilize to help children learn! Teachers have to take the initiative. The class where I volunteered went to the grocery store last year, and the kids learned a lot about the food and how it gets to the store. We even got to taste some of the vegetables that were unfamiliar to some of the children.

DANIELLE: It sounds like fun, getting away from school. I used to love that when I was in elementary school. But from what Dr. K. said, it sure takes a lot of time to organize something like that. It has to be worth the effort. They could go to the grocery store with their moms. What are some other places that you think would be good for little kids to visit in *this* city? There must be something pretty interesting here.

Unique Community Features

ASK YOURSELF

Can I write a description of my town or community that highlights both its usual and uncommon aspects? What makes my community unique? (Try writing a description.)

Communities share in the process and responsibility of educating children.

Each community is different from the next, although there are always some commonalities. For instance, most towns and cities have a school, a library, retail stores and businesses, and government agencies. Each locale also has a history and consists of particular individuals. Perhaps the best place to start determining what resources are available in your community is to determine what typical and unique features characterize the community.

If Danielle pursued her question about interesting community sites, she might discover that some cities have books or pamphlets that describe places and activities of particular interest to children. Looking in bookstores for such references may assist you in identifying unique community resources. If no such reference exists, finding resources related to the unique features of your location can be enlightening. Following is an example of a community description and resources:

The climate in Arizona is quite hot because it is located in the Sonoran Desert. Using just that knowledge, there are multiple avenues one might take to find resources unique to children and families in this community. One of the most enjoyable for children is the park system, which features water activities. There is a

---

CITY LISTINGS FROM TELEPHONE BOOK

Abuse/Assault Services	Parks and Recreation
Airports	Police
Arts Commission	Postal Services
Fire Department	Recycling Center
Fish and Wildlife	Services for Individuals with
Libraries	Special Needs
Mayor's Office	Youth Programs
Museums	

---

desert botanical garden that engages visitors in becoming detectives in discovering unique features of plants that allow them to adapt to the desert. There is also an archaeological site in Phoenix that invites children to simulate what archaeologists do in digging for the artifacts left by the Hohokam Indians, who developed a canal system to supply water. These are just a few of the many types of resources that characterize this location.

In addition to unique features, you can investigate typical resources to add to your store of information. These resources can usually be found in the telephone book under government agencies or in other city reference materials. Look in the White Pages of your telephone book under the city name to find a great deal of basic information, which is helpful especially if you are new to the community. A sample from one telephone book includes the categories in the accompanying box.

Many city government agencies and services have brochures or other printed materials, may provide speakers, or oversee sites for potential field trips for children. Alternatively, other businesses or community sites may be listed in newspapers or other resources. Again, these sites might be places to go with children or places where you can acquire needed materials. The following box provides a sample of what a search might yield.

BUSINESSES AND COMMUNITY SITES

Botanical garden	"Junk" stores
Children's bookstores	Lumberyard
Conservatory	Teacher resource stores
Ethnic stores or museums	Thrift shops
Factories	Toy Stores
Farms	Universities or colleges
Grocery stores	Zoo
Imaginariums	

Finding Resources in Unusual Places

ASK YOURSELF

What are some unusual sources of materials that I have discovered? How might I think of other sources to investigate? (Remember to share some of these with us via email. See page 8).

Following are some examples of unusual sources of materials and information that students have discovered in the past:

▸ Casinos. Because casinos must replace decks of cards often, they may be willing to donate used decks to teachers who can use them to help children learn math.
▸ Retiring teachers. They often are very happy to pass on materials that they have developed or collected over the years.
▸ Garage sales. Students say that when they are searching for inexpensive materials, estate sales, garage or yard sales, and swap meets often have interesting items for sale, including children's books and games.

CONSTRUCTIONS

1. Organizing and Listing Community Resources

Using the relevant preceding categories and any that you added to our list, fill in the specific names and addresses of community resources. Compare your list with a classmate's and draw on each other's information to fill in even more categories.

2. Working Collectively

Following the collective approach suggested earlier, divide new sources or ideas among group members, then call or visit various sites to determine what resources are available for teachers and children. Jot down that information. In a similar fashion, brainstorm ideas of unusual sources and see what you can discover. Include any Web sites you discover.

Teachers must take the initiative to find unusual community resources.

The suggested sites give you a start in developing an awareness of resources and places that may be available in your community. Have an enjoyable time creating your community resource file.

EDUCATIONAL TECHNOLOGY RESOURCES

Earlier, Dr. K. assigned the students the task of looking up resources on the Internet. She also asked them to write their reactions and thoughts about this task in their journals. When the class met again, Dr. K. asked for a volunteer to share his or her reflections. Without any hesitation, Amy volunteered her journal entries. Let's read a couple of her entries to see her reactions and thoughts as she investigated Internet resources on early childhood.

> I have only been familiar with a computer for a short time. Although I took a superficial course, I find, like anything new, I needed to give myself time to explore. I found myself avoiding the project initially, due to my beginner status with computers. Then I put my fear aside and created a window of time to just explore the Internet. I was shocked at how many sites came up for early childhood education—almost 1.5 million! "Wow," I thought, "how am I going to get through this assignment?" Then I discovered the amount of junk that clogs the system, the litter on the information superhighway. Then I thought, "Great, with all of this junk, how am I going to access quality information, which was my assigned task?" I found one good site in two hours of looking! I was exhausted at the two-hour mark.

> (One week later) Funny how the foreign language of Web addresses starts to become familiar. I look at it as learning a new language. It takes time, contemplation, and the willingness to take the risk to "speak." I happened upon a search engine, something called WebCrawler. Now I had spent quite a bit of time on the Web and easily took the risk of clicking on it. Earlier in my journey, I would have been afraid that I would get lost and never find my way back. At any rate, I took the risk on WebCrawler and found this to be the most successful medium to find desired information. Because I was looking for specific academic-quality sites, I could type in a topic like "collaboration in early education" and the crawler found matches. Once I got on the crawler, my assignment went faster and I had a lot of quality information. I found in surfing the Net I had to be willing to investigate a broad circumference of knowledge before I could get specific. I'm not very good at this yet, but I'm getting better!

We assume that many of you, like Amy, have at least some familiarity with computers and the Internet. If so, think back to your first forays on the Web. Did you also find that making sense of the computer and the Internet was a humbling and time-consuming task?

This last section of the chapter encourages you to become more familiar with electronic means of accessing resources in early childhood education. Why should you be asked to include resources from the **information superhighway**, including the Internet? The answer is easy: The information superhighway is a key for teaching and learning now and in the future. As Amy indicated, the best way for most of us to learn about this network of resources is to set aside time to explore. This can be daunting for the computer novice, but once you start, you will learn fairly rapidly. Further, technology will accommodate learners at almost every level. Even if you are a master at accessing resources via the computer, you will undoubtedly be challenged to find newer and better sources and sites to include in your

Computer technology provides young learners with exciting learning possibilities, but they must be assessed thoughtfully.
(© Elizabeth Crews)

collection. Before we begin our discussion of resources, however, a further point must be considered.

Using Technology with Young Children

How computers are used with young children is a controversial issue that is addressed in Chapter 6. As you will see, NAEYC has issued a position paper on the appropriate use of computers with young children. In addition, research conducted on the use of computers with children has provided important guidelines for your consideration. Being knowledgeable about the issues surrounding computers and the use of related resources is critical for teachers of young children. This issue is important to mention here because the selection of software, CD-ROMs, and Internet sites is vast and highly variable in quality. (See the suggested references for selecting software on pages 87 or 270.) Understanding the controversy about the use of computers with children is essential in making a decision about using or purchasing software or other computer-related materials. The resources described here are primarily those that other experts, teachers, and parents have recommended. As we said at the beginning of this chapter, your own experience with and informed assessment of available resources are the most powerful starting points in resource selection.

The Information Superhighway

What is the information superhighway? While serving as vice president, Al Gore first used this phrase to describe all the new means of communicating electronically (AT&T Learning Network Community Guide, Home Page, 1998, p. 29). Though commonly considered to be the same as the Internet, it is more than that. It includes **networks** accessible through telephone, cellular phone, broadcast, cable, and satellite systems. **Appliances** are the devices used to connect to the networks so that you can access, send, and receive information on the superhighway. Appliances include telephones, fax machines, cellular phones, pagers, computers, modems, CD-ROM drives, televisions, radios, and videoconferencing monitors (AT&T Learning Network Community Guide, Road Map, pp. 5–6). All of these devices can be considered teaching and learning tools. For example, think of the variety of ways that these appliances could be used or linked to broaden the communication between teachers and parents or to bring information into a classroom of children.

The computer, because it integrates many of these appliances, has the potential to replace previous forms and means of communication and information transfer. Although children can use the computer to play computer games and to practice basic skills, it presents far more interesting and exciting learning possibilities. In the following section, we provide some starting points for finding computer-related resources. Because computer and computer-related resources change on a daily (indeed, hourly) basis, these are only initial suggestions. We also provide a list of Web sites where you can access current information.

The Internet. Because of its power, we turn first to the Internet as a resource. The Internet can be considered the network of networks, linking people around the world through computers. According to Alvin Toffler (1990), access to information is the key to success in the next century:

> The second priority (after education) involves the speedy utilization of access to computers, information technology, and the advanced media. No nation can operate a 21st century economy without a 21st century electronic infrastructure. This requires a population as familiar with this infrastructure as it is with cars, roads, highways, trains, and the transportation infrastructure of the smokestack period. (p. 369)

Simply stated, the world's information infrastructure is the Internet (Van Horn, 1995). Because Toffler's projection appears to be true, prospective teachers must use the Internet and other computer-related resources for their own learning, as well as for instruction with children. What can

Information and resources available to teachers through technology are increasing rapidly and offer a means to access other resources worldwide.

you do on the Internet that is related to your professional development? At the time this is being written, you can send and receive electronic mail (E-mail); order and purchase materials and information; get news immediately; find discussion groups on any early childhood topic (including constructivism); transfer files; and access databases, card catalogs, and software. You can get technical assistance, find on-line educational magazines and journals, investigate guides to on-line libraries and museums, and enjoy video and audio presentations. You can also enter classrooms, both for adults and children, and visit educational sites worldwide. In fact, you can take courses through distance learning and download lesson plans. In the very near future, we will have electronic books that are commonly downloaded from the Web. By the time you read this, there will be even more uses (Van Horn, 1995, p. 572; AT&T, 1998, Road Map, p. 6).

The most efficient way to begin searching for resource topics and sites on the Internet is to start with an abbreviated list of the search engines currently available. By going directly to search engines, your research will be more focused and less time-consuming than Amy's. But be aware that these engines will take you to locations that contain huge amounts of information about a multitude of topics. The accompanying box lists some of the most popular search engines.

SEARCH ENGINES

Altavista (**www.altavista.digital.com**)
Excite (**www.excite.com**)
Lycos (**www.lycos.com**)
Netscape Navigator (**www.netscape**)
Yahoo! (**www.yahoo.com**) and Yahooligans! (**www.yahooligans. com**) specifically for children

If you want additional assistance, a tutorial on the use of search engines is available. "How to Search the World Wide Web: A Tutorial for Beginners and Non-Experts" can be found only on the Internet at **http://www.users.ids.net/~davehab/**.

CONSTRUCTIONS

1. Exploration

Set aside some time to play on the Internet. Investigate the Internet using one or more of the search engines.

2. Discovery

See what can you find in the way of sites that are useful to you as a teaching resource. Be sure to jot down the site(s) you find so that you can return later.

Web Sites for Teachers

Early Childhood. Of particular interest to us, as authors of this book, is the first site: Houghton Mifflin's Teacher Education Station, a resource for teachers and teacher educators. The address is **http://www.hmco. com/college**; click on "education." You can find lengthy information about topics such as "project-based learning space," and you can get thumbnail sketches from its free "concept carts." There you might want to look up "technology as a tool." Each cart has three subsections: (1) background knowledge, (2) what it looks like in the classroom, and (3) resources that are both print and electronic. You also can click on links to other relevant Web sites. To link to the authors of this book, and to provide direct feedback to us about it, go to the "connections" column and click on "contact authors," or find our book in the "tickets" area, which has a link to our E-mail addresses. We hope to hear from you.

The Web sites for NAEYC (**http://www.naeyc.org/naeyc**) and ACEI (**http://www.udel.edu/bateman/acei**) were mentioned earlier in this chapter. Both of these sites provide early childhood teachers with specific information about the professional field of early childhood education. Because of these organizations' foundational work in early childhood education, we highly recommend that you browse these sites early in your search for resources.

Another site that is interesting and helpful to prospective teachers is the ERIC Clearinghouse on Elementary and Early Childhood Education at **http://www.ericece.org**. This site allows visitors to investigate a vast database of information about early childhood education. (Searching this way would please Danielle, who dislikes going to the library.) There is also the World Association of Early Childhood Educators to explore, at **http:// www.waece.com**. Another powerful professional site is the Children's Defense Fund, at **http://www.childrensdefense.org**. This education and advocacy organization provides a voice for America's children. Particular attention is given to the needs of poor and minority children and those with disabilities.

Early Childhood Special Education. To locate information about children with special needs, refer to the Council of Exceptional Children (CEC),

Division of Early Childhood (DEC), at **http://www.soe.uwm.edu/dec/dec.html**. There you will find selections about the CEC and DEC, professional standards, a job bank, publications and products, and information about children with special needs. A second site with this focus can be found at the ERIC Clearinghouse on Disabilities and Gifted Education, **http://www.cec.sped.org/er-menu.htm**. Selections include information about the clearinghouse, the ERIC system, a database search mechanism, special projects, links to other information sources, list servers, and information about upcoming conferences. A final site in special education is Marc Sheehan's Special Education Page, at **http://www.halcyon.com/marcs/sped.html**. This site allows you to link to many other special education sites and even has a selection for lesson plans. More teacher Web sites are listed in the Resources section at the end of this chapter. Perhaps you would like to suggest other teacher Web sites to us that you find especially helpful. You can add to our list by going to the Houghton Mifflin site (see p. 81) and supplying us with a complete address for the site.

Web Sites for Children. One of the most interesting educational sites for children is Exploratorium, found at **http://www.exploratorium.edu**. This museum in San Francisco has around five hundred interactive exhibits. Kids learn by doing! Another location that has the mission of fostering literacy, artistic expression, and cross-cultural understanding is Kids Space, at **http://www.kids-space.org**. Here children can share their creativity with other children around the world. A fun site for children and parents that includes video clips is Gumby Central, at **http://www.gumbyworld.com**. Visitors can send Gumby postcards to family and friends. For older children in the early childhood age range, try KidsClick, at **http://www.sunsite.Berkeley.edu/kidsclick**. A joint project of the University of California–Berkeley and Sun Microsystems, this site provides children help with their homework.

A final suggested Web site for children (and their parents and teachers) who are seeking volumes of information is Encarta, at **http://www.encarta.msn.com**. Encarta Online is an on-line encyclopedia with links to other sites for further exploration.

Computer-Related Resources. The superhighway also provides for learning through multiple modalities. Multimedia technology has allowed for the inclusion of visual, auditory, and graphic input and output. Software programs that use CD-ROMs and videos are an increasingly commonplace means of gaining information. This is as true for adults as for children. Here are a few multiple-media suggestions to enhance your professional development and to investigate for use with children.

A company called Classroom Connect, at **http://www.classroom.com**, has developed a link to help K–12 teachers achieve their goals for students. The major focus is helping teachers use the superhighway in their classrooms. This site offers teachers the opportunity to contact colleagues online to discuss using the Internet in the classroom, and it provides a list of innovative educational products. One example of these products is an Internet video series that provides hands-on instruction for how to use the Internet with children in the classroom. The videos show how to link students to the world and get Internet-wide responses to questions. They also include ideas for curriculum integration and showcase Internet projects with children in other classrooms. One product that has received particular attention is the Quest series, which takes children on powerful interactive Internet adventures in Africa, the Galápagos Islands, and Australia (Classroom Connect, 1998).

Another example of a multiple-modality program designed for children is *The San Diego Zoo Presents . . . The Animals* (Software Toolworks, 1992). Children can "visit" the zoo and see and hear the animals, all courtesy of CD-ROM. They can watch animals on videotape and read about the animals as well. They can even create their own tour of the zoo. A second suggestion, *Millie's Math House*, comes again from Edmark. Here children can explore math concepts along with interesting characters. They can solve problems and enjoy the music as well.

One of the most useful resource guides for software is *Educational Software Preview Guide* (International Society for Technology in Education, 1999). This guide, which has sections for early childhood/preschool and older children, lists software for the disciplines of math, science, language arts, and social studies. Although the guide does not evaluate the products available, these lists will help you begin the evaluation process. For example, many computer stores have demonstration programs to preview, but it helps to know something about the products before you preview them. The guide includes publishers' addresses and national educational software distributors. To order this annual guide, go to **iste@oregon.uoregon.edu**.

These are just a few suggestions out of thousands of products. We encourage you to spend some time becoming familiar with teaching possibilities using these and other technology tools.

The future of education is about to be revolutionized by the innovations of the superhighway. We hope that you, as a teacher of the future, are as excited

Teaching is a relationship-based activity: One-on-one interaction is important for young learners.

about the possibilities as we are and that this section has given you the desire and foundation to become a connected teacher. However, even with all the electronic possibilities, we want to remind you that teaching is a relationship-based enterprise. The Velveteen Rabbit (M. Williams, 1922/1969) knew that the critical part of being "real" develops from hours spent together in person-to-person contact. Although the computer enables teachers and children to do many things, it cannot replace that contact, which is especially important in the early years. This chapter has presented a variety of resources for you to consider as you build your professional knowledge base about early childhood education. Your constructions and experiences are the foundation for becoming that real teacher you envision.

SUMMARY

> Information, resources, and support are found or created by the actions each person takes. They are based on the individual's knowledge, past experiences, interactions, and needs.

> Important human sources of information, resources, and support are ourselves, our peers, early childhood professionals, friends with different challenges and cultural backgrounds, and individuals with expertise in the community.

> Students' parents and family members provide information and resources that cannot be acquired from any other source.

> Joining with other individuals in professional organizations introduces students to the culture of the early childhood profession and the invisible university.

> Books and other printed material provide beginning teachers with knowledge of long-standing and current practices in the field of early childhood education.

> Knowledge of children's books assists teachers in reaching children through both fantasy and fact, integrating content across disciplines, building community with children and families, and promoting literacy.

> Creating a professional library and a collection of materials and resources promotes personal growth in the field.

> Knowledge of sites and resources in the local community enables teachers to use the community in educating children.

> Technology provides novice teachers access to a vast number of resources that may be helpful in multiple ways.

CONSTRUCTIONS

1. Organizing

The constructions in the chapter have encouraged you to organize sections of your professional library and resource collection. You may have several different collections and lists, as well as ideas written down to work on later. For this construction, bring all those pieces together in a coherent, clearly organized resource kit that you can add to as you progress. We have provided examples of how to organize such a kit, but you may want to use another system to coordinate the various parts of this personal resource.

2. Expanding Your Resources

As you read the following chapters, pay particular attention to the references and resources provided. The authors have carefully chosen these professional references because they contain valuable information. Go to the original citation to read more about ideas that are of particular interest to you or that will strengthen your background in an area unfamiliar to you. You might also find lists or other items in the chapters that you would like to photocopy or use with an overhead projector later on. Add these to your resource file as you complete the course.

RESOURCES

Basic Books and Documents

Beaty, J. (1996). *Preschool appropriate practices* (2nd ed.). Orlando, FL: Harcourt Brace.

Bredekamp, S., & Copple, C. (Eds.). (1997). *Developmentally appropriate practice in early childhood programs* (Rev. ed.). Washington, DC: NAEYC.

Derman-Sparks, L., & The ABC Task Force. (1989). *Anti-bias curriculum: Tools for empowering young children*. Washington, DC: NAEYC.

Eddowes, E., & Ralph, K. (1998). *Interactions for development and learning: Birth through eight years.* Upper Saddle River, NJ: Prentice-Hall.

Fields, M., & Boesser, C. (1998). *Constructive guidance and discipline: Preschool and primary education* (2nd ed.). Upper Saddle River, NJ: Prentice-Hall.

Gonzalez-Mena, J. (1993). *Multicultural issues in child care*. Mountain View, CA: Mayfield Publishing.

Labinowicz, E. (1980). *The Piaget primer: Thinking, learning, teaching*. Menlo Park, CA: Addison-Wesley.

Moyer, J. (Ed.). (1995). *Selecting educational equipment and materials for school and home.* Wheaton, MD: ACEI.

Paley, V. G. (1990). *The boy who would be a helicopter.* Cambridge, MA: Harvard University Press.

Shore, R. (1997). *Rethinking the brain: New insights into early development.* New York: Families and Work Institute.

Trawick-Smith, J. (1997). *Early childhood development: A multicultural perspective*. Upper Saddle River, NJ: Prentice-Hall.

Children's Literature

(Note: The following resources provide titles and review or summary information about many children's books, often including how to incorporate literature when teaching children. In addition to these books, the journal *Childhood Education* regularly reviews new literature for children.)

Glazer, J. I. (1991). *Literature for young children* (3rd ed.). New York: Macmillan.

Huck, C. S., Hepler, S., & Hickman, J. (1993). *Children's literature in the elementary school* (5th ed.). Orlando, FL: Harcourt Brace.

Raines, S. C., & Canady, R. J. (1991). *More story stretchers: More activities to expand children's favorite books*. Mt. Rainier, MD: Gryphon House.

Journals and Professional Magazines Related to Early Childhood Education

American Music Teacher
Educational Leadership (See special issues on early childhood education [1986] and integrating technology in teaching [1997].)
Elementary School Journal
Journal of Health, Physical Education and Recreation
Journal of Learning Disabilities
Journal of Negro Education
Music Educator's Journal
Pre-K Today
School Arts: The Art Education Magazine for Teachers
Teaching PreK–8

Resources for Computer Software

(Note: In addition to the *Educational Software Preview Guide*, mentioned on page 83, the following resources provide titles and descriptions of software and often provide information about using software with children.)

Grabe, M., & Grabe, C. (1996). *Integrating technology for meaningful learning.* Boston: Houghton Mifflin.

Only the Best Guide to Software (http://www.asce.org). Go to ASCD Select
   Online to access
Recommended Starter Software K–6 (http://www.highscope.org/).
Technology journals that frequently review software:
   CD-ROM Today
   Computers in the School
   The Computing Teacher
   Electronic Learning
   Journal of Computers in Mathematics and Science Teaching
   NewMedia Magazine
   Technology and Learning

Web Sites

Books and Libraries

Amazon.com **(http://www.amazon.com)**
Internet Public Library **(http://www.ipl.org)**
Libraries for the Future **(http://www.inch.com/~lff/lffhome.htm)**

Children and Families

Interesting Places for Kids **(http://www.crc.ricoh.com/people/steve/
   kids.html)**
Family.Com **(http://www.family.disney.com)**
Kidlink **(http://www.kidlink.org)**
Kidscom **(http://www.kidscom.com)**
National Center for Fathering **(http://www.fathers.com)**
Parent Soup **(http://www.parentsoup.com)**
Parenttime **(http://www.parenttime.com)**

Computers/Internet

AskEric **(http://ericir.syr.edu)**
Evaluating Internet Resources: A Checklist
   (http://infopeople.berkeley.edu:80000/bkmk/select.html)
How to Critically Analyze Information Sources
   (http://urisref.library.cornell.edu/skill26.htm)
International Society for Technology in Education (ISTE)
   (http://isteonline.uoregon.edu)
No Wonder **(http://www.nowonder.com)**
Online Internet Institute (OII)
   (http://prism.prs.k12.NJ.US:70/0/Ollsignup.html))
ZD Net **(http://www.zdnet.com)**

Early Childhood Resources

National Organization of Child Development Laboratory Schools
(http://w3.aces.uius.edu/HCD/CDL/noecdls/nocdls.html)
Organization Mondiale pour l'Education Pre-Scolaire OMEP—U.S. National Committee (a unit of the World Organization for Early Childhood Education)
(http://www.omep-us.crc.uiuc.edu)

Museums

Impact Guide to Museums on the Web
(http://www.sils.umich.edu/impact/museums/)
Museums on the Web
(http://curry.edschool.virginia.edu/~lha5w/museum)

PART 2

Children

*T*HE FOUR CHAPTERS *in Part 2 of this book offer perspectives on the children who frequent the early childhood programs for which you are preparing to teach. These four chapters provide the information and experiences to help you begin to transform your currently held ideas and beliefs into more coordinated understandings of children. Chapter 3 introduces you to children in many settings, discusses how they grow and develop, and offers information on how different educational settings facilitate children's development. Chapter 4 explores children's thinking from a constructivist perspective and helps you advance your thinking about the kinds of knowledge children hold and how that knowledge changes over time. Chapter 5 describes how views of children have changed over time, and provokes you to think about how those views translate into your personal philosophy about the care and education of young children. Chapter 6 informs you of some of the major issues facing children and families today. This chapter provides insight into how early childhood professionals help children and families deal with some of these issues. We trust that you will find the children in these chapters as intriguing and personable as we do.*

3

Observing Children's Development in Early Childhood Education

• •

This chapter presents images of children from different cultural backgrounds, with different kinds of abilities, and at different levels of development to help you construct a deeper understanding of the types of children with whom you might work. Most beginning teachers are eager to visit early childhood settings so they can observe teachers in action. This chapter invites you to set aside what you may learn from observing the teacher to focus on what you may learn from observing the individual children in early childhood settings. To do this, we offer dialogues among children in a variety of early childhood programs. We challenge you to notice that although children of the same age may be similar in many ways, they are all individuals who differ from each other in many ways. We visit children in an infant program, a toddler program, a preschool program, a public school kindergarten classroom, and a second-grade classroom in a public primary school. This chapter will help you construct a more advanced understanding of the following issues:

▶ How children within settings are alike and different
▶ How children across settings are alike and different
▶ How each setting is adapted to meet the physical, social, cognitive, and individual needs of the children
▶ How each setting responds to the cultural differences and special needs of the children

INTRODUCTION

Dr. K. has asked the class to visit a variety of early childhood settings that serve children of different ages. The purpose of the visit is for the students to become familiar with the developmental and individual characteristics of the children in each setting and to determine how each setting meets the children's developmental and individual needs. Dr. K. has asked that the students, working in pairs, visit at least two different local programs so that they can exchange points of view. She leaves the students to make their visitation arrangements.

TILLIE: Well! I don't see why we have to go observe in those infant and toddler programs. All that's going on there is baby-sitting, and I didn't come to college to learn how to be a baby sitter.

ZENAH: Oh, Tillie, don't be so negative. I think it's just amazing how much those little ones can learn.

TILLIE: Maybe so, but I don't think it takes a college education to change a diaper. I think I'll visit the preschool.

ERIC: I was thinking that I might like to visit an infant program, because I've never been around children that young. I worry that I might not be able to hold them correctly. They seem so fragile and helpless.

DANIELLE: I'll go with you to see the infants. I think they're so cute, and at least I won't have to think of clever questions to ask them.

CHILDREN IN INFANT PROGRAMS

Eric and Danielle visit the local public school's early education program, which has a full-day infant program that serves infants from six weeks to eighteen months of age. The building has observation booths that allow visitors to observe the entire infant classroom without disrupting the children and caregivers. Eric and Danielle enter the observation booth and begin to look around the infant room. Danielle notes one teacher changing the diaper of an infant girl. While she is changing the diaper, she is talking to the infant, explaining everything that she is doing. "Now a little wipe to make sure you are clean. Now I'm putting on the clean diaper. And now you are ready to play!"

DANIELLE: Gosh, Eric, look at all the stuff that teacher is doing just to change a diaper. It looks like an operating room in the hospital with those latex gloves she's wearing. And why in the world is she talking to that baby like she thinks the baby understands? Don't you think it's a bit much?

ERIC: I don't know, Danielle. Look at how that infant seems to be listening to every word she says. And look, now that the teacher has stopped talking, it looks like that little tyke is trying to talk back. Listen to the cooing sounds she's making.

DANIELLE: Yeah! It's almost like they are having a conversation.

ERIC: Yeah! And did you notice how carefully the teacher put the dirty diaper in that covered pail? Now she's recording the diaper change on that chart on the wall.

DANIELLE: Wow, I never dreamed that changing a diaper could be so complicated and could possibly be a learning experience as well.

ERIC: Hey, Danielle, look over there by the beds. That little boy is pitching a real fit. I don't think he likes it here. It looks like his mother is trying to get him to go to sleep and he keeps screaming.

DANIELLE: Yeah! Wonder what's wrong? That's the problem with infants! They can't talk, so you can't figure out what they want.

ERIC: But look! He's stopped crying. He stopped the minute that other little boy was brought in. Look at him now! It almost looks like he's smiling.

(At this point, the caregiver places the two infant boys on the floor facing each other.)

ERIC: Look, Danielle, it looks like they're playing together. That second little one looks like he's trying to give his rattle to the first.

DANIELLE: Yeah, and listen to the gurgling sounds the other is making! I wonder if infants can really have friends. Hey, where did the mother go?

These conversations reflect how many students feel when they first enter an early childhood program. Their main objective is to teach children in public schools, starting with kindergarten, and they view work with infants as baby-sitting. Eric and Danielle have never considered working with infants as teaching, but as they observe in this center, they begin to question some of their earlier notions. We leave Eric and Danielle in the infant room and take this opportunity for you to advance your understanding about the developmental characteristics of the infants in this center.

Developmental Characteristics of Infants

ASK YOURSELF

Why does the caregiver spend so much time diapering the infant? What do I know about why she wears gloves and records the change on the chart? And why does she tell the infant everything she is doing? Is this overkill, or is there something that I need to know about this?
....

> The earliest period in the life of the infant is one of rapid growth and development.

Infants in infant care programs range in age from around six weeks to eighteen months of age. Usually the infant enters the program when the mother's maternity or father's paternity leave ends. The length of time a child remains in an infant care program varies according to how programs are organized.

The earliest period in the life of the infant is one of rapid growth and development. Although the words *growth* and *development* are often used interchangeably, *growth* refers more to a change in size, such as height and weight, whereas *development* refers more to a change in the complexity or organization of actions and ideas. The developmental sequence is the same for all children, but the developmental rate differs individually because of each child's biological inheritance and the environmental conditions under which the child is raised.

Physical Characteristics. Infants are busy at work from the time they are born. They listen to the sounds around them, they look at everything they can see, they flail at and grasp objects, and they put everything in their mouths. At six weeks weeks of age, infants have little voluntary control over their **reflex actions,** but by the time they leave this infant care program, most will be walking. This amazing metamorphosis includes developing processes as complicated and necessary as eye control, holding the head erect, reaching out and grasping, sitting upright, and transferring and manipulating objects. By the end of the children's first year, they will be able to use their fingers with precision and stand and walk with support. All of this is accomplished through the infants' own sensory and **motoric** activity as they interact with their physical environment. Three major growth processes govern the infant's ability to coordinate the actions of their bodies and the objects about which they are curious.

> ▸ The control of the body begins at the head and proceeds downward, so that control of the walking muscles is one of the last to be managed. This is referred to as the **cephalocaudal** process.
> ▸ The control of the body begins with the middle of the body and proceeds to the outer parts. That is, development proceeds from the use of the torso to the use of the extremities, such as the fingers. This is referred to as the **proximodistal** process.
> ▸ The control of the body progresses from more general motor control, such as crawling, to more specific fine motor control such as holding a rattle. This is referred to as **motoric refinement.**

These three processes allow us to discern how children in the infant center are developing physically. All of this activity is integrated by the infants' inborn curiosity about the objects and people in their environment. They use all of their sensory receptors to build their impressions of their physical and social world. Benchmarks to look for when observing infants' physical development are presented in Table 3.1.

Cognitive Characteristics. The infant's early activity facilitates **cognitive development** as well as physical development. According to Piaget, cognitive development is a continuous process that begins at birth and continues through adulthood. Infants fall into the first of Piaget's four stages in the development of thought, the one he refers to as the **sensorimotor stage.** During this stage of cognitive development, infants do not think as we understand the

Infants use all of their sensory receptors to build impressions of their physical and social worlds.

Cognitive development is a continuous process that begins at birth and continues through adulthood.

TABLE 3.1 Benchmarks in Motor Development from Birth to Eighteen Months

Age	Gross Motor Activity	Fine Motor Activity
Birth to 6 months	Lifting head Supporting own weight Turning over from front to back Supporting own head Sitting with support	Swiping at objects Involuntary grasping of objects Reaching for toys
6 to 12 months	Turning over from back to front Sitting alone Crawling with hands and feet Pulling up to stand Standing alone Initial walking with adult or bed rail support Crawling up stairs	Moving toy from hand to hand Voluntary grasping of objects Using thumb and forefinger to grasp
12 to 18 months	Walking between chairs or low tables Rolling balls Walking without support Squatting without falling Climbing into and onto furniture	Throwing objects from chair or bed Dropping toys and picking them up Using fingers to eat Stacking blocks and knocking them over Using a cup for drinking Using a spoon

term, but rather use all of their senses and a limited number of reflex actions (the first schemata) to adapt to and organize the world around them. These first **schemata** are the beginnings of the intellectual structures by which all intellectual development is adapted and organized. Piaget classified sensorimotor activity into six sequential levels, which he grouped according to the increasing complexity of the patterns of activity (see Table 3.2). The important characteristics of each level document the infant's movement from the use of reflex activity through object permanence to representational thought. The first five of these stages describe the intellectual development of infants from birth to eighteen months of age.

Cognitive development is an internal process in which children are the active constructors of their knowledge. You will learn considerably more about this process in Chapter 4, but for now we want you to understand that children learn as they act on their environments. This action is the source of their intellectual development, and it begins at birth.

Recent brain research supports the work of Piaget in that it explains how the important work infants do facilitates cognitive development. This research suggests that infants learn better if they are deeply interested in what they are doing. Additionally, research suggests that the more of this interesting experience children have in the early years, the greater the number of

TABLE 3.2 Characteristics of Sensorimotor Development (Ages Birth to 2)

Stage	Defining Characteristics	Examples
1. Reflexes 0–1 month	Reflex actions	Sucking, grasping, crying, vocalizing, body movement, movement of arms and legs.
2. First achieved adaptations Primary circular reaction 1–4 months	The child differentiates the object to be sucked or grasped. The infant reproduces an activity in order to reproduce the sensation that it brings.	Infant rejects pacifier or fingers when he wants milk. Thumb or pacifier sucking is controlled by infant.
3. Secondary circular reactions 4–8 months	The beginning of intentionality: The infant reproduces the effect of the action by repeating the action, and thus rediscovers the means that cause the result.	When infant in bed kicks her legs, the mobile swings back and forth. Infant watches the mobile, smiles, and kicks her legs again.
4. Coordination of secondary schemata 8–12 months	The infant can differentiate means and ends of actions and can apply this schema to new situations.	Infant can use his lifting schema to lift the pillow as a means to get the toy under the pillow. Lifting is used as a means to get the toy (which is the end goal).
5. Tertiary circular reactions 12–18 months	The discovery of new means through experimentation. Variation in the means leads to variation in the results. Variation is pursued for its own sake.	Infant rolls different objects under different conditions and watches to see what happens.
6. Invention of new means 18–24 months	Cognitive representation. New means through mental combinations. Can evoke objects not present and anticipate action plans.	Infant sees a cookie out of reach, picks up a long stick, and uses it to bring the cookie within her grasp.

Source: Adapted from *Constructive evolution: Origins and development of Piaget's theory* by Michael Chapman. Copyright © 1988. Reprinted with permission of Cambridge University Press.

neural connections their brains will form. Thus all infants go through the same process in early brain development, but the kind of experiences a child encounters during this period will influence the number of neural connections made, which in turn influences the child's cognitive development.

The two most important cognitive steps infants complete during this stage of development are **object permanence** and the ability to invent new means to solve problems. Object permanence refers to the awareness that objects exist even when they cannot be seen. You can determine when a particular infant has reached this step by hiding a play object and observing whether the child searches for it. As object permanence develops, the child uses it to solve the problem of finding missing objects. However, at this point the infant is limited to searching for things only where they have disappeared earlier, rather than where she last sees it disappear. Through unsuccessful searches using this process, the infant gradually refines her schemes for finding objects by experimenting with new means rather than habitually using the old means. Through this trial-and-error experimentation with objects, the infant invents solutions to new problems, an important step in her intellectual development.

Infants move from being asocial at birth, through feelings related only to self, to true social relations with others.

Social Characteristics.

Through their own activity and their interactions with others, infants move from being asocial at birth, through feelings related only to self, to true social relations with others. Adults find it difficult to believe that the infant is asocial at birth, because they find the infant responsive to their faces and voices. However, at birth the infant's smile is reflexive. He has no sense of others as adults would like to think. The social characteristics of infants fall into three major categories: characteristics of social cognition, characteristics related to language learning, and characteristics related to feelings, or **affective development**.

Social Cognition. The construction of knowledge about self is part of cognitive development. Infants move from a state of total **egocentrism,** a lack of awareness of anything but their own point of view, to the knowledge of self as an object that is separate from other objects in the world. The construction of self-identity is a major task at this stage. At around ten to twelve months of age, infants begin to differentiate themselves from objects in their environments. By eighteen months, infants have differentiated themselves and others as permanent objects. This allows for the development of self-perception. Once this differentiation begins, infants may experience separation and stranger anxiety. Separation anxiety relates to the distress children have when their parents leave them, and stranger anxiety relates to the apprehension children feel when they see a face that they do not recognize.

Language Learning. Watching an infant construct language is a fascinating experience because he accomplishes so much in such a short time. During their first six months, infants are very busy making and listening to sounds. As they listen, they are actively discriminating between human and other sounds, as well as between different rhythmic and intonational patterns in the human voice. As they play, they experiment with all the sounds the human voice can make in a highly random way, and they seem to have little control over the sounds they make.

Piaget suggests that children construct social schemata in the same way they construct schemata about the world of objects. (© Elizabeth Crews/ The Image Works)

Around six months of age, there is a significant change in their vocalizations. At this point, infants begin to use only the sounds of their own language, and they work to bring the sound patterns under greater control. These sound patterns are speechlike in that they are organized in syllable-like combinations (for example, ba-ba-ba), with the use of intonational features such as pitch, rhythm, and stress. If you listen carefully, you will be able to discern which kind of sounds an infant is producing.

As infants continue to experiment with these sound patterns through **babbling,** they produce wordlike sounds such as "ma-ma" or "ga-ga." Adults often respond to segments of this babble as real talk. They smile and repeat what the child says or urge the child to say it again. These adult-child interactions help move the infant to real speech—the ability to consistently use the same groups of sounds to symbolize a consistent meaning. Infants continue this kind of babbling, interspersed with the use of one-word expressions that have different meanings depending on the context. For example, "milk" may mean "I want some milk," or it may mean "Take that milk away!" The meaning is conveyed through intonation and body language. At this point, infants understand many more words than they can produce. The language of the young child is representational as it represents one object or action from the child's experience. You will learn more about the representational nature of language in Chapter 4.

Affective Development. The first signs of an infant's emotional development begin between one and four months of age. At this time the smile, which was present at birth, begins to be used to signal feelings of contentment. There are two kinds of feelings that begin during this period. The first of these feelings are perceptual, responses to stimuli such as feelings of pleasantness, pain, discomfort, and pleasure. The second kind of feelings result from the differentiation between needs and interests (Piaget, 1981) and range from contentment to disappointment. These feelings are not perceptual in nature, but they do go beyond the immediate need to the whole experience.

Infants between eight and twelve months use their feelings to help them determine goals and the means by which they can achieve those goals. For example, playing with an object may bring pleasure, so the infant's goal is to get that object, or an infant may repeat behaviors she knows will bring adult attention.

From twelve to eighteen months, infants begin to build social relations with others. As they learn to differentiate self from others, they develop feelings about those they like and those they fear. It is at this time that the social smile is a genuine response to the caregiver's smile. The two infants Eric and Danielle observed in the infant center exemplify how infants use feelings to achieve their goals and to express their liking of each other.

Individual Characteristics. Jerry, the first child Eric observed, comes from a two-parent home where both parents work. He is the youngest of three children and has been in a full-time care program since he was six weeks old. He is nine months old, measures thirty-one inches in length, and weighs twenty-two pounds. Jerry is rather shy and has recently developed separation anxiety, the fear of separating from familiar adults. Quantavious, the child who played with Jerry, comes to the program two days a week. He is the first child in his family, and his mother wants him to socialize with other children. Quantavious is also nine months old, measures twenty-seven inches in length, and weighs eighteen and a half pounds. Quantavious is very active, sociable, and outgoing. Both boys enjoy playing together and love opportunities to explore new toys.

Individual differences result from many factors, including heredity, culture, gender, and birth order.

Individual differences that make every child unique result from many factors, including heredity, culture, gender, and birth order. In addition to these differences, each child is born with a different temperament. **Temperament** refers to a person's patterns of functioning or responding, which start at birth and continue throughout life. Temperamental characteristics include the manner in which an infant adapts to new situations, the degree to which he persists in activities, the ease by which he is distracted, and the kind of mood he exhibits. In the above example, we find two infant boys of about the same age who are different in size, in affective development, and in temperament. One is shy and has separation anxiety; the other is outgoing and more sociable.

MULTIPLE PERSPECTIVES

From the Field

Marti White is the director of the Auburn City School's employer-supported child-care program in Auburn, Alabama. She holds a bachelor's degree in early childhood education and has completed work toward a master's degree. Her center is going through *STEPS to Accreditation,* a system of support, technical assistance, and recognition to encourage and assist child-care centers in attaining national accreditation by NAEYC. Florine Fuqua is an infant teacher at the UAW Chrysler Corporate Child Development Center in Huntsville, Alabama. She holds a bachelor's degree in social work and child development. This box presents two perspectives of the children served in infant centers.

Marti White

Our infant program serves children from six weeks to no more than eighteen months. We serve them in two different rooms that I refer to as the infant room (six weeks to twelve months) and the creeper room (twelve months to eighteen months). In the infant room, we presently have five children. We will have a sixth coming in November.

In the infant room, we have Sylvester and Thomas. Sylvester is eight months with brown hair and brown eyes. He is the biggest infant in our class. Sylvester's mother and father are both in the athletic field, and you can see that athletic prowess in Sylvester. He was born with a cleft palate and has had a tough life so far. He is tough because he has had to be tough. He has already had two surgeries, and he is going in for the final one soon. The difference the surgery has made is just amazing. Sylvester is a very friendly, outgoing child, who is just about as round as he is tall. And he is so very friendly. He comes into the room, and he just lights up. He enjoys lots of interaction with people and is not easily upset by strangers. He is not walking yet, but he is trying to crawl. He gets so frustrated. You'll see him on the floor trying to pull up, falling, and then trying to pull up again. It is such a process! There is frustration, and then you can see that sense of pride when he accomplishes something. Sylvester is beginning that process right now.

Thomas has blond hair and blue eyes and is about the same age as Sylvester, but different in many ways. When I think of Thomas, I think of pleasant. He has a very sweet nature and is so appreciative of everything we do. When you talk with him, he is willing to help by cooing or babbling when you stop. When you walk over to him, his face looks like he is saying, "Welcome to my world!" and he gives you a beautiful smile. Thomas interacts with others in the classroom. He smiles, coos, and responds to any interaction with his body. He wiggles in pure enjoyment, and watching him is pure delight.

ASK YOURSELF

Can infants really learn at this age, or are they merely being cared for? Does it really make a difference how I interact with these children? Do I want to teach in an infant program? Why or why not?

In the creeper room, we have Josh. Josh is very responsive but is particular about who to trust and who not to trust. He is learning to walk and is very confident in that area. He can pull up on things and can stand alone, but he hasn't taken a step yet.

Florine Fuqua

I had two difficult children in the center that no one in the center wanted. They cried all the time, and no one could do anything with them. I was able to work with them, to love them, to spend time with them, and to kind of go back to the beginning with them and redevelop things that I thought were missing. So in other words, I had to go back and undo what someone else had done. The most wonderful part was seeing the result after I had worked with them. They are so wonderful; all they really needed was patience. They needed someone to love them, to hold them, and to teach them certain things.

How the Setting Accommodates Infants' Needs

Infants need human and physical environments and curricula that meet their developmental and individual needs.

Infants are different from toddlers and preschoolers and need human and physical environments and curricula that meet their developmental and individual needs. Creating a healthy, safe, loving, and stimulating environment for infants is challenging for even the most experienced infant teachers and caregivers. In light of the most recent research on the brain, the environment must hold the infant's interest for sustained periods of time. The caregiver is the most significant other in the infant's early growth and development. On the one hand, she is responsible for providing a nurturing, caring environment. On the other hand, she is responsible for the infant's early education. With that in mind, we have chosen to use the terms "teacher" and "caregiver" alternately to reflect this dual responsibility.

Meeting Infants' Health and Safety Needs. Meeting the infant's health and safety needs is a major responsibility of the infant program. Some health and safety standards are required by state licensure regulations, and others are guided by criteria for quality early childhood programs, such as those put forth by the National Academy of Early Childhood Programs (1991), the center accrediting project of NAEYC. Health and safety standards govern the safety of indoor and outdoor environments, record keeping, safety in transportation, and all routines that reduce infectious disease and prevent injuries and accidents.

Infant programs require initial immunization records and regular health evaluations. Caregivers keep daily records of feeding, diapering, resting, and medications administered, such as the one in Figure 3.1.

Figure 3.1 **Infant Room Daily Report**

Infant's Name Molly _____ Date 12/18/2000_____

BABY SEEMS

(Active as usual)

A bit fussy

Not acting as usual

Very busy

taking toys

off shelf

BABY SLEPT

(Soundly)

Did not sleep well

Time baby woke up

_____

_____

_____

BOTTLES

6 oz at 10:40

6 oz at 1:30

4 oz at 5:30

___ oz at ___

SOLID FOODS

Cereal or meat

Cracker at 9:00
1/2 jar Chicken Rice
stuffing at 11:55

Fruit

Peaches at 4:30

_____ at _____

Vegetables

_____ at _____

_____ at _____

OLDER BABIES

Breakfast

(Ate good portion)

Ate all

Ate none

Lunch

(Ate good portion)

Ate all

Ate none

except rice

DIAPER CHANGES

10:00 wet

12:40 wet

1:00 BM

3:30 wet

_____

_____

NEEDS

Diapers

Bottom Wipes

Bottle Liners

Jar Food

Cereal

Formula

Extra Clothes

Diaper Ointment

ACCIDENTS TODAY

_____

_____

_____

_____

COMMENTS

Molly stood by the

bouncing chair

today for a few

minutes

_____

_____

MEDICATION

Dosage	Time	Given by

Infants learn about themselves as they explore their images in mirrors. *(© Elizabeth Crews)*

Teachers reduce infectious diseases and provide a healthy environment by implementing licensing standards in the diaper-changing process, following stringent hand-washing procedures, disinfecting mouthed toys every day, administering medicine only from prescribed medications after receiving written permission from parents, and keeping the cribs sanitized. Caregivers attempt to prevent accidents by the careful selection of nontoxic toys with no removable small parts, the removal of broken toys, the use of shatterproof mirrors, and the selection of furniture that meets safety standards.

Meeting Infants' Social Needs. Infants need an environment that provides for consistent care by a primary caregiver on a daily basis, opportunities for social interaction with adults and other children, and a responsive environment that meets their individual needs. If these three needs are met, infants typically will develop from egocentric beings to those who seek out and enjoy relationships with others.

A *primary caregiver* is one who has the main responsibility for a small group of children on a regular basis. Teacher to child ratios recommended for infant programs by the National Academy of Early Childhood Programs

(1991) are 3:1 or 4:1. State standards are often somewhat higher, ranging from 4:1 to 6:1 or more. Lower ratios are desired, as they provide infants with the security of a known continuous caregiver and help alleviate stranger and separation anxiety, which often occur between eight and twelve months of age.

Infants are active participants in their environment. They have individual and developmental needs that caregivers respect. Caregivers respond to these needs in many ways. They follow individual sleeping and feeding schedules rather than trying to impose a general schedule on all. They use daily routine events to engage in face-to face interactions with the infants. They talk with them during feeding and diaper changing, telling them what they are doing and what they will do next, and waiting for the infant to take a turn in the conversation. When the child responds, the caregiver smiles and continues the conversation. The caregiver listens for and attends to the infant's cues, moving her to different places in the room, holding and comforting her if needed, and responding to her cries in a warm and caring manner.

Social interaction for infants includes interacting with self and with others. Room space is arranged so that children can play by themselves or observe others in the room. Teachers periodically move infants so that they sit or lie face to face with other infants or so that they see objects from a different perspective. Shatterproof mirrors are secured on the floor and walls so that infants can view themselves from many perspectives. Being around other infants and being able to view themselves in different mirrors facilitates differentiation of self from others.

Meeting Infants' Learning Needs. The infant curriculum facilitates children's construction of three different kinds of knowledge: knowledge about things that exist in their physical world, knowledge about social conventions such as language and manners, and knowledge about how things relate to each other. You will learn more about these kinds of knowledge in Chapter 4. Infants learn primarily through play, experimentation, and actions based on interest. Actions based on interest occur when something unusual happens that intrigues the child. For example, an infant swings his arm randomly and suddenly hits the mobile. The mobile swings and attracts the infant's attention. The infant then attends to the mobile and tries to make it swing again. This differs from play and experimentation in that the infant is interested in solving a problem. The curriculum is implemented through the way the teacher schedules routines, the way the caregiver interacts with the infants during those routines, and the way the teacher arranges the environment to engage and sustain interest.

> ### FACILITATING INFANT PROBLEM SOLVING
>
> 1. Teachers facilitate the development of searching behaviors by placing the infant's favorite toy on the left side one day and the right side the next day and by playing games such as hide-and-seek.
> 2. Teachers facilitate the development of means-end behaviors by allowing the infant repeated opportunities to act on mobiles and visual displays.
> 3. Caregivers facilitate the physical development of the infant by placing him in spaces where he can move freely without fear of his safety and by having different kinds of things he can crawl on, under, through, and over.
> 4. Teachers facilitate the social development of the infant by engaging her in one-on-one conversations using turn taking and by responding with delight when she takes a turn.
> 5. Caregivers facilitate language development by providing the infant with face-to-face interaction using finger plays, songs, and books and by playing games such as peekaboo.

Infant rooms have different kinds of play areas that encourage different kinds of actions, such as crawling spaces with hard surfaces, big cushions and carpet in areas where infants can look at board books, and areas where they can see themselves and others through the use of mirrors and pictures. Walls and furniture are colorful and inviting, and there are enough windows for children to enjoy the out-of-doors. Playgrounds are easily accessible for infants to go outside to play on blankets or in strollers.

Meeting Infants' Personal Needs. Teachers use several methods to meet the personal needs of the infants in their care. They do not force a general schedule on the children, but rather respond to the infants' schedules for feeding, napping, and playing. They respect the infants' cries as indicators of real problems or needs and give comfort or soothe them when they are distressed. They respect the parents' culturally different ideas about what is appropriate and work with the parents to find solutions that consider both points of view. They understand that developmental rates may differ and that these differences do not necessarily reflect delay.

CONSTRUCTIONS

Observation

Work in teams of two or three and complete observations of three infants in infant programs.

 a. Each team member selects three children. One child should be six weeks to four months of age, one four to twelve months of age, and one twelve to eighteen months of age.

 b. Observe each infant for at least thirty minutes, taking notes on all you see.

 c. Try to identify each infant's level of physical, cognitive, and social development.

 d. Try to notice individual temperament and personality characteristics.

 e. Compare and contrast your observations across the three ages with the other members of the team to see how the infant characteristics are similar and different.

 f. Prepare a written report explaining your findings. Be sure to discuss how the perspectives of the three children observed by each team member contributed to the final report. Be sure to assign a pseudonym to each child observed.

 g. Be prepared to discuss your findings in class.

CHILDREN IN TODDLER SETTINGS

Amy and Zenah visit the toddler program located in their university's child and family study center. This center has an observation booth, which they use so that they can observe without disrupting the children and teachers.

ZENAH: Boy, I'm glad the kids are wearing their nametags. It will make our observations so much easier.

AMY: Yes, and look, Zenah, the whole room is set up with different areas, just like we talked about in class. That must be the home living center, and there is the center for building with soft foam blocks and for playing with those cube blocks that have spaces to crawl through, an area for looking at books, for painting and using Play-Doh, for playing with sand and water, and for eating snacks. Boy, there are lots of things for these kids to do.

ZENAH: Yeah! Look at those three climbing through the cube blocks and those two playing in the home living area.

AMY: I think I just saw one of the toddlers, Charles, experimenting with those foam blocks. First he picked up two of them and banged them together. They made a funny slapping noise, and he laughed. You could tell he really liked it. Then he put down the block in his right hand and picked up a smaller one and started hitting those two blocks together. It didn't make as much noise, and he dropped it immediately. Now he's using that larger block and banging them together again. He looks so satisfied.

ZENAH: Yeah, but he is looking at that kid over there, Darius, who is building a tower of blocks. Look, now he is walking over there. Oops, he just knocked the tower over with his foam blocks.

AMY: And they are both giggling and rebuilding the tower together. It didn't seem to bother Darius.

(Three little girls playing in the home living center capture Zenah's attention. This dramatic play area has been set up with dolls, a crib, and a number of items for playing hospital.)

ZENAH: Amy, look at those kids in the home living center. Christina just picked up that doll, looked at it, got a red marker, and made red spots on the doll's face.

(As they observe, Christina hands the doll to Cynteria, who puts a doll blanket around her shoulders and begins to listen to the doll's heart with a cup from the dishes in the center. Then she tells Christina to put the baby to bed. Both place the doll in the crib, and then Christina picks up the baby, gets in the crib, and holds the baby. Cynteria walks over to the mirror. She looks at herself with her cape and cup and decides she needs a hat. She finds a Burger King crown in the prop box and puts it on. Then she goes back to the mirror and checks herself out. Brandy brings the doll she has been playing with to Cynteria. Cynteria looks at the doll and puts a Band-Aid on its arm. Christina gets out of the crib and goes to the toy phone. She picks it up and pretends to listen. Then she hands the phone to Cynteria.)

ZENAH: I think this is what Dr. K. means when she talks about **symbolic play.** Look at how Cynteria is using the cup as a stethoscope. It looks like Christina and Brandy are role-playing parents and Cynteria is a doctor or a nurse.

AMY: Probably a doctor. Kids are used to seeing female doctors today.

(Amy's attention then moves to the sand table, where Zack is filling his cup with sand. He fills and pours, fills and pours. Roland comes to the table and begins sifting the sand with his fingers. Then he makes paths in the sand and makes sounds like a car as he moves his finger through the sand. Next he picks up a truck from the shelf and uses it to make tracks in the sand. Zack goes to the shelf and gets a car. Roland picks up the cup Zack was using and begins to make sounds like a steam shovel as he digs a deep hole in the sand.)

AMY: There is symbolic play going on at the sand and water center, too, Zenah. I just saw Roland pretend his finger was a car moving along a road. At first Zack was experimenting with pouring, but after he watched Roland, he began to play with a car. Isn't it fascinating how that idea was transferred from Roland to Zack without language?

ZENAH: Yeah. You know, it really helps when you can actually see what you are learning about in class. I remember that those pouring activities are absorbing to children of this age because they help the child exercise his grasping and releasing. Oh, look! *(Laughs.)* Over here at the art center. That little Brandy put on her own smock and opened the paint cup. She put a few long swipes on her paper, and then she looked at her hand and began painting it. She put her hand on the paper and made her handprint. Look at her! She is very excited about her discovery and has asked for more paper.

ASK YOURSELF

Was I able to note examples of children learning through play, experimentation, and actions based on their interests? How did the room arrangement facilitate that kind of learning? What kinds of questions did these scenarios raise for me?
....

(Amy notes that as the children play, the two teachers check and change diapers, check to see if Brandy needs to "go potty," and chart the routines. Snack time comes, and all the children wash their hands, come to the snack table, and sit down. Each child is offered banana pieces with the peel still on, and each takes one. They take one or two crackers and their juice in small paper cups. All peel their banana pieces with great interest. Brandy says, "Nana, nana," and the others follow along in the chant. After their snack, they wash their hands again and go back to play.)

The observations Zenah and Amy have made of the toddlers will help them better understand what toddlers are able to do independently and under the guidance of a competent caregiver. However, they have many new questions about what toddlers know and can learn based on some of the things they have observed. We leave Amy and Zenah in the toddler center and take this opportunity for you to advance your understanding about the developmental characteristics of the toddlers in this program.

Developmental Characteristics of Toddlers

Toddlers are usually defined as different from infants by their ability to move. The age range by which toddlers are defined ranges from eighteen to thirty-six months of age. This stage continues to be one of rapid growth and development. Toddlers are becoming far more mobile than infants, and they are making a transition from sensorimotor intelligence to preoperational thought. Most enter a toddler program in stage six of sensorimotor development and gradually, as their thought process becomes representational, advance to the preoperational stage, where thought is no longer tied to immediate action. Piaget's **preoperational stage** includes children from two to seven years of age, although these age parameters describe only the ages when typically developing children exhibit the characteristics of this stage (see Table 3.3). Again, it is important to remember that within this age

TABLE 3.3 Characteristics of Preoperational Development (Ages 2 to 7)

Characteristics	Definitions	Examples
Representational thought	Child can mentally bring to mind images of past events and objects that are not present.	Deferred imitation, symbolic play, drawing.
Oral language development	Egocentric speech—lacks intent to communicate (ages 2–4). Social speech—intentionally communicative (ages 4–7).	While building with blocks, "And then this one." To another child, "Want to play cards?"
First moral feelings	Child has become aware of rules and wants to play with others. Child is not concerned about winning.	Children play until all the lotto cards are filled rather than stopping when the first card is filled.

Source: Adapted from *Piaget's theory of cognitive and affective development* (5th ed.) by Barry J. Wadsworth. Copyright © 1996. Published by Longman Publishers.

range, the developmental sequence is the same for all children, but the rate at which they develop differs according to an individual child's biological inheritance and the environmental conditions under which the child is raised.

Physical Characteristics. Toddlers exude physical energy and are constantly on the move as they continue to refine their gross and fine motor skills. By eighteen months, most children are walking without support. By nineteen to twenty months, many will start adapting their walking schemata by walking backward and walking up stairs. These accomplishments will soon be followed by attempts at running and jumping. All of this is accomplished through their playful motoric activity as they interact with their physical environments. Toddlers want to climb on everything, and their boundless energy allows them to repeat patterns of activity over and over. As they exercise each of these gross motor abilities—walking, running, jumping, climbing—they begin to develop the ability to balance on one foot for short periods of time.

A toddler's throwing abilities grow from a simple push of a ball on the floor to holding the ball on the chest and pushing it forward. Catching develops a bit later, and their first schemata consist of closing their arms around the ball as it hits their chest. By this age, toddlers begin to use beanbags and smaller objects for throwing and dropping games that require some control to hit a target or drop an object in a box. They also are beginning to coordinate their fine motor skills, such as eye-hand coordination. They enjoy using chalk, markers, and crayons on large boards or easels, an activity that helps them refine this coordination.

Toddlers exude physical energy and are constantly on the move as they continue to refine their gross and fine motor skills.

Young toddlers are making the transition from sensorimotor intelligence to representational intelligence.

Cognitive Characteristics. Young toddlers (eighteen to twenty-four months) fall into the last of the sensorimotor stage and are in the process of making the transition from sensorimotor intelligence to *representational intelligence*. Once this transition is made, they no longer have to rely on motoric or sensory experimentation to devise new means to solve problems, but can act out new means in their heads through internal representations of the action schemata. Piaget identified this transformation as the ability to mentally image objects that are no longer present in the sight of the child and to image possible solutions for finding those objects. This ability to mentally evoke ideas, actions, and objects that are no longer present is referred to as *representational ability*. This ability will be explained more fully in Chapter 4, but we want you to begin to construct understanding of internal and external forms of representation.

Older toddlers (twenty-four to thirty-six months) begin to refine their representational ability, an important development that occurs during the preoperational stage. Early use of this representational ability allows toddlers to move beyond the immediacy of the here and now. The earliest external form of representation is called **deferred imitation.** This occurs when the child imitates an action that happened at a much earlier point in time. For example, when one of the authors' grandsons, Alex, was two years old, he was playing with her car keys while she talked with his mother. After exploring the keys for a while, he picked them up, walked to the door, put a key up to the keyhole, and tried to turn it. This is significant in that through an internal representation, he was able to remember a past action he had seen and to copy it.

Symbolic play is another early form of external representation. In symbolic play, the child takes an object and uses it to represent something else. For example, in the toddler room Amy and Zenah visited, Cynteria used the Burger King crown as a nurse's or doctor's hat and a cup as a stethoscope. Roland was engaging in symbolic play when he made the sound of a car as he ran his finger through the sand.

Mental images are another form of representation. They differ from deferred imitation and symbolic play in that they are internal forms of representation. We cannot observe children's mental images, but they too are imitations of sensory perceptions. If you were to close your eyes and image your mother, the image would not be a direct copy of her face, but it would bear some resemblance to what she looks like. According to Piaget and Inhelder (1969), these preoperational images are like a photograph, a quick nonchanging image.

Drawing is another external form of representation. However, for most toddlers drawing is not representational. Drawing becomes representational to the child when the child talks about what it represents. Most children do not

Toddlers explore the physical properties of things by pounding, throwing, banging, and pouring.
(© Elizabeth Crews)

draw images that are considered representational (they bear some resemblance to the thing represented) to adults until the later part of the preoperational stage. Spoken and written language are also forms of representational ability and will be discussed in a later section and in Chapter 4.

Children learn by acting on objects and by observing the immediate result of their action.

Toddlers are intensely inquisitive about the things in their environments, and they are eager to explore the physical properties of things by pounding, throwing, banging, pouring, and stepping on them. Charles was experimenting with the sound the blocks made and the force it took to knock the blocks over, and Brandy was experimenting with printing. The thought process of the early preoperational child is egocentric in nature. That is, children at this level of development think that everyone thinks as they do and that everyone knows what they know. This egocentric thought process is not selfish or intentional, but rather it is due to the fact that children have not yet differentiated their thoughts from others'.

Social Characteristics. Through their own activity and their interactions with peers and adults, toddlers move from feelings related only to self to true social relations with others. The social characteristics of toddlers fall into three major categories: characteristics of social cognition, characteristics related to language learning, and characteristics related to feelings or affective development.

Social Cognition. As you can see from Amy and Zenah's observations, children construct knowledge about their social world through their social experiences with others. Cynteria, Christina, and Brandy are playing what they know about the chickenpox, doctors, using the telephone to communicate, and Band-Aids. These representations imitate what they have observed through their interactions with others.

At around two years of age, children begin to have a concept of self. They start using "me" and "mine" as words to describe themselves and objects that belong to them. According to Brazelton (1974), two-year-olds know what belongs to them and what belongs to someone else. Additionally, this sense of self accounts for toddlers' desire to do things for themselves. We often hear them exclaim, "I do it!"

Darius and Charles give us a good picture of peer social relations at this age. Notice how they spent a significant amount of time playing by themselves. Then, when Charles knocked Darius's tower down, Darius didn't get mad. They giggled and built it back up. Toddlers spend the majority of their time in solitary play, but there are many times when two-year-olds play together. Darius and Charles rebuilding the tower is a good example of this.

Language Learning. The preoperational stage is the most significant period for language development. Toddlers fall within the early half of the preoperational stage. During this very early stage of cognitive development, toddlers, without any direct instruction, construct the system of language used by those around them. They learn this oral language as they interact with other language users. They learn language as another means to reach a goal, such as getting a glass of milk. Language learning is one way children adapt to their social worlds.

During this period, children acquire all but the most complex sounds in their language, such as *f, th, sh, ch, r, l, oy,* and *ay.* For example, a toddler may say "ting" for "thing" or "wabbit" for "rabbit."

Toddlers' first stage of using language for meaning is the one-word stage. During this stage, the number and kind of words acquired and the different ways of using them show rapid development. By three years of age, toddlers will understand and use as many as five hundred to one thousand words. These early vocabulary words include a significant proportion of nouns, many action words, some social-conventional terms ("bye-bye"), and locational terms ("up," "down,") and terms of negation such as "no!" These words are used as a means to reach a goal (saying "milk" to mean "Please get me some milk!") and to describe an experience to another person (saying "hot" after placing a hand in the bath water). Toddlers use what they know to express myriad meanings.

Toddlers' first use of syntax, or meaningful combinations of words, comes between eighteen and twenty-four months, when they combine two words to make their intended meaning clearer (for example, "allgone juice," "more cookie," "doggie bye-bye"). These combinations increase to three and four words over the next year ("Daddy wiping our car"). Additionally, they begin to understand and use some markers for plurals, possessives, and past tense.

Affective Development. Mental representation allows a child to recall and revisit his feelings. Because of this, feelings can last longer than the experiences that caused them. Feelings become more stable and consistent over time, which allows for the development of mutual respect between the child and those he likes. The first real social feelings have begun by age three. These feelings are often demonstrated through symbolic play. We saw this in the opening example, when Amy and Zenah watched three little girls care for sick dolls.

By contrast, feelings of anger, disappointment, and fear are shown through aggressive behaviors, such as pushing another child, taking a toy from another, or shouting "No!" to the teacher. During this stage, children often shift quickly from one feeling to another and are very demonstrative about their feelings. They seek social interactions with adults and peers.

ASK YOURSELF

How can I best nurture the growth and development of toddlers? How would I discipline toddlers who are crawling in places they are not supposed to go? Would I like to work in a toddler center? Why or why not?

Individual Characteristics. Individual differences become increasingly apparent in the toddler room as children begin to build their constructions of self. During this stage, they begin to notice how they are similar to and different from others. Additionally, they display significant differences in the rates by which they develop linguistically, cognitively, and physically. They differ in their play preferences, in their need for a highly predictable environment, in how they adapt to new situations, and in how much environmental stimulation they are able to tolerate. Some of these differences are related to cultural backgrounds. As suggested in Chapter 2, teachers need to spend time reading and in the neighborhood to become aware of the different cultural values and expectations parents have for their toddlers. For example, Heath (1983) found that although low-income African-American parents in South Carolina provided a wealth of oral language interactions for their children, they did not expect the children to ask questions until they were much older.

How the Setting Accommodates the Toddlers' Needs

Toddlers are different from infants and preschoolers and need human and physical environments and curricula that meet their developmental and individual needs. Creating a healthy and safe environment for toddlers is as challenging as creating one for infants, but more attention must be paid to creating an environment that supports the toddlers' learning needs. Much consideration has to be given to how the environment will hold the toddlers' interest for sustained periods of time. The caregiver is still the most significant other in the toddler's early growth and development. However, the role of peer interactions takes on more importance during this stage.

Meeting Toddlers' Health and Safety Needs. Meeting toddlers' health needs continues to be a major responsibility of toddler programs and is guided by the same standards mentioned earlier. However, at this level caregivers try to help the toddlers learn how to follow some simple procedures that minimize health risks. Some of these procedures include hand washing before eating, hand washing after using the toilet, putting mouthed toys in the cleaning solution, and covering your mouth when coughing or sneezing. Another major milestone during this stage is making the transition from using diapers and pull-ups to toileting.

Many potential safety problems arise due to toddlers' mobility and curiosity. These new behaviors lead to falls, cuts, and injuries from outdoor play apparatus such as swings and slides. Most of these accidents can be prevented by following licensure standards, by considering the need for sturdy furniture and safety flooring, by examining your room and eliminating possible sources of trouble, and by carefully monitoring the children at all times.

Meeting Toddlers' Social Needs. Toddlers also benefit from an environment that provides a primary caregiver for consistent care on a daily basis, opportunities for social interaction with adults and other children, and a responsive environment that meets toddlers' individual needs. If these three needs are met, toddlers will continue to develop significant social relationships.

The teacher to child ratio recommended for toddler centers by the National Academy of Early Childhood Programs (1991) is 6:1. State standards are somewhat higher, ranging from 6:1 to 8:1 or more. Lower ratios provide for more quality time for adult-child interaction. This is particularly important during this period of rapid language development.

Since toddlers have the desire to do things themselves, the classroom should offer multiple opportunities for independence. Classrooms should have distinct areas for children to play in, and materials should be accessible. Sinks and toilets should be child-size, and snack time should allow children to make choices and to help themselves. Remember how Brandy and her friends enjoyed peeling their own banana pieces? Consistent daily routines and stable classroom environments help toddlers feel secure, as they are able to predict when things will happen and where things are.

Children at this age enjoy participating in finger plays and songs with a small group for a short period of time. This kind of activity helps toddlers relate to other children. They also love to hear stories about other children like themselves.

Meeting Toddlers' Learning Needs. Toddlers continue to be problem solvers and need environments that facilitate problem-solving activity. Toddler rooms should provide a variety of materials for experimentation, such as stringing and pop beads, blocks of many different kinds, wooden puzzles, pegboards, woodworking tools, inclined planes and pendulums, light tables, and opportunities to play in sand and water. The daily schedule should provide ample time for exploration and experimentation. In addition, the environment should provide opportunities for toddlers to explore living things through bringing live plants and animals into the classroom, and by providing sufficient outdoor experiences for this kind of exploration. Opportunities to play different kinds of searching games should continue.

As the toddler refines representational ability through symbolic play, the caregiver needs to provide dress-up clothing, dolls, stuffed animals, and furniture and tools. Representational ability is also enhanced through opportunities to listen to stories and revisit those stories independently. Toddlers should be offered opportunities for painting, drawing, and using writing materials.

To refine motor skills, the teacher should provide many opportunities to throw objects such as beanbags and balls of different sizes and weights and to play games that allow children to run and chase each other. The program should include opportunities to develop more complex motor abilities, such as walking the balance beam, jumping, and marching.

Toddlers expand their ability to use oral language through authentic language situations. The caregiver needs to provide many opportunities to engage all toddlers in authentic conversation. This can happen as they focus on interesting observations together or share an experience. For example, they are watching balls roll down an inclined plane, and they discuss which balls roll the fastest. The caregiver should model games for interaction, such as "Whose name is Christina?" to which Christina should answer, "My name is Christina!" or other simple games such as Simon Says.

Meeting Toddlers' Personal Needs. As the teacher comes to know the toddlers for whom she has primary responsibility, she is able to respond to their individual, cultural, and special needs. She respects each toddler's food preferences and activity selections and recognizes these as indicators of a developing conception of self. The teacher adapts the schedule to meet individual needs, while also maintaining consistent routines. For example, the teacher provides a choice at snack time and implements the "No thank you" helping (a small portion for tasting) at lunch to accommodate individual food preferences and still provide a healthy meal. Additionally, if she has a child who has difficulty resting during rest time, she might let the child look at books quietly on his cot while the others sleep. She uses the knowledge she has gained about the cultural and individual needs of the toddlers to create an environment that is culturally sensitive.

Two significant problems can arise that require special attention: biting and temper tantrums (Weiser, 1991). These problems may result from the toddlers' developing sense of self, from their inability to use language to solve problems, or from a number of other problems relating to individual temperament, frustration, or stress. Piaget would suggest that children who use these behaviors should suffer the logical consequence of being removed from the group until they can control their behaviors. This removal would be supervised by the toddler teacher, and both the teacher and the other children talk with the child, so that the child begins to understand the impact his or her behavior has on others.

CONSTRUCTIONS

1. Research

Select one of the ideas in the toddler section that intrigues you and become the class expert on the topic. Select from topics such as temper tantrums, egocentrism, transformational reasoning, or oral language development, to name just a few.

2. Research

Read as much as you can on the topic you have selected, using the resources listed at the end of the chapter or other resources you identify in your library.

3. Observation

Observe in a toddler program to determine whether you see examples of the topic you have selected.

4. Writing

Write up your findings and share them with the class.

CHILDREN IN PRESCHOOL SETTINGS

Tillie and Eric visit a private preschool that organizes children from three to five years of age in multiage classrooms of seventeen to twenty children. It's morning center time as Tillie and Eric walk into the room. The two teachers, Mrs. B. and Ms. R., welcome them into the classroom and invite them to interact with the children. Tillie notes that it looks like the pictures of preschool classrooms she has seen in textbooks, except for the woodworking center. There it is, and two children are wearing goggles and using real child-size hammers, saws, wood, and nails. Eric observes that two other children are playing at the water table, another is painting at the easel, two are working with clay, and two others are drawing pictures and making books in the writing area. A student teacher is reading a book to two children in the reading area, four children are playing dress-up in the creative dramatics center, and two boys are playing with the unit blocks. There are seventeen children in this classroom.

Mrs. B. invites Tillie to help with the morning snack. Tillie notes a community helpers' chart that has pictures of children who are daily helpers. She spots the snack helpers, wonders what they do, and decides to call them to the table first. Tillie invites the children to sit at the snack table as she begins to hand out paper plates and napkins.

SNACK HELPER: I'm supposed to do that. She helps, too!

TILLIE: Not today. I'm doing it. You just got to come over first since you're the snack helpers. *(She counted each child as she handed out a plate.)* You're one. You're two. You're three.

SNACK HELPER: No, that's not right. We do it. We hand out everything. Wait. *(Leaves the table and goes to the teacher for clarification.)*

CHILD 3: No, I'm four.

TILLIE: No, you're three.

CHILD 3: No, I'm four. We just had my birthday party. I'm four!

TILLIE: Whatever! *(Continues to hand out plates.)* Where was I? Oh, yeah. You're five.

(While Tillie works at the snack table, Eric moves to the area where two children are working with unit blocks. He listens to them talking.)

PATRICK A.: We've got two Patricks in our class.

CARL: No, You're Patrick.

PATRICK A.: I know, but see that boy over there? He's Patrick, too.

CARL: No, you're Patrick.

PATRICK A.: No, see he's Patrick, and I'm Patrick. My mama told me he could be Patrick, too. See, he's Kara's brother. So he's Kara's Patrick.

ASK YOURSELF

What is the problem here? Where did Child 3 get this idea? Would other children respond in a similar fashion?

· · · · · · · · · · · · · · · ·

CARL: What?

PATRICK A.: Yeah, I'm Mama's Patrick. Kara's Patrick goes to school here, too.

CARL: Oh!

(Eric is puzzled by the children's conversation. He wonders, "What are those two kids talking about? Don't they know that there can be more than one Patrick? Don't they understand that they are something outside of their names?" He is stuck. The more he thinks about their conversation, the more confused he gets. Then he chuckles and mumbles to himself, "I wonder what Dr. K. knows about this." Ms. R. asks Eric to supervise the children's hand-washing procedures before lunch. She refers him to the instructions posted on the wall above the sink.

When they return from lunch, Ms. R. asks Eric to supervise hand washing again and to assist the parents coming to pick up their children from the morning session. Mrs. B. tells Tillie that several children will be arriving from Head Start for the afternoon session and asks whether she would like to go outside with her to greet them.)

TILLIE: Sure. So, you have some children who are here all day, some only in the mornings, and some only in the afternoons? You mean some of these kids spend all morning at Head Start and then all afternoon here?

MRS. B.: That's correct. Let's greet the children as they get off the bus with a song. Just follow along.

(The children join Tillie and Mrs. B. in singing as they greet each other and go into the building.)

MRS. B.: Let's have our afternoon circle time. Tillie, will you please pass out the carpet squares?

TILLIE: Everyone takes one piece. Wait, let's play a game. Which color do you want, Nikki?

NIKKI: Lellow.

TILLIE: Okay, good. That's the top one. Which one for you, Scott?

SCOTT: The purple one.

ELI: I already wanted that one *(referring to the dark purple)*.

SCOTT: There are two purples. See, a light one and a dark one.

ELI: I have five more before my purple one.

TILLIE: Scott, how many carpet pieces before your light purple one?

EMMA: That's called lavender.

SCOTT: Two.

TILLIE: No. That is not right. There are seven.

SCOTT: No, two.

MRS. B.: How clever, Scott. Your lavender one is the second one after Eli's dark purple one.

TILLIE: But that's not right.

MRS. B.: It depends on which question you're answering, Tillie.

(The children get their carpet pieces, join Ms. R. in the area of the room designed for large group activities, and begin their afternoon ritual of greetings, story time, review of the work done earlier, and planning the afternoon activities to follow naptime. Tillie and Eric listen and watch. Once large group ends, the children take their naps. Scott doesn't sleep, and Mrs. B. allows him to look at books on his cot.

When naptime is over, the children choose their projects, and center time starts again. Ms. R. invites Eric to join her in supervising some of the proj-ect work, and Mrs. B. asks Tillie to assist with snack time again. Tillie asks one of the children from the morning Head Start program if she would like a snack. The child nods her head. Tillie notes that the child seems very hungry and decides to question her about her lunch.)

TILLIE: What did you have for lunch today?

BLAIR: I didn't have any.

TILLIE: I thought you ate lunch before coming here.

(Blair nods her head yes.)

TILLIE: So, what happened today?

BLAIR: I just didn't get any. I'm so hungry. Can I have some more?

TILLIE: Sure!

(Mrs. B. watches. She makes a note to ask Blair about lunch later. Blair's mother ar-rives early to pick up Blair, so Mrs. B. goes over to check on lunch and get Blair ready to leave.)

MRS. B.: Blair, I heard you didn't have lunch today. *(To Blair's mother.)* Did I miss a note about lunch at Head Start today?

MOTHER: No, they served lunch.

BLAIR: We had lunch—that stuff I don't like.

MRS. B.: I thought you told Miss Tillie that you didn't have lunch.

BLAIR: I did tell her I didn't have any.

MOTHER: Blair, did you lie?

BLAIR: No! I told Mrs. B. we had lunch.

MOTHER: But what about the helper? Did you lie to her?

BLAIR: Yes, but she didn't punish me.

MRS. B.: Oh, I see! So since Tillie didn't punish you, it was okay to tell a lie?

BLAIR: *(Smiles as she gets her papers from her cubby, puts on her coat, and takes her mother's hand to leave.)* Yeah!

MOTHER: Blair!

MRS. B.: *(To the mother.)* Don't worry. Blair and I will talk about lying and getting punished tomorrow. She is not being bad! Good-bye. Good-bye, Blair. See you tomorrow. Remember, you will still have time to help make the strawberry preserves for our general store.

As Eric and Tillie return to class, Tillie thinks about Dr. K.'s discussion of reality and existence. She also remembers her discussion with the preschool teacher about how we come to know and what we know to be true. She thought those questions and ideas were just lectures professors used to bore their students. Now here they were in a classroom.

ERIC: Tillie, why did those boys think that they couldn't have but one Patrick?

TILLIE: I think they were trying to figure out whether a person's identity is tied up in their name or themselves.

ERIC: Wow! Listen to Tillie! The professor!

TILLIE: No, I'm not joking! What did you make of the conversation?

ERIC: I'm not sure, but it made me realize that I need to do more listening.

TILLIE: That's where I've been making my mistake. I've tried to make the kids learn what I thought they should know. I should have been listening to them.

ERIC: And could you make sense out of what they were saying if you did?!

TILLIE: Well, not always, but I think that I could learn more if I listened more.

Through participation with the preschool children, Eric and Tillie realize there is much more they need to know about how children learn. They have many new questions about why children respond in ways that are so very different from the ways adults respond. We leave Tillie and Eric on their way to class and take this opportunity for you to advance your understanding about the developmental characteristics of the preschoolers in this program.

Developmental Characteristics of Preschoolers

The center Eric and Tillie visited serves preschoolers three to five years of age in multiage classrooms. Children in each classroom fall into the preoperational stage of development and are continuously developing their ability to represent ideas and events both internally and externally. While considerable growth occurs during these three years, it is slower than during the preceding three years. Again, it is important to remember that within this age range, the developmental sequence is similar for all children, but the rate at which children develop differs according to biological inheritance and environmental conditions.

ASK YOURSELF

What is the difference between facilitating learning and teaching children what I think they ought to know? How do these ideas fit with my conception of teaching? Have I ever tried to understand something from a child's perspective?

Preschoolers develop large motor skills, like jumping, through a variety of planned activities. *(© Elizabeth Crews)*

Physical Characteristics. Preschoolers continue to refine their gross and fine motor skills. Locomotion abilities increase from walking heel-to-toe to running with agility, from skipping unevenly to skipping with speed and agility, and from jumping to hopping and leaping. Their climbing and balancing abilities become more coordinated, and their ability to endure without becoming tired increases with age.

At this age, the motor development in the arms, hands, and fingers, as well as in the legs, feet, and toes, allows children to participate in activities ranging from lacing cards (cards that outline simple pictures with perforations that can be connected with a shoe string) and playing with pegboards and small Legos to other fine motor activities such as drawing, coloring, and cutting. They become better able to dress and undress themselves using buttons and zippers and to tie their shoes. They have refined their catching ability, so they are able to adapt their catching schemata to accommodate to the size of the ball.

The representational ability of preschool children has become increasingly complex.

Cognitive Characteristics. Preschool children are still in the preoperational stage, but their representational ability has become increasingly complex. Their symbolic play is organized around social and cultural themes, and their drawings are becoming more realistic in appearance as well as intent. One of the major representational tasks children have to accomplish during this time is the ability to differentiate the *signified* (the thing being represented) from the *signifier* (the symbol used to represent the thing). This is what was occurring in the conversation Eric overheard between Patrick A. and Carl. Young children think that their names (the signifier) are part of them or belong to them (the signified). Therefore, from this perspective there can be only one Patrick. When another child with the same name enters the class, it causes a conflict in the children's thinking about the relationship between a name and the thing the name represents. Because Patrick has already had to resolve the conflict, he has begun to make this differentiation and now explains it to Carl.

Although the thought of the preoperational child is still egocentric during these years, it is not as consistently egocentric as it was earlier. For example, a preoperational child may be able to differentiate between self and others but not be able to differentiate between his own thoughts and the thoughts of others. Reasoning in the later part of the preoperational stage becomes more intuitive, but children still do not question their own reasoning about undifferentiated ideas. The characteristics of preoperational thought include transformational reasoning, centration, and reversibility (Wadsworth, 1996).

CHARACTERISTICS OF PREOPERATIONAL THOUGHT

▸ Lack of transformational *reasoning*. Transformational reasoning refers to a child's ability to reason about transformations, or changes. For example, if you put five chips out in front of a four-year-old child and ask the child to tell you how many chips there are, he or she might count them and tell you five. Then, telling the child to watch carefully, you move the five chips around on the table without removing any of them and without adding any to them. After you stop moving them, you ask the child to tell you how many there are now, and the child will not be able to respond without counting them again. Here the child focuses on the perceptual final state of the chips as if it were independent of the state that he or she first counted. Children at this stage lack the ability to integrate the steps in the transformation and therefore focus on just one state at a time. This kind of reasoning is apparent in the problem Tillie had with Child 3 at the snack table. Child 3 had not differentiated the symbol that represented her age (four) from herself. Four named her, and she was not able to think about being any number but four. She could not be three, as Tillie kept insisting. She was not able to think of successive states of number and could not understand what Tillie was doing.

▸ **Centration** refers to the child's attention to only one attribute of an object or a set of objects without consideration for the other attributes of the same object or set of objects. For example, suppose that you have two water glasses that are the exact same size and as the child watches, you fill each glass with the same amount of water. You ask the child if there is the same amount of water in each glass and she responds "Yes." Then you pour the water from one of the water glasses into another water glass that is taller and more slender in circumference than the other two glasses. You ask the child if there is still the same amount of water in both glasses and if she responds "No" you ask her to explain. If centration is a characteristic of the child's reasoning she will respond that the water in the slender glass is higher than the water in the other glass. Her reasoning has centered on only one attribute, the height of the water, without considering the circumference of the glass.

▸ Lack of **reversibility**. Reversibility refers to a child's ability to reverse a thought back to its starting point or to understand that the starting point and the end result are all one operation. Reversibility is required to understand that if I put two and three together to get five, there is also the possibility of taking five apart to get two and three. Lack of reversibility is the problem Scott had when he said there were only two more carpet squares until his purple one. He was not able to go back and include Eli's five and his two, so the question he answered was how many more carpet squares until his purple one after Eli received his.

Play becomes the means by which preschool children learn to interact with each other in meaningful and enjoyable ways.

Social Characteristics.   Three- through five-year-olds are able to form true social relations with peers and are able to play with each other for longer periods of time. Play becomes the major avenue by which preschool children learn to interact with each other in meaningful and enjoyable ways. Parten (1932) studied the development of children's social behaviors in play. Her classification scheme, shown in the box on page 124, is still considered appropriate and sound today.

Social Cognition.   Children continue to construct social knowledge related to self and others. During this time, they begin to become more aware of how they are similar to and different from others, as well as how others

---

DEVELOPMENT OF SOCIAL PLAY BEHAVIORS

‣ Solitary play. A child plays entirely alone. This play may be experimental or symbolic in nature.

‣ Onlooker behavior. A child is interested in watching the play of other children but does not enter in the play.

‣ Parallel play. Children who play in close proximity to each other and use the same play materials but do not attend to each other or attempt to coordinate their play. They may use language, but there is no attempt to communicate.

‣ Associative play. A group of children use the same materials and interact with each other, but there is no common agreement about how the play is to take place.

‣ Cooperative play. A group of children work together to establish how the play is to be organized, how the play is to proceed, and how players will interact. Language is used to negotiate and communicate.

---

are similar and different. They use these relationships of sameness and difference to begin to categorize people into groups. Edwards (1986) identified four attributes by which children organize others: age, gender, race, and familial and friendship connections. Children judge age by perceptual characteristics, such as wrinkles or hair color. However, they also center on height as a predictor of age. For example, a four-year-old might say that his father is older than his grandmother because his father is taller. Gender identity at this stage is determined by perceptual clues such as clothing and hairstyles, and children think that gender can change when these characteristics change. Racial identity is similar to gender identity. During this period, children are able to identify and label people according to racial characteristics (Katz, 1983), but they still do not understand the permanency of racial identity. Familial and friendship relations begin to be constructed during this period. Children will use familial terms such as "brother" and "grandmother," but they do not understand the underlying kinship relation. For example, Tommy tells you that he has a brother named Jimmy. But when you ask him whether Jimmy has a brother, he will say no.

Language Learning. The preoperational stage is the most significant period for language development. By the end of this period, preschoolers have acquired almost all of the language system into which they were born. In English, they acquire all but the most difficult **diphthong** sounds and one or two complex grammatical structures. This acquisition of language makes children's ability to think faster and more powerful. During this age span, they increase their vocabulary considerably both in new vocabulary terms and in the construction of new meanings for acquired terms.

Affective Development. Piaget suggested that preoperational children's ability to reason morally is not due to a feeling of necessity to do what is just, right, or honorable, but rather to a fear of being punished by the authority to whom they must be obedient. Tillie was upset when Blair lied to her about not having had any lunch. Mrs. B. understood that Blair didn't think it was so naughty to lie to Tillie because Tillie wasn't aware that she was lying. Although Piaget described this reasoning as prenormative, children do advance their concepts of rules, justice, and intentions during this period.

Individual Characteristics. Individual differences become even more apparent in preschool children. The range of developmental differences becomes greater, and some children exhibit special needs that require identification and adaptation. These differences may be in physical, social, or cognitive development. Temperamental characteristics become more stable during this time, and children begin to differ markedly in personality. Cultural differences become more apparent to children, and differing cultural norms can cause conflicts with other children.

> The range of preschool children's developmental differences becomes greater, and some exhibit special needs that require identification and adaptation.

ASK YOURSELF

What have I learned about how preschool children think? How will that knowledge guide my teaching decisions? Would I like to work in a preschool center? Why or why not?
....

CONSTRUCTIONS

Reflection and Journal Entry

Reflect on what you have learned about the thinking of preschool children. What characteristics surprised you? What characteristics do you want to know more about? What questions do you have based on what you have read? Record your answers in your journal.

How the Setting Accommodates Preschoolers' Needs

Preschoolers are different from infants and toddlers and need human and physical environments and curricula that meet their developmental and individual needs. Creating a healthy and safe environment for preschoolers is important, but helping preschoolers assume responsibility for caring for their own health and safety is an important change. Teachers must consider how to manage time, space, materials, and people to meet the children's needs.

Meeting Preschoolers' Health and Safety Needs. Tillie and Eric were surprised to see the use of a woodworking center in this preschool. Many

Preschool children construct considerable physical knowledge as they engage in carefully supervised woodworking projects. *(Janet Taylor)*

teachers avoid this center because they fear accidents. Teachers need to encourage and support risk taking that is age appropriate. They do this by providing activity centers such as woodworking and providing the kind of supervision and safety equipment necessary to minimize the risks. Mrs. B and Ms. R. have provided safety goggles and child-size tools, and they supervise the children to help them learn the appropriate ways to use the tools.

Teachers continue to encourage and supervise hand-washing, tooth brushings, and toileting routines to minimize infectious disease transmission. They use latex gloves at all times when bodily fluids might be transmitted, and they teach children the appropriate procedures to follow when accidents cause bleeding.

Meeting Preschoolers' Social Needs.

Preschoolers still benefit from an environment that provides one primary teacher for consistent care on a daily basis, opportunities for social interaction with adults and other children, and a responsive environment that meets their individual needs. If these three conditions are met, preschoolers will continue to develop significant social relationships.

Teacher to child ratios for preschool classrooms recommended by the National Academy of Early Childhood Programs (1991) are 7:1 for a group size of fourteen, 8:1 with a group size of sixteen, 9:1 with a group size of eighteen, and 10:1 for a group size of twenty. State standards are somewhat higher, ranging from 10:1 for three-year-olds to 20:1 or more for four- and five-year-olds.

Teachers can meet the social needs of preschoolers by establishing a constructivist sociomoral classroom (DeVries & Zan, 1994).

SETTING UP A SOCIOMORAL CLASSROOM

The classroom atmosphere is organized:

- To meet children's physiological, emotional, and intellectual needs
- To foster peer interaction
- To promote child responsibility

In this classroom, children and teachers:

- Respect and value differing points of view
- Use conflict resolution when problems arise that disrupt the social bonds that have been formed
- Learn from the natural consequences that ensue when social bonds are broken

Source: DeVries, R., & Zan, B. (1994). *Moral Classrooms, Moral Children*. New York: Teachers College Press.

Meeting Preschoolers' Learning Needs. Play is the medium through which preschoolers learn. Center time and project work allow children many opportunities to play with different kinds of materials and content areas. Children learn through active education, and the elements of active education (interest, cooperation, and experimentation) should be connected in the context of play (Chaille & Silvern, 1996). Active education through play allows children to construct all kinds of knowledge and to better understand the physical and social worlds in which they live.

Teachers organize the classroom into different learning areas so that children can identify a place where they want to work. Areas may include a woodworking area, a reading area, a writing and drawing area, a construction and block area, a dramatic play area, an art area, a puzzles and games area, a natural science area, a computer area, a project area, and a sand and water area. Each of these areas should be well equipped with interesting open-ended materials that allow for experimentation and invention. Teachers need to set up procedures that allow for children's choice of activities, supervision, and interacting with children in each area.

Teachers organize time so that there is a balance between indoor and outdoor play, active and restful times, and individual and group times. Curriculum content is integrated through project work and themes so that children begin to make connections across disciplines.

Meeting Preschoolers' Personal Needs. Teachers meet children's individual needs as they interact with children on a daily basis. Teachers get to know children well so that they can greet the children individually each day with a reminder about something that occurred the day before. Teachers

Figure 3.2 **A Preschool Teacher's Anecdotal Record**

9/15/2000	Neelia and Carmen were discussing family pictures. Neelia said, "That's me and that's Kaya. And I don't know that girl [someone else in picture]". Then she asked, "What's his name?" about Carmen's picture.
9/16/2000	Neelia unbuttons and rebuttons very small buttons on her shorts/overalls! She shows patience and persistence.
9/17/2000	Neelia walked along the cubbies, touching each apple shape as I said the children's names. Neelia saw another child's toy lying on a toy shelf. She called the teacher over, "Kari," and pointed.
9/18/2000	Neelia had trouble sharing the pieces of the game at small group today. She would share with the teacher but not with other children. She was persuaded to share.
	During the guitar sing-along with Michelle Sennett, Neelia watched carefully but didn't seem to join in the singing. At one point she looked around at the other room's cubbies. She noted they had leaves instead of apples.
9/18/2000	Neelia refers to children in the other classroom as "the big kids."
	Neelia used three arc-shaped blocks to build a bridge.
9/21/2000	Neelia spent a lot of time in the "hospital" today. She dressed up as a nurse. She wore a stethoscope and used the hypodermic needle to give "shots."
	Neelia was attentive when the public health nurse told us about doctor visits. She stepped on a scale, was measured, allowed the nurse to shine a light in her eyes.

communicate with parents when they arrive and leave so that they can address individual needs. Remember how Mrs. B. checked the lunch problem with Blair's mother and reminded Blair about an event to anticipate for the next day? A teacher spends time with each child on a regular basis. She keeps records on things that she observes and follows up on situations that need to be addressed (see Figure 3.2).

Teachers consult with specialists in determining adaptations needed for children with special needs, and they work with children in the activity centers so that the human and physical environments are sensitive and responsive to these children. The books and other play materials reflect children from a variety of cultures and present the cultural **ethos** or values in authentic and interesting ways.

MULTIPLE PERSPECTIVES

From Children

Amanda Branscombe interviewed Misty, age four; Shandell, age three; and Adam, age five, to see what they thought about their preschool experience in the child and family study program she directs.

AMANDA: Tell me about your school.

MISTY: We play in preschool. Drums, computers, bikes, the mirror one, sand. We eat and have naptime. Sometimes we cook. We eat snack, and we eat mashed potatoes. Every day we have a buffet. We decided we wanted a buffet, and we planned it with Moe [the teacher], and now we have a buffet.

AMANDA: Shandell, what about your school?

SHANDELL: Yeah! We play, you know all that stuff. We eat, too. We all have to have a "no thank you" helping. You know, like with cabbage, we get a "no thank you" helping. But now I like cabbage. When I was three, we made my cake here. I really like the computer 'cause we have to take turns. I like to play bears. They tickle me.

AMANDA: Bears?

SHANDELL: Yeah, you know, the grandma and baby bear. They wait for the school bus, and then they get on and the door shuts.

AMANDA: Oh, you mean *Just Grandma and Me*. [CD-ROM of Mercer Mayer's book].

MISTY: We have to sign our names for the computer. We have to ask that way. Then we get on and you punch things in, and then you get what you want. Like you punch in some lines and get a picture. And then you can punch some more and color it.

AMANDA: What do you mean punch?

MISTY: You know, with that mouse that doesn't look like a mouse. You punch it and make stuff happen.

SHANDELL: Yeah! You can even make the whole thing go away and make the tray come out and put a new one in.

ADAM: I like the toys. I like the games, too. I really like the bike riding and the races. You know, I'm going to get to cook my own cake for my birthday and give it to my friends here.

AMANDA: What makes a good teacher?

MISTY: I don't know. Moe just waits for us. You know, when we're not ready to quit playing and she wants us to quit playing. She just waits.

SHANDELL: Julia and Kathy [two other teachers].

AMANDA: What do you like about them?

SHANDELL: They let us take turns. They sit with us. They love me.

ADAM: 'Cause they [Moe and Janice] let me play cars and roll on the floor. They aren't like my other daycare, 'cause they don't make me sit in the bad boy's chair. They don't make me get sad faces on my papers. I can paint whatever I want.

• •

CONSTRUCTIONS

Observation

Working in teams of two or three, complete three observations of preschoolers in preschool programs.

a. Each team member should select three children. One child should be thirty-six to forty-four months of age, one forty-four to fifty-two months of age, and one fifty-two to sixty months of age.

b. Each team member should observe preschoolers for at least thirty minutes, taking notes on all you see.

c. Each team member should interview each child using one clinical procedure you learned in Chapter 1. Each team member should interview and observe three different children, but all should use the same clinical interview.

d. Tape-record and transcribe your findings.

e. Compare and contrast your observations across the three ages with the other members of the team to see how the preoperational characteristics are similar and different.

f. Prepare a written report explaining your findings. Be sure to discuss how the perspectives of the three children contributed to the final report. Be sure to assign a pseudonym to each child observed.

g. Be prepared to discuss your findings in class.

CHILDREN IN KINDERGARTEN SETTINGS

Danielle and Amy enter the kindergarten classroom just as center time is over. They glance around the room and note that it looks very much like a preschool classroom. Amy reminds Danielle that Dr. K. is having them

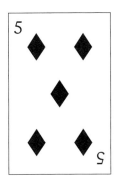

Figure 3.3

Kamii War Cards
Kamii designed the War card decks so that they do not have face cards, and the number of symbols on the card matches the quantity represented by the numeral on the card. A deck of War cards consists of 40 cards: 10 red cards, 10 blue cards, 10 black cards, and 10 green cards of numerals 0 through 9. These cards are used to play War and Double War, as shown.

observe in a constructivist kindergarten. Both say that they didn't expect it to look so much like a preschool classroom. Two children are playing math games in the math center. Danielle nods to the children as she thinks, "That's different. No folder games, and they're not even doing worksheets to reinforce what they learned during the game." Four others are acting out their version of "Little Red Riding Hood" in the creative dramatics area. Amy points out that this teacher has a woodworking center as well as art, writing, listening, and computer centers.

Danielle decides that she wants to go over to the math center, where the two children are playing cards. Amy follows her.

DANIELLE: Those cards look funny.

AMY: You remember, Danielle, those are the Kamii cards [Kamii & De-Clark, 1985]. They have a card that's a zero and a card that's a one, and they don't have any face cards in the deck [see Figure 3.3].

DANIELLE: Oh, yeah! We buy them in our math curriculum course.

AMY: Let's watch and listen. I think they're playing War, and I want to video this.

(The children are indeed playing the card game War.)

BRIAN: Your turn.

KIKI: I already put down that five. It's your turn.

(Brian looks at his card and tries to pull the next card.)

KIKI: You can't do that. That's cheating. Put your card down. Okay, it's a three.

(Brian reaches for the pair of cards.)

KIKI: I win that. Look. *(Points to the symbols as he counts.)* You got one, two, three dots on your card, and I got one, two, three, four, five. I got more than you. *(Picks up cards.)*

(The boys begin to play their next hand, but Brian doesn't have any more cards. Kiki gives him several of his.)

KIKI: Here. Here are some you can play with.

BRIAN: *(Puts down his card, a nine.)* I win.

KIKI: Wait till I put mine down. *(Turns over a five.)* Yeah! You win that one. See—one, two, three, four, five, six, seven, eight, nine. One, two, three, four, five. You've got more.

(Amy glances over at the children at the water table. She sees two children pouring water into a water wheel. She begins to watch and film the conversation. The children play in silence for about five minutes. Finally, Amy interrupts by asking what they're doing.)

CHILD 1: Playing

CHILD 2: Making the wheel turn.

CHILD 1: Playing. See how fast I can make it go?

CHILD 2: Yeah. I can make it go faster.

(Amy decides that she'll just film, as her question didn't get her the information she wanted.)

DANIELLE: The children's actions are speaking louder than your question and their answers, aren't they? Remember what Dr. K. said about good questions and being able to observe their actions as well as listen to their words!

Both Amy and Danielle decide to see what the children are doing in the writing center. Just as Amy is getting the camera ready and Danielle is sitting down, the teacher begins a transition song. As she and her assistant help the children clean up, she explains to Danielle and Amy that shared journal (Taylor, 1984) is a daily event in their classroom. She explains that the children tell stories about events in their lives and question each other to get more details. Then she explains that once the story sharing is completed, the teacher leads the children through negotiating which story they will write about that day.

One girl tells a story about how she cut her finger on a piece of glass, and a boy tells about how he got sick and had to miss school. Amy and Danielle watch and help as each child writes the title of his or her story on the board before the teacher begins the negotiation. This is what the children write:

1. gtkut   for the first story
2. got sic   for the second story

TEACHER: We need to decide what we are going to write about today. Which story do you think we should write about?

CHILD 1: Got sick.

CHILD 2: Got sick.

CHILD 3: Got sick.

CHILD 4: Got cut.

CHILD 5: Got sick.

CHILD 6: Got cut.

TEACHER: Why do you think that, Clay? Why do you think we should write about getting cut?

CHILD 6: 'Cause she got hurt.

TEACHER: All right, but what about Antonio? He was hurt too, wasn't he?

CHILD 6: He's through with it [meaning that he is not sick anymore].

TEACHER: But he shared about getting sick. Didn't you share about getting sick, Antonio? You had a stomachache.

CHILD 7: That's bad!

TEACHER: What's bad?

CHILD 7: Getting sick.

TEACHER: Getting cut is bad, too, isn't it?

CHILD 2: Uh-huh. It hurts.

TEACHER: Why is getting cut bad, Jessica?

CHILD 8: 'Cause it bleedin'.

CHILD 9: Just is.

CHILD 1: 'Cause it hurts.

CHILD 10: 'Cause they get to have a Band-Aid *(inaudible)*.

CHILD 3: 'Cause it hurts.

CHILD 5: 'Cause it hurts.

TEACHER: Okay, do you think Antonio's stomachache hurt?

MANY: Yeah, yeah, yeah, yeah.

CHILD 10: Mine hurt, too!

CHILD 3: 'Cause I don't know what to do!

TEACHER: Why do you not know what to do?

CHILD 3: 'Cause they're both important!

TEACHER: How are they both important?

CHILD 10: 'Cause one was sick. I mean, both hurt.

CHILD 11: 'Cause they were both hurt.

CHILD 10: 'Cause they both had medicine. They were both hurt.

CHILD 2: 'Cause Antonio threw up.

CHILD 3: 'Cause they were both sick.

TEACHER: So how are you going to decide which one to vote for?

CHILD 6: Raise our hands.

TEACHER: How are you going to decide, though? How are you going to decide?

CHILD 5: Try thinking hard.

TEACHER: But when you are thinking, what's going to make you decide which one is better to write about?

CHILD 4: Just thinking.

TEACHER: Why, David?

CHILD 10: 'Cause a little cut hurts a little, too, but sick is a really, really big hurt. But I think "got sick" is more important, because I, um, throwed up. My brother was sick, too.

TEACHER: Who agrees with David?

(Many hands.)

TEACHER: Bridget, why do you not agree? Why do you think getting cut is a better story?

CHILD 4: It could have gone between my fingers.

TEACHER: It could have gone between her fingers. She would have had to have stitches.

CHILD 2: Tyler, in Miss Shartel's class, had to have stitches.

(The teacher closes the negotiation, reminding the children it is time to vote. One child counts and writes 12 for "got sic" and 2 for "gtkut." Then the children begin writing the story in their journals.)

DANIELLE: Let's ask them what they think about shared journal.

AMY: Check with the teacher first.

DANIELLE: She said that we could ask. Are you ready with the camera?

(They move over to a group and ask what shared journal is and whether it's work or play.)

CHILD 1: Shared journal stories are work! No, play! They're play, 'cause you get to write stories. Well, they're kinda stories. We share about good stuff, bad stuff, important stuff, new stuff. Then we write. Journal stories have pictures and words. Lots of them. They're true stories, some of them.

CHILD 2: Shared journal is work, 'cause kids gets up an' shares their story what happened . . . what happened to them. I'm making a book, but kids at shared journal gets up and share. They tell their story what happened at home and what happened to them. Then we write. I like shared journal.

CHILD 3: I like shared journal. I like reading them, 'cause I want to learn about my friends. In journal, if you don't want to write about your friends, you don't have to. Just don't vote for them. Like yesterday, we wrote about Brad fell down the steps. See, Brad tells his story. Then his story makes us sad, so we say, "I'm sorry that Brad fell down the step like that." You draw like Brad holding a newspaper, and he fell down the steps. He's falling. The picture helps you remember what Brad does.

DANIELLE: Wow! Did you hear those little kids? I didn't think they could do stuff like that.

AMY: You know, Danielle, these children in this classroom seem to be continually constructing knowledge through social interaction and **disequilibration,** just like Dr. K. said they would.

DANIELLE: Don't forget she mentioned maturation as well.

AMY: Right, and the interaction between all of those factors.

DANIELLE: Yeah. The process is sure active!!

(Both students have been waiting for writing time. Amy and Danielle observe several children writing.)

CHILD 1: I'm gonna write about I got a new kitten and I went to a wedding. First the kitty and then the wedding. The kitty's a her. We might sell its baby. It is gray and white.

CHILD 2: You didn't tell us enough of that story.

CHILD 1: Now I'm gonna write about Laura and her boyfriend got married. *(Talks as he writes and draws.)* Laura used to live with Mrs. Smith. She was dressed in white, with a headpiece with white flowers in a circle on her head. We were watching. They had a cake with a heart on top. It was big! They cut the cake. The boy touched Laura's face with icing. He put the frosting on her nose! She put it on his nose, too!

CHILD 2: Grownups don't do that!

CHILD 1: But they did! I don't know whether the girl bride threw her flowers. We just ate snack, and we played.

CHILD 3: Where?

CHILD 2: We went on-stage where they got married. Then a boy, Seth, he went over to Laura, and they kissed. Jane and Susan were there throwing out flowers. The boy and girl got married. When we were through eating cake at snack, we saw Laura's car. If they opened the doors, balloons would fly out. It was covered with that white stuff. I don't know that much about weddings. I just ate cake and watched.

CHILD 7: What day was it? You always forget to tell us the day.

CHILD 1: Saturday.

CHILD 2: Sounds like a TV show to me!

(All of the children continue to write and draw in silence. Danielle and Amy thank the teacher, pack up their equipment, and wave to some of the children. Once outside, Danielle surprises Amy with the following comment.)

DANIELLE: I just don't know whether those kindergarten kids are getting all they need to get in that classroom. They just talk and play.

AMY: But, Danielle, we learned that while academic kindergartens appear to be the answer, they aren't. Don't you remember?

DANIELLE: Okay. But what about Lisa Delpit's [1995] writings about African-American children in settings like this one? She doesn't think that this kind of kindergarten is right for them.

AMY: Delpit and many others have said this. But doesn't the research support both points of view?

DANIELLE: Well, I'll have to think about it.

CONSTRUCTIONS

1. Research

Read one article supporting Lisa Delpit's view that a constructivist kindergarten is not appropriate for African-American children and one supporting a constructivist point of view. Interview two kindergarten teachers for their points of view.

2. Comparison

Compare and contrast the various points of view. Try to determine major points on which they agree and disagree.

3. Writing

Draw conclusions about what you found and write a position statement that coordinates the points of view.

4. Sharing

Be prepared to present your statement in class.

Developmental Characteristics of Kindergartners

The kindergarten classroom Amy and Danielle visited serves seventeen children who turned five before the school year began. Children in this classroom range in age from 5.1 (a child who turned five on August 31) to 6.0 (two children who turned five on September 2 and 16 of the previous year). Most of these children fall into the preoperational stage of development. A few are transitional, between preoperational and **concrete operational** thought, the next Piagetian stage. Again, it is important to remember that within this level, the developmental sequence is the same for all children, but the rate at which children develop differs according to biological inheritance and environmental conditions.

Physical Characteristics. Kindergarten children do not differ dramatically from preschoolers. They gain around three to four pounds and grow two to three inches taller per year, and many will lose their first tooth during this year. They continue to refine their gross and fine motor skills. They are able to balance better on either foot and to throw and catch objects more successfully. They are highly active, but they tire easily. They are better able to dress and undress themselves, including using buttons and zippers, and but many still do not know how to tie their shoes. Their fine motor coordination has developed to the point that they are able to use scissors to cut a continuous line without completely closing the scissors. They are able to control pencils and crayons to draw and write straight lines, curved lines, and all combinations of these.

Cognitive Characteristics. Kindergarten children's symbolic play is increasingly cooperative, and their drawings have become much more realistic in intent and form. One of the major representational tasks children begin to undertake in kindergarten is the use of written language as a representational mode. Learning how the written language system works in reading and writing will occupy the thinking of kindergarten children throughout the year.

Although the thought process of the kindergarten child is still egocentric, some children begin to play games with rules. They begin to question the reasoning of others and therefore are becoming more able to question their own reasoning. For example, when Brian picked up the cards, Kiki challenged him and used counting to prove to Brian that he had more dots. He was not at the point where he could simply say, "Nine is more than five," but he could use an empirical test to prove that he was right. This kind of empirical test is characteristic of the transition to concrete operational thought. Notice that Brian did not question Kiki's thinking or his own, nor did either child play to win. Although most of their responses were still egocentric, Kiki's thought process was beginning to transform. This example highlights the continuous nature of cognitive development. Children continuously construct new and transformed schema, so that by the end of the preoperational period, a child's thought process is significantly different from that of a two-year-old.

Social Characteristics. Kindergarten children are becoming more social, and their conversations are more communicative. They enjoy sharing stories with their friends, and they love having stories about others read to them. Social groups are highly flexible, and children change friends frequently.

Social Cognition. Play in kindergarten can be solitary, associative, or cooperative. Some kindergarten children are beginning to understand the need for cooperation. Kiki understood that in the game of War, the person with

> Learning how the written system of language works will occupy the thinking of kindergarten children throughout the year.

the highest or greatest number takes both cards. He challenged Brian when Brian attempted to take the two cards with his five to Kiki's nine. However, Kiki didn't have a fully coordinated set of rules. When Brian had no more cards, Kiki didn't claim a win, but rather gave Brian some of his cards so that they could continue playing. Kiki didn't care that the goal was to win the game; his goal was to continue to play the game for the fun of it. Other children in the same classroom were engaged in solitary play at the water wheel. They were experimenting with making the wheel turn, but there was little evidence of cooperation. Gender roles become more defined at this age; girls begin to play more with girls, boys more with boys.

Language Learning. As evidenced through the shared journal process, kindergarten children advance their ability to represent their experience through stories. At the beginning of the year, their stories may be only one sentence, but by the end of the year, they are able to tell stories that have a sequence of events, main characters, and substantial detail. Additionally, they are learning how to differentiate between telling and asking sentences as they engage in conversation about the stories shared.

The children in the example are constructing hypotheses about what makes a good story, and these constructions give rise to hypotheses that the children invent and use as they decide which events in their lives are of interest to others and which are not. The first hypothesis they construct is that their story is a good story. Next they hold that a story is good if it describes something they have experienced. For example, a child shares that she lost her first tooth. Another child says, "I did, too! Did yours hurt?" This matching of experience makes a good story from the children's perspective. The main hypothesis this class is using at the present time is the bad hypothesis. Children decide that good stories are about bad things that happen to them and their families and friends. It is apparent that Child 10 was using the bad hypothesis when he argued that a little cut was not as bad as being sick. Child 4 tried to make the cut story worse by saying that the knife could have gone between her fingers. Even more important is the fact that both stories were about bad events in the children's lives. The bad hypothesis is significant because it reflects the beginning of an appreciation of what makes good literature. When we consider the Greek or Shakespearean tragedies, we know that they produce the greatest feelings of empathy for others. Through this process, children begin to develop an appreciation for literature that is timeless.

Kindergarten children use oral language and drawing to help them begin to use written language as a representational form. They share oral stories, then they draw pictures of a story and try to put some writing with the pictures. They develop their writing schemata, as they are able to segment the

Kindergarten children learn to consider other points of view and begin to realize that not everyone thinks as they do and knows what they know.

sounds in the words they say and to relate those sounds to the letters they use to write those sounds down. In the example, using *gt* for the word *got* shows that the writer heard two sounds in the word *got* and used the corresponding letters to write those sounds down. This child had already learned a great deal about written language.

Affective Development. In kindergarten, children are learning to consider the points of view of others and to realize that not everyone thinks as they do or knows what they know. Additionally, they are becoming more able to respond empathically to other children's situations. When the children were responding to questions about the shared journal process, Child 3 demonstrated empathy when she said, "I'm sorry that Brad fell down the step like that." Most kindergarten children are imaginative, curious about the world they live in, and eager to learn new things.

Individual Characteristics.

Most kindergarten classrooms serve some Caucasian and some African-American children, and depending on where the school is located the percentage of each group will vary. Chinese, Indian, Hispanic, Native American, Japanese, Korean, Taiwanese, Vietnamese, and children from other ethnic backgrounds are usually minorities in these classrooms. Many children come from contrasting religious backgrounds that value different kinds of behaviors. Thus some children may view assertiveness as a valued trait, while other children may think of it as highly undesirable.

ASK YOURSELF

Starting with the awareness of diversity constructed in Chapter 2, what do I know about religious and cultural beliefs that differ from my own? How can I go about learning more about these different ideas? How will I know when a behavior is culturally or religiously motivated?
....

CONSTRUCTIONS

Journal Entry

Think about all the character traits that you value in children and all those that you do not value in children. List some of each. Then think about all the people you know who are from backgrounds that are different from yours. Try to determine what influenced your selection of character traits and think about how you will deal with children who do not value the same kinds of behaviors that you do. Share your findings with a peer.

How the Setting Accommodates Kindergartners' Needs

Kindergartners' needs are not that different from those of older preschool children, and they require human and physical environments that are very similar to preschool environments. However, because most kindergartens are situated in public schools and follow the guidelines of the state board of education rather than the office of human resources, many people think that they should be more academic in nature and less based on play.

Meeting Kindergartners' Health and Safety Needs.

Kindergarten children are screened before or during their entrance into the kindergarten classroom. Parents provide immunization records upon entry, and screening procedures usually check the children's vision, speech, and hearing. Referrals to other agencies are made if problems are detected. Teachers or school nurses are trained to check for head lice, ringworm, scabies, and other contagious diseases, and to inform parents when problems are detected. As in preschool, teachers continue to supervise hand-washing and toileting routines to minimize infectious disease transmission, and they continue to use latex gloves at all times when bodily fluids might be transmitted. Children are instructed in the appropriate procedures to follow in case of a fire, a bomb threat, a hurricane or tornado, or an intruder in the school.

Teachers implement a social-moral atmosphere to meet kindergartners' social needs.

Meeting Kindergartners' Social Needs.

Teacher to child ratios vary from state to state. Because research supports the fact that lower ratios produce better learning results, many states are implementing group sizes of seventeen to twenty. This ratio gives teachers more time to meet the personal and social needs of the children. Teachers implement the same social-moral atmosphere described earlier in this chapter to meet children's social needs. This atmosphere helps children learn how to be friends and how to make friends. It helps them face differing points of view and come to understand how to consider those points of view in decision-making. It helps children construct shared meaning, resolve conflicts, and determine the rules by which they are to be governed.

Meeting Kindergartners' Learning Needs.

While play continues to be an important medium through which kindergarten children learn, other forms of active education begin in the kindergarten classroom and provide the foundation for the primary grades. These forms of active education, which Piaget referred to as *active play*, include project work, group problem-solving activities, and drama. The curriculum revolves around themes or topics that appeal to the interest of the children. They use math and science to solve problems related to their project work, and they read, write, and draw to communicate what they are learning about the topic.

Whether for a full-day or half-day kindergarten, teachers plan the daily schedule so that it allows for a balance between large group, small group, and individual time; indoor and outdoor time; and activity and rest time.

Teachers are careful to allow sufficient time for sustained project work, music, and physical education. They divide the room into different areas to support the learning needs of the children. There is usually an area for reading, writing, art, construction, experimentation, and for displaying the children's work.

Meeting Kindergartners' Personal Needs. Kindergarten teachers plan routines and procedures for children to use the toilet when they need to rather than making them adhere to a rigid schedule. Similarly, they plan open snack times so the children can eat when they are hungry. Teachers find ways to allow the children to have some personal space in the room, where they can go when they need to be alone. As in preschool, teachers meet with parents and specialists to address each child's personal needs.

Teachers allow the children to make choices and don't require them all to do the same thing at the same time. Children can make choices about the materials they use, the area in which they work, and the people with whom they work. Teachers establish an environment that is sensitive to the children's cultural and religious backgrounds and ensure that the materials are multicultural in nature.

CHILDREN IN PRIMARY SCHOOL SETTINGS

Zenah and Tillie are nervous about visiting the primary school, even though it is considered to be a model school. As they check out the video camera, they discuss with Dr. K. the fact that the other students went to classrooms that were identified as developmentally appropriate and had graduates of their program teaching the children. They note that they don't have a placement like that.

TILLIE: Will this lower our grade if we can't find a classroom you like? You know, one with centers and woodworking and stuff? I know they won't have that, 'cause I've worked as a teacher's aide in these schools, and I can tell you that kids have to do real learning when they get in primary school.

DR. K.: Don't worry about the grade, Tillie. I have picked a classroom that's more like the ones I discuss in class. Just enjoy your visit and videotape what you want us to see.

ZENAH: Will we get to work in the classroom like the others?

DR. K.: You may do more observing, but you may get to help with an individual child or a small group. Just go and see what happens!

After Zenah and Tillie arrive at the school, the teacher explains to Tillie that after morning announcements, they are going to open the class with a math review. Tillie and Zenah observe that the classroom is attractive, even though it is a little crowded with twenty-five second-graders, two gerbils, a teacher, and a volunteer. The teacher seems to have a developmentally appropriate classroom. She has an area designated as the reading/writing workshop, a building construction area, and a science area. They count five multimedia computers networked to a server. They also see a printer and scanner next to the computers. The desks are flat so that they can be clustered into a large table or separated into individual desks. The children's work is aesthetically displayed on the walls. The television monitor that is mounted in one corner of the room has been turned on.

TILLIE: Look, Zenah, that math review is going to be on television.

ZENAH: I think I've heard about this school's program for student broadcasting.

MRS. M.: We televise our morning announcements. Mrs. Ling's class is in charge of today's announcements. It shouldn't take long.

ZENAH: Talking heads!

TILLIE: My friends won't like this. What's this have to do with learning second-grade stuff?

ZENAH: Look! Wow! What an opening! Looks like they've used a Power-Point package on the computer to help with their opening.

TILLIE: This looks like real TV! Commercials and everything. Can we get the video to tape this?

ZENAH: I'll try!

(Both watch and attempt to video. The announcements last about ten minutes.)

ZENAH: Wow! That's fantastic!

TILLIE: Yeah! This must be some kind of magnet school for television or technology.

MRS. M.: *(Having overheard the students' conversation.)* No, this is part of our media center's program. We think that the students need to be makers as well as consumers of multimedia events. Tillie, come on over and join us for the math review.

TILLIE: Do you use a curriculum like Saxon Math or Mathematics Their Way or a textbook series?

MRS. M.: Well, some of us designed our curriculum around the National Council for Teachers of Mathematics standards. We use lots of Constance Kamii's work, like *Young Children Continue to Reinvent Arithmetic*. We also use the cognitively guided instructional ideas from the University of

Wisconsin–Madison and a little of the early work of Marilyn Burns. We like to have the children work with real problems and do lots with games. Let's watch the children as they lead the math review.

TILLIE: You mean you don't teach.

MRS. M.: Well, I do, but not like you mean.

LEADER: It's time for math review. Everybody ready?

CLASS: Ready!

LEADER: My problem that I have for you today is forty-two take away twenty-seven.

TILLIE: This is too easy for them. They should have had this last year.

ZENAH: Are you sure? *(To the teacher.)* Have they had this yet?

MRS. M.: No, but let's watch and see what happens.

CHILD 1: I think we should start with forty take away twenty is twenty.

CHILD 2: No, don't you remember? Our first-grade teacher said we always had to start on the right side. But how can we take seven out of two? That can't be done.

CHILD 3: I don't know. I guess we'd have to take it out of the forty.

CHILD 4: But how would we do that?

CHILD 1: Well, forty-two take away seven. *(Counts on fingers.)* Forty-one, forty, thirty-nine, thirty-eight, thirty-seven, thirty-six, thirty-five. Thirty-five!

CHILD 2: But I don't think that's right. Last year I learned you had to take ones away from ones and tens away from tens.

CHILD 1: *(Ignoring Child 2.)* And then thirty-five take away twenty is fifteen. I think the answer is fifteen!

CHILD 2: That makes sense. I just don't think it's right. We aren't supposed to do it that way.

CHILD 3: But I think the answer is right, so what difference does it make how we do it?

CHILD 2: What do you think, Mrs. M.?

MRS. M.: Well, tell me how you figured this out.

CHILD 3: He counted backward.

CHILD 2: Well, if we do it his way, you could count the whole twenty-seven backward. That's not how I learned last year.

CHILD 3: Let's see. Forty-two, forty-one . . . *(and so on to 15).*

MRS. M.: Let's put your solution on the board and see what everyone thinks.

CHILD 1: Okay! *(Puts his solution on the board.)*

MRS. M.: Did anyone come up with a different answer?

TILLIE: *(Whispering to Zenah.)* Oh, brother! She's letting them do this wrong. That little girl was right about the ones and tens. Do you think Mrs. M. will correct them before this lesson is over?

ZENAH: Listen! Let's see what happens. This is really interesting!

MRS. M.: *(To the class.)* There are many different ways to solve a problem. One way is no better than another if you can explain it. Does anyone want to try another?

CHILD 2: Yeah! I want us to try thirty-five take away twenty-seven.

(The children finish their work on the problem. The teacher announces that it's time for the readers and writers workshop.

Tillie and Zenah begin to pack up their camera. They are both puzzled but are afraid to ask the teacher about the math lesson. Finally, Zenah decides to question her about "the right way" to solve a problem. The teacher suggests that they read Kamii's book and then return for another observation. They thank her and leave.)

Developmental Characteristics of Primary School Children

The second-grade classroom that Tillie and Zenah visited is housed in a public elementary school. The children in this classroom range in age from 7.1 to 8.0. Many of these children fall into the concrete operational stage of development, while a few are transitional between preoperational and concrete operational thought. Again it is important to remember that within this grade level, the developmental sequence is the same for all children, but the rate by which children develop differs according to their biological inheritance and the environmental conditions under which they are raised.

Physical Characteristics. Physical growth seems to slow down in the primary grades, except for occasional growth spurts in the extremities. Primary children will gain one to two pounds a year, will grow a few inches taller, and will lose their baby teeth during this period. Their gross motor abilities are highly coordinated, and they enjoy participating in games and sports that allow them to use these abilities. Their fine motor skills become more controlled, so that they are able to participate in activities such as sewing and paper folding with ease. They continue to be highly active, and they do not tire as easily. Depending on cultural and environmental circumstances, some second- and third-grade females may begin to show signs of early puberty.

Physical growth seems to slow down in the primary grades, except for occasional growth spurts in the extremities.

Cognitive Characteristics. First-, second-, and third-grade children are moving into or are at the concrete operational stage of reasoning. Although this stage reflects a qualitatively different kind of reasoning from the preoperational stage that precedes it, it develops very gradually over time. Piaget (1981) defined **operations** as internal systems of actions that are mentally reversible. At this stage, operations are *concrete* in that they can be applied only to problems that exist in reality. According to Piaget, operations have four defining characteristics: They are actions that can be completed in

TABLE 3.4 Characteristics of Concrete Operational Stage (Ages 7–11)

Operations	Definitions	Examples
Reversibility	Mental ability to move backward in thought.	"It is still five, because it was five when I counted before you moved them."
Identity	Mental ability to reason about constancy.	"You are really still my daddy even though you look like Santa."
Compensation	Mental ability to reason about constancy.	"There are still just as many red chips as black. This one just looks like more because there is more space between the chips."
Conservation	Mental ability to hold something constant through transformations.	"There is still the same amount even though you changed the container, because you didn't add any more or take any away."
Classification	Mental ability to group things according to similarity and difference and according to subordinate relationships.	"There are more plants than tulips, because tulips are just one kind of plant."
Seriation	Mental ability to order objects along a dimension.	"This spoon is longer than that spoon but shorter than this one."

thought, conserve or hold something constant through transformations, are reversible, and never exist alone. Concrete operational thought includes reversibility, the ability to take all relevant factors into account, the ability to attend to transformations, and the ability to base problem solutions on reason instead of perception (see Table 3.4).

These characteristics can be demonstrated best in the conservation of number task. A child who originally agrees that two rows of five chips are equal in number is asked to watch while an adult spreads out the chips in one of the rows so that the row appears longer. The child is then asked if the rows still have the same number of chips. Whereas the preoperational child would notice that one row looked longer and therefore reason that it must be longer, the concrete operational child would tell you that they are still equal. Her reasoning would be either "If you moved them back, they would still be the same"; "You didn't add any or take any away"; or "It just looks like more because there is more space between them." Notice in this reasoning the ability to take all relevant factors into consideration, the ability to attend to the transformations, and the ability to base the solution on reason rather than perception.

Two logical operations that are constructed during the primary years are classification and seriation. **Classification** refers to the ability to group things according to their similarities and to understand the principle of

Two logical operations that are constructed during the primary years are classification and seriation.

class inclusion (for example, there are more animals than there are birds, so since birds belong to the class of animals they are a subgroup of animals). **Seriation** refers to the ability to organize and order things along a dimension, such as height, weight, or length. Counting backward, as one of the children was doing, documents her understanding of these two operations, because number includes both operations. Classification relates to the fact that four is included in five and six but is not all of five or six. Seriation relates to the fact that five comes after four but before six.

Social Characteristics. Primary-grade children are highly social, and egocentrism is replaced by sociocentrism. They enjoy playing games with rules, and they recognize that the rules can be changed if all the players agree on the changes. They are more competitive, and they play to win as well as for the fun of playing. Their friendships are based on relationships that have been constructed over time and are stable, and they are able to understand and consider their friends' points of view. They love telling stories and jokes, writing, drawing, singing, and participating in dramatic activities.

Social Cognition. Let's return to the students attempting to solve the problem forty-two minus twenty-seven. They were able to consider not only the relevant factors related to the problem but also each other's points of view. They were able to communicate their points of view through language and to argue their ideas through social interaction. According to Piaget, true cooperation can occur only between those who consider themselves equals. He suggested that children will not argue and hold fast to what they think if they are interacting with someone they consider above them in authority. The teacher in this second-grade classroom allowed the children to debate among themselves, an example of cooperation from a Piagetian point of view.

> According to Piaget, true cooperation can occur only between those who consider themselves equals.

Language Learning. Primary-grade children's oral language is well developed. They have acquired all the grammatical structures and are capable of using highly complex sentence combinations. They are able to tell stories that have complex plots and well-developed characters. Their hypotheses about what makes a good story have grown to include things that are bad, funny, and unique and that make you feel good. Their major goals during this period are learning how to apply these oral language abilities to written language. The many children are not yet able to express their thoughts in a clear, logical fashion in written language. Additionally, they are making the transition from the primary to the cursive form of handwriting.

Affective Development. During this period, children construct their *will*, a sense of obligation to do what is right according to their values. This requires them to struggle between what one wants to do and what one should do. They are also developing a more relative moral stance that includes intention as a criterion for making judgments about naughtiness. Their understanding of what a lie is will change considerably during this period, but they will not yet construct an adult conception of a lie.

Another affective characteristic developed during this time is a beginning sense of autonomy. Remember from Chapter 1, autonomy refers to the ability to make decisions about what is right in the moral realm and what is true in the intellectual realm. Autonomy requires that a person has considered all points of view and has based her judgments on self-constructed norms. Although children in this age group are not completely autonomous, they are making a shift from heteronomous obedience to forms of mutual respect between equals. One day one of the authors' grandsons came home from school, and his mother greeted him quite excitedly with a letter from Santa. Seth took the letter and began to read it. He looked up at his mother and said, "I don't think that this letter really came from Santa. It must have come from one of his helpers." When his mother asked why he thought that, he replied, "Because it is postmarked New York, and Santa doesn't live in New York. Besides, he didn't send Ben [his brother] one, and I don't think Santa would send one to me without sending one to Ben." This example documents the transition from obedience to autonomy.

Individual Characteristics.   The older children get, the greater the developmental differences among them. Piaget identified four factors that account for this wide range of developmental differences. The first factor is *biological maturation*. Children need different amounts of time to explore ideas, to try out hypotheses, and to construct knowledge. Biological maturation is different for every child. The second factor is *social interaction*. Again, depending on their home and school environments, children will differ in the amount and quality of social interaction they have had. The third factor is *physical experience*. Children differ greatly in the kind and quality of physical experiences they bring to the classroom. The last factor is what Piaget referred to as **equilibration,** and he considered it to be the most important factor. Equilibration is sometimes referred to as self-regulation, as it is the factor that coordinates the other three factors. Again, you will learn more about this factor in Chapter 4.

How the Setting Accommodates Primary School Children's Needs

Good constructivist classrooms are designed to accommodate all the needs of primary school children. These classrooms are developmentally appropriate in their approach to curriculum practices, and they foster the children's

---

The older the children get, the greater the developmental differences among them.

ASK YOURSELF

Do children in the primary grades have the right to make autonomous judgments about what is right or what is true? How will doing this help them come to understand what society holds to be right or true?

academic, social, affective, and physical growth through both the classroom environment and the curriculum.

Meeting Primary School Children's Health and Safety Needs.

As in kindergarten, teachers and school nurses continue to check for head lice, ringworm, scabies, and other contagious diseases and to inform parents when problems are detected. Teachers continue to model and supervise hand-washing and toileting routines to minimize infectious disease transmission, and they use latex gloves at all times when bodily fluids might be transmitted. Children are instructed in the appropriate procedures to follow in case of a fire, a bomb threat, a hurricane or tornado, or an intruder in the school. Additionally, concepts related to nutrition, drug abuse, personal hygiene, and dental health are integrated into the daily curriculum.

Teachers meet children's learning needs by allowing them to use what they know to solve problems about what they do not know.

Meeting Primary School Children's Social Needs.

Teacher to child ratios are set by state boards of education, but generally speaking they seem to increase at each grade level. First-grade ratios range from 17:1 to 20:1 or more, second-grade from 18:1 to 20:1 or more, and third-grade from 20:1 to 25:1 or more. These ratios are based on either daily student attendance or daily student membership. The rationale used by state departments of education seems to be that as children mature, they are better able to take care of many things independ-ent of the teacher. Therefore, ratios can be higher. Teacher to child ratios recommended by NAEYC are 15:1 to 18:1, or 25:2.

Teachers implement a social-moral atmosphere (DeVries & Zan, 1994) to meet the children's psychosocial, affective, and personal needs. This kind of classroom promotes social negotiation as a daily activity, values students' questions and thoughts, and expects students to be responsible and self-regulated. Additionally, this atmosphere promotes cooperation between peers and fosters the development of moral reasoning and relationships.

Meeting Primary School Children's Learning Needs.

Teachers meet the children's learning needs by providing instruction in a way that allows all children to use what they know to solve problems about what they do not know. The curriculum is organized around important topics that include the literacy, mathematics, science, or social studies content recommended by national and state standards.

Literacy and language needs are met through the use of a workshop approach. A readers workshop engages children in reading quality literature about topics of interest to them and in sharing perspectives on books, authors, and themes. A writers workshop engages children in authentic expository and fictional writing. Mathematical learning needs are met through solving prob-

Playing math games allows children opportunities to construct mathematical knowledge in authentic ways.
(© Elizabeth Crews)

lems related to daily living activities, playing math games, and solving problems that arise in project and theme work. The creative arts are integrated throughout the curriculum. Science and social studies are integrated in themes and project work. For example, a third-grade class is doing a theme on Australia. Through their reading, they determine that a red kangaroo can jump around forty feet in one leap. They wonder how many leaps they would have to take to jump forty feet. The teacher and children figure out how to mark off forty feet, then each child jumps while the others count. The children graph the results. Then they wonder how the kangaroo can jump that far. Through reading for information, they understand that the kangaroo propels itself with its tail. They wonder how they might use propulsion to improve their jumps. They measure their jumps with and without a running start and compare the distances. They test their jumps using simple propulsion with an apparatus similiar to a teeter-totter. They read Australian literature and determine how those books differ from and are similar to American books in illustrations, writing style, and content. They have questions and find Australian pen pals and use the Internet to answer some of their questions. They make topological maps of Australia and Tasmania. As you can see from this example, the curriculum is integrated around these themes and project work.

Essential to meeting the learning needs of primary children are endless opportunities for social interaction, authentic experiences with aspects of the physical world, and experiences that raise questions and challenge children's thinking. With these factors in place, teachers can interact with all the children, adapt the curriculum to their individual needs, and provide the materials and environments that help children construct their understandings of the world.

Meeting Primary School Children's Personal Needs. The children in primary classrooms demonstrate significant individual variability. Recognizing this variability is essential in providing for individual needs. Teachers establish a classroom environment in which children learn to respect and value all members of the classroom. Through topic work, teachers use a variety of strategies to help children learn about each other and appreciate how they are different academically, culturally, religiously, and in gender. Group work helps students get to know all the children in the classroom.

Teachers adapt the classroom environment to accommodate the needs of all the children, including those with special needs. They plan flexible schedules that allow time for children's individual physiological schedules.

SUMMARY

- The early childhood years are years of rapid growth and development.
- Young children grow physically from reliance on reflex and sensory activity to the use of complex gross and fine motor coordination.
- Young children grow socially from pure egocentrism to the ability to engage in genuine social relationships.
- Young children grow intellectually from the logic of action to the logic of concrete thought.
- Young children grow emotionally from early feelings of pleasure and pain to the capacity for genuine differentiated emotional responses.
- Programs that serve young children vary according to the ages of the children served.
- Programs adapt to the needs of the children served.

CONSTRUCTIONS

1. Reflection

Go back to one of the conversations in this chapter. Read it and reflect on the teaching/learning process it describes. Do you agree or disagree with this approach?

2. Analysis

If you had your own classroom, how would it look? First, draw the design of the classroom. Next, represent that design through two more media (for example, use a computer to design it, and then make a shoebox diorama). Be sure that you include places for electrical outlets, cabinets, sinks, tables, and bookcases.

3. Writing

What would the children and teachers say in your classroom? Write the dialogue for a lesson. How is this similar to or different from the conversations in this chapter?

4. Site Visit

Visit an infant program, toddler program, preschool, kindergarten, and primary school classroom in your community. Write observations using the guidelines provided in Chapter 1. After the observations, compare and contrast the five settings.

5. Reflection

Review the chapter. Why did the authors include a chapter like this? What points or conversations really caused you to pause and reread particular sections? How do you think you'll use the information in this chapter to help you with the rest of your course?

RESOURCES

Child Development

Books

Allen, K. E., & Marotz, L. R. (1994). *Developmental profiles: Pre-birth through eight.* Albany, NY: Delmar.

A comprehensive look at developmental characteristics of children through eight years of age. Particularly helpful in providing normative profiles at each age level.

Labinowicz, E. (1980). *The Piaget primer.* Menlo Park, CA: Addison-Wesley.

An excellent reference for students interested in learning more about Piaget's explanations of cognitive development.

Lindfors, J. W. (1987). *Children's language and learning.* Englewood Cliffs, NJ: Prentice-Hall.

A comprehensive look at how children learn language and communication ability. Particularly useful are the end-of-chapter suggestions for how early childhood students can learn from children.

Web Sites

National Center for Infants Toddlers and Families
   (http://www.zerotothree.org/)

This Web site provides a wealth of information for those dedicated to the healthy development of infants and toddlers. It allows you to choose either "For Parents" or "For Professionals." Both provide information on programs and services, a resource list, and a bookstore.

www.ed.gov/MailingLists/EDInfo/msg00272.html

The Web site of the educational information mailing list archive of the U.S. government.

What New Brain Research Tells Us About Young Children

Excerpts from the transcript of the April 17 "White House Conference on Early Childhood Development and Learning: What New Research on the Brain Tells Us about Our Youngest Children."

Early Childhood Practice

Books and Journals

Bredekamp, S., & Copple, C. (1997). *Developmentally appropriate practice in early childhood programs* (Rev. ed.). Washington, DC: NAEYC.

This publication provides national guidelines for practice that is thought to meet the developmental and individual needs of children. It will help students expand on the information presented in this chapter.

Chaille, C., & Britain, L. (1997). *The young child as scientist* (2nd Ed.). New York: Addison-Wesley.

A wonderful application of constructivist theory to the teaching of science. Easy to read and full of good ideas for the classroom.

Delpit, L. (1995). *Other people's children: Cultural conflict in the classroom*. New York: The New Press.

Useful to students who want to know more about this opposing point of view. Questions whether constructivist approaches are beneficial to African-American children.

Edwards, C., Gandini, L., & Forman, G. (1998). *The hundred languages of children*: *The Reggio Emilia approach—advanced reflections* (2nd Ed.). Greenwich, CT: Ablex JAI Press.

This book is particularly helpful for those interested in working with the preoperational child. It helps students understand representational thought and how to provide experiences that allow children many symbolic ways to show what they know and to use new media to rethink ideas.

Fields, M. V., & Boesser, C. (1998). *Constructivist guidance and discipline*. Upper Saddle River, NJ: Merrill.

This text is particularly useful in helping novice teachers manage children. It shares the constructivist approach to discipline.

Fields, M. V., Spangler, K. L., & Lee, D. M. (1991). *Let's begin reading right*. New York: Macmillan.

A constructivist approach to early reading and writing. Excellent in helping the student deal with issues of invented spelling and composition.

Kamii, C., & DeVries, R. (1980). *Group games in early education*. Washington, DC.: NAEYC. Kamii, C., & Joseph, L. L. (1989). *Young children continue to reinvent arithmetic—2nd grade: implications of Piaget's theory*. New York: Teachers College Press. Kamii, C., & Livingston, S. J. (1994). *Young children continue to reinvent arithmetic—3rd grade: Implications of Piaget's theory*. New York: Teachers College Press.

These three texts are particularly helpful to those who wish to take a constructivist approach to the teaching of mathematics. Each provides specific games that achieve particular educational goals.

Ryan, K., & Cooper, J. M. (1995). *Those who can, teach*. Boston: Houghton Mifflin.

The standard reference work on teaching methods, presenting methods from a variety of learning perspectives.

Web Sites

Early Childhood Educators and Family Web Corner
   (http://www.nauticom.net/www/cokids/)
This Web site provides all kinds of information for teachers. Articles about practice, a calendar for each month, and conference announcements are available here.

Project Construct National Center
   (http://www.projectconstruct.org/)
This Web site provides information for those who are applying constructivist tenets in the classroom. It includes resources, news, and support.

4

Children as Sense Makers

· ·

In Chapter 3, we described how young children grow and develop in many ways and how different educational settings facilitate that development. We also introduced the notion that all development is continuous. For example, we discussed the operations of existing structures that affect children's capacity for thought at given ages. The aim of this chapter is to discuss the development of thought so you can advance your thinking about the content and functional aspects of thought as they relate to the structures of thought presented in Chapter 3.

Piaget raised two questions when he studied the young child's ability to make sense of the world: First, how does the child's intelligence develop? Second, how does the child's reality develop (Gruber & Voneche, 1977)? When he raised those two questions, Piaget had to look at how the child used continuity, transformations, and coordinations in the categories of correspondences, classification, conservation, ordering, symbolic representation, simultaneity, and causality. We would like you to use Piaget's two questions to guide you as you consider how the child constructs knowledge. Doing so will make you more aware of how different children's thinking is from adults and how you might view teaching if you begin with children and what they know.

After reading this chapter, you should be able to discuss these topics:

▶ **The three kinds of knowledge as identified by Piaget**
▶ How a child's intelligence develops
▶ How a child's reality develops
▶ How a child functions as a social being

INTRODUCTION

Piaget noted that intelligence has three components that are equally necessary for thought to develop: structures, function, and content. Remember, you cannot really separate these three components. We separate them only to discuss them so that you can understand how thought develops.

According to Piaget, cognitive development has three components: structures, function, and content.

You may remember from Chapter 3 that the **structures** of thought are the organizational components, or *schemata,* of cognitive development that help us understand why certain behaviors occur. The **content** of thought is what children know. It is observable behavior and varies from child to child, activity to activity, and age to age (Wadsworth, 1996). The **function** of thought relates to the processes by which thought develops, which are assimilation and accommodation. Structures and content change with age, but the way thought functions does not. Understanding the function of thought helps us address questions such as the following: Why do children speak? How do children construct tools that help them understand their worlds? How do children develop tasks that help them discover their worlds? Do children and adults think in the same ways? To address such questions and understand the function of thought, you will need to think about the interplay between function, content, and structures and realize that that interplay causes the structures of thought to change (Inhelder, de Caprona, & Cornu-Wells, 1987).

ASK YOURSELF

Who was Piaget? Was he a teacher? A researcher? Where and when did he do his research and writing? Why is his research so important to us today?
. . . .

Piaget's Path to His Study of Intellectual Development

How many of you realize that Piaget began his career as a biologist? Between the ages of eighteen and twenty-one, he focused his biological studies on the mollusks that were found around Neuchâtel, Switzerland. Mollusks are a large group of mostly shelled and aquatic invertebrate animals (squid, snails, and clams). From his research, Piaget decided that the biological aspects of the mollusks adapt to their environment. For example, he learned that if you move a mollusk from one kind of lake water to another, over time its shell will change, or adapt to, the new environment (Wadsworth, 1996).

Piaget learned about adaptation from his study of mollusks.

Piaget's study of mollusks caused him to hypothesize that the biological functions of the human body were useful in studying intellectual processes. To him, intellectual processes were the adaptation to the environment (Wadsworth, 1996) and the organization of that environment. In other words, Piaget saw the biological aspects of humans as directly connected to their intellectual aspects. His early work in the biological sciences led him to his interest in the nature of knowledge. Because Piaget wanted to get at the roots of knowledge, he hypothesized that children's thinking was as close to

Children learn when they have a need to know. (© Jean-Claude LeJeune/ Stock Boston)

the beginnings of human thought as he could get. To test his hypotheses, Piaget began his study by focusing on how children construct their understanding of time, space, and causality. Questions such as, "How does the child's intelligence develop?" and "How does the child's reality develop?" arose from Piaget's study of biology and his interest in the nature of knowledge.

The Role of Adaptation in the Functioning of Intellectual Structures

Piaget believed that just as the body has physical structures such as kidneys and lungs, the mind has mental structures called schemata.

Unlike Darwin, who believed that species evolve in response to their environments, and unlike Skinner and Watson, who believed that the environment shapes the individual's behavior, Piaget maintained that the organism is the one doing the adapting to the physical environment and then organizing it. The processes involved in adapting are those of the individual taking something in and interpreting it on the basis of existing cognitive

The child had to accommodate his thinking about the relationship between puppies and grown dogs when he experienced the conflict that not all dogs grow as big as his dog. *(Amanda Branscombe)*

An organism uses assimilation and accommodation to adapt to its environment.

structures (assimilation) and then, if it doesn't fit, changing those existing structures (accommodation). Piaget believed that just as the body has physical structures such as kidneys and lungs, the mind has mental structures called schemata. Even though a schema isn't observable, he believed, it still exists. For example, the lungs are bodily structures whose function is to allow us to breathe. Schemata are hypothetical structures that are ever changing and become more complex and defined as a child ages and experiences new stimuli. At birth, the schemata is reflex. As the child develops and adapts, the schema changes (Wadsworth, 1996).

For the organism to adapt to its environment, it uses assimilation and accommodation to establish equilibration. Equilibration is the process of balancing between assimilation and accommodation. If the organism experiences disequilibration, it experiences a form of cognitive conflict or cognitive imbalance that requires accommodation so that a new state of balance or equilibration can be achieved. Assimilation and accommodation are the mechanisms that control equilibration. **Assimilation** is the internal process a child uses to take something in and interpret it on the basis of his existing cognitive structures—in other words, to put new information into what he already knows so that it can be used. For example, Gaines, a two-year-old, saw a miniature dachshund and assimilated it into what he knew about small dogs and puppies. After all, it was small like his Weimaraner's puppies. **Accommodation,** another component of adaptation, happens if the incoming information doesn't fit the existing structures of what the child already knows. It is the actual change or modification of the existing schemata to manage the incoming information. Several months passed, and Gaines saw the miniature dachshund again. His Weimaraner puppies had grown to be almost as tall as his brother, George, but the dachshund had stayed the same size. He looked at the dachshund and asked, "Why won't your puppy grow up?" When the owner replied that the dachshund was grown, Gaines looked puzzled and said, "How can he be? He's still little." Later that day, Gaines said, "I get it! Dachshunds stay little. My Weimaraner gets big." He reorganized his schemata to accommodate the new information from his experience with miniature dachshunds.

Gaines constructed knowledge for himself. His environment and the cognitive conflict within that environment created an opportunity for him to make new inferences. This story demonstrates the principle of children constructing knowledge and thereby making meaning. This principle is essential for a constructivist teacher to understand. Children construct knowledge by acting on their environment. Their actions can be mental, physical, or both. Along with development, the actions cause the child cognitive conflict, or disequilibration, which causes him to assimilate and accommodate information within that environment. Such actions lead to the transformation or reconstruction of the child's schemata. Children's constructions of knowledge can be grouped into three kinds of knowledge, which are discussed in the next section.

CONSTRUCTIONS

1. Journal Entry

Write a journal entry about intellectual processes. Be sure to consider the following questions. How do you think children's intellectual processes develop? Do you think the brain evolves, reacts to the environment, or adapts itself to the environment?

2. Journal Entry

After reading about accommodation and assimilation, reflect on those processes. Create a journal entry that describes what you understand about them. The entry can be a drawing, cartoon strip, chart, or written reflection. You could even write a mock dialogue or interview with accommodation and assimilation. Consider these two questions, as well as your own ideas, as you create your entry: Do you think there has to be a balance between accommodation and assimilation? What would happen if a person just assimilated or just accommodated?

THE THREE KINDS OF KNOWLEDGE

Dr. K.'s students are puzzling over the need to learn about knowledge and intelligence in order to teach young children.

TILLIE: I just don't get it. I mean, I can memorize the information in the book and write the papers like Dr. K. wants, but I don't get the purpose for us studying about children's intelligence.

DANIELLE: For once we agree! I thought counselors gave you an IQ test to place you in a gifted program or a magnet school. If you scored high enough, your parents bragged about it. Teachers need to know how to teach.

ZENAH: Intelligence and how intelligence develops is important knowledge for teachers. When we begin our teaching with the child and what the child knows, we have to understand intelligence. I don't mean scores on an IQ test. I mean how intelligence develops.

AMY: I think I agree with Zenah. I got interested in this stuff when I was observing in the preschool last month. I think adaptation to the environment is important.

TILLIE: Well, I know it's continuous! I learned that.

ERIC: Amy, what's happening to you? You were so into constructivism. Why the big change?

TILLIE: Well, I talked with some teachers I know. They said I need to have all kinds of kits and materials made before getting a job. When I told them we were learning about intelligence and how to observe, interview, and question, they just laughed.

ZENAH: They're just threatened by what they don't know. Their professors probably used approaches that were based on behaviorism and sensory learning. There's nothing wrong with those approaches, but they start with the teacher or a published curriculum. We are starting with the child and what the child knows.

AMY: When you graduate from this program, you'll know what you need to know. I've heard that people from this program get hired first!

DANIELLE: You bet! That's why I stayed here when my boyfriend transferred to the college in our hometown.

ZENAH: Back to intelligence! I don't understand this idea that children construct knowledge.

ERIC: I think the notion that children construct knowledge is a key principle to using constructivist teaching principles.

ZENAH: Why?

ERIC: Well, do you remember me telling you about my visit to the preschool? We saw children signing their names for roll in the mornings.

Some of them would scribble or put a mark on the page. Others would put some letters or a picture of a face. Julia and Kathy [the teachers] accepted their efforts to sign their names and, over time, offered examples of the conventional spellings of their names. Like Julia and Kathy had each kid's name printed on their cubby, had each kid's name and picture on a card for the choice board and helper chart, and had each kid's name on language experience charts. After several weeks, we saw accommodation occurring as the kids began looking at those cards and charts and discussing that that was the way to draw their names. They began to apply what they were learning by adding letters to their names when they signed roll. They even began to spell their names conventionally. Like—remember Tillie?—we could read several names before we left. So, over time, the children constructed knowledge about ways to sign their names.

TILLIE: Why didn't those teachers just teach them? That's what the teachers I talked to said we should be learning to do.

AMY: It doesn't work that way. I've tried! Believe me! When I was an aide, I tried to make kids write their names, but it didn't work. My teacher and I took recess away, sent notes to their parents, made them write their names over and over, and it didn't work. What I saw Julia and Kathy doing worked. The kids were doing the thinking and deciding that they wanted and needed to write their names.

To understand the origins of intelligence, we must examine Piaget's classification of the knowledge children construct: physical knowledge, social (conventional) knowledge, and logico-mathematical knowledge. He based his classification on children's continuous actions on their environment, which lead to the development of structures from the interplay between content and function. **Physical knowledge** is knowledge of objects in external reality (Kamii & Ewing, 1996, p. 262). It is constructed through observation and acting on an object, because the ultimate source of physical knowledge is partly in the object itself. It's as if the object "tells" or "shows" its physical properties when the child acts on it. For example, the color, texture, and weight of a ball are physical properties that are in external reality. Knowing that a ball will bounce when dropped is also physical knowledge. What the child learns from the object could be considered the content of physical knowledge. Kamii and Ewing used the term "partly" because they wanted to point out that logico-mathematical knowledge also has a role in physical knowledge. To make sense of a ball, you have to have a classification framework that allows you to distinguish a ball from other objects.

Social knowledge, also called conventional knowledge, is knowledge of culture, its values, and its conventions (Kamii & Ewing, 1996). For example, holidays, written and spoken language, moral codes, and rules of conduct (holding the door for an older person or sending a thank-you note when you receive a gift) are examples of social knowledge. We learn social knowledge partly from people in our culture (externally) and partly from logico-mathematical knowledge (internally). There is no physical or logical reason that people in the United States celebrate Thanksgiving on the fourth Thursday in November; however, people in our culture agreed on that date. Words such as *one, two, three, four,* and *five* also are social knowledge. The underlying notions about numbers is **logico-mathematical knowledge,** but the sets of words used for counting are specific to a culture's language. Just as the underlying framework for physical knowledge is logico-mathematical knowledge, the underlying framework for social knowledge is logico-mathematical knowledge. For example, to recognize holidays, we have to categorize words (Kamii & Ewing, 1996).

Social knowledge is necessary and useful. It gives names to objects (baseball game) so that a person doesn't have to hold all of the attributes of an object or rules of a game in memory when comparing. It allows one to communicate and function within the culture. One important aspect of social knowledge is that it can be learned but not constructed. For example, reading and writing are examples of social knowledge. You learn to read and write in the language of your culture. Another important aspect to remember is that when social knowledge is placed in a logico-mathematical framework, a child can use that knowledge to go beyond it rather than simply applying it because the culture says so. For example, a child might learn other countries celebrate a holiday similar to Thanksgiving in the United States. Through categorizing words used to represent holidays that celebrate giving thanks, children use logico-mathematical knowledge.

Unlike social knowledge and physical knowledge, which are obtained from the external world, logico-mathematical knowledge is knowledge we create internally through **reflective abstraction.** It is based on the coordination of actions that occurs internally rather than on the object itself (as with physical knowledge). For example, the relationships of same/different, some/all, and part/whole are internal relationships we make. If you have a red block and a blue block and you think they are *similar,* it is because you internally created the relationship of *similarity* between the blocks (Kamii & Ewing, 1996). The important point here is that you put blocks in this relationship internally, thereby creating it in your mind. You were able to put them into relationship because of the continuity of the materials (you had the opportunity to work with those blocks day after day rather than experiencing new materials each day). You could have coordinated relationships of *twoness, difference,* or *weight* with those same blocks.

Piaget classified knowledge into three parts to help explain the difference between the thinking that children do when they use simple abstraction, when they reflect on their actions and the organization of those actions, and when they learn about their culture.

As you put those blocks into relationships, you learned about them. As you read earlier in this chapter, what you learned is what Piaget called the content of thought. In logico-mathematical thought, content relates to relationships like same/different, more than/less than, and some/all. In physical and social knowledge, content relates to what you have learned from objects and people in the external world. Your earlier experiences with the content help you know how actions relate to each other so that you can coordinate relationships into elaborate ones. For example, the more children coordinate same/different and more than/less than with beads, the better they will understand how those actions relate to each other. Over time and with experiences with the beads (continuity of materials), the children will construct notions of class inclusion (there are more beads of all colors than red beads) (Kamii, 1986, p. 8).

The three kinds of knowledge are essential to understanding Piaget's notions about how young children construct knowledge. He classified knowledge into three parts to help explain the difference between the thinking that children do when they use simple abstraction, when they reflect on their actions and the organization of those actions, and when they learn about their culture. At this point, you might be wondering whether there are other aspects of children's thinking you need to know about to understand how children construct knowledge. As mentioned earlier in this chapter, over time the intellect adapts to the environment and organizes its experiences, which creates knowledge. For the intellect to do that, it uses the processes of assimilation, accommodation, transformation, coordination, and continuity.

THE INTELLECTUAL DEVELOPMENT OF VERY YOUNG CHILDREN

The Intellectual Development of Infants

How does intelligence develop? Do very young infants use assimilation and accommodation as they adapt to the environment? If so, how? Very young infants reach or grasp for an object, such as a rattle, and use action and sensory awareness at the perceptual level to discover and understand how that object functions. For example, the rattle is an object to hold or shake. How does the rattle help the infant's intelligence to develop?

The growth of children's intellect is an internal process of self-construction governed by existing cognitive structures and how those structures function. The growth happens in relation to the world and is a process that has evolved in such a fashion that its results are biologically and socially adaptive. In other words, infants experience their worlds and adapt to that world. Children's increased height and weight is an example of biological and social adaptation. Because of society's interest in and study of the role of nutrition in children's growth, parents and schools now provide children with more nutritious diets than in the past. Just as the mollusks' shells changed because of changes in their environments (different lakes' water), children's bodies have changed because of changes in their diets. They have adapted by becoming taller and heavier than they were several hundred years ago.

Piaget, Sinclair, and other constructivists have characterized children as young scientists who use observation, hypothesizing, and experimentation to assimilate objects and events into their structures and to accommodate those schemata to the new information. To understand why researchers such as Piaget and Sinclair would think of an infant as a scientist, you must consider the notions of continuity in the development of the cognitive structures of children from infants to adults (Piaget & Garcia, 1989, p. 263); of exploration and experimentation through action; and of the use of hypothesis testing, which creates awareness, and cognitive conflict, which advances thinking.

Let's join Dr. K.'s class as they continue their discussion of children's thinking.

DR. K.: I would like you to react to the following observation I made in the infant center last week. When the infant teacher put a drum close to Matt, a seven-month-old, he reached for it, pulled it over to himself, and accidentally tapped the top. It made a sound. He looked surprised and tapped it again. Sound! The teacher said, "Look, he's playing the drum! Mattie, you're playing the drum. When he gets older, he'll be in the marching band just like his father." She viewed Matt's action as symbolic and as a deliberate attempt to play the drum. What was really happening in this situation was that Matt was using sensory awareness and reflex action to experience an object. He was associating the object with the action and the sound, but he was not using the object to stand for any action or event.

DANIELLE: Dr. K., you talk about that baby as if something was happening in his brain. We all know that babies don't think. Well, maybe this new brain research I read about in *Newsweek* suggests that they think, but they don't talk, so we don't know what they're thinking. I was babysitting for this three-month-old last week, and all she did was cry and sleep. I got so tired of feeding, changing, rocking, and checking her as she slept that I didn't know what to do.

AMY: Sometimes I get so exasperated with you, Danielle, I don't know what to do. Babies may not think the way we do. Piaget and other researchers have made us aware of the complex nature of their brains. Look at what Mattie was doing.

Children are young scientists who use observation, hypothesizing, and experimentation to assimilate objects and events into their structures and to accommodate to the new information.

ZENAH: Amy, you're right. I remember when my babies were a few months old. If they were hungry, when they saw me picking up a bottle and pouring formula in it, they'd start crying, because they knew they were about to get a bottle. At one point, every time a strange person came into the room, they bawled. They used the actions and objects as a signal for them.

ERIC: I think that stranger reaction happens before two years of age. We talked about that in my child development class. It happens because babies begin to recognize the people around them all the time and get scared when they don't recognize a face. All of this relates to what Dr. K. is talking about when she says very young infants wait and react. Later on, they begin to anticipate, act, and search. Your babies were searching for a face they recognized. They anticipated a bottle.

TILLIE: Yeah! You know, Dr. K. also talked about something called object permanence. I wonder whether the baby just wakes up one day and has it, or whether it's like the baby cutting a tooth.

AMY: From my understanding of object permanence, it takes place over time. You know, the baby has to understand that when she puts a toy down and the infant teacher takes it away, the toy still exists and can be played with later that day.

TILLIE: Okay, Amy, enough! I think it's time for Dr. K. to do some explaining.

ASK YOURSELF

How do children construct tools that help them understand their worlds? Are invention and representation examples of tools infants use? How do children develop tasks to discover their worlds?

Invention and Representation as Functions of Infants' Intellectual Development

Invention and representation are necessary for children to construct reality.

Invention and representation are both necessary for the child to construct reality. How do infants use these functions to construct the external world? How do infants view objects and information about those objects, such as a rattle? Interestingly enough, Piaget's research found that what he calls **object concept** is constructed little by little. Furthermore, it is connected to children's spatial constructions and ability to form relationships. At first, infants form recognizable pictures that have no permanence or spatial organization. For example, infants recognize a nipple or a sound. At another point, infants use that earlier recognition to learn more about the object. They grasp, pull so they can see, and hold, which allows them to begin to establish some continuation and organization with regard to the objects they recognize. At this point, they do not look for the object when it's absent. Next, infants look for objects that have disappeared, but they look only within their visual field. This suggests that they are aware that those objects exist separate from themselves, even though the objects are out of sight.

Sinclair (1995) observed young children engaging in such actions as early as four months of age. However, age is not as important as the fact that in-

Infants construct actions that lead to more elaborate thought. *(© Elizabeth Crews)*

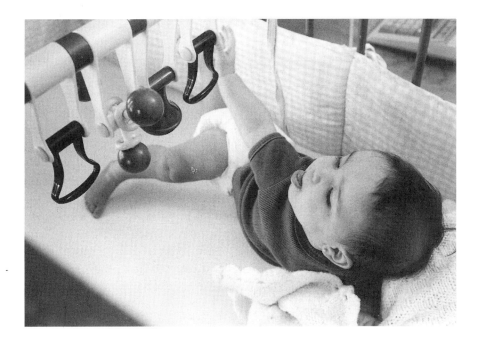

fants construct actions that lead to more elaborate scientific thought patterns. We have all observed infants as they stare at an object or a light, turn to find a distracting noise, or turn to find a familiar sound. We also have seen infants close their hands on an adult's finger and suck it. We have watched as infants visually follow an object and then reach for it. To a caregiver, such early actions are stories to tell family members. To psychologists, these actions represent inborn, or innate, patterns much like nesting patterns in birds.

Next, infants begin to combine patterns. When an infant looks and then reaches for an object, she is making her first coordination of two patterns (the act of looking and the act of reaching). Once she has created this new pattern, she repeatedly uses it to experience more objects. With these actions, the infant is assimilating a variety of objects into her cognitive pattern. The assimilating of all the objects at the same time causes the infant to accommodate the objects to her first pattern of looking and reaching. Once this has occurred, she has used practical adaptation (Gruber & Voneche, 1977; Sinclair, 1995). In other words, the infant has extended inborn or already mastered patterns to new objects and new events, while coordinating those patterns and accommodating them. She is establishing the foundation for later sense making, which demonstrates the necessity of continuity in her constructions.

Repetition of an action is the rudimentary beginning of the cause and effect pattern in humans.

Around four and a half months of age, infants begin to act on objects in ways other than reaching and grasping. Such actions are evidence of **intentionality.** For example, an infant might hit an object with his hand, become interested in the action, and repeat it. This action shows that he is reproducing new and interesting events by intentionally applying earlier patterns or by combining patterns. When the hitting becomes as intentional and repetitive as the grasping, the infant has constructed a different cognitive pattern. The new pattern, repetition, is the rudimentary beginning of the cause and effect pattern (I caused this action. What will be the effect? Let me test it again and again and again.), which moves children to more experimentation through elaboration of their actions.

Around eight months of age, infants extend looking for an object to looking behind doors or under chairs. When this happens, we know that they can hold images of the object in their minds even though the object is absent. To do this, infants must coordinate the object's movement, which Piaget calls *logic in action,* as well as hold an image from the past in their minds.

Once infants are aware that objects exist outside themselves and can invoke the images of those objects when the objects aren't present, they actively attempt to create systematic changes in the materials or objects they are investigating. This action results in groping, which Piaget views as essential in the "formation of networks of meaning" (Gruber & Voneche, 1977, p. 218). For example, eight-month-old Michael had been sitting by a Pat Mat, patting the surface so that the colorful objects in the liquid moved. On Monday, the infant teacher brought in a sensory quilt that had squares of different textures and colors. Michael sat on the quilt and attempted to pat it as he had done the Pat Mat the week before. Another infant used groping when, after pushing a beach ball and watching it roll, she attempted to push her cereal bowl and make it roll.

As infants get a little older, they will not only reach for an object but also attempt to swing it. If the first object hits another object by accident, the infant experiences a momentary action that is a glimmer of her future use of it as a tool to make her arm longer and thereby reach further (remember the earlier example with Mattie and the drum). When infants do this, they are creating tools that function to help them discover their worlds.

When infants fully and internally construct the notion of the object within the world, it shows their ability to coordinate, combine, and order internal mental representations.

Sinclair (1995) notes that around eight months of age, infants' ability to coordinate more than two patterns allows them to begin to understand that they are doing something to cause an object to move. This is the earliest notion of separating self from another and ordering. What is meant by "separating self from other"? When an infant first encounters an object, it's just an extension of self, part of the infant like an arm or a leg. After experiencing it over time, the infant begins to anticipate the object. Next, he experiments with the object and its properties to know what might happen when he uses it. Finally, he fully and internally constructs the notion of the object within the world, which shows his ability to coordinate, combine, and order internal mental representations (Gruber & Voneche, 1977). Many researchers feel that this is the most important aspect of intellectual development at this age.

Infants use one more step in their use of the roots of representation. Once they have constructed an awareness of the images of objects and an awareness of their knowledge of the objects' existence, they can evoke those images even though the objects aren't present. When this occurs, they begin to intentionally initiate an action or behavior. For example, as an infant Gaines repeatedly touched, twisted, and rubbed the tablecloth at the dinner table. For months he had enjoyed the feel of the cloth. Although he pulled the cloth and watched as objects on the table moved, he did not repeat his action every time he saw the tablecloth. When he was around eight months of age, he purposefully pulled the cloth to move the flower arrangement on the table. Although he gave no indication that he was attempting to figure out what was causing the flowers to slide closer to him, he did imitate his own movements to create the action again. Thus he demonstrated intentionality. His actions suggested that he realized he did the acting, not someone or something else. It also indicated that he was beginning to separate himself from others.

ASK YOURSELF

Reflect on these observations. When children construct a need and a purposeful way to use tools, such as a table-cloth and a stick, they open up endless opportunities for exploration. Think of the importance of the beginnings of intelligence for the children in your classroom. Think of the role continuity plays in intelligence. Did you realize that we build from what we know? Thus the four-year-old builds from what the infant constructed.

This example is similar to Piaget's observation of his son, Laurent, as he played with a short stick that accidentally hit a toy hanging out of reach. Although he continued to hit the toy, when he tired of the hitting action, he did not return to that action after a rest. Several months later, Laurent reached for and used a child's wooden cane that Piaget had put within his reach to strike objects that were out of reach. Finally, much later, he intentionally used a stick to get a toy that was out of reach. He then tested his hypothesis that the stick helped obtain the object by using it in various situations at different times (Gruber & Voneche, 1977). Laurent continued to elaborate his experimentation with the stick as a tool, and through awareness of its uses, he discovered new purposes for it.

By age two, an infant's continuous elaboration of direct action patterns on her environment has evolved from using reflex actions such as "empirical groping" (Gruber & Voneche, 1977) to using perceptual and motor actions that allow early internal representations and sudden inventions. In other words, two-year-olds do what we call thinking (Piaget & Inhelder, 1969). For the first time, infants can use a rudimentary form of **invention.** They do this by thinking about a whole sequence of actions, mentally combining those actions, and using those thoughts rather than having to rely on every detail of each step of each action. This kind of thinking allows infants to use invention and representation as they choose. You will learn more about how constructions of invention and representation are elaborated in the intellectual process later in this chapter.

CONSTRUCTIONS

1. Journal Entry

Write a journal entry in which you reflect on the similarities and differences between infants at four months and infants at eight months.

2. Observation

Visit a center that provides infant care. Observe the infants at the center. Look for their attempts to reach, grasp, use tools, and repeat actions.

3. Journal Entry

Reflect on your understanding of how reaching, grasping, using tools, and repeating actions relates to the functional aspect of intellectual development.

Causality as a Function of Infants' Intellectual Development

ASK YOURSELF

Can infants solve problems? Do they use tools to help them with exploring their worlds? Do they see themselves as causing events? Do they socially interact with others? Do they have feelings? Do they make friends? What do causality and social interaction have to do with intellectual development?

· ·

Infants see themselves as causing all events or activities.

Another important aspect of intelligence is the understanding of causality. We mentioned it briefly when we were discussing infants' use of objects as tools in the previous section. Although causality is continuously developing, it becomes clearly apparent in seven-month-old infants. What Piaget meant by **causality** is that infants see themselves as causing all events or activities. Children focus on each part of an event or activity but do not realize that one part causes another. As infants elaborate their schemata about causality, they move from the notion that they caused the activity or event to realizing that other objects or people beyond themselves caused it. Once children have some representational competence (ability to evoke internal images), causality can be elaborated even more. Children begin to investigate rudimentary cause and effect relationships. The following observation of Gaines exemplifies a child's use of causality.

When Gaines was sixteen months old, his cousin and her friend took him outside to play. As the two adults watched, he became fascinated with the watering hose on the porch. He found that when he lifted the hose, water would sometimes trickle out and make a wet spot on the cement. Second, he learned that if he swung the hose, water might trickle out. Third, he observed that sometimes when he played with the hose, nothing would happen. As he intently engaged in his play, his cousin turned on the water faucet. Suddenly, there was a stream of water. She then turned it off. He continued to play, only to find another stream of water coming from the hose. He stopped his play, looked around, saw his cousin's hand on the

Toddlers use rudimentary cause and effect relationships to satisfy their need to know and create hypotheses. *(© Bob Daemmrich/The Image Works)*

faucet, smiled, walked over to the faucet, put his hand on it, and then returned to the porch and his play. Once his need to know how and why the water came from the hose was satisfied, he went back to his play. As he played, he would occasionally look at his cousin and the faucet. His hypothesis about the water and his play with it would lead him to his next puzzle. How could he make the water come out of the hose?

Causality, just like other aspects of children's thought, continues to develop well into formal operational thought.

Social Interaction as a Function of Infants' Intellectual Development

ERIC: I wonder how language develops.

DANIELLE: You need to have language before you can have thought.

ZENAH: I don't think that hypothesis will work in all situations, Danielle. For example, how can deaf people think if they need to be able to talk before they think?

AMY: I agree with Zenah. Many people have the mistaken notion that a person has to be able to talk before he can think. Let's ask Dr. K.

TILLIE: She'll just turn your question around. You know she never answers a question.

ERIC: Well, I'm going to see what she says when I ask her about language, 'cause I want to hear her perspective, not just read the stuff in a book. *(Raises his hand and asks the question.)*

DR. K.: How does language develop? Let's see. You really want me to answer this question, right? Not turn around and ask you one—right? Before I answer the question, you might raise a question about the role of the infant as a social being and how language fits into that role. You also may want to consider communication and language in the infant's role as a social being.

TILLIE: What do you mean, a social being? Isn't language part of logico-mathematical knowledge?

DANIELLE: Do you mean that you think language is social knowledge?

DR. K.: I want you to consider the role of the infant as a social being. Think about that.

At first infants use reflex reactions in response to adult sounds, but not in a social way.

Infants are not born social (Piaget, 1963), but they are born into a world of social networks. The earliest sounds they hear are those from people telling stories about their births, recounting daily events, and talking about the do's and don'ts of their worlds. Because infants use reflex reactions at this point in their development, they react to the adult sounds, but not in a social way. As they get older, they continually react to, adapt, and become part of their social worlds by engaging in social behaviors, telling and listening to stories, asking questions, and making friends.

Thanks to researchers such as Brazelton, Sinclair, Stambak, and others, we now know that newborn babies are attempting to enter those social networks at a much earlier age than people previously thought. They are doing more than just sleeping, eating, and dirtying diapers. For example, infants begin using a social smile (implying communication) at around six weeks of age. Two-to-three-month-old infants realize that it is not the pain or discomfort that they feel that makes a parent come to them, but rather their cries (Sinclair, 1995). Thus we are learning that infancy is an important period of social development for children and an equally important period for early childhood educators to study. It is the time when infants begin to use adaptations (a smile, crying, babbling and words, steps, and so on) and patterns of adaptations to interact with their physical and social worlds.

At the same time infants are expanding their growth in intelligence through patterns of action, they are expanding their social knowledge by acting on their social environments. Their interaction with their social worlds allows them to learn about their cultures' laws, values, symbols, language, and rituals. As a result of acting on their social worlds they learn to collaborate with others, experience reciprocity of perspectives, and thereby construct a reality in which their own thought is not absolute (Gruber & Voneche, 1977).

Infants begin developing their representational competence before the third month of their lives. When they respond to others by imitating their actions (for instance, sticking out their tongues in response to an adult's action), infants are engaging in the rudimentary aspects of *deferred imitation*. Later, when they clap their hands together to imitate an adult playing patty-cake with them, they are demonstrating more elaborate forms of deferred imitation.

Language, another form of representation, plays a major role in infants' ability to act on their social worlds. Up until seven or eight months of age, infants experiment with cooing and babbling. Around seven or eight months many of them attempt to imitate sounds such as "da-da" and later, "ma-ma." In addition, infants attend to their mothers' words, not the contexts in which their mothers use them. Both of these attempts indicate that infants have some comprehension of situations before they are able to produce words. By nine or ten months of age, infants begin to show some signs of understanding the words being said rather than the situations in which they are said. Furthermore, they begin to use "no" and other one-word refusals. This suggests that they have some awareness that they are communicating a message to another person. Their actions offer even more support for the hypothesis that infants are aware that they are separate from others.

By sixteen months, some children are combining words in such a way that they show they have separated one object from another, have used creativity with their combinations, and are attempting to communicate. Such representations are called one-word sentences and are used by infants to have needs met, to express emotions, and so on.

When Gaines was sixteen months old, he loved orange and apple juices. He did not like milk. He and his mother had the following conversation.

GAINES: Juice!

HIS MOTHER: Milk?!

GAINES: No! Juice!

HIS MOTHER: Milk!

GAINES: No white juice! Juice!

Another example of communication and social behavior occurred when Gaines, age nineteen months, was shopping with his mother. As they hurriedly walked through a large store, Gaines spied his favorite series of books, the Spot books by Eric Hill. He said, "Mama! Pot! Mama! Pot! Pot!" His mother replied, "Gaines, they don't have Spot books here. Come on!" He stated, "No! Pot! Pot!" Once she saw the books, they went over and bought a book. In this example, Gaines was demonstrating early social behaviors and feelings that related to his likes and dislikes. When he and his mother were in the store, he saw the Spot books and recalled that he liked these books. Then he communicated that preference to his mother through language.

Language plays a major role in infants' ability to act on their social worlds.

Around age two, children begin using two-word sentences and then short complete sentences. When they begin using two-word sentences, children really begin working on *syntax* (word order) and *morphology* (the smallest unit of meaning in language). Gradually, children acquire more and more complex grammatical structures. As they expand their use of language, they are better able to function socially and use notations for relationships and classifications.

As social beings, infants not only reach out to others in their environments, but they also begin to develop their understanding of themselves and their feelings. During the first three or four weeks of their lives, infants use instinctual drives and reactions to feel. Over the next four months, their feelings become connected to their satisfaction. They react if they are hungry or wet, dry or comfortable. They can demonstrate relaxation, stress, or tension. For example, if they hear other infants crying, they become distressed and cry. At this point, they still view these feelings as part of their own bodies and actions. Around eight months of age, infants begin to experience feelings of success or failure. For example, you remember how Laurent and Gaines were able to use their tools to make something happen. Their actions caused them to feel success. At this point, infants also begin to feel affection for others. No longer are they simply using others to meet their needs so that they feel good (for instance, dry or content). For example, if two infants are playing, they will smile at each other, comfort each other, and babble. Infants at this age also begin to show preferences, have likes and dislikes, and decide what they will and will not do.

CONSTRUCTIONS

1. Research

Find an article about infant brain research and read it. Compare and contrast what the article says with what Piaget thought about infants' intelligence.

2. Journal Entry

Reflect on your notions of how infants think. Contrast those notions with what you've read. Draw a representation of your thinking.

3. Reflection

Review what you have learned about logico-mathematical reasoning and the intelligence of infants. As you review, consider your understanding of reflex action, object concepts, spatial constructions, causality, assimilation, accommodation, and continuity.

THE INTELLECTUAL DEVELOPMENT OF TWO- TO SEVEN-YEAR-OLD CHILDREN

Children between the
ages of two and seven
move from perception
to operation through
coordination.

ASK YOURSELF

How do toddlers think?
How does their intelli-
gence develop? What
happens to them as so-
cial beings? How do
toddlers use representa-
tion and invention? Is
their use of representa-
tion and invention dif-
ferent from that of
infants? How does a
toddler's thought
process relate to the de-
sire to teach children in
the primary grades?
....

The construction of thought is continuous. It begins with infancy and continues throughout life. For thought to continue to advance, children must
experience *disequilibrium* through puzzlement and conflict, so that they assimilate and accommodate the new information. When children are between the ages of two and seven, their thought is still tied to perceptual
activities, even though they are able to represent actions internally. To advance their thinking, children need numerous experiences that cause them
to question their own reasoning. At this point in their thinking, children
have to have experiences that challenge their thinking, their perspectives,
and their roles.

Earlier in the chapter, we talked about infants' inability to separate or
differentiate themselves from objects (rattles, people, bottles) in their environments. Infants begin to make this construction through repeated interactions with the objects. Children between the ages of two and seven must
engage in the same kinds of continuous experiences so that they can move
beyond believing that their thoughts or perspectives are the only ones. By
doing this, they are able to move from perception to operation through
coordination.

Toddlers' content and structure of thought is different from very young
infants, even though they use assimilation and accommodation to adapt to
their environments. Through the use of physical knowledge during infancy,
toddlers have constructed early structures that move beyond the reflex actions of the infant (see Table 3.2 on page 96). Although their thoughts are
still tied to perceptual activities, those activities no longer have to be immediate or based on motoric actions. According to Piaget, toddlers have constructed three very important, observable patterns by eighteen months of
age. The first is the ability to solve a problem without trial and error. For example, at eighteen months of age, Oh-Lin was working with a simple five-
piece puzzle. Rather than attempting to match the puzzle piece to the space,
she looked at the space, looked at the pieces, and carefully selected one that
matched the space. Such actions indicate that she was using experimentation and planning that required looking into the future. The second pattern
that toddlers demonstrate is that they begin classification by knowing. For
example, when they see something that is round, they know it can be rolled.
When they see something square, they know they can make it slide. The third
pattern is that toddlers can and will use representation to solve a problem or
get a result. They do this by making something present (through symbols
such as words, actions, and images) that isn't actually there.

Children need to question
their own reasoning.
*(© Elizabeth Crews/
The Image Works)*

Semilogic as a Function of the Two- to Seven-Year-Olds'
Intellectual Development

Toddlers have the ability to solve a problem without trial and error, begin classification by knowing, and can and will use representation to solve a problem or get a result.

Eric, Amy, and Zenah are meeting at the student union to discuss a presentation they are planning on ways toddlers think. Tillie and Danielle have just dropped by to see what they are doing.

DANIELLE: How's the presentation coming?

ERIC: Okay! We thought we'd show a video of two- and three-year-old children and ask questions.

TILLIE: What good is that going to do us? I think you're just trying to get out of work.

ZENAH: You're right, Tillie. Eric is just teasing you. We plan to give scenarios and show the video, as well as talk about this period of development.

AMY: We really want you to understand children's use of representation during this period. But we also want to discuss children's lack of ability to take the perspectives of others—their efforts to decenter, transform, and conserve.

TILLIE: Well, we talked about representation with infants. Why are we talking about it again?

AMY: We want you to understand that representation, like causality and other aspects of intellectual development, occurs throughout our lives. It's a function of intelligence and doesn't end with a certain stage of development.

ASK YOURSELF
How do I think about the processes of correspondences, reversibility, conservations, and classifications as they relate to semilogical thought and intellectual development? (See Chapter 3.)
....

DANIELLE: What do you mean by decentering, transforming, and conserving?

ERIC: I guess you'll have to come to class to hear our presentation.

As children reach the ages of two to seven, their thinking is semilogical. Because they don't reflect, their logic is *unidirectional* (goes one way) rather than reversible. They do not question their own ideas, thoughts, and actions. Even when the evidence shows children that their thinking is erroneous, they believe that it is correct. Although their logic is only semilogical, they are actively constructing more elaborate notions about correspondences, functional relationships, order and seriation, and classification; understanding states and attributes; abstracting meaning; and raising questions about the past and future (Robinson, 1996).

Correspondences. Children between the ages of two and seven begin to create or make correspondences. These **correspondences** are comparisons that are horizontal in organization and do not create transformations or modifications (Robinson, 1996, p. 14). For example, children make one-to-one correspondences when they match napkin, silverware, and cups to each family member's place mat when they set the table. They have great difficulty if the family is having a guest for dinner, because adding a place setting requires a modification of their correspondences. Children also form correspondences when they learn to read and write.

Following a sequence of events within a *transformation* (which can be organized as hierarchical and vertical comparisons) is another important conflict children between the ages of four and six begin to coordinate. Children at this age focus on each separate event rather than on the relationships between the events and the process that causes an object to transform through a series of related events. For example, four- and five-year-old children draw a pitcher in a stance that shows the ball being released and then a hitter after the ball has been hit. Their cognitive development does not allow them to draw the sequence of events that occurs when a pitcher throws a ball and a batter hits it.

Reversibility is an essential process within the ability to follow a transformation. Reversibility means that children can follow their line of thought back to its beginning. This is very difficult for children because so little of what they experience in their physical environments is reversible. For example, the water runs out of the faucet. They can't make it go back into the faucet. Between the ages of two and seven, children begin to raise questions and become aware of experiences that cause them to puzzle over their earlier ideas that were bound by what they could see. The children's questions and testing of the answers to those questions lead them to new constructions of reversibility.

Two- to seven-year-olds' thinking is semilogical in that it is unidirectional (goes one way).

When children can follow their line of thought back to its beginning, they are using reversibility.

Children between the ages of four and seven elaborate their earlier notions of ordering relations. They use linear ordering and convert circular arrangements into linear ones and vice versa (Robinson, 1996, p. 16). No doubt you have seen children order their toys at various points in their play. For example, Ally, at age five, lined her dolls up on a table before beginning her play episode. As she played, she would take one down, play with it, and then return it to its place. Music, repetitive stories, chants, and patterning activities are other examples of children's efforts to order (Robinson, 1996).

Just as reversibility is a construction of intellectual development that begins to develop between the ages of two and seven, notions of conservation also begin to be elaborated. **Conservation** is the child's ability to understand and conceptualize that the amount or quality of matter stays the same regardless of any changes in the quantity. It relates to correspondences in that it is a state (liquid, gas, whole, part, powdered, solid, and so on) within a correspondence. For example, you have the same amount of clay regardless of whether you make it into a sausage or a pancake. Because children between the ages of two and seven concentrate on one attribute that they can see, they are "tricked" by their own thinking. For example, if young children are given a pint milk carton that is short and squat rather than tall and slender, they cry because they think the teacher has given another classmate more milk. They aren't capable of understanding that a pint is a pint, regardless of the container. If the teacher provides the children with a water table that has pint-size containers of varying shapes and sizes, and if the child chooses to go to that center and act on those materials, he will begin to construct new notions about liquid and containers. Cooking is also a valuable activity for children as they develop their notions about conservation. During this age span, children puzzle over and self-regulate their notions of conservation of number, area and volume by acting on objects and events. We cannot teach children to conserve; they must construct their own notions through acting on materials.

Classification is another aspect of cognitive development that children between the ages of four and seven begins to develop. Although they have the roots of classification at a much earlier age, their cognitive structures begin to change and advance at this age. A child becomes interested in the attributes of objects and their similarities to other objects. Once this occurs, the child begins to group the objects (color, size, shape, function, use, state, and so on).

When children begin to construct notions about conservation of identity and classification, they begin to consider possibilities or ideas other than their own. This construction is essential for a child to advance in his thinking. Once the child considers alternatives, he begins to anticipate, predict or hypothesize, solve problems, and link events to past events. He also begins

When children begin to group objects (color, size, shape, function, use, state, and so on), they are classifying.

to make choices. For example, a four- to-seven-year-old child will roll a toy car over a pretend highway. Then he will use another pretend highway (another possibility) to reach the same point. Another example is, when a four- to seven-year-old child goes shopping. She will pick one item to buy, then find others that are equally interesting. She will talk about ways she could use each item and finally make a decision.

You must remember that children between the ages of two and seven don't have the complete constructions necessary for transformation, coordination, and continuity. Even though a child might tell an adult the "correct" answer to a question, he does not have the understanding necessary to explain that answer in a logical manner. For example, Seth, at four, often used semilogic as he explained events to adults. He loved baseball and spent hours hitting the ball. As he hit, he often said to the pitcher, "I've hit three balls and missed two. That makes five." Seth also loved candy. One Easter season, his grandmother had an Easter egg tree with candy Easter eggs on her dining room table. Seth came for a visit and found the eggs. He carefully counted the eggs and noted, "There are eight eggs here." His grandmother heard him counting and came over. She said, "Are you sure you found all of them?" Seth looked again and found three more buried in the decorative grass. He said, "There are eight here, and three more make eleven. Eleven eggs for me. The Easter Bunny left me eleven eggs. Did he turn flips in the front yard when he left?"

Although Seth was counting and giving the correct answer, he had no real logic for his responses. He needed logical necessity or precise quantification to explain his solutions in a logical manner.

Let's go back to the students, who are discussing their assignment to interview children about thinking.

AMY: Eric, what questions did you use to get at children's thinking?

ERIC: Not the right ones! I got the craziest stuff.

TILLIE: Me, too! I got stuff like "Sometimes I get sick and take medicine and get well." I thought, "What does this have to do with thinking?"

AMY: What question did you use?

TILLIE: How do babies think? When I asked that, this girl says, "Say please, and that's thinking." Now what am I supposed to learn from that?

AMY: I tried that one, too, and got some interesting stuff. When I asked Jenny, she said, "Sometimes it just hits me. When I was at Patti and Phil's house, they have a new baby. I don't know. I just do it. Like when I was a baby, I did it. When I was born. I was a baby and then Mariah was born, and she was a baby and I'm grown up!"

DANIELLE: How old is Jenny?

AMY: She's four and a half.

DANIELLE: I asked Michelle, who's five. She said, "They think, well, they poop in their diapers a lot. That's what I know about babies. And . . . and God made the languages. He just sat up there and made them up. He put them in our mouths, and they just come out."

ERIC: Well, I asked Katie. I think she's about five. She's really smart. She said, "I just think in my head. I don't know how it works, but sometimes it hurts to think. I have a friend named Sage, and she has a baby. I play with her and her baby sometimes. Babies crawl on the floor and drink a bottle. They think funny! My daddy makes my mind work."

TILLIE: The thing I don't understand is why children can respond with something that makes sense when you ask them about a holiday like Thanksgiving but can't when you ask them how they think. The same day I was asking those questions about thinking, the teacher had the children tell her what they were thankful for. One said, "I'm thankful for my family." Another said, "I'm thankful for the turkey we're going to eat." Another one said, "I'm blessed with my family and my dog."

ERIC: Did you ask them what being thankful meant?

TILLIE: No, because they knew. Just look at their responses.

AMY: Their responses were based on social knowledge. Thanksgiving is a cultural event. The children had been taught facts about Thanksgiving and were also imitating what they had heard adults say about Thanksgiving. I don't think their responses had anything to do with their ability to reason.

The accompanying box contains a transcript from the oral storytelling part of the shared journal process, which is a daily ritual in many preschool and primary classrooms (Taylor, 1984). Once the children have shared the stories, they all write and draw about one story. This transcript demonstrates how children who are five and a half to six years of age use semilogic in the story and their discussion, even though their reasoning on certain Piagetian tasks is more logical than semilogical.

MULTIPLE PERSPECTIVES

From Children

The Fight

By Chad

This morning, someone hit me on the bus. It was a boy. I punched him in the stomach. He hit me. I punched him three times. Somebody cried, but

I didn't. The other boy started it. His name is Tommy. His real name is Thomas. My sister didn't see it 'cause she was already at school. The bus driver didn't see it 'cause she was driving. My cousin saw it, and that's bad for me.

(Children's comments during the storytelling event)

CHILD 1: You don't have to scream the story! Just tell us. Now, tell us more.

CHILD 6: What day was it?

CHAD: I already told you. Today! This morning!

CHILD 1: You are not suppose to fight!

CHILD 7: I want to write about the fight.

CHILD 1: A fight is so bad. What if some big boy comes and hits you? Then you'll be sorry.

CHILD 2: I don't want to write about that. I want to write about Daniel's baby being sick. That's important.

CHILD 3: I want to write about the other story 'cause Jamie was a hero when he put the fire out. I don't want to write about no fight.

CONSTRUCTIONS

1. Journal Entry

Revisit the stories about children's reasoning in this section. Write a journal entry in which you try to explain how each story exemplifies some aspect of children's reasoning.

2. Journal Entry

Use the transcript of "The Fight" and answer the following questions. What did you learn about the child's ability to tell a story or recount an event? Was Chad attempting to communicate? Were his classmates attempting to communicate? What did you learn about the children's reasoning? Did you see contradictions? Did you see the children trying to take on others' perspectives? How well did the children use language? Did they ask questions? Make judgments? Did they use logical reasoning or semilogical reasoning?

3. Research

Read about some of Piaget's conservation tasks. Pick one or two and administer them to at least six children who are about five years of age. Write up your observations and share them with a classmate.

Representation and Social Interaction

ASK YOURSELF

When children use representations of thought, how do these representations relate to social relationships?
....

Children between the ages of two and seven use several forms of representation: deferred imitation, symbolic play, drawing, mental images, spoken language, and writing.

Representation. Two- to seven-year-olds' elaboration of the function of representational competence gives them the ability to initiate conversations, communicate through various forms of representation, and elaborate their social networks. The early use of representation, which Piaget calls the semiotic function, allows infants to begin problem solving and representing objects and events internally. In other words, the semiotic function separates thought from action (Gruber & Voneche, 1977). Toddlers elaborate those early schemata. They begin to use representations of thought so that they can elaborate social relationships or coordinate their thoughts with others.

Children begin to engage in several forms of representation between the ages of two and seven. These include deferred imitation, symbolic play, drawing, mental images, spoken language, and writing.

Deferred Imitation. Deferred imitation is the first form of representation you can observe. As we mentioned earlier in this chapter and in Chapter 3, you can observe the beginnings of deferred imitation when infants imitate adults' actions. Around the age of two, children have completed most of the understanding necessary to engage in deferred imitation, and they begin to imitate someone or some action intentionally when the person or action is no longer present. For example, one teacher began singing the cleanup song to signal the end of free play, while the other teacher took the tray with plates, cups, and snacks to the table. Darius went over to the dramatic play area and gathered blocks and other objects. Once he had his hands full, he went to the dramatic play table and used the objects to prepare the "snack table" for "snack." When he finished, he sat down and pretended to eat. Although children begin their imitation when the model is present, they will either continue it or imitate solely in the model's absence. They remember. According to Piaget, such deferred imitation is the beginning of external representation.

Symbolic Play. Symbolic play, or pretending, is another form of representation that is part of the semiotic function. Symbolic play is very important to children, because they may know more than what their mastery of language allows them to relate to others. It is a way for children to present ideas, elaborate thoughts, express concerns, and represent rituals within their communities. For example, Gaines got on his pedal tractor, checked the gas gauge, got off the tractor, pretended to put gas in the tank, got back on the tractor, and then pretended to crank it. He played out the entire ritual of servicing a vehicle. Another example that is not so obvious occurred in the toddler program of a child-care center. George stomped around the room. He rushed up to everyone, stared at them, and tried

Symbolic play, a form of representation, is part of the semiotic or symbolic function. *(© Elizabeth Crews)*

ASK YOURSELF

In Chapter 3, we learned about representations of thought. Now we are thinking about it again in terms of intellectual development. Why?

· ·

to scratch them. Several of the children begin to cry and push him away. The teacher puzzled over George's actions until she remembered that his mom had said they had watched the movie *The Lion King*. George was pretending to be a lion. Because children have no intended audience, an observer may not be able to figure out what they are imitating, as was the case with George.

Drawing is another form of representation. Children begin with "scribble drawing" rather than drawing realistic pictures. This is because they draw what they think rather than what they see. Usually children at two or two and half years of age begin to attempt representing their thoughts realistically. An interesting aspect of young children's drawings is the lack of visual perspective. A four-year-old child considers only one perspective. For example, the child will draw a profile of a face with two eyes or a chimney that is perpendicular to the roof, rather than to the ground (see Figure 4.1). Until after age four, children draw closed circles when representing squares, rectangles, and circles, and they draw open curves when making crosses or arches. They may imitate drawing a square but they are not capable of drawing a square they mentally represented correctly. They are capable of using topological relationships such as proximity, separation, and enclosures. In other words, they are not capable of using Euclidean, or projective, properties in their pictures (Gruber & Voneche, 1977).

Figure 4.1
A young child's drawing typically lacks visual perspective.

Mental images are internalized imitations that are much like pictures or drawings. They are not actual copies of an experience. Although they have some resemblance to what they represent, they are imitations of perceptions. Because of this, mental images are often thought of as symbols. Furthermore, the images are static rather than representing motion. By seven, children can use these properties and their drawings are more representational. They still do not consider perspective, and their drawings often show the inside of a house along with the garden.

For a child to construct reality, he experiments with invention and representation. Toddlers use invention for purposes other than mere discovery (Gruber & Voneche, 1977). They also use it to solve puzzles or problems. For example, when a toddler is faced with a problem to which earlier solutions don't apply, she must invent a solution using mental combinations to see which ideas might succeed and which might fail. Because representation accompanies invention, the toddler has the ability to try out a sequence of actions internally rather than through actual, hands-on experimentation. Invention and representation are both necessary for the toddler to construct reality. Needless to say, the toddler's use of invention and representation is much more elaborate than the infant's efforts to use them as ways to discover and explore her world.

The use of mental images allows children to think about things not present in time or space. For seven-year-olds, mental images allow for the comparison of their mother's face with their friend's mother's face to advance their conception of mother. *Spoken language* allows children not only to open a conversation but also to sustain one, even if they use one-word utterances. Around the age of two, children begin using two-word sentences and then short complete sentences. Two-year-olds, unlike infants, use language to imitate as well as to represent objects with symbols—spoken words. Language development occurs rapidly once children begin working with language and experience the social interactions that result from their use of it. According to Piaget, language provides children with a vehicle for socialization beyond actions, the ability to use internal representations rather than just perceptual and motoric actions, and an internal system of signs that can be used for thought (Piaget, 1967).

> Piaget said, "Language does not constitute the source of logic but is, on the contrary, structured by it."

Spoken language is essential for children. It appears about the same time the other forms of semiotic thought appear. According to Piaget, "Language does not constitute the source of logic but is, on the contrary, structured by it" (Piaget & Inhelder, 1969). Think about this quote. Many people misunderstand Piaget's ideas about language. He is saying that cognition can develop without spoken language. Language is a form of representation, but it is not necessary for the development of intellectual functions. Those functions began developing as actions long before age two, which is the typical age for a child to begin using language. Although language gives children the power to represent their thinking, the other means of representation are just as important in helping children move into more advanced forms of reasoning.

Social Interaction. In addition to developing their abilities to represent, children begin to develop **social feelings.** Just as the roots of representation can be found in infants' imitative actions, so can the roots of social feelings. And just as we can identify the roots of social feelings in infants, we can also identify the ages of two to seven as the time when children begin to represent and recall feelings. For example, Cody, a three-year-old, hadn't seen the child-care director in a few days. The director joined the children for lunch and sat by Cody. He looked at her and said, "I remember you had lunch with us afore. You sat by Rachel."

> Between the ages of two and seven, children begin to experience moral feelings.

Between the ages of two and seven, children also begin to experience **moral feelings.** For example, children will begin to construct notions about right and wrong, such as it's wrong to lie to their parents but not to their playmates. They view good and bad as how well they follow instructions. When asked about the rules for a game, children are unaware of any rules or use habit or their own ideas as guidelines for playing. Another social concept that children begin to consider is who's at fault when there is an accident. At first children do not understand the concept of intention because of their inability to take the perspectives of others. Children at this age believe in "an eye for an eye." As they experience repeated social situations and social interactions, they move to understanding that others have points of view and intentions.

Children begin to develop a sense of duty or social responsibility at this age. For example, Seth's grandmother has an elderly neighbor whose nickname is Bunny. One afternoon, Seth, age three and a half, and his grandmother saw that neighbor's screen door ajar. In an attempt to imitate adult conversation and to show concern for the neighbor, Seth said, "How's Rabbit?"

Seth had constructed the beginnings of a sense of duty: He was concerned about someone outside the family but within the neighborhood. He felt some obligation to know about the neighbor's well-being because she was the age of his great grandmother who was ill.

CONSTRUCTIONS

1. Journal Entry

Write a reflection that explores how you thought children developed a sense of responsibility. How did you think they made and understood rules? How did you think they learned to play games? Which games did you think they learned first and why?

2. Research

Design your own game, or select a game that you think four-year-olds would play. Have several children play, then record your observations of their attempts to understand directions, follow rules, make rules, and play the game. Repeat this with five-year-olds and then seven-year-olds. Discuss your findings with your classmates.

THE INTELLECTUAL DEVELOPMENT OF SEVEN- TO ELEVEN-YEAR-OLD CHILDREN

Usually by age eleven, children have the potential to think logically.

Just as with younger children, children between the ages of seven and eleven construct their reasoning in a continuous fashion. Usually by age eleven, they have the potential to become logical thinkers. At age six, children's reasoning is still tied to the context and the concrete object, as we saw in the Multiple Perspectives box on pages 178–179. At this point, children are trying to use two different results or situations at the same time *(simultaneity)*, but they think of them in static terms. They attend to the figural appearance rather than the meaning of the action. For example, a six-year-old girl, when asked her blood type, responds, "Warm."

Children progress in their thinking between the ages of seven and eleven because their thinking allows contradictions between perception and reality. The children themselves cause the contradictions by composing and changing the composition of the mental groupings within their schemata (remember the puppy and miniature dachshund). They do this by adding to the groupings and looking at the inverse and reciprocal relationships within them.

At this point in children's intellectual development, their thoughts are no longer controlled by perceptions. This is because they are able to decenter through considering others' points of view, as well as conserve, have reversibility, and attend to transformations. The result of this new reasoning is that children begin to construct notions about seriation and classification. As with the other operations, this process begins long before the children establish an equilibrium with these two constructs.

Seriation is the mental ordering of objects according to physical characteristics, such as differences in size, weight, length, and so on. Before four years of age, when asked to order objects, children have no planned order. Around four or five years of age, children order according to pairs in a linear fashion. By age seven, many children have some schemata, but their schemata have no transitivity, and they can't mentally order more than three objects. Finally, around seven or eight, most children can accurately order ten or more objects.

When children use classification, they are mentally grouping objects according to similarities (Wadsworth, 1996, p. 98). Just as with every other construction, children have early, less refined schemata for classification. For example, when children are four or five, they classify two objects at a time. When they classify those two objects, they do it on the basis of a similarity that they decide on in that moment: Two objects may be classified based on color, then the next objects may be classified based on shape. Around seven years of age, children use the notion of collections of like objects that are similar. They do not use the notions of class and subclass. By age eight, children are beginning to use class inclusion. At this point, they understand differences as well as similarities and use relationships between those differences and similarities in their constructions of classification schemata.

> Seriation is the mental ordering of objects according to physical characteristics.

CONSTRUCTIONS

1. Journal Entry

How does the information in this section help you shape your ideas for planning lessons? For example, would you teach seriation? Why or why not? What does class inclusion have to do with writing a lesson plan?

2. Research

Try some of the Piagetian tasks we've mentioned in this chapter. Observe how children think during those tasks. Talk with your classmates about your findings.

3. Research and Compare

Rather than using formal Piagetian tasks, think of experiences in the classroom that you might use to observe children as they attempt to seriate, classify, or conserve. Write them down, then observe to see if you could learn the same kinds of information from those experiences as from formal tasks.

The Function of Social Interaction

As children develop and have opportunities to interact with others, they construct more elaborate notions of being social. They also move from what Piaget called egocentrism to **sociocentrism.** When a child functions as a social being, she can assume and understand the viewpoints of others. Now she understands that rules are not absolute or unchanging, but rather serve a purpose in helping children to play a game properly or helping people to work together. Cooperation, reciprocity, and winning become desired aspects of games as well as life. In addition, accidents are viewed differently. Now, because children can take the viewpoints of others, they recognize that intention is important. If someone bumps a child, he can consider the intention of the bump rather than just react to the action.

Children around age eight begin to demonstrate autonomy in their thoughts and interactions with others (see Chapters 1, 3, and 11). Just as with other constructions children make, autonomy is a continuous process that begins at an early age and moves through various levels of "wrongness" as the children interact with others in their environments. For example, younger children accept rules as edicts handed down from a higher, more powerful authority, such as God, parents, or the government. They don't reason about the rightness or wrongness of the rule but simply obey (heteronomy).

Around age eight, children begin moving into the notion of respect between equals by separating from earlier notions of total obedience to others. At this age, children also begin to consider their wants and desires in relation to others. They begin to consider that their choices must be based on more than what they want. They construct the notion that lying is wrong. As they move into adolescence, they move from "lying is wrong" to "lying is wrong because it destroys others' trust." As they elaborate all of

Around age eight, children begin to demonstrate autonomy in their thoughts and interactions with others.

As children have opportunities to interact with others, they construct more elaborate notions of being social and moving into a sociocentric perspective. *(© Elizabeth Crews)*

these ideas, moral autonomy advances, and children begin to coordinate their reasoning with the reasoning of others. This moves them to more advanced levels of thinking.

According to Piaget, children from ages seven to eleven are in transition between semilogical and logical thought. They have developed logical operations to use when acting on real problems with limited variables or on observable events or objects in the present. They are no longer anchored in perception. This transition period is very important to children, because their thought becomes an internalized system of actions that has the ability to reverse, follow transformations, conserve, and use classification (Piaget, 1981). In this period, children decenter from action even more than at earlier ages, which allows them to become social beings.

Let's return to several members of Dr. K.'s class, who are discussing their own thinking in view of their earlier class discussion about children's thoughts.

DANIELLE: I know early childhood education includes children from birth to age eight. But how do *we* think? I learned something about formal operational thought in my educational psychology class, but nothing that really fit into what we've been learning about intelligence. How do children from eight to our age think? I mean, I never took calculus and hated math. Maybe my thought process is concrete operational. It would be such an embarrassment if Dr. K. asked me a formal operational question, and I couldn't answer it.

TILLIE: I agree with Danielle. I worry about whether I should even be a college student and whether others will laugh at me because I'm older. The thought of some college professor embarrassing me by showing you how dumb I am scares me.

ERIC: I think Dr. K. wants us to think about how we think in relation to how children think. You know, she wants us to act like scientists who test their hypotheses rather than letting our feelings rule us.

ZENAH: I know what you mean, Tillie! We've all had those fears. But let's do what Eric is suggesting and recall some of our observations from our visits to the schools.

TILLIE: Okay, Eric! Let's play scientists! I read somewhere that children start thinking when they're around five to seven years of age. Until then, they're just children. They certainly aren't scientists.

AMY: I read that, too. But, remember, Dr. K. said that Piagetians call such thinking semilogic.

TILLIE: I thought we were hypothesizing, not saying what we've read.

AMY: We are, but you have to read, question, and use reflection, as well as test your ideas. What I read said that many cultures view the age of six as a time when children's behaviors change enough that they begin to be formally considered workers, helpers, and learners in their cultures.

ZENAH: Wait a minute, Amy! Listen to Tillie. I agree with her. We do need to read, but we also need to coordinate that with our observations. Remember, we are discussing what we saw at the schools. We are comparing the children's thinking to our thinking.

AMY: I know, but I think we have to consider the information we read along with our observations. Otherwise, we'll just base our discussion on perceptions, not reasoning.

ERIC: We might as well let her talk. She's just got to tell us what she learned!

AMY: But semilogic is a construction before formal operational reasoning. We need to know about it in order to talk about our reasoning. Around age eleven or twelve, children begin to construct reasoning that is more adultlike. This reasoning is more abstract and frees children from depending on the isolated experience to make sense of a situation or problem. I am not saying that the eleven- or twelve-year-old's quality of the content and function of thought is that of an adult! But I am saying that the structures necessary to think like an adult are in place.

ASK YOURSELF

Do I share Tillie and Danielle's fears? How do adults think? If intellectual development is continuous, how does an adult's thinking differ from a child's thinking? Why does it differ?
....

TILLIE: You just memorized that for the test. I want to go back to Danielle's fears about whether we are formal operational thinkers.

ERIC: Okay! Let's try a few of the tasks that Piaget used for formal operational thought and see what happens.

DANIELLE: No way!

ZENAH: No, Eric! Let's talk about our observations. Tillie, do you remember when you observed the children talking about lying and knowing more than one Patrick? We all giggled at their reasoning.

DANIELLE: Were we using formal operational thought?

ERIC: Not when we giggled! But we were when we recognized that the children were working on what reality is.

ZENAH: We are using formal operational thought now as we recall, reflect, and question what the children were doing. We are recalling past events, dealing with abstract concepts, and questioning. In fact, we have posed and are discussing the abstract question, "Do all people think alike?"

AMY: Yes, we are dealing with the way our thought functions for us.

The Function of Intelligence After Age Eleven

Formal operational thinkers use not only facts from the real world but also deductive reasoning, possibilities, probabilities, and combinations.

Because the purpose of this chapter is to discuss the intellectual development of children from birth to age eight, we will offer a very brief glimpse of what Piaget identified as formal operational thought. **Formal operational thought** begins around twelve years of age and may not be fully developed until well into adulthood. It builds on and extends concrete operational thought, which was discussed in Chapter 3. Formal operational thought allows you to understand, reason, coordinate, and draw conclusions using the abstract as well as the real. Formal operational thinkers use not only facts from the real world but also deductive reasoning, possibilities, probabilities, and combinations. They also can use reasoning that moves from specific to general and can explore possibilities in concrete as well as hypothetical terms. Consider your own ability to think about abstract problems, such as word problems in math, problems in the future, and hypothetical situations. Because of your ability to use reflection, hypotheses, and deductions, you can learn and use information from lectures, books, and other problems. For example, you can use algebra as a means of representing your knowledge and reasoning. The term *reflective abstraction* is used to describe these processes. Reflective abstraction is the use of reflection or abstract thought to create new knowledge from existing knowledge.

Although formal operational thinking begins around age twelve, not all twelve-year-olds think at the formal operational level, and those who do think at this level do not use such reasoning all of the time. With formal operational thought, many adolescents are capable of abstract thinking and of learning in a classroom setting, just as you experienced in your high school algebra class or the first years of college. They have moved through many levels of "wrongness" (Kamii & Ewing, 1996) by constructing, elaborating, refining, and differentiating earlier notions. In other words, they are capable of using reflective abstraction.

As adult thinkers, most of us are capable of reflective abstraction. We can abstract information from lectures, textbooks, and hypothetical problems. We are freed from the present reality, which allows us to reflect and coordinate several points of view. We may not be formal operational in all areas, but we will be in the ones in which we've had the most experience and the most opportunities to construct notions that allowed our thinking to reorganize and create more complex structures.

SUMMARY

▸ Piaget classified knowledge into three categories: physical knowledge, social knowledge, and logico-mathematical knowledge.

▸ Physical knowledge is knowledge of objects in external reality.

▸ Social, or conventional, knowledge is knowledge of culture, its values, and its conventions.

▸ Logico-mathematical knowledge involves internal relationships and the coordination of those relationships that people create.

▸ The content of logico-mathematical knowledge includes the relationships of same/different, some/all, and part/whole. Development of logico-mathematical knowledge depends on continuity.

▸ The processes of adaptation, assimilation, accommodation, continuity, transformation, coordination, and conservation are necessary for children to reason.

▸ Piaget maintained that the organism adapts to the physical environment and then organizes that environment. This is a continuous process.

▸ Preoperational thought develops between the ages of two and seven.

▸ Semilogic or concrete operational thought occurs before formal operational reasoning. Around the ages of five to seven, children begin using semilogic.

▸ Concrete operational thought is transitional thought between infants' and toddlers' thought and formal operational thought. Seriation (ordering objects according to differences), classification (grouping objects according to similarities), and conservation are three constructions that children finalize during this period.

▸ Conservation means that a child can conceptualize the amount of a quantity of matter regardless of any changes in the perception of that quantity.

▸ Reflective abstraction is necessary for formal operational thought. It is the use of reflection or abstract thought to create new knowledge from existing knowledge.

▸ Formal operational thought begins around twelve years of age and may not be completed until well into adulthood. It builds on and extends concrete operations. By this we mean that individuals can really understand, reason, coordinate, and draw conclusions using the abstract as well as the real.

▸ A person may not be formal operational in all areas, but he will be in the ones in which he has had repeated experiences and opportunities to construct notions that allowed him to reorganize and create more complex structures.

CONSTRUCTIONS

1. Analysis

Reflect on the following dialogue and analyze the social world of these six-year-old children. How did it come into existence? What do these children know about birthday celebrations? How did they learn? What do they know about discussions and taking turns? About language?

TAMMY: I gonna have—

CHAD: I know.

ELLEN: I know.

SCRAP: Well, we wanna hear about it.

CHAD: My mama told me about it.

SCRAP: Is today your birthday?

TAMMY: It's Saturday at two.

SCRAP: My mama's got to work.

MARY: My mama and daddy work, and I can't come.

TAMMY: I'm gonna have games, and I'm gonna give—

ASHLEY: We're gonna win prizes. We know.

TAMMY: Ya'll can go inside, too.

SCRAP: Can we play outside as long as we don't hit your plants?

AMBER: Yes.

MARY: Can my brother go to play with Cory?

SCRAP: Can my brother, Chris, come? He's mean!

TAMMY: Only the kids. Only the little kids and kids in our class. Not the big kids.

JAMIE: Are we gonna have any cake?

TAMMY: No, we are gonna have Angel A'lot.

SCRAP: Real angels?

TAMMY: Yeah, and balloons. It's Angel A'lot. You put Jell-O, strawberries, and cream.

SCRAP: Jell-O is better.

TAMMY: It's gonna be lots of fun. Everybody is going. We are going to get on the bus and go down to my memmie's. All the balloons and stuff will be way up high so ya'll can't get them.

2. Journal Entry

Stop, reflect for a minute, and then write a journal entry about thinking. Do you think the young children you know think differently from you? If so, how? Write several examples to support your view. If not, how is their thinking like yours? When is it like yours?

3. Analysis

Reflect on the section about formal operational thinking. Analyze the following examples and explain why a person would need to be formal operational to understand them. Think about what young children might say if you asked them to analyze the passages. Share your analysis with others in the class.

    a. "In the field of world policy I would dedicate this Nation to the policy of the good neighbor—the neighbor who respects himself and because he does so, respects the rights of others—the neighbor who respects his obligations and respects the sanctity of his agreements in and with a world of neighbors" (Franklin D. Roosevelt, First Inaugural Address).

    b. Every early childhood student has great opportunities.
      Some early childhood students are poor.
      Therefore some poor people have great opportunities.

    c. All dogs are carnivorous.
      My dachshund is a dog.
      Therefore my dachshund is carnivorous.

RESOURCES

Forman, G., & Kruschner, D., (1977). *The child's construction of knowledge: Piaget for teaching children.* Belmont, CA: Brooks-Cole.
An excellent reference for students interested in learning more about constructivist teaching and behaviorism.

Labinowicz, E. (1980). *The Piaget primer.* Menlo Park, CA: Addison-Wesley.
An excellent reference for students interested in learning more about Piaget's explanations of cognitive development.

Lindfors, J. W. (1987). *Children's language and learning.* Englewood Cliffs, NJ: Prentice-Hall.
A comprehensive look at how children learn language and communication ability. The end-of-chapter suggestions are particularly useful for early education students.

Piaget, J. (1970). *The science of education and the psychology of the child.* New York: Viking.
A good beginning point for students who want to read Piaget's original writings. It is a must read for students who want to become constructivist teachers.

Piaget, J. (1932/1965). *The moral judgment of the child.* New York: Free Press.
Because Piagetian texts are translations, they are often difficult to read. Beginning students of Piaget's theory and research should choose texts they find accessible. *The Moral Judgment of the Child* is such a book. Not only is it interesting, but it is also relatively easy to read.

Wadsworth, B. J. (1978). *Piaget for the classroom teacher.* New York: Longman.
An excellent reference for students interested in learning more about Piagetian theory. The text is reader-friendly and includes various Piagetian tasks.

Wadsworth, B. J. (1996). *Piaget's theory of cognitive and affective development.* (5th ed.). New York: Longman.
This reference provides a detailed explanation of Piagetian theory. It serves as a foundation for constructivism.

5

Views of Children Over Time

· ·

This chapter invites you to visit children throughout history to help guide you as you develop an awareness of the issues young children have faced and continue to face. This will help you address the questions "What is childhood?" and "How has the conception of childhood changed over time?"

Why should the history of children and childhood be important to you? A culture's child-rearing practices, traditions, and rituals are related to how that society values children. Those practices, traditions, and rituals evolve over time. In addition, the way children are valued determines the ways the culture or society socializes and educates them. Our classroom practices are influenced by how we, as members of a particular culture, value children.

A constructivist perspective maintains that today's notions of social and cultural behavior are built from the past. For you to think about what you value and where you fit in the early childhood profession, you must consider a historical perspective of childhood and children so that you can advance your awareness of these issues:

▶ Definitions of childhood
▶ How people learned about childhood in the past
▶ Historical, cross-cultural child-rearing practices
▶ Historical and cultural perspectives of childhood
▶ Historical and cultural experiences of children
▶ How early childhood teachers can use a historical understanding of childhood to become better teachers

194

INTRODUCTION

The class members are reminiscing about their childhoods.

ZENAH: I've been going around to all the different schools today trying to figure out the best place for my baby. I don't mind moving if it means he'll be better off. It's just so hard to decide.

DANIELLE: Is it really that big of a deal?

ZENAH: It's always been the toughest decision for me whether it's childcare, nursery, or baby sitters. There is nothing easy about deciding on child-care. Wait till you have a kid!

ERIC: With most parents working now, it seems like we're rushing our kids to grow up faster—putting them in fancy preschools and expecting them to read by age five.

AMY: It would be nice if we could all raise our kids ourselves, but it's not a compromise many people can make anymore.

ERIC: You mean it's not a compromise many *will* make. I think fancy cars and houses have become a lot more important than time with our children. I think we need to reevaluate our priorities.

TILLIE: Okay, Eric. I better see you putting your career on hold as soon as your first child is born.

ERIC: Well, I guess there isn't an easy solution.

DANIELLE: I feel terrible for these kids today. Guns everywhere, all the abuse and neglect. Teenagers are killing their own babies! When I was a little girl, things were so much simpler. Mom made dinners with desserts. We ate at the dinner table with a tablecloth. Then Daddy would read us a story before he tucked us into bed. Do you remember all of those Dr. Seuss books?

ERIC: Boy, I do! My mom would read me two every night. *The Cat in the Hat,* and *Green Eggs and Ham.* But Dad was never home that early. Now that I think about it, I don't know when he came home. Whenever I needed a spanking, I guess.

TILLIE: I know what you mean, Eric. Mama comes in; the sitter walks out. I can't remember anyone ever reading me a story. I don't even think Mama had enough money to buy a book. She had more to worry about than tucking us into bed—like the welfare folks putting us in foster care. I think kids may be luckier today with all of the child-care services and business freebies. It's harder for them to be overlooked and ignored.

AMY: Let me tell you something. Money sure doesn't ensure that a child will be given sufficient attention. My parents had it all! The cars! The house! All the right clothes! They definitely thought they provided for me. Every toy I could want! Baby sitters galore! But I'd give it all back in a heartbeat for one Dr. Seuss book with Mom or Dad. I hope kids have it better today.

ZENAH: I had my grandmother! She couldn't read or write. My dad was in the fields from first light until dark. My mama was a maid in town. She cooked *that* family's breakfast and stayed until *those* babies went to bed. By the time she got home, I was usually asleep. But my family valued me and wanted me to have more than they had. I can remember my mama saying I was her "special gift" and she was going to take care of me. So maybe we're all right! Maybe it's not about now or then. Maybe it's the individual experiences of each child and the people they encounter in their lifetime that makes up their idea of childhood. Some have it good. Some have it bad. But it's within all of us to make it better for the kids today.

AMY: Right, Zenah! You know, the interesting thing about our discussion is that we all remembered events from our childhood, but none of us said anything about how old we were when the events happened.

ERIC: What does how old we were have to do with anything?

AMY: I think it has a lot to do with childhood. Like how many years do children experience childhood? Why does NAEYC say age eight is the end of early childhood? Is it a cultural definition, or does it have some biological basis?

DR. K.: Amy's questions reflect some of the things we need to think about as we study the history of children and childhood.

ASK YOURSELF

What do I remember about my childhood and my interactions with my parents? How old was I when the events I remember took place? When do I think my childhood ended? On what did I base my decision?
....

THE CONCEPT OF CHILDHOOD

Historians consider childhood a relatively new concept.

Many of you might assume that "childhood" is a well-known concept that identifies the period of life before adulthood, but might find it difficult to suggest exactly when childhood ends and adulthood begins. Most of you would be surprised to know that some historians consider childhood a relatively new concept that grew out of cultural changes during the seventeenth century (Aries, 1962). This section is designed to introduce you to different ways childhood has been viewed over time and to help you understand how historians have studied the data to examine and document these historical notions.

Definitions of Childhood

The class discussion ended with the realization that the student's memories of childhood focused on different ages, some remembering events around ages four or five, and others remembering events around age twelve. The students also concluded that the parent-child relationships in their families were very different and led to different conceptions of childhood. This discussion raises the question of what constitutes childhood: Does it exist, and if it does, how is it defined and when does it end?

Historians and scholars have begun to address these questions about children and childhood. Some study childhood from the parents' and other adults' perspectives, while others attempt to study it from children's points of view (Johnson, 1990). Some describe it as a period of life that differs from adulthood (Aries, 1962; deMause, 1982); however, they disagree as to when the conception of childhood first came into being. Aries suggests that "in medieval society the idea of childhood did not exist" (p. 128). By contrast, deMause suggests that the concept of childhood has evolved throughout history as parental child-rearing modes "began to develop the capacity to identify and satisfy the needs of their children" (p. 61).

As you consider multiple perspectives about the history of childhood, remember that the constructivist perspective holds that you should look back into your own childhood and what you and your family valued so that you can begin to know who you are today. You want to consider not only your own past but also the pasts of others from your community and state.

Along with the historical perspective of childhood, consider a biological perspective. As we will see, humans have changed in appearance over thousands of years, and biology is closely linked to culture and history. Age and maturation are common ways by which childhood has been defined over time. Other definitions of childhood have been based on the time when the individual achieved a certain biological or social milestone, such as the ability to care for oneself, the ability to read, the ability to exist independent of the parent, or the ability to produce children.

According to Piaget, there is a biological explanation for why age and maturation have been used to define childhood. Until around two years of age, a child is in the sensorimotor stage of intellectual development. During this period, the child is not able to hold ideas about actions or objects in memory. Consequently, when we try to remember back to our childhoods, we can evoke images only of those events that occurred after our thought process became representational. Maturation is one of the four factors you learned about in Chapters 3 and 4 that foster intellectual development. Intellectual development is requisite to reach some of the milestones defining the end of childhood, such as the ability to read. Biological maturation is necessary to reach other milestones, such as producing offspring.

NAEYC's and ACEI's definitions of early childhood (see the accompanying box) fit with Piaget's preoperational stage of representational thought, and ACEI's definition of later childhood fits with Piaget's concrete operational thought. Although age is used in the definition, it is based on the child's growing ability to reason—that is, her intellectual development.

> Biology is linked to culture and history in the definition of childhood.

DEFINITIONS OF CHILDHOOD

Historical

Birth to the ability to "live without the constant solicitude of his mother, his nanny or his cradle-rocker" (Aries, 1962, p. 128)

Birth to six or seven years of age, when the child can talk (Aries, p. 21)

Birth to about thirteen years of age, or when the child begins to develop sexual characteristics (Gutek, 1972)

Birth to seven, when the child has the physical ability to work (Aries, p. 26)

Birth to when the child is able to reproduce

Birth to when the child is able to survive independent of the parent

Birth to the ability to read (Postman, 1982)

Modern

Early childhood: birth through age eight (National Association for the Education of Young Children [NAEYC])

Early childhood: birth through age eight; later childhood: age eight through adolescence (Association for Childhood Education International [ACEI])

Birth to about eighteen years of age, or when the child has completed a period of schooling or training

Birth to eighteen or twenty-one years of age, or when the child can legally vote and drink alcoholic beverages

---

CONSTRUCTIONS

Journal Entry

With a classmate, use a semantic map, or web, to brainstorm your own definitions of childhood. Once you and your partner have completed the brainstorming, write separate definitions of childhood. Revisit each definition to see if you can identify your underlying values.

Primary and Secondary Sources of Research on Childhood

Although there is a growing interest in the evolution of childhood, the subject still has much to be explored. Sources of information are limited, and what we

Sources of information on the evolution of childhood include art, literature, music, and codes of law.

know is based on inferences from the materials available. As historians continue to carefully analyze materials to address questions that emerge, we will come to understand more about earlier views of childhood (Abrahamse, 1979).

Historical anecdotes, literature, art, and music are essential ways to learn about children who lived hundreds of years ago. Those accounts are called secondary sources. The primary sources are actual records or accounts that document events. For example, some primary sources that help us study childhood in different periods of history are letters, biographies, laws, codes of law, and legal transactions, such as the sale of property and medical records.

If we look at a culture's laws and legal issues, we can discover culture's rules for children's behavior and considerations for children's lives and well-being. For example, when we read the laws of a society, we can learn whether that culture allowed its members to sell a child, kill a child, or refuse to feed a child (Bar-Ilan, 1996).

By studying the medical records of the historical period, we can learn about birthing procedures, childhood diseases and treatments for those diseases, and child-rearing practices. For example, when we look at records from the fourth century, we learn that **wet-nursing** was a common practice in the Byzantine Empire. We also learn about the emotional relationships between parents and their children. If we read some of the records from the sixth century in the Byzantine Empire, we learn the role of religion and magic in treating children's illnesses. People in that era believed that the parents' sins caused the Devil or demons to make their infants have fevers and illnesses. Children over four years of age were responsible for their own illnesses. Exorcism was a recommended practice to help children regain their health (Abrahamse, 1979). According to Johnson (1990), more is known about the history of childhood in England, France, and the United States than in other parts of the world. For this reason, the information provided in this chapter focuses primarily on those countries.

ASK YOURSELF

What significance does the historical treatment of children have on how early childhood educators teach? How will I teach? How will the treatment of children throughout history influence how I think about children and childhood? How have we changed biologically?

ANCIENT TIMES

This section discusses child-rearing practices in prehistoric and early Greek, Roman, African, and Asian societies. Drawing from a wide variety of sources, Lloyd deMause (1982) identified six modes of parent-child relations that represent a "continuous sequence of closer approaches between parent and child" (p. 61) since the birth of Christ. These developmental modes, presented in Figure 5.1, have advanced at different rates in different families, economic classes, and cultures. Each mode is based on adults' views of children and childhood and identifies the child-rearing practices resulting from those views. All of these practices are still used today in some

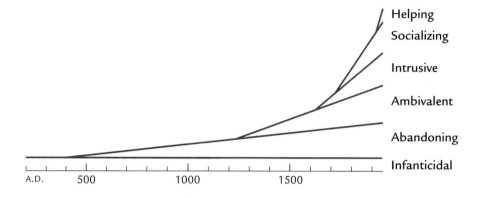

Figure 5.1

The Evolution of Child-Rearing Modes

families and to some degree in all societies. (You will learn more about some of the practices in Chapter 6.) The time periods of these modes are based on when deMause first found evidence of them. We will refer to these modes as we discuss each historical society and time.

Although some child-rearing practices are common to all cultures, others differed from culture to culture. **Infanticide** and **incest** were common in most early societies, while the practice of **foot binding** of girls was particular to a few. Nurturance of the young was another characteristic common to most early societies. All early societies had some form of family structure (Murdock, 1949), the smallest of which was the **nuclear family**. The nuclear family was organized around four basic functions: the management of sexual relationships, the bearing and raising of children, the transmission of culture through some form of education, and the economic subsistence of the family through the division of labor between the spouses. Women's tasks, such as food gathering and preparation and textile making, were economically productive and compatible with caring for children. Men's tasks, such as hunting for provisions and keeping the family safe, were not compatible with caring for children.

> Infanticide was a common practice in many early societies.

Prehistoric Societies

Due to climatic changes, prehistoric families moved from being tree dwellers to living on the open savannas. This brought about biological changes, as well as changes in their economic subsistence patterns. Biological changes included increased cranial size and decreased pelvic size, which caused infants to be born earlier and to remain dependent longer (Lee, 1982). Humans developed **small kinship groups** to reproduce more humans, nurture infants, protect themselves from wild beasts and natural elements, and obtain food.

Infanticide was a common practice from the beginning of these family groups until around the fourth century A.D. According to deMause (1982), infanticide was based on the view that the child was evil because he was evidence of parental intimacy. In addition, parents were unable to separate themselves from the child. This double image of child as evil and parent as child created anxiety that could be resolved only by killing the child. The killing was not out of the parent's anger toward the child, but rather out of a need to eliminate the thing causing anxiety. Needless to say, infanticide had a profound effect on siblings. DeMause reports that children who were considered less than perfect were drowned, exposed without shelter or clothing, or starved. Children also were used as sacrifices and were often sexually assaulted.

As humans moved from the hunting and gathering stage of civilization to the farming stage, family lifestyles became more complex. For example, families began to join other families to form tribes so that they would have workers for their farms, be able to trade their products, and be able to protect themselves from outsiders. Although parents still killed their children, these new living arrangements forced people to begin to find ways to care for sufficient young to sustain their societies. To have productive adults within these societies, families needed to tend to the health and education of their children. Over time, families improved their nutrition, health care, and lifestyles. These improvements resulted in each succeeding generation of children being taller and in life spans growing much longer.

CONSTRUCTIONS

Research

Look up information about early humans, their families, and their child-rearing practices. Have a discussion with a classmate in which you mention the facts that surprised you and why they surprised you. Discuss the ways in which the family structures of these early humans differed from today's family structures. In what ways were they similar?

Ancient Greece

Many ancient Greek stories and plays mention infanticide.

Many ancient Greek stories and plays recount infanticide. You may recall reading a Greek myth in which Medea was so angry with her husband that she killed their children and fed them to him. Although the image of Medea might be thought of as an exaggeration of the child-rearing practices of

Young male citizens of Greece were taught to read in their homes. *(© Corbis/Bettmann)*

ancient Greek society, it does capture the notion that killing children was a common enough practice to be presented in literature.

The effect of infanticide in ancient Greece was so strong that families were exceptionally small and rarely kept more than one female offspring (Langer, 1974). It is no wonder that around 400 to 300 B.C., Plato, Aristotle, and other Greek scholars began writing about the importance of childhood and of educating children for their roles in society. They realized that if society continued to practice infanticide, there would be very few people for future civilizations. These scholars' teachings and writings caused people to reconsider their ideas about killing their offspring.

Child-rearing practices in Greece were dependent on the gender of the child, whether the child was born to slaves or citizens, and whether the child was Athenian or Spartan. Slave children had to perform adult work. By contrast, young male citizens were schooled and received military training, while young female citizens learned household chores. Parents were the first teachers, and children were expected to carry on the family's role in society (Barnes, 1992).

Both Plato and Aristotle were in favor of educating children before age six. Aristotle favored cultivating the individual's talents and abilities, while Plato favored taking children away from parents and educating them to be

strong citizens of the state. Plato also favored educating girls, but this idea was never implemented (Osborn, 1991).

Ancient Rome

Greek child-rearing practices influenced Roman societies, and infanticide was present in ancient Rome as well. The father of a Roman family had absolute authority over the household and held the power of life and death over the family. This is called *potestas paterfamilias*. Infanticide was not considered wrong, and children were often used as sacrifices to the gods. These practices were justified as effective ways to control population. Not until Christianity and Judaism emerged as major influences did Roman societies change their attitudes about infanticide (Langer, 1974).

The Roman family served as the basic educational unit, and children were expected to bring honor to the family. Male children were taught to work on the farm, and female children were taught to perform household tasks. Emphasis was placed on teaching children to be pious and serious about their work (Barclay, 1959).

Ancient African Societies

There were many ancient African cultures (Egypt, Nubia, Ethiopia, Somaliland, Kenya, Mali, and others), and most viewed children as gifts or rewards who received places of honor in the family and culture. Because of this, Africans saw children as human beings who had identities even before birth (Pearce, 1977). A pregnant woman was highly valued and nurtured because of the fetus she carried. Once born, a child stayed with the mother or a sibling or close relative, observed the daily activities of the tribe, explored her environment at will, and socialized with everyone in the tribe. As children grew older, they learned through participation, play, observation, and imitation. Songs, stories, rituals, dances, and work were part of that learning. African societies viewed cooperative learning, community membership, attachment, and establishing bonds as essential for young children (Hilliard, 1992).

In light of these views, it is hard to believe that infanticide and female genital mutilation were practiced in these societies. Indeed, Egypt, Ethiopia, Somalia, and Kenya continue the practice of genital mutilation today. Genital mutilation, the removal of part or all of the external genitalia, was usually completed between the ages of four and twelve and was meant to preserve the girl's chastity. Infanticide was practiced more often on female offspring, as families preferred male children who could inherit the families' wealth and continue the family name.

Ancient Asian Societies

Ancient Asian societies included China, Japan, Korea, Mongolia, the Philippines, Cambodia, Laos, Malaysia, Singapore, Thailand, Vietnam, and Tibet. Confucius (c. 551–479 B.C.) was one of the most important influences on the thought of many Asian societies. He placed great emphasis on the extended family and on respect for one's elders. The Asians who followed his teachings taught their children to obey, respect, and care for older people. These societies also were patriarchal, and sons were considered part of a family's wealth (Yang, 1992). Even so, infanticide was widely accepted in China, with female offspring being more expendable than males. "In the seventeenth century, Jesuit missionaries to China were horrified to find that in Peking alone several thousand babies (almost exclusively females) were thrown on the streets like refuse, to be collected each morning by carriers who dumped them into a huge pit outside the city" (Langer, 1974, p. 354).

Until their children were six and entered school, Asian parents humored them and had a family member nurture them. Because of the importance the society placed on formal schooling, parents wanted their children to achieve. Schooling was designed to instruct children in the strict rules of the Asian culture and obedience to the hierarchy of the culture and the family. Children quickly learned that they were expected to bring honor, not shame, to the family and culture.

CONSTRUCTIONS

1. Research

Choose one of the many ancient societies not discussed in this section (for example, the Aztecs, Incas, Maya, or groups of people connected by religion such as the Hindus, or Muslims) and research its early child-rearing practices through laws, art, literature, and historical documents.

2. Analysis

Analyze the child-rearing practices you find for evidence that might support the society's conception of childhood. Also analyze the origins of the practices.

3. Comparison

Compare your culture's child-rearing practices with those included in this chapter. What similarities and differences can you find?

Let's join the students as they discuss the practice of infanticide.

AMY: Boy, all that discussion of infanticide made me wonder about what's going on with kids today.

DANIELLE: Yeah! Hey, did you all hear about that girl who had a baby at the prom, threw it in the trash, and then went back to the dance? Can you believe someone could do that?

TILLIE: Well, what about abortion? It's the same thing, except the baby is killed before it's born. How can women do that when there are so many people wanting to adopt babies?

AMY: Tillie, what if I was pregnant, and I just wasn't ready to be a mom? It is the woman's body, you know.

DANIELLE: That's true! So many children are born into homes where they are unwanted and mistreated. I think in some situations abortion may be in the best interest of the unborn child as well as the mother.

ZENAH: When I found out I was pregnant, I didn't think twice. I knew God had given me a gift. I had to be a good mom, and I've done my best. I wish everyone would realize motherhood is a privilege, not a burden.

ERIC: Well, I don't want to get into that abortion debate, but I do know that our society should value children more. Even though infant mortality rates are down, doctors and researchers should do more research on sudden infant death syndrome and diseases that affect young children.

DANIELLE: I guess there are many things to consider when becoming a parent—more than I ever imagined.

AMY: Don't you wonder when our values begin to influence child-rearing practices?

TILLIE: Yeah, but I'll bet they started with Christianity! I know that is where I get my beliefs!

DR. K.: One of the perspectives I'd like for you to consider is that as we read about the historical modes of child rearing, we realize that those modes didn't end with a particular era. They are still part of the way many in our society value children today.

THE FOURTH TO SEVENTH CENTURIES

Abandonment began around the fourth century A.D.

The second historical child-rearing mode, **abandonment** (deMause, 1982), began around the fourth century A.D. Up until that time, none of the ancient societies thought infanticide was wrong. Early Christian leaders began to view children as having souls and "denounced infanticide as a pagan practice and murder" (Osborn, 1991, p. 14). Consequently, parents began to abandon rather than kill their children. They gave them to the church (nuns and priests), put them out to wet-nurses, or apprenticed them to the local lords of the manor. Other forms of abandonment included **swaddling** them and hanging them on a post so that they could not move, putting them in baskets in public places, or letting them remain in the home with no support. Children continued to be viewed as having been born evil, and beating was used as a form of discipline to make them good.

The Jewish Influence

"Among the Jewish people, as among other peoples, children were beaten or even killed—a practice that gained the approval and encouragement of the social authorities." (Bar-Ilan, 1995, p. 1) Infanticide was present in ancient Jewish families, and the Jewish scriptures, the Torah and the Talmud, document that parents and teachers beat their children for disciplinary reasons and that some children were severely hurt or killed.

Jewish families "considered themselves a people with a special destiny" (Barnes, 1992). In many ways Jewish families were like their non-Jewish neighbors in that they farmed, made household utensils, and hunted for provisions. Their children were educated in performing the same tasks as the adults in the family. These families differed from their non-Jewish neighbors in that the parents and the communities in which they lived shared the responsibility of educating the children in the religious beliefs that made them different from other people.

The Christian Influence

The early Christians started the battle against infanticide.

The early Christians started the battle against infanticide and played a major role in changing society's views of childhood through child-god images and new moral teachings. One of the basic tenets of the Christian movement was that "a little child shall lead." It was taken from the early Christian idea that each child was special, different, and separate from adults. For example, when Jesus was a child, his wisdom was viewed as superior to that of the priests in the temple.

By the fourth century, this new image of children caused government leaders to enact laws to protect children from infanticide and abandonment. In 318 A.D. the Roman emperor Constantine declared that killing a child was a crime (Osborn, 1991, p. 14). By 322, the Theodosian Code offered food and clothing to parents who could not afford to raise a child. From 474 to 523, the Burgundian Code protected the property rights of children and provided for the care of "foundlings," children who had been abandoned (Kroll, 1977).

ASK YOURSELF

How do societies' views change over time? What are some of the major influences that advance people's thinking about the treatment of children? Is it hard for me to understand how people could kill or abandon their children?
....

The **personification** of the child as saint, such as the "child-god, mythical child, wonder child or **primordial** child" who had superhuman powers (Jung & Kerenyi, 1963) that helped him survive the untold sufferings of society, began to appear in early Byzantine hagiographies (Abrahamse, 1979). These worshipful biographies were of child saints who chose to be prepared not for life in the world, but for eternal life in heaven. These personifications permitted adults to treat children as if they were separate from the world and helped justify the practice of abandonment as opposed to infanticide. These religious influences began to change society's views of children and their child-rearing practices through the seventh century.

THE MIDDLE AGES

Although the practice of abandonment emerged prior to the Middle Ages, which began around the eighth century and continued until the fourteenth century, there was still a high incidence of infanticide at this time. The forms of infanticide became more subtle, however, because of laws against the outright killing of children. Two new forms of infanticide used during the Middle Ages were exposure and overlaying (Osborn, 1991). *Exposure* refers to leaving a child outside, exposing her to the elements, and then claiming her death as accidental. In *overlaying,* a child was suffocated between the parents while sleeping. If the parents could claim that the death was accidental, they were not punished.

During the early part of the Middle Ages, children continued to be viewed as evil and the embodiment of original sin. The concept of childhood was lost (Braun & Edwards, 1972), and children were depicted in paintings and tapestries as little adults, with adult behaviors and facial features (Osborn, 1991).

The concept of childhood was lost during the Middle Ages.

There was little regard for the education of children during this period. The schools of antiquity had been lost, and parents were in charge of educating their children to be prepared for life after death. There was some education for young boys who wanted to become monks.

In the latter part of the Middle Ages, the depiction of the child saint brought about the idea of childhood innocence as embodied in Christianity. Two themes regarding childhood emerged during this time. One was the role of nature and naturalism with regard to children, and the other was the role of affectivity toward children. **Naturalism** in this context refers to valuing things that belong to the natural world as opposed to things made by humans. Consequently, the ancient schools were thought to be pagan, because reading and writing were not natural. **Affectivity** refers to the belief

Fourteenth-century art
captures the acceptance
of the right of the mother
to love the child.
(© Culver Pictures)

that it was permissible to care about young, innocent children. Religious leaders sought to become like little children and taught adults that childhood innocence was a model for living. St. Francis of Assisi, born about 1182, was one of the leaders who exemplified these themes. He combined a love of nature, a simple faith, and a childlike dependence in his approach to life. He founded the Franciscan Order, a religious order of monks who spoke in the natural language of the people and modeled a childlike dependence on God. Additionally, Roman popes during this time used names such as Innocent to capture the pervasive notion of childhood innocence. The societies of the Middle Ages continued to elaborate the themes of naturalism and affectivity.

Toward the end of the Middle Ages, the conflict between the two depictions of childhood—one of innocence and one of evil—gave rise to the third child-rearing mode, **ambivalence** (deMause, 1999). The first evidence of this mode was in the twelfth century. The solution to the conflict was to educate children so as to rid them of evil, but at the same time to love them. According to deMause (1982), at this time there was an increase in child instruction manuals and a beginning of the "close-mother image" in art. Until this time mothers were not seen in close proximity of the child, as the child represented her sin. At this point art depicted mothers holding their babies.

THE FOURTEENTH TO SIXTEENTH CENTURIES

This was the time of the Renaissance and the Reformation. European society was changing dramatically due to Johann Gutenberg's invention of the printing press and movable type in the mid-1400s.

The Renaissance

The printing press and movable type caused dramatic changes in people's views of childhood.

The Renaissance has been considered the period of enlightenment. Because of newer ways to print classical texts from the ancient world, scholars began to revisit the writings of Plato, Aristotle, and their counterparts. People began to believe in their abilities again, and the government was once more controlled by the state. People also began to view themselves as microcosms of the larger natural world, or macrocosm. Because of this view, scientists in medicine and psychology were beginning to consider the connections between humans and the physical world and to attribute ailments to something other than witchcraft. Science replaced theology, and life had order. The king was the head of state, and God was the head of the universe. There was a rise of the middle class and a glorification of earthly things. Although deMause (1999) has characterized the early part of this period as one of ambivalence toward children, most historians have viewed it as a time for celebration of the sensuous and naturalistic aspects of childhood. This celebration can be seen in art, music, and literature.

As mentioned earlier, Christianity suggested that it was permissible to show affection for children. The numerous images of the holy mother, Mary, and her child, Jesus, in the art and literature of the Renaissance encouraged mothers to show their love for their children. During the Renaissance, children became part of their parents' emotional lives. Because of this, parents had to assume responsibility for molding their children so that they fit into the family. Instruction manuals on how to raise children became important.

The state and man controlled education, not God. Furthermore, that education was to focus on earth not the afterlife. Erasmus, a leader of the humanistic movement, felt that love and a deep concern for children should motivate parents and teachers. He held that children had innate abilities that could be brought out and developed under the guidance of loving

Renaissance art cele-
brated childhood. Here
children are being taken
to school. *(© Corbis/
Bettmann)*

teachers. He thought that discipline should be taught by example rather than through punishment and coercion. He was the forerunner of the child-centered movement in early childhood education.

The Reformation

Many historians cite the Reformation of the sixteenth century as the beginning of the early modern image of childhood. The Reformation was necessary to rebuild Christianity in the Western world after the Protestants broke with the Roman Catholic Church.

Closer emotional
bonds were formed be-
tween parent and child
in the intrusive mode,
prevalent during the
Reformation.

Although infanticide, abandonment, and ambivalent modes of child rearing were still prevalent during the Reformation, the **intrusive** mode (deMause, 1999) began to emerge in the sixteenth century. This child-rearing practice began when parents were able to see children as individuals separate from themselves. Rather than swaddling children, parents let them crawl freely on the floor. Parents were closer to their children physically and were able to use this closeness to show affection. Consequently, closer emotional bonds were formed, and true empathy between parent and child began in this period. However, parents were still ambivalent about whether children were born evil or innocent, and they had to find new ways to control children and to make them obedient. These methods included praying with their children, threatening them with hell, and beating them for behaviors parents considered evil or disobedient.

The invention of movable type during the fifteenth century made the printed word more readily available to more people. In 1442, the first in a series of small books for children was printed. These books were called hornbooks, and they "usually consisted of the alphabet, vowels and consonants, the Lord's Prayer, and/or some biblical verse" (Osborn, 1991, p. 21). In 1521, Martin Luther completed a German translation of the New Testament. The Old Testament was translated in subsequent years. Mass publication of the Bible for individual study brought about the expansion of literacy. Luther was an advocate of state-supported schools and massive public school attendance. He believed in the layperson's right to read and interpret the Bible.

The advent of printed material and the belief in people's right to read and interpret the Bible caused a shift from relying on the oral tradition to gather information to relying primarily on one's own ability to gather information through reading. Learning to read and think independently helped people begin to construct new ways of thinking about time, space, and causality.

ASK YOURSELF

How do views of childhood change as cultures advance their scientific and practical knowledge? Why do I think this is so?
....

THE SEVENTEENTH AND EIGHTEENTH CENTURIES

The seventeenth and eighteenth centuries in Europe and America are known as the early modern period. During this time, the transition to modern thought began. Commonly held views were a mixture of those left over from the Renaissance and new ones formulated during this period.

The Role of Literacy

Literacy had a big influence on society during the seventeenth century.

As literacy began to become prevalent in the Western world, people began to think about children differently. They saw young children not as little adults, but rather as children whose thought process relied on the natural, magical, semilogical, purposeful, and concrete. Since children could not read and reasoned differently from adults, they were no longer included in polite adult society. For them to join adult society, they had to be educated out of childhood reasoning and taught to read. In most instances, however, only male children of upper-class families had the luxury of going to school. Orphans and paupers had to assume work responsibilities in the adult world without being educated. Consequently, they remained forever outside

ASK YOURSELF

What assumptions does Pepys make about poor children? What assumptions do I make today?
....

of polite society. Samuel Pepys's entry in his diary describes such a child/adult and his view of work:

> 25th [March, 1660/1]. Homewards, and took up a boy that had a lanthorn, that was picking up of rags, and got him to light me home, and had great discourse with him how he could get sometimes three or four bushels of rags in a day and got 3d. a bushel for them and many other discourses, what and how many ways there are for poor children to get their livings honestly. (Witherspoon & Warnke, 1963, p. 651)

The Role of Science

The seventeenth century also saw the establishment of the foundations of modern science. Sir Isaac Newton invented differential calculus and with others created classical physics, which was not challenged until the twentieth century. The heliocentric theory of Copernicus, the discoveries of Galileo, the work of William Gilbert on magnetism and electricity, and the work of William Harvey on the circulation of the blood brought an end to many ancient views. These discoveries fostered a new appreciation of scientific inquiry based on experience, careful observation, and experimentation. They also allowed people to question the authority of earlier philosophers and religious leaders. This freedom of thought in science allowed for more imagination related to children and childhood and led to changing views in this area.

Sentimentalizing Childhood

Parents' ability to differentiate themselves from children, which was a new idea in the sixteenth century, supported the prevalent view of children as distinct entities. This ability fostered the thinking about childhood as a time with less responsibility, a time of innocence that can never be recaptured.

The scientific discoveries of the seventeenth century created conditions that made average people wonder where they fit in the world. It is no wonder that they looked at childhood in sentimental and idealized terms—just as they looked at the days before these discoveries. Seventeenth-century literature is filled with examples of adults' need to sentimentalize childhood and recapture their "lost innocence." Henry Vaughan did this in his poem "Childhood" (Whitherspoon & Warnke, 1963, p. 989):

> I cannot reach it; and my striving eye
> Dazzles at it, as at eternity.
> Were now that chronicle alive,
> Those white designs which children drive,
> And the thoughts of each harmless hour,
> With their content, too, in my power

Quickly would I make my path even,
And by mere playing go to heaven.

Dear, harmless age! swift span
Where weeping Virtue parts with man;
Where love without lust dwells, and bends
What way we please without self-ends.

An age of mysteries! which he
Must live twice that would God's face see;
Which angels guard, and with it play,
Angels! which foul men drive away.

How do I study now, and scan
Thee more than e'er I studied man,
And only see through a long night
Thy edges and thy bordering light!
Oh for thy center and midday!
For sure that is the narrow way!

Changing Views of Childhood

Parents began to view children as an important part of the family unit. This view also caused a change in people's views about infanticide, abandonment, and punishment. Furthermore, they began to question the merits of such practices. Sir Frances Bacon characterized these concerns when he wrote "Of Parents and Children" in about 1612. The first paragraph exemplifies how people had changed their views of the children's place within

Seventeenth-century art reflects how childhood was sentimentalized. *(© Culver Pictures)*

the family. The second reflects the role of incest or heredity, depending on how it is interpreted.

ASK YOURSELF

What do I think Bacon was referring to when he wrote the second piece? On what do I base my interpretation? Is Bacon's view child-centered or adult-centered?

The joys of parents are secret, and so are their griefs and fears; they cannot utter the one, nor will they not utter the other. Children sweeten labors, but they make misfortunes more bitter; they increase the cares of life, but they mitigate the remembrance of death. . . .

Men have a foolish manner (both parents, and schoolmasters, and servants) in creating and breeding an emulation between brothers during childhood, which many times sorteth to discord when they are men, and disturbeth families. The Italians make little difference between children and nephews, or near kinsfolks; but so they be of the lump, they care not, though they pass not through their own body; and, to say we see a nephew sometimes resembleth an uncle, or a kinsman more than his parent, as the blood happens. (Witherspoon & Warnke, 1963, p. 42)

Educational leaders of the period were changing their views of childhood. Comenius, a Moravian bishop, designed the first children's textbook, *Orbis Sensualium Pictus* ("The Visible World in Pictures"), in the 1600s. John Locke, an English scholar, suggested that people use the scientific method for observing children. Jean Jacques Rousseau held that the child had to be removed from society until ready for adulthood. You will learn even more about this movement in Chapter 9 on the history of professionals in early childhood education. Note that the themes of literacy, the scientific approach, and the separation of child and parent were all addressed by these educators.

The socializing mode began during the late eighteenth century.

In the late eighteenth century, another child mode began to emerge, the socializing mode (deMause, 1999). In this mode, the mother was thought to have "a deep, unquenchable love for her offspring" (p. 665), reflecting the sentimentalizing of childhood. This affection for children changed the parents' view of child rearing. They began to see it as an opportunity to guide, train, teach, and socialize their children. Harsh modes of discipline started to disappear and were replaced by gentler guidance methods. This view emphasized psychological, rather than physical, discipline. During this period, the father's role began to take on new meaning, and some fathers helped with child-care activities. According to deMause, this mode is still the one used most widely in the Western world.

Colonial America

As colonists moved to America, they established a lifestyle revolving around their religious views. Their child-rearing practices were based on the common conception of children as sinful. Although the socializing mode was emerging, parents' discipline practices were severe and abusive and children were whipped and beaten regularly.

In northern New England, there was a strong emphasis on literacy so that everyone would be able to read the Bible. The Old Deluder Satan Act, which required every town with fifty or more households to have a school, was passed in Massachusetts in 1647. The purpose of schooling was to get rid of Satan and bring children to God. Schools were publicly supported and taught religion.

In the South, tutors were hired to educate wealthy landowners' sons. The schools that did exist were private, and only young men were eligible to attend. Poorer boys and all girls were educated in their homes whenever possible. Southern colonists held the same view of children as ignorant and evil, and discipline was as harsh as in New England.

CONSTRUCTIONS

Journal Entry

Reflect on what it means to sentimentalize children. Can you think of instances of this in contemporary views of childhood? If so, write about them. What effect do you think this has on children? Compare your journal reflections with a peer's reflections and with someone who is of another generation.

THE NINETEENTH CENTURY

The Spirit of the Time

The romantic movement was a rebellion against scientific objectivity.

During the nineteenth century, the romantic movement was a rebellion against the scientific objectivity of the Age of Reason. In Europe, it was a time of unity: unity with nature, fellow humans, and the supernatural. Many artists and scholars viewed experience as the way to unity. The desire for unity helped many parents change their perspectives of children and move to the socializing mode. They wanted to help their offspring rather than conquer them by beating them into submission. They began to view child rearing as an opportunity to guide, train, teach, and socialize the child.

Poets such as William Wordsworth saw the child as the "real" philosopher and a personal guide to self or unity. Writers such as Ralph Waldo Emerson saw the child as uncorrupted by "custom." Even Sigmund Freud saw the role of the young child as the key to unity in the adult's personality.

The romantic movement occurred later in America than in Europe. In America, it was a time of great westward expansion. It was also the period when the North and South debated the issue of slavery and finally split over this issue. In American literature, this was the first highly creative period, although little was written about children.

Socializing the Child

You might think that the scholars and poets of the romantic period would have brought adults and children closer together, but that's not what happened. Although adults valued children from a cultural perspective and sentimentalized them from a literary perspective, they distanced themselves from their own children. On the one hand, parents saw themselves as socializers of their children. On the other hand, they wanted a social life of their own. They wanted to give their children the opportunity to play and discover the universal laws of nature, but only as the children were educated could they began to join the world of adulthood and reason.

Educational leaders thought that parents needed help in raising their children to adulthood. They also held that all children needed to be educated to be productive members of society. These ideas helped establish the notion of public and private elementary and secondary schools for all children. Johann Pestalozzi, a Swiss educational reformer, had a deep and loving concern for children that motivated him to establish schools for poor children. Friedrich Froebel, a German educator, held that children were born good and that schools should help that goodness unfold. He started the kindergarten movement in 1837. Johann Herbart, a German philosopher, devised a scientific method to develop the character of young students. You'll learn more about some of these educational innovations in Chapter 9.

About 1800, the United States began to develop a unique system of education—one similar to European systems but different in many respects. Education was marked by a broader curriculum, a transition from a religious emphasis to one of democracy, good citizenship, more public support of education, and a system of free elementary and secondary schools. Although many schools were available to children, parents still relied on beatings to keep children under control.

ASK YOURSELF

Have I ever thought that the child-rearing practices of today will affect practices in the future? What does this mean to me as a future teacher or parent?

THE TWENTIETH CENTURY

As you read this section, think about the common images of childhood during the last century. Examine the roles of family values, childcare, medical care, education, food, housing, and our "impatient society" in shaping late-twentieth-century images.

In the early part of the twentieth century, young children were expected to work long hours.
(© Brown Brothers)

The First Fifty Years

In 1900, Ellen Key stated that the next hundred years were going to be the "Century of the Child" (Osborn, 1991). Children of the early twentieth century were born between the Industrial Revolution and the technological revolution. They were born before the automobile, the television, and the computer. Additionally, during the early part of this century, children were raised mostly in small towns or on farms, had many siblings and two parents, and put in long hours of work in coal mines, on farms, in sweatshops, and on street corners shining shoes. In the 1930s, compulsory school attendance laws and state child labor laws reduced the number of children in the work force.

The kindergarten movement began during the early 1900s. You will learn more about this movement in Chapter 9, but for now we want you to know that this movement had a significant impact on advancing our thinking about childhood. A similar nursery school movement occurred in England to improve the health and welfare of young children there. This movement influenced American child-care leaders.

During the first fifty years of the twentieth century, five White House conferences on childcare and child development were held, myriad child labor laws were passed, and nursery and child-care programs were established for young children. Two professional organizations were started to support children and families—the International Kindergarten Union and the National Association of Nursery Educators.

The Second Fifty Years

The helping mode emerged during the second half of the twentieth century.

The last child-rearing mode, the helping mode, emerged at the midpoint of the twentieth century (deMause, 1999). In this mode, helping parents attend to the children's goals at each stage of life rather than attempting to socialize them into adult goals. Children are empowered to explore their own capabilities as they grow and are loved unconditionally. Parents are careful not to intrude on children's personal lives.

National Initiatives. In the second half of the twentieth century, people continued to build from the socializing mode to the helping mode. Today we have variations on the helping mode, in that we see children as competent beings, controllers of their own worlds, and little adults. We provide more and more protection and power through laws and agencies. For example, today's children can "divorce" their parents. They also have the right to court-appointed representatives whose sole purpose is to represent their needs, desires, and perspectives.

Children with special needs are protected by laws such as Public Law 94-142, the Education for All Handicapped Children Act, passed in 1975, which places children with special needs, ages three and up, in appropriate services, programs, and educational settings. Public Laws 99-457 and 99-371 expanded earlier efforts by giving federal funding to state and local agencies to help disabled children from birth to school age receive services and education. According to Bredekamp and Copple (1997), the Americans with Disabilities Act and the Individuals with Disabilities Education Act now require that all early childhood programs provide reasonable accommodations for children with disabilities or developmental delays.

National initiatives support the community role in rearing children.

Educators, philosophers, therapists, researchers, politicians, and the public at large view children as part of the community and its future. First Ladies Barbara Bush and Hillary Rodham Clinton have supported projects and written about the importance of an entire community taking on the task of raising children. Acts such as the Child Care and Development Block Grant Act of 1990 and the Family and Medical Leave Act of 1993, as well as passage of additional funding for Head Start, support this movement toward community support for rearing children.

Childhood Needs. Environmental changes continue to cause even more biological changes in children and adults. For example, many young girls and boys are entering puberty at much earlier ages. Although the causes of this are not clear, some research attributes the early onset of puberty to environmental estrogens, which result from the breakdown of chemicals in products ranging from pesticides to plastic wrap. Real estrogen is used in many hair products marketed to African Americans. The relationship between cumulative, multiple environmental factors and the onset of puberty continues to be studied.

In the future, all children will need quality care while their parents or guardians work. Child-care providers will need additional financial support, supplemental medical care from sources outside the federal government, supplemental sources of food and lodging as federal funds are cut, supplemental sources of education, and more agencies to provide after-school care and safety. This is the profession's current perturbation. Children need our help; they are our future. Although they are capable beings who are growing and developing, they aren't adults in little bodies who can do everything adults can do. Many people hope that society will take on the Piagetian premise that we need to focus on the growing child and the laws of development rather than on producing adults in children's bodies (Gruber & Voneche, 1995, p. 695).

MULTIPLE PERSPECTIVES

From a Researcher of Psychohistory

Child Rearing as Historical Change

Lloyd deMause is the director of the Institute for Psychohistory, editor of the *Journal of Psychohistory,* and founding president of the International Psychohistorical Association. Following is his essay "Women and Children at the Cutting Edge of Historical Change."

The evolution of childhood from incest to love and from abuse to empathy has been a slow, uneven path, but one whose progressive direction is, I think, unmistakable. This evolution of parent-child relations is, I contend, an independent source of historical change, lying in the ability of successive generations of parents to live through their own childhood traumas a second time and work through their anxieties in a slightly better manner this second time around.

It is in this sense that I say that history is like psychotherapy, which also heals through revisiting one's childhood traumas and reworking earlier anxieties. If the parent—the mother, for most of history—is given even the most minimal support by society, this evolution of child rearing progresses, new variations in historical personality are formed, and history begins to move in new, more innovative directions.

The crucial relationship in this evolution is the mother-daughter relationship. If little girls are treated particularly badly, they grow up to be mothers who cannot rework their traumas, and history is frozen. For instance, although China was ahead of the West in most ways during the pre-Christian era, it became "frozen" and fell far behind the West in evolutionary social change after it adopted the practice of footbinding girls. Similarly, the clitoridectomy of girls in Moslem societies has inhibited their social development for centuries, since it likewise puts a brake on the ability of mothers to make progress in caring for their children. Clearly, different groups have moved different distances up the ladder of psychological evolution, since some contemporary groups still practice brain-eating as our Paleolithic ancestors did, and different subgroups of our more advanced nations still terrorize and abuse their children in ways identical to those that were commonplace centuries ago, producing the "historical fossils" we now call borderline personalities and other severe character disorders.

The "generational pressure" for psychological change is not only an independent historical force—originating in inborn adult-child striving for relationship—it occurs independent of social and technological change, and can be found even in periods of economic stagnation. My "psychogenic theory of history" posits an evolutionary historical tendency to move from need to love and from symbiosis to individuation, with new variations of historical personalities selected by local environmental conditions. This theory suggests that a society's child rearing practices are not just one item in a list of cultural traits, but—because all other traits must be passed down from generation to generation through the narrow funnel of childhood—actually makes child rearing the very basis for the transmission and development of all other cultural traits, placing definite limits on what can be achieved in the material spheres of history.

Regardless of the changes in the environment, it is only when changes in childhood occur that societies begin to progress and move in unpredictable new directions that are more adaptive.

That more individuated and loving individuals are ultimately more adaptive is understandable—because they are less under the pressures of infantile needs and are therefore more rational in reaching their goals.

But that this childhood evolution—and therefore social evolution—is terribly uneven is also understandable, given the varying conditions under which parents all over the world have to conduct their child rearing tasks.

• •

Childhood Today.   Today's configuration of families and society's changing views of family are important in understanding today's children. Today's families may consist of a mother, father, and their offspring; a mother

The current configuration of families helps us understand childhood today.

and her offspring; a father and his offspring; a parent, her significant other, and the offspring of either or both adults; same-sex parents and their offspring; adoptive parents and their offspring; multigenerational families; and so on.

Just as the configuration of families has changed from the traditional two-parent nuclear family, so have the attitudes about parenting and children. Society's attitudes toward children have changed in such a way that deMause (1999) refers to them as being in the helping mode. Attitudes have become "pacified," "sentimentalized," or "feminized" (Johnson, 1990). They are pacified in the sense that parents no longer flog or beat their children, but instead use more passive means to guide their behavior. They are sentimentalized in that parents have affection for their children and are willing to show honest affection. They are feminized in that they reflect what is commonly referred to as "good mothering," even though the father may provide that care.

Society has extended the period called childhood in terms of how long a child is dependent on his parent(s). For example, more and more children are continuing to live at home with their parents while attending college or working. The cost of rearing and educating children has changed society's views of their worth and purpose. Today parents invest large sums of money in their children's futures (Johnson, 1990), while the children rarely contribute to the economic sustenance of the family. The traditional view of the family as an economic unit and the idea that parents have children to participate in the work force have changed due to three factors: (1) overpopulation and the availability of workers for the work force; (2) the shift from a farming economy to a service- or technology-oriented economy; and (3) the shift from three major classes to a society of haves and have-nots.

Because of the attitudinal and configurational shifts in families, a multidimensional perspective of childhood is necessary to understand today's children. All of the six child-rearing patterns identified by deMause (1999) coexist in today's society. According to deMause, the evolution of childhood is extremely uneven. Childhood is viewed in terms of ecological factors, political-economic conditions, and ideologies (Johnson, 1990). Childhood today depends on the place where the child is being reared and by whom. It depends on whether the class structure in which the child is being reared supports modern child-rearing practices and the cultural ideology or religion of the child's family.

NAEYC helps families provide better opportunities for children.

Today we have the ideological support from NAEYC, which provides information to families so that they can provide better opportunities for children. When you become a teacher of young children, this commitment will help you support parents as they make important decisions regarding children and childhood.

ASK YOURSELF

Was Ellen Key right—was the twentieth century the "Century of the Child"? If I think so, on what do I base my opinion? Can I predict what the next century or the next millennium might hold for children and childhood?

NAEYC'S COMMITMENT TO CHILDREN

It is important to acknowledge the core values that underlie all of NAEYC's work. As stated in the association's Code of Ethical Conduct, "standards of ethical behavior in early childhood education are based on commitment to core values that are deeply rooted in the history of our field. We have committed ourselves to

- Appreciating childhood as a unique and valuable stage of human life cycle
- Basing our work with children on knowledge of child development
- Appreciating and supporting the close ties between the child and family
- Recognizing that children are best understood in the context of family, culture, and society
- Respecting the dignity, worth, and uniqueness of each individual (child, family member, and colleague)
- Helping children and adults achieve their full potential in the context of relationships that are based on trust, respect, and positive regard"

(Feeney & Kipnis, 1992, p. 3)

Additionally, we have ideological support from the United Nations Convention on the Rights of the Child. This convention, adopted in 1989, has almost universal ratification with the exception of the United States and Somalia. The convention guarantees children all of the rights listed in the following box.

UNITED NATIONS CONVENTION ON THE RIGHTS OF THE CHILD

- Affection, love and understanding
- Adequate nutrition and medical care
- Protection against all forms of neglect, cruelty, and exploitation
- Free education and full opportunity for play and recreation
- A name and a nationality
- Special care if disabled
- Relief in times of disaster

> ‣ Education to learn to be useful members of society and to develop individual abilities
> ‣ Upbringing in the spirit of universal peace and brotherhood
> ‣ To enjoy these rights regardless of race, color, sex, religion, or national or social origin
>
> Source: Stroud, M. [1993]. *Reaching the children: In celebration of the rights of the child.* New York: United States Committee for UNICEF.

CHILDREN'S VIEWS OF CHILDHOOD

Now that we have studied adult views of children and childhood, let's look at children's views of childhood. This is a very difficult task for many reasons. Children's thought differs from adult thought, so what they say and do must be interpreted with care. Some children's lives are so filled with violence that they can't get interested in talking with others. Some are so involved in shouting profanities, throwing the magnetic board at the teacher and bruising her leg to the point that she has to go to the emergency room, or backing another child into a corner and trying to stab him with scissors that they won't talk about their childhood. These are examples from real classrooms. The next are snippets of real stories told by children. Some of them have been passed down for generations, and some are contemporary aspects of childhood.

Children can give us wonderful insight into the experience of childhood.

In Vivian Paley's book *Wally's Stories* (1981), Wally and his classmates address the difficulty of understanding what it's like to be a child and think like a child:

WALLY: People don't feel the same as grown-ups.
TEACHER: Do you mean "Children don't"?
WALLY: Because grown-ups don't remember when they were little. They're already an old person. Only if you have a picture of you doing that. Then you could remember.
EDDIE: But not thinking.
WALLY: You never can take a picture of thinking. Of course not. (p. 4)

To introduce you to how children view childhood and being a child, we have organized this section around several themes that seem to be common to all children: safety, power and control, the need to be loved, pleasure, insults, and wonder. We use songs, games, literature, interviews, and samples of children's writing to exemplify those themes.

The first theme of childhood is *safety*. For children to feel safe, they must have their basic needs for food, shelter, and clothing met. They also need to know that they are safe from harm that may come from adults, other children, or nature. Vivian Paley is a celebrated kindergarten teacher who captured the voices of her children as they told and acted out stories and discussed serious topics in her classroom. *Wally's Stories* (Paley, 1981) provides several examples of children addressing the issues of safety and basic needs. One such example is the children's discussion of the story "Hansel and Gretel" and the fear of being abandoned.

ELLEN: It's too scary. I don't want to hear it.

KIM: Me too.

WALLY: It's not too scary for me. Just a little bit too bad.

EDDIE: Well, I want to hear it.

TEACHER: Which part is too scary? Maybe we can change the scary part.

ELLEN: Being lost and also the bad mother and father part.

TEACHER: Not the witch? Well, why don't I change the first part of the story then? There was a wicked witch who put a spell on a father and mother and made them leave Hansel and Gretel in the forest even though they didn't want to.

ELLEN: No. That's not good.

WALLY: Have them just get lost and the parents don't even know.

DEANA: They could be looking all over for them every day.

TEACHER: Once upon a time there was a poor woodcutter and his wife and they had two children named Hansel and Gretel. One day the children took the wrong path in the forest and got lost. The mother and father looked everywhere but they couldn't find them.

LISA: And they said, "If we find our dear children we'll never yell at them or argue or spank them ever again. We promise."

ELLEN: No, I still don't want it. Because I can remember the real words how it goes.

EDDIE: Well, I do want to hear it.

TANYA: You can't Eddie. We have a rule not to make people feel bad.

EDDIE: Okay. I'll tell my mother to read it to me. She likes it too. (pp. 179–181)

Another example of children's need to feel safe can be found in a narrative of a six-year-old kindergarten child. Because he is talking about what happened to another child, he is able to "express relief that his friend was not harmed, provide commentary on the cause and prevention of such a tragedy, and assure himself that such a disaster could never happen to him" (because his house was made of brick) (Branscombe & Taylor, 1988, p. 107).

ASK YOURSELF

What made the Hansel and Gretel story so frightening to some of the children? Is it too scary to have the children have to face the witch (magic) alone? What does this dialogue tell me about children's basic needs?

Justin's house burned
He couldn't help it.
Justin could have burned down too.
He's lucky.
They think somebody set it.
Then cops came and got 'em.
I came by Justin's house one day.
If it had been brick it wouldn't have burned.
My house is brick.
I'm sad for Justin cause his house burned.

Another theme is *power and control.* Children want to have some power and control over their environments and over others. Some of them may choose to use unacceptable and dangerous means, such as the third-grader in this true story (taken from an interview with the teacher).

> I used to have twin brothers, but they got burned up the day our house caught on fire. I got myself out but couldn't get my brothers out. My mama was working. She left me to take care of them . . . like she always does.
>
> Them kids at school get up in my face now and say I killed my brothers. Well, I'm gonna kill 'em. I got my mama's butcher knife hidden under this coat. It's the long one she uses to cut up chickens. The next time one of them gets in my face, I'm gonna kill 'em.

Others use their wit to gain power and control over others. For example, Josh, a first-grader, used his wit and intellect when his teacher was attempting to teach letter recognition and phonics with flash cards. She held up a card that had the letter *P* and a picture of a pig. She asked. "What do you see in the picture that starts with the letter *P?*" Josh, who was already reading at the third-grade level and was rather perturbed at having to participate in this elementary ritual, responded, "Pork!" His classmates giggled in delight as his teacher corrected him, "No, Josh, it's a pig! You know that. Why did you say pork?" Josh responded, "The letter is *P,* and pork starts with the "p" sound just like pig. And, after all, pigs are pork!" Again, his classmates giggled, and the teacher couldn't argue because, of course, Josh was right.

The third theme is children's *desire to be loved,* accepted, and liked. As children wrestle with feelings of being loved or not loved, they differentiate them from feelings of being bad or not liked. Many times children use the opposite of being loved or having friends as a way of explaining belonging and being loved. In 1947, Iona and Peter Opie captured these characteristics of children when they published a new genre of childhood rhymes. Unlike rhymes written by adults for children, these rhymes and sayings were made up by children and were passed down from one generation to the next without adult intervention. A new edition of this collection, illustrated by Maurice Sendak, was published in 1992. The following examples, the first from Opie and Opie's 1992 collection (p. 111) and the second from Vivian Paley's *Wally's Stories* (1981, p. 150), show how children attempt to address their needs for love and acceptance.

> Nobody loves me,
> Everybody hates me,
> Going in the garden
> To-eat-worms.
> Big fat juicy ones,
> Little squiggly niggly ones.
> Going in the garden
> To-eat-worms.

TEACHER: How do you know if somebody likes you?

TANYA: When you think that there's someone that doesn't like you . . . well, you don't have to worry about that so much.

KIM: Maybe they might not like you but later they will.

EDDIE: If he talks to you a lot he likes you.

DEANA: I chase him and he doesn't run after me.

WALLY: Watch a person and see if they stay and play.

EDDIE: I know the boy next door is my enemy because we know we're enemies.

ELLEN: They say bad words to you if someone doesn't like you.

A fourth theme for how children view being a child or living their childhood is *pleasure*. Children find pleasure in play, whether it is language play, playing alone in the yard, or playing with peers. Children's songs and rhymes capture their pleasure. Some of the Opie and Opie (1992) chants reflect the children's love for rhyme and repetition through language play. Following are two examples of such language play.

> I was in the garden
> A-picking of the peas.
> I busted out a-laughing
> To hear the chickens sneeze. (p. 29)

> I asked my mother for fifty cents
> To see the elephant jump the fence;
> He jumped so high he reached the sky
> And didn't come back till the Fourth of July. (p. 31)

A fifth theme is the theme of *insults*, teasing, and mockery. It could be part of the theme of power and control or the theme of pleasure, but because it is such an integral part of childhood, we made it into its own category. Peers, teachers, and adults in general can be the targets of these insults. Opie and

Young children invent and pass on numerous clapping games that reflect their views of the world.
(© Elizabeth Crews)

Opie (1992) provide some of the best examples of children's insults that have been passed down from one generation to the next. The first verse below is one of the childhood expressions that started the Opies' collection. Iona Opie wrote, "These are the lines that brought us under the spell of the schoolchild lore. We were leaning out of a window of our country home one evening in 1946, when a small boy went by intoning them. They seemed to us strange, primitive, and utterly fascinating." (p. 143).

Tommy Johnson is no good,
Chop him up for firewood;
When he's dead, boil his head,
Make it into gingerbread. (p. 33)

He that loves Glass without G
Take away L that is he. (p. 81)

I beg your pardon
Grant your grace;
I hope the cows
Will spit in your face. (p. 62)

The sixth and final theme is *wonder,* curiosity, or questioning. Children spend much of their childhoods wondering about the supernatural, nature, their friends, and thousands of other things. They shape their wonderment into games, questions, and poems. Following are some poems and letters written by children.

The World
Why does the World turn around in a circle?
Why is it shaped that way?
Why do they call it the World?
And why don't we live on Mars instead of the World?
Why?
Why?
Why?
I want to know Why.
Why do we call them states? And countries?
I want to know Why?
Please tell me.
Why?
Why?
Why?
Tell me
Why?

Jessica [age 7]

Dear Sean,

Thank you for your letter. I do not like football. Do you love Power Rangers? Do you have a pet? Do you love cats for a pet? We have been learning about New Zealand. We are going to the zoo Wednesday.

Your friend,
Sean [age 6]

Dear John,

Thank you for writing this letter. Do you like climbing trees? We are learning about New Zealand. Have you seen *Jaws,* the movie? It is cool. Guess what? There is no snakes in New Zealand.

Your friend,
Kyle [age 6]

Knock Knock
Who's there?
Orange.
Orange who?
Orange you glad to see me?

Trey [age 5]

We have used representations of children's voices to help you become aware of issues that are important to children. Note that all six themes relate to aspects of the human condition.

CONSTRUCTIONS

Journal Entry

Reflect on the six themes discussed in this section. Try to remember an instance of each theme from your own childhood or from a child you observed, then record it in your journal.

This chapter has presented a brief look at children and childhood throughout the ages. The constructivist perspective of becoming aware of your past so that you can use that knowledge can help you construct a deeper understanding of young children, values about them, and ways to educate them.

SUMMARY

▸ Childhood has been defined in many different ways throughout history.

▸ Early childhood is currently defined as birth through eight years of age by the two major professional organizations that study children and childhood.

▸ Primary sources such as diaries, interviews, letters, and medical and legal records, and secondary sources such as art, music, and literature provide information about young children and childhood.

▸ Historically, children have been viewed differently according to how parents' child-rearing patterns have advanced.

▸ Child-rearing modes have evolved from the practice of infanticide, through abandonment, ambivalence, and intruding, to socializing and helping.

▸ Our views of children have changed from viewing children as evil projections of our own misconduct, through viewing children as evil embodiments of original sin and later as the epitome of innocence, to viewing them as innately good.

▸ Child-rearing modes have advanced as societies have moved forward scientifically, socially, and technologically.

▸ A multidimensional perspective of childhood is necessary to understand today's children.

▸ Children's views of childhood can be found in their oral expressions, writing, jokes, and games.

▸ Children's views of childhood can be organized around several themes that seem to be common to all children: safety, power and control, the need to be loved, pleasure, insults, and wonder.

CONSTRUCTIONS

1. Analysis

Write a letter to a friend explaining how your views of children have changed as a result of studying the history of children and childhood.

2. Research

Identify key issues that you think early childhood educators will face in the next twenty years. Use the Internet if you have access to it. Join others who are using this textbook and share your ideas.

3. Advocacy

Make a pamphlet that provides glimpses of children for local and state government officials.

RESOURCES

Books

Beatty, B. (1995). *Preschool education in America: The culture of young children from the colonial era to the present*. New Haven, CT: Yale University Press.

An excellent historical account of childhood in America. It provides an in-depth account of the child-rearing modes and expectations of children in early colonial days.

Cable, M. (1975). *The little darlings: A history of child rearing in America*. New York: Scribner's.

This book will extend your understanding of children's behaviors and child-rearing patterns in the United States.

Wortham, S. (1992). *Childhood 1892–1992*. Wheaton, MD: ACEI.

Well written and easy to read. A good source of information on the modern period.

Web Sites

Child Welfare League of America **(http://www.cwla.org/)**

This organization is devoted to the health and welfare of children and families in need.

Lloyd deMause's "The Evolution of Child-rearing Modes" **(http://cnet.unb.ca/orgs/prevention_cruelty/modes.htm)**

A wonderful source of information about child-rearing practices from a psychohistory perspective.

Meir Bar-Ilan **(http://faculty.biu.ac.il/~barilm/home.html)**

The Web site of an author who has many publications in Hebrew and English on children in Jewish antiquity.

National Network for Family Resiliency
(http://www.nnfr.org/nnfr/)

This organization supports the prevention of family violence and provides a number of resources on family resilience and economics.

United Nations Convention on the Rights of the Child
(http://www.unicef.org/crc/statas.htm)

Provides information related to the implementation of the United Nation's Declaration of the Rights of the Child.

6

Exploring the Lives
of Young Children
and Families

● ●

This chapter presents some of the major issues facing children and families today, as well as ways early childhood professionals can help families cope with difficult situations. These issues have been around for a very long time and continue to challenge teachers today. For example, as you recall from Chapter 5, issues of child abuse and violence have deep historical roots. This chapter will also help you to think about the multiple perspectives involved in issues. A constructivist perspective focuses on co-ordinating multiple viewpoints to enhance understanding, which in turn leads toward possibilities for resolving issues. This chapter will help you to construct a deeper understanding of these areas:

▶ Some of the major issues affecting children and families today, such as violence, child abuse, and the use of technology in early childhood programs
▶ How to coordinate multiple perspectives on issues
▶ How early childhood teachers can help children and families address issues in constructive ways

INTRODUCTION

The class is discussing the importance of teachers' sensitivity to diversity in family beliefs.

DANIELLE: I think parents need to realize that the teacher is in charge of what happens in the classroom.

AMY: But what if a parent can't go along with what the teacher's doing because it's against a religious belief?

TILLIE: But we just learned that church and state are supposed to be separate, so teachers don't talk about religion at school now.

AMY: Well, I know a teacher who believes it's important to give children choices, and she lets them choose among activities. She had a parent complain that she didn't want her child to be given choices because in her religion children are taught to obey adults and do as they're told.

DANIELLE: But it's the teacher's classroom, and she can't react to every parent's religious beliefs. She has to teach the way that she knows is best for the children.

TILLIE: Well, I think that teacher has to listen to that parent and make an exception for that child. Otherwise, the parent will complain to the principal about the teacher.

AMY: But if the teacher does what the parent wants, the other children will be penalized and not allowed to have choices.

ERIC: And other parents might get upset because their children aren't allowed to make choices. Then they could complain, too.

DANIELLE: I was in a class in elementary school once, and a child couldn't participate in holiday activities like Christmas parties because his religion didn't believe in doing that. My teacher would send him to the office when we had such parties.

AMY: I wonder if he felt left out and angry. Dr. K., what does a teacher do in that situation?

Considering multiple perspectives is important.

This discussion addresses the issue of differing religious and educational beliefs and their potential to affect an educational program. Considering multiple perspectives on issues may not give you an immediate solution to a problem at hand, but it will deepen your understanding of the situation. When teachers and families experience conflicts in beliefs, it is critical that all parties involved listen to each other and attempt to understand each others' perspective. Listening and putting yourselves in others' shoes is the first step toward understanding beliefs different from your own. When teachers and families listen and understand each other, even though they may not agree, they can discuss alternative solutions until they reach one that is acceptable to all. Teachers and parents who are able to share their

Early childhood programs work with families on overcoming difficulties. *(© Elizabeth Crews)*

Issues affecting families include violence, poverty, and abuse.

perspectives, consider each other's points of view, and make a decision based on what is best for the children will be able to work together in overcoming difficult issues.

In the previous discussion, an agreed-upon compromise may be for the teacher to guide this child's choices, while the parent visits the program on a regular basis to observe the effects of the program on promoting respect for self and others. In the case of holiday celebrations, the teacher may plan alternative celebrations other than holiday parties. For example, some schools have a game day in celebration of friendship, in which everyone can participate. Or teachers could provide some activity choices in which no one is left out of the action.

ISSUES AFFECTING YOUNG CHILDREN AND FAMILIES

ASK YOURSELF

What would I do as a teacher if a parent's religious beliefs conflicted with my teaching practices? What do I consider the most significant issue facing children today?

In this chapter, you will find examples of issues that affect children and families and ideas for addressing them. You will begin to see that early childhood programs can play a positive role in helping families overcome difficult situations. Issues affecting families today reflect the broader issues inherent in society, such as violence, poverty, drug and alcohol abuse, and diverse perspectives, including religious beliefs, that result in conflict among groups. Societal issues as they affect families are brought to school by children who attempt to cope as best they can with the tensions in their lives. Teachers are not immune from these issues, either on a personal level

ISSUES FACING FAMILIES TODAY

Violence	Drug and alcohol abuse
Child abuse	Diverse values
Time and work pressures	Health care
Poverty	Teen parents
Divorce	Technology
Homelessness	Conflict over religious beliefs

Overcoming Issues: The Silver Lining

Issues	What Teachers Can Provide
Violence at home and in the community	Peaceful classrooms
Poverty	Equity in learning opportunities
Child abuse and neglect	Care and compassion for children in a safe classroom
Homelessness	Sense of belonging to a classroom community
Stress and pressure	Time to explore and think
Fear, anger, and shame	Respect, acceptance, and self-worth
Cruel adults	Adults who listen and understand

in terms of their own experiences and histories or professionally, as they attempt to work with diverse families who may not always see the world as they do.

MULTIPLE PERSPECTIVES

From the Field

We asked first-grade teacher Kristi Dickey what she considers the most significant problem children have to deal with today. She said:

Families today feel stressed.

I had children who were rushed all day from one event to another. There doesn't seem to be as much relaxation at home. Families don't read much together. The pace is too fast today. There is a lot of stress from rushed life. We had children who were away from home from 7:30 A.M. to 5:30 P.M., in childcare before and after school. There were children who were at school before I was and there longer than I was. I don't think kids do as much with their families at home as they used to. I think children are ignored a lot and made to be very independent at a young age. Some families never seem to have time at home.

Kristi told us that she recognized she has no control over changing the home lives of her first-grade children. She does what she can, within the time she has them each day, to provide a relaxed, accepting environment for children to pursue their interests with her support and guidance. She hopes that the positive effects of her program will sustain them through the difficult times outside her classroom. She gets to know each child as a unique person by spending time interacting with the child and carefully listening to him. Her children have learned that there is an adult in the world who cares for them and is available to help them learn what is important for them to know. They learn that they can talk to her and she will understand.

• •

Quality early childhood programs offer lasting benefits to children and are cost-effective to society.

Early childhood education offers hope to troubled children and families. It has been demonstrated numerous times that children who are at risk for school failure and who participate in quality early childhood education can succeed in school and become self-sufficient, socially responsible adults (Schweinhart, Barnes, & Weikart, 1993; Schweinhart & Weikart, 1997). Because quality early childhood education has long-lasting effects, children who participate require fewer special education services, retention in grades, and help from social service agencies. They get in trouble with the law less often, have fewer teenage pregnancies, and are more likely to become contributing citizens through employment. It has been estimated that for every dollar going toward quality early childhood education for at-risk children, there is a return to taxpayers of more than seven dollars in terms of savings on special education and special services, including institutionalization (Fuerst & Petty, 1996; Schweinhart, 1994). That is quite an endorsement for early childhood education! Think of the positive impact you could have as an early childhood teacher.

MULTIPLE PERSPECTIVES

From the Community

My name is Caryn Bruckheimer, and I work at the Emergency Family Center of the American Red Cross in New York City. The center serves ninety homeless families, women and children only. Many of the women are in the center because they are homeless as a result of battering or spousal abuse. The usual length of stay is about six months. There is an on-site daycare, as well as many programs for the families, including recreation and after-school care. We try to create a home-like atmosphere, avoiding institutionalizing the families in any way.

Shelters for families pro-
vide temporary homes.
(© J. Berndt/The Picture
Cube)

Our main goal is to relocate the family to permanent housing as rapidly as possible.

Teachers will find that the children in this center respond most positively to a low-gear, sensitive, and respectful approach. Voice tones need to be carefully modulated. Many of these children have been exposed to the brutalities of life and have seen very severe situations. These children benefit from reading and writing about homelessness. It helps them understand their condition better and live with it more meaningfully. Artwork often reflects this theme. Children are encouraged to speak about what caused them to become homeless, thus helping them overcome the stigmatization. This is incorporated into the entire curriculum.

Homeless children re-
spond best to a calm,
respectful approach.

We often find the children to be very guarded, vigilant, sometimes highly aggressive (as a prevention to violence), and other times quite withdrawn. Other behavioral factors include depression and inability to concentrate. Much of this is due to conditions to which they are exposed, as well as to a reaction to the caregiving they receive. Many parents are so distraught with their situation that they are unable to focus on their children and attend to them normally during this traumatic time. Naturally, this exacerbates the behavioral difficulties a great deal. It should also be noted that children who are victims of fire and other natural disasters tend to manifest behaviors which are reactive to the trauma.

We teach the staff that success is measured in small doses and to look for success in unexpected places. For example, if within six months a child has gained significant vocabulary since arrival at the center, you consider this as quite a success. This does not necessarily mean the child will leave your program on grade level, and you should not aim for this type of success. Rather, progress is measured in smaller goals. Another example would be if a child is assessed as being significantly delayed in development, and when the child leaves your program, you have arranged for a complete evaluation at a clinic or similarly appropriate site, then you have been successful. You may never know the results of the evaluation or the treatment plan, but you have benefited the child tremendously by identifying the problem and offering a future assistance arrangement. This is quite a success as we see it.

Sometimes it is hard to believe what these families endure. As a result, I believe it makes you a more caring and sensitive professional. There is a tremendous feeling of having helped and feeling that they could not have done this without you. When I began, I saw an opportunity to work with children who needed me, and I never thought it would develop into this professional relationship which has lasted so long and which has been so satisfying. Those of us who do this work have a saying which goes something like this: "Please put us out of jobs and out of business." I guess that says it all.

● ●

ASK YOURSELF

In what ways does Caryn Bruckheimer have a positive impact on children and families?
....

The fastest-growing poverty group in America is children.

Children today are the same as children have always been in their need for love, protection, health, nutrition, and a sense of belonging. But conditions in communities have changed. The fastest-growing poverty group in America is children. One in every five children lives below a subsistence level. Families with children make up more than 36 percent of the homeless population living in shelters (Children's Defense Fund, 1998). Many schools provide academic help to homeless children, but only a few provide comprehensive approaches to education such as shelters within schools (Nunez & Collignon, 1997). In addition, many families today, especially single-parent families, are unable to meet children's basic needs for care and emotional support. Children do not leave these difficulties at home. They come to school with these needs.

CONSTRUCTIONS

Research

Visit a homeless facility in your community. As suggested in Chapter 2, gather information on services provided to families in your area and incorporate it into a resource file for use with parents. Volunteer some time to work at one of the agencies that helps families.

VIOLENCE AS AN ISSUE

We revisit students Amy, Eric, and Tillie on their way to a Monday class.

ERIC: Hi, Amy, Tillie! Did you have a good weekend?

AMY: I had a very disturbing experience at the mall this weekend. I hope Dr. K. will let us talk about it in class.

TILLIE: What happened? Was there a fight?

AMY: Not exactly. I walked into a women's restroom, and there was a child screaming inside a locked stall. There was an adult woman with her in the stall, and I was the only other person in there. The girl sounded like she was about six years old, and she kept pleading with the woman to stop hitting her. But the woman just kept on, and she wasn't just hitting, she was beating this child!

ERIC: How horrible! What did you do?

AMY: I didn't know what to do! The child screamed every time she was hit. I went up to the stall and asked if there was a problem, and the woman said no. She said it was a matter of proper discipline and that she was teaching her granddaughter a lesson. And she kept beating that screaming child. I was so upset. I didn't know what to do. I didn't know if I should stay there and keep talking to her or go get the police or mind my own business!

CONSTRUCTIONS

Journal Entry

Write a journal entry about any experiences you had as a young child in which you were physically "disciplined." What do you remember about the experience? If you were Amy, what would you have done in her situation?

Whether they want to or not, early childhood teachers deal with many different issues every day. Some are more difficult to deal with than others, such as children who are physically or emotionally abused by their parents or someone in or close to their family. Thinking about all the issues facing families today may seem overwhelming and can even lead to despair. However, a more realistic view of the situation provides hope, in the sense that every day teachers have opportunities to help children deal with these issues in a safe, nonthreatening environment where they can relax, have their needs met, and learn positive strategies for coping with their worlds.

NAEYC developed a position statement on children and violence that tells teachers what they can do to help children who are exposed to violence (see the box below). The research cited in this paper clearly shows the important role of quality early childhood education in preventing and helping children overcome the negative effects of violence in society, the media, homes, and the community. This document encourages schools and other programs for children to prohibit corporal punishment, which teaches that physical solutions to problems are acceptable. Children who have warm, nurturing relationships with teachers and positive early schooling experiences are better able to cope with the effects of violence. Early childhood teachers also can help families find constructive ways to cope with stress.

> The NAEYC position statement on violence encourages early childhood programs to prohibit corporal punishment.

NAEYC POSITION STATEMENT ON VIOLENCE IN THE LIVES OF CHILDREN

NAEYC is committed to actions that support families, such as the following:

Increase awareness on the part of families about the profound effects of violence on children.

Support the critical role that parents play in promoting the development of prosocial behavior.

Collaborate with parents to bring about changes needed in local communities to prevent violence.

Support the importance of the parental role in the lives of children by providing education for parenthood, helping parents develop positive parenting skills, and supporting proven programs that prevent child abuse and neglect.

Increase the ability of families to find and use community resources to support and protect children and families.

Source: NAEYC. (1993, July). Position statement: Violence in the lives of young children. *Young Children, 48* (6), p. 83.

MULTIPLE PERSPECTIVES

From the Community

Bert Franks is a police officer who teaches the Drug Abuse and Resistance Education (DARE) and Gang Resistance Education and Training (GREAT) programs in a medium-size school district.

Young children need caring adults who listen.
(© Elizabeth Crews)

The most significant problem children have today is violence. Even in a small town, kids are bombarded with it day in and day out in the media, on TV, video games, and in entertainment. It's such a part of our lives that I think kids have a hard time learning that violence only makes the problem worse.

Violence is more graphic today. You see in video games someone ripping out someone's skull and spinal column to hang up for everyone to see, and kids think that's cool. I worry that it is so much a part of their lives and many see it as a solution. I will pose a situation to them about someone who calls them a name in front of friends or gets after them, and what will they do? Eight times out of ten they say, "Beat him up! You gotta fight them because you've got to teach them not to do that to you." You have to wonder, if that's the solution they have for problem solving and conflict resolution, then what's their solution going to be when they get older and are having a more intense problem with a spouse or with other people in relationships?

In working with young children, I think it's important to listen to their stories. Children love to tell stories. During a recent program with kindergartners, they really wanted to tell me stories about drugs. A lot was what they had seen on TV and what they had heard from friends and some of the misconceptions they had. One said, "Those drugs can really hurt you bad! I saw my grandma when she took so much of this, and it was really bad for her." I could really help them understand more realistically what drugs were about by dealing with their stories and dispelling some of the misconceptions they had. Their stories represent the kinds of personal experiences they have had, but they may not necessarily have had a chance

Violence is more graphic today.

Children need to talk about their personal experiences.

to integrate it or put it all together. And you can work with that and help them understand better so that they will be better prepared for difficult situations.

CONSTRUCTIONS

Reflection

Do you agree with Officer Franks that violence is the most difficult problem facing children today? Have you ever witnessed a violent act? How did it make you feel? Did it help to tell your story about it to someone? How do you think a child who witnessed violence would feel? What can teachers do to help?

The Effects of Violence on Children

Violence in homes, communities, and the media is a common concern of families and early childhood educators. Violence is not just an inner-city problem. It occurs in rural and suburban areas as well. Each day in our country, approximately fifteen children are killed by guns and at least thirty are wounded (Children's Defense Fund, 1998). James Garbarino (1992) and others have identified **post-traumatic stress syndrome/disorder,** similar to what occurs in war-torn countries, in inner-city children exposed to extreme violence. These children become sad, aggressive, and apathetic after continuous exposure to violence. They expend most of their energy trying to cope with these disturbing experiences and have little left for schoolwork. Consequently, they typically do not do well in school because they are preoccupied with the horror of violence and their attempts to adapt to it. Children who experience or witness a violent event are more likely to be depressed, have excessive worries about dying or being injured, and suffer from low self-esteem. Child abuse, a form of violence, has increased significantly. Since 1980, reports of abuse and neglect have almost tripled. Each year between 1986 and 1993, more than 2 million children have been reported abused. Since 1993, the figures have risen to more then 3 million per year (Children's Defense Fund).

Some children, in reaction to violence, are in a continuous state of stress and worry about being safe; they find little pleasure in activities others find joyful. They are sometimes identified by teachers as being overly aggressive and hurtful to others. In their play, they may act out violence they have experienced or witnessed as a means of coping or attempting to control it.

Violence or trauma can cause post-traumatic stress syndrome/disorder.

Early childhood teachers can provide safe environments for troubled children. (*© Elizabeth Crews*)

What Teachers Can Do

According to the work of Susan Craig (1992), teachers are in a special position to have a significant impact on children living with violence. Such children view life as something that happens to them rather than as something they have control over. Teachers can help them learn that what they do affects what happens to them. Teachers can provide environments that are safe, predictable, and consistent and that give children a sense of purpose.

Traumatized children benefit from predictable routines.

Predictable routines help children to develop a sense of cause and effect relationships—that one object or event is directly related to another. For example, in an early childhood classroom, they may learn that cleanup time always follows working at centers or learning stations. This routine helps them understand that some environments are stable, not chaotic and unpredictable. Most academic tasks require an understanding of the sequential ordering of events and the ability to set goals for oneself. Children who are victims of violence and a chaotic environment often have not developed the ability to infer sequence and cause and effect relationships. Teachers can engage children in setting both short- and long-term learning goals so that they will eventually learn that they do have some control over certain aspects of learning, such as learning to read.

Children from chaotic environments where violence is common tend to live in the present moment with little thought of the future. They tend to be so preoccupied with the violent reactions of others that they fail to differentiate a sense of self. It may be difficult for them to understand that materials and resources are available for more than the present moment and it is not necessary to grab them up before others do. Delay of gratification requires thought focused beyond the present moment and immediate desire. Teachers can help children develop a sense of self and the ability to delay gratification by reassuring them and encouraging them to think about the future and to consider the views of others and how their behaviors affect others. They will eventually learn that needs and desires can best be met in cooperation with others (DeVries & Zan, 1994). The accompanying box provides examples of what teachers can do to meet the needs of children living with violence.

> **Children from chaotic environments often focus on the present with little regard for the future.**

EDUCATIONAL NEEDS OF CHILDREN LIVING WITH VIOLENCE

Needs	What Teachers Can Do
Sequential learning	Predictable routines and schedules
Cause and effect	Safe environment for risk taking
Goal setting	Group problem solving
Delay of gratification	Cooperative learning
Awareness of self	Focus on active participation
Self as object (little self-individuation)	Provision for individual interests
Language development	Social interaction

Some children are resilient in overcoming the effects of violence and trauma. Others can learn to be resilient with the help of caring adults. The most important way for a child to overcome the effects of trauma is to have an adult in her life who sends a strong message of care, support and **unconditional positive regard.** This adult may or may not be a member of the child's family. The caring adult may be a teacher, minister, social worker, or friend. To regard a child *unconditionally* means that you care for the child regardless of the circumstances and that you communicate to the child that your caring has no strings attached. You may not like or approve of the

> **Children exposed to trauma can be helped by a relationship with a caring adult.**

child's behavior, but you do like the child and are there for her. The accompanying box lists general principles of therapeutic support for children who have been exposed to trauma. Think about specific ways you could implement these principles in the classroom.

It helps children to talk about the violence in their lives.

PRINCIPLES OF THERAPEUTIC SUPPORT FOR CHILDREN EXPOSED TO TRAUMA

1. Healing begins with relationships. The adult helping relationship is the most powerful tool we have to help children heal from traumatic events.
2. Help children reestablish a sense of safety at home and at school. Provide a highly structured and predictable environment for children. Emphasis should be placed on routine and predictability.
3. Give children permission to tell their stories. It helps children to be able to talk and draw about the violence in their lives with trusted adults.
4. Pay attention to the language you use. Young children often have a literal interpretation of language. Use simple, straightforward language with children.
5. Give parents help and support. Family members need information about how young children accommodate to trauma, what the symptoms of exposure to trauma are, and how they as caregivers can help the child feel more secure. Help parents understand that young children think differently than adults and need careful explanations about scary events.
6. Elicit an understanding of the particular meaning of the trauma for that child. Correct the cognitive distortions that children may have about the traumatic event.
7. Foster children's self-esteem. Children who have lived through traumatic events need reminders that they are competent, successful, and important.
8. Help children make a contribution to their social network.It can facilitate the development of resilience and build self-esteem.
9. Don't try it alone. Identify and collaborate with other caregivers in the child's life.
10. Heed your own feelings of helplessness and hopelessness. Get support from colleagues, supervisors, friends, and family.

Source: From Principles of Therapeutic Support for Children Exposed to Trauma, Child Witness to Violence Project, n.d. Boston: Boston City Hospital.

CONSTRUCTIONS

Journal Entry

Write a journal entry about your own resilience in meeting the demands and traumas you have experienced. You might want to list those things you have found to be most helpful to you in overcoming difficulties. Reflect on how you might encourage young children to develop similar helpful responses to trauma.

Violence has a numbing effect on children and adults.

Issues that are pervasive in society today affect us all. Violence is an issue that many early childhood teachers find troubling. Children and adults are constantly bombarded by violence in children's homes, local communities, TV news, movies, video games, sports, and TV programming often targeted at children, such as violent cartoons. Violence has a numbing effect on children and adults, creating a sense of hopelessness and apathy after continuous exposure. The effects of violence on children have been characterized by numbness, a vacant look in the eyes, alienation, and the inability to concentrate on school activities. Children who are in constant danger of being harmed in the community concentrate their energies on worrying about what may happen to them and have little interest in, for example, doing math problems. They don't see math as something that can help them overcome their immediate concerns.

A child whose home life consists of continuous abuse from parents learns to be constantly alert for signs that the next blow may be forthcoming. An abused child may live in a hyperalert state, which can result in highly distractible behavior at school, little interest in schoolwork, and an initial view of the teacher as an unpredictable person who needs to be watched and controlled. Building trust becomes an essential goal of a teacher attempting to work with an abused child. Seeing children with physical wounds such as bruises and burns and realizing that the child's parents or other family members have caused these hurts can anger any teacher. Having several children in various abusive situations can seem overwhelming to a teacher. Having to report suspected child abuse can be even more overwhelming.

MULTIPLE PERSPECTIVES

From the Field

Kindergarten teacher Laura Hines recalls feeling overwhelmed by the numerous children she has cared for who have suffered from abuse at home.

I used to get really frustrated. Now I know there is something I can do in addition to reporting child abuse. I give these children a safe and caring program for several hours a day and hope they learn there are some safe and interesting places where they will be cared for and that it will help them cope with their stressful home lives. I used to want to take them all home with me. I know I cannot do that, and getting depressed about their situations does not help me or them. I give them my best for the time they are with me, and that's what keeps me going back—that I can make a difference in their lives.

Sometimes I worry about other teachers who seem oblivious to children's pain, possibly because they have very full and busy lives with their own families to care for. Perhaps they've just seen so much that they've become hardened. I hope I never get so cold and hardened that I could ignore the pain I see every day. I want to be there for my children to show them I care about them, to listen to what they want so much to talk about, and to provide a place where they feel safe.

• •

MULTIPLE PERSPECTIVES ON ISSUES

In this book, an **issue** is defined as a problem or concern, such as child abuse, that (1) has a high impact on children and teachers, (2) is enduring and has existed for quite some time (child abuse dates back to ancient times), and (3) is something that a teacher must do something about (such as the legal and ethical responsibility to report suspected child abuse and neglect). Can you think of other issues that fit this definition?

Major issues such as child abuse, poverty, and homelessness cut across various aspects of life, including education, health, economics, politics, and religion. For any issue, there are wide-ranging implications. Can education prevent poverty? How does poverty affect health? Are certain groups more likely to experience poverty than others? How does legislation influence poverty? Any issue can be seen from multiple perspectives, as the following case study shows. As you read it, identify as many perspectives on the incident as you can. Remember that there can be multiple perspectives on any issue.

Martin: A Case Study

Karen's Perspective.   Karen is a beginning preschool teacher. The eighteen children in her program manifest a broad range of special needs and developmental delays. She is a careful kid watcher, always tuned in to what children say and do. She has noticed something she does not understand

Teachers don't always recognize symptoms of abuse.

about one child since he entered the program several weeks ago. A three-year-old boy, Martin, comes to the program each day with unusual-looking markings on his arms. These markings are oval in shape and about the size of a dime. Sometimes they appear bright red and shiny, but other times they are brown and almost look like scabs have formed. Karen has never seen markings like these and doesn't know what to make of them or the fact that they seem to come with regular frequency, especially on Monday mornings after the child has been home for the weekend.

Karen has noticed things about Martin's behavior as well. Although she tries hard to engage Martin in conversation and play, he seems to avoid Karen by backing away from her, lowering his head, and avoiding eye contact. He doesn't seem interested in play with the other children and tends to go off by himself. When Karen moves near Martin to try to get him interested in an activity, he sometimes crouches away from her as if to avoid being touched. When she asks if something is wrong, he is silent and looks away.

Recognizing her need for assistance, Karen mentions what she has observed about Martin to the other teachers. She tells them she is having a hard time engaging him in activities. Jamie, another preschool teacher, suggests that Martin may be suffering from child abuse. She volunteers to observe Martin, because she has experience in identifying and reporting abuse. After her observation, Jamie tells Karen that she suspects Martin is an abused child and that the markings are a result of cigarette burns. The abuse may be more frequent on the weekends when Martin is with his parents and family tensions are high. Jamie encourages Karen to report the abuse to the preschool director, who will report it to the local department of human services. Jamie also urges Karen to keep written records documenting each time she observes markings on Martin or unusual behavior.

Karen takes Jamie's advice. She keeps a running record of what she observes and informs the director of each incident of suspected abuse. She also attempts to get closer to Martin and build a trusting relationship with him. She plays alongside Martin and tries to converse with him about his play and about what he is interested in. She often shows affection toward Martin to let him know she cares about him and is there if he needs her. She also tries to serve as a role model for Martin's mother when she comes into the classroom. She tries to build communication with Martin's mother and is friendly and approachable in case the mother wants to talk.

One day after the suspected abuse has been reported several times, Martin's mother storms into the preschool claiming she knows that Karen has reported her for child abuse, which she has not committed. She angrily tells Karen that Martin has allergies and the markings on his arms are a result of allergic reactions. She threatens Karen with bodily harm if Karen ever reports her again.

The preschool director overhears the incident with Martin's mother and reassures Karen that she has done the right thing in reporting the suspected abuse. The director says that if the markings are due to allergies, it will come out in the social worker's investigation. The director tells Karen that she has known many abusive parents who deny the abuse and become defensive and angry. She says that although teachers are legally responsible for reporting suspected abuse and neglect, nothing may come of the case because of the backlog of cases at the department of human services and because the first priority of the department is to preserve the family. She cautions Karen to consider that Martin's mother may withdraw him from the program to escape from Karen's watchful eye.

Karen has mixed feelings about the situation. She feels good that she has done the right thing in reporting the suspected abuse. She also feels angry that more is not being done to prevent child abuse and to investigate this situation. She is sad that she may lose Martin just when she is beginning to gain his confidence and help him develop some interest in the program. She thinks more should be done to help this child.

> Teachers are responsible for reporting suspected child abuse.

CONSTRUCTIONS

Reflection

What can Karen do? What would you do? What is the right thing to do? Consider this situation from as many perspectives as you can. What is Karen's perspective? The mother's? Martin's? Other perspectives?

The Director's Perspective. I have been a preschool director for about fourteen years and have seen child abuse become much more frequent today than in the past. My major role is to provide a safe and appropriate program for the children. Working collaboratively with parents is essential. In general, parents are cooperative and supportive of our programs. Occasionally, we notice what may be child abuse because of suspicious physical markings or unusual behavior in a child. It is our legal and ethical responsibility to report all incidents of suspected abuse. I usually make a call to the department of human services. Sometimes we know that they do an investigation, because we hear from them or from the parents. Other times it seems as if they do nothing about the report because the signs of abuse continue. They tell us that the department is understaffed and overworked.

They respond immediately if the case is life threatening. If it is not, it may take months for them to respond, because they do not have the staff to cover all the reported cases.

Meanwhile, we continue to report additional incidents and to work with the child and family as best we can. We do tell parents when they enroll their children that we are legally obligated to report all cases of suspected abuse. We realize that sometimes what appears to be abuse turns out to be something else. But it is best for the child in the long run to report it than not to report it.

In Martin's case, I think Karen did the right thing legally and ethically. I phoned the department of human services each time that Karen told me about any suspected abuse. Eventually, the department did investigate the parents. While they do not tell the parents who reported the suspected abuse, Martin's mother correctly guessed it was Karen and reacted in a typical fashion for abusing parents: She denied the charge and attributed Martin's condition to allergies. Abusive parents often try to cover up or deny what they are doing to their children. Parents need to realize that we are responsible only for reporting suspected abuse, not for providing evidence that abuse has occurred.

Open communication with parents suspected of abuse is important.

Keeping open communication with parents you have reported for suspected abuse is difficult. Usually, and unfortunately, they leave the program, and we never see them again. When they do stay, we try our best to work with them by serving as role models for appropriate ways to interact with children and by providing as much information as we can on services and agencies that will give them the help they need to stop the abuse. Like Karen, I have also been threatened by accused parents. I have been to court several times to testify on behalf of a child in our program. Most of the time, the child is not taken out of the home. The department of human services tries to keep the family intact and to help parents learn to overcome their problems. It is difficult to watch a child struggle while this is happening. You wish you could take them home with you, but you can't. So you hope the child will benefit from your program and be able to develop ways to cope with other aspects of life.

If it appears that Martin's mother may try to make good on her threat to Karen, we will notify the police. Early childhood programs must be safe for children and teachers. I have worked with the program much longer than Karen, and I understand that in the long run, children and families do benefit in numerous ways from participation in our programs. It is hard for Karen to watch what is happening to Martin. But eventually she will see that Martin will respond to her, develop ways to cope, and learn that preschool is a safe and interesting place to be.

Considering Various Perspectives on Martin's Case

Reporting child abuse is a legal and ethical obligation.

In deciding that Martin may be suffering from child abuse and that she would report the suspected abuse, Karen took various perspectives into consideration. First, she did not understand what was causing Martin's unusual markings and behavior. She sought help from others who might know, including more experienced teachers. She conferred with other teachers and the preschool director to understand Martin's situation better. She wanted to help Martin learn that preschool was a safe place where he could do lots of interesting things. She wanted him to learn that he did have control over what happened to him at preschool and that he did have choices about what he wanted to do. She wanted him to learn that he was a contributing member of the classroom, accepted for himself and respected by others. She decided to report the suspected abuse because she thought it was the right thing to do on Martin's behalf and that it would likely result in Martin getting the help he needed at home. In addition, she knew she was legally obligated to report it.

Karen was disappointed when nothing was done immediately to help Martin. She felt that more should have been done on his behalf. The threat of bodily harm from Martin's mother did not deter her from continuing to report the suspected abuse, but she was uneasy that she might lose Martin from the program. She tried to maintain a positive and nonaccusatory relationship with Martin's mother so that she could continue to work with Martin and to provide a positive role model for his mother. She also wanted to keep an open mind that the markings could have resulted from an allergic reaction. Her responsibility was not to make that judgment, but to keep communication open with Martin's mother so that Martin could continue making the gains she was seeing. She finally accepted the idea that she might lose Martin from the program. She decided she would try to find out where Martin might go next so that she could continue to provide assistance on his behalf. She was hopeful that he might go to another preschool or program where teachers would be sensitive to his needs and that he would continue to make progress.

ASK YOURSELF

What is my perspective on Martin's case? Do I think Karen did the right thing? (Discuss this case with others to get additional perspectives.)

CHILD ABUSE AND NEGLECT AS AN ISSUE

After you have considered multiple perspectives on child abuse from the teacher's, parent's, and director's points of view, it is important that you understand how early childhood professionals define this issue. The accompanying box contains a formal definition generally accepted by professionals.

A DEFINITION OF CHILD ABUSE AND NEGLECT

Definition

Child abuse and/or neglect is any action or inaction (by someone responsible for the child) that results in the harm or potential risk of harm to a child. It includes:

Physical abuse (cuts, welts, bruises, burns)

Sexual abuse (molestation, exploitation, intercourse)

Physical neglect (medical or educational neglect, and inadequate supervision, food, clothing, or shelter)

Emotional abuse (actions that result in significant harm to the child's intellectual, emotional, or social development or functioning)

Emotional neglect (inaction by the adult to meet the child's needs for nurture and support)

Indicators of Child Abuse

Bruises or wounds in various stages of healing

Injuries on two or more planes of the body

Injuries reported to be caused by falling but that do not include hands, knees, or forehead

Oval, immersion, doughnut-shaped, or imprint burns

Reluctance to leave school

Inappropriate dress for the weather

Discomfort when sitting

Sophisticated sexual knowledge or play

Radical behavior changes or regressive behavior

Child withdraws or watches adults

Child seems to expect abuse

Revealing discussion, stories, or drawings

Source: From "Child abuse and neglect," by B. J. Meddin and A. L. Rosen, 1986, *Young Children, 41* (4), pp. 182–184.

Legal and Ethical Responsibilities to Report Abuse and Neglect

All states have laws against child abuse and neglect. Each state has policies for legal intervention and has designated a state agency to intervene when children have been abused or neglected or are at risk for abuse or neglect. The agency's first priority is to make reasonable efforts to preserve the family. Everyone, especially doctors, nurses, and teachers, is legally responsible for reporting suspected abuse to the appropriate agency. Schools and child-care programs have set procedures for reporting. The first step is usually the child's teacher reporting suspected abuse to the school principal or program director, who then calls the responsible agency, such as the department of human services. Teachers should follow up to make sure a report has been made. Teachers can be held liable if suspected abuse is not reported. Evidence that abuse has occurred is not required for reporting; only reasonable cause to believe that abuse has occurred is required. All cases of suspected abuse or neglect should be reported. Individuals reporting are immune from any civil or criminal liability. Not to report suspected abuse is a violation of the law.

> **Evidence of abuse is not required for reporting; reasonable cause is enough.**

The agency will investigate the reported abuse. Response time is based on risk of harm to the child. Cases that are life threatening have priority and are investigated quickly. Caseloads are usually very heavy, sometimes resulting in long delays in investigations. Teachers should continue to report incidents, because it is often the accumulation of reports that leads to action on behalf of a child.

Helping Children Who Are Abused

ASK YOURSELF

What would I do if I suspected that:
- A young child was locked in a closed car on a ninety-degree day?
- A mother refused to seek necessary medical treatment for a child?
- A parent failed to send a child to school regularly?
- A young child in my care had numerous bruises on his body?
- A parent slapped and spanked a child in the grocery store?

As you may recall from Chapter 5, child abuse has been an issue throughout history. Our ideas about what defines child abuse have also changed. Even today, there is not complete agreement among parents on what child abuse is. For example, cultural differences in child-rearing practices lead to different conclusions about spanking. Some parents advocate spanking children while others view it as abusive. When children are harmed, early childhood professionals are in a critical position to recognize and report suspected abuse. It is important to know that children have a great deal of potential for resilience. Between one-half and two-thirds of children from abusive families grow up to lead productive lives. One reason for their success is having caring relationships with adults. The most important help to a child who is suffering the effects of violence, including abuse, is an adult who cares. Having a caring adult in his life tells the child that he is worthwhile and valued. This *unconditional positive regard* is critical as it enables the child to overcome the effects of abuse. An early childhood teacher can be the caring adult who makes an important difference for an abused child. As a teacher, you cannot solve the child's problems, but you can help the child learn to cope.

Healing begins with relationships. Early childhood teachers are in a key position to have healing relationships with children. Teachers with an ethic of caring relate to children in ways that convey compassion, understanding, respect, and interest. They send the message that they will not give up on the child and that they are available to help.

Unconditional positive regard helps children to heal.

When children's homes are in violent turmoil, other places can sometimes substitute and provide a feeling of home as a secure and caring place to be. Church, child-care, and school programs can become safe havens for troubled children. Such programs can provide children with clear expectations, developmentally appropriate activities, and opportunities to maximize feelings of coping and self-esteem. In general, schools are one of the safest places for children—much safer than homes.

Troubled children need programs that are structured, have predictable daily routines, set clear limits, and provide consistency in rules and discipline. Teachers can help children cope by listening to them, being emotionally available to them, reassuring them, and helping them find ways to feel effective and activities that are personally interesting to them. They can help children find ways to be in control, such as planning and finishing an activity of their choice. Teachers can encourage children to use language to express feelings and ideas to others in appropriate ways rather than using it to distance themselves from others. They can help children learn that violence hurts and that people have the power to make choices about how they will act and how they want to be. Teachers can plan a peaceful curriculum to help children overcome the effects of abuse.

A Peaceful Curriculum

Give reassurance and physical comfort.

Teach ways to avoid becoming a victim of violence.

Provide opportunities for children to write, dictate stories, or create pictures reflecting their experiences.

Read books that deal with some of children's fears and discuss how the characters react.

Encourage expression of feelings.

Give opportunities and props for the reenactment of experiences through storytelling, dramatic play, and expressive art.

Provide opportunities for making choices, problem solving, and cooperative play.

Engage children in decision-making, rule making, and rule enforcement.

Use materials and activities that provide a tension release: water, sand, clay, Play-Doh, music, and movement activities.

Encourage constructive conflict resolution by helping children work through problem solving by considering all viewpoints and deciding on what is best for everyone involved.

CONSTRUCTIONS

Journal Entry

Write a journal entry about the peaceful curriculum described in the box on page 254. In what ways would this kind of environment have benefited you as a child?

Teachers who are having difficulty relating to abused children may first need to reflect on violence in their own personal histories and to discuss their feelings with caring adults or helping professionals. Teachers can try to put themselves in the children's shoes to better understand their behavior. Teachers participating in Choosing Non-Violence, an educational approach developed by Rainbow House and tested for four years in Chicago's Head Start and child-care centers, worked through the series of questions listed in the following box. Rainbow House is a social service agency in Chicago that helps women and children who are victims of domestic violence by providing shelter and support services.

VIOLENCE IN SOCIETY

How would you answer these questions?

How do I support or buy into violence in our society?

What violent TV shows do I watch and say I enjoy?

How may I be affected by what I see and hear?

What toys of violence do I buy for children I love?

Do I believe there may be a connection between these toys and the violent responses I see in children?

What movies showing violence get my money and attention?

Do I take children along with me to see adult-rated movies portraying violence?

How do I use my age, my size, or my voice to intimidate or control children?

What words expressing violence do I use with my partner? My child?

What stories do I read to children? What messages do children get from them?

Do I analyze these messages with them?

Source: From "Children surviving in a violent world—'Choosing Non-Violence,'" by A. Parry, 1993, *Young Children, 48* (6), p. 15.

CONSTRUCTIONS

Interview

Interview a child abuse counselor to learn more about his or her job and how teachers can help abused children.

Research

Gather information about services available to help abused and neglected children in your community. Add this information to your resource file.

TECHNOLOGY AS AN ISSUE

Tillie and Danielle are discussing a class assignment.

DANIELLE: Why the long face, Tillie?

TILLIE: I'm having a tough time with this class assignment. I'm supposed to go to the computer lab, review three pieces of software for young children, and evaluate whether they're appropriate to use with young children.

DANIELLE: Sounds like it could be fun! What's the problem?

ASK YOURSELF

What criteria do I already know for evaluating the appropriateness of software for young children?

TILLIE: The problem is I have no idea how to decide whether software is appropriate for young children. I've seen children using software on computers, but I don't know how to judge it.

DANIELLE: Maybe you could approach it in terms of what you like in software programs. Have you thought about what interests you?

TILLIE: Well, I like programs with good graphics, lots of action . . .

Some children may know more about technology than teachers.

You may recall, from Chapter 2, suggestions for educational technology resources. In addition, it was mentioned that technology is an issue in early education. Today almost all homes in America have TV sets, and an increasing number have computers accessible to young children. It is not unusual for some children to know more about using computers than their teachers. Children are often the ones who program the home VCR or teach parents how to play video games. Technology in the form of TVs, VCRs, video cameras, calculators, computers, the Internet, video games, and robots is increasingly finding its way into the lives of young children, especially in affluent homes where parents can afford the latest gadgets. The role of technology in education has been controversial since the advent of educational television, teaching machines, and computer-assisted instruction, which many feared would remove the need for teachers. Technology has been slow to arrive in public schools, partly because of its controversial nature and partly because of its cost.

The role of technology in early childhood programs is controversial.

ASK YOURSELF

What role do I think technology should play in programs for young children?

Some educators fear that technology in the form of computers will replace teachers in the near future. Others fear that computer programs are just another, more expensive form of electronic ditto sheet and not developmentally appropriate for young children, who they think benefit more from play and interactions with other children and real objects. Still others see an untapped potential for the use of technology to enhance children's knowledge construction. Regardless of the viewpoint, it is doubtful that technology is merely a passing fad. It is likely to become increasingly important in the workplace, at home, and even in the classroom.

Early childhood educators will continue to debate the appropriateness of computer-based instruction, especially for the youngest children. There is also an increasing concern for equity in access to technology. Will schools help equalize computer use, or will they widen the gap between those who can afford computers and those who cannot? The issue of technology will have a significant impact on today's children, because what happens in classrooms affects children's long-term learning and later employment opportunities. In addition, technology is an enduring issue that will be with us far into the future. It is an issue that requires action from teachers, who are in positions to decide on the appropriate or inappropriate uses of technology. Consider the following two scenarios.

The Computer Lab

Teacher Libby Baker takes her second-grade children to the school's computer lab at their allocated time every Tuesday and Thursday from 2:00 to 2:30 P.M. The children work on computer exercises selected by the school's computer teacher to reinforce their skills in language arts and arithmetic. The children work individually at computer terminals and on programs that record their errors and reinforce their responses with pleasing graphics and sounds for correct responses or unhappy faces and repetition of the exercise for incorrect responses. Libby can review individual children's error profiles to confirm the extent of their learning of specific skills.

The children are not allowed to talk to each other, but they can ask a teacher for help. Libby has noticed that some children do not seem to read or respond to the computer instructions, but instead repetitiously press the return key to keep the program moving along. A child will occasionally ask a question relating to the procedure for following the program, but rarely is there a question about the content of the lesson. The children do not talk much about their experiences on the computers either during the lab or later in the classroom.

Computers are often used to reinforce skills.

Libby was not responsible for choosing the computer programs adopted by her school's curriculum committee. She tries to use them as best she can, but they are not always related to other classroom activities she has planned. She wonders to what extent the children are benefiting from computer lab time. The programs resemble pages from workbooks that drill children on certain skills and incorporate external rewards from the teacher for correct responses. A child's involvement amounts to selecting one response among several as she would on a multiple-choice test.

The Writing Center

Second-grade teacher Nadine Skinner has equipped a writing center in her classroom with two connected computers that are linked with the school's library computer, as well as with the computer at a local university that provides for Internet access. The writing center also contains a printer, a variety of paper, folders, markers, pencils, staplers, and other materials for the children's use. There are large blocks of time during the day when the children can choose to work in the writing center either alone, in pairs, or in small groups.

Computers can be used to encourage creative writing.

The activity in the writing center seems to have an organic flow, as children get ideas such as working on stories, poems, drawings, or articles for a class newsletter, which emerges by the end of each day. Children also use the center to write their own books, study published authors, collect information for projects from the available databases, create recipes, write to their pen pals or their fifth-grade study buddies, or play math games. The children initiate whatever they work on in the center. They are not given specific assignments, but are encouraged to use the center to read, write, compute, create, pose questions, and collaborate. Although the area is designated as the writing center, children also incorporate math, science, social studies, art, and music as they do project work such as the production of the newsletter.

The children talk and collaborate in the center and are occasionally joined by Nadine as she monitors their projects or asks them questions to encourage thinking about the work from a variety of perspectives. Nadine has noticed that the children have learned more about using the computer than she knows herself. For example, the children figured out how to use the word-processing program to make double columns for the class newsletter. She also has noticed they are very skilled at retrieving appropriate graphics to illustrate a story or poem.

Another thing she has observed is how the children use the center as a tool for connecting all aspects of the curriculum. For example, when there was a local bombing, the children used the writing center to produce a newsletter describing the disaster, what the community was doing to help,

During project work, children pursue answers to their own questions. *(© Ellen Senisi/The Image Works)*

and their own reactions to it. In addition, they used the center to produce get-well cards and drawings for the disaster victims. They also used it to research disasters so that they could better understand what had happened in their community.

Nadine can evaluate the children's newsletters, stories, and so on, for the reading and writing skills she is mandated to teach. By collecting samples of their work at various times during the year, she can document their progress.

CONSTRUCTIONS

Analysis

Think about your reactions to the descriptions of the computer lab and the writing center. Which environment is more child centered? Which environment promotes more creativity in computer use? If you were a child, in which environment would you most like to spend time?

Considering Various Perspectives on Technology

Some educators view the role of the computer as useful for drill and practice on skills instruction. This view reflects a behavioristic approach: The teacher determines skill objectives, presents computer programs for practice, evaluates children's errors, rewards correct responses, and corrects incorrect responses. Children follow instructions and answer a series of multiple-choice questions on the skills they have been taught by the teacher or the program. Skills are taught in isolation, with follow-up practice and monitoring by the teacher. Children work individually and are individually assessed.

Other educators take a different view of the computer as a tool through which children can create and construct knowledge, answering their own questions and pursuing their own interests individually or in collaboration with others. Children choose topics, questions, or projects to pursue using the computer to gather information or to generate written copy or graphics. For example, project work on the topic of duck eggs may take children to the computer to find information on incubation periods, types of duck eggs, or recipes using duck eggs. Children may use the computer to write stories or poems about duck eggs. Children may generate a duck egg questionnaire to use to ask other class members to estimate how many ducks will hatch from a certain number of eggs. Children may program the computer to draw eggs of various shapes and colors. These activities are child initiated and child regulated, with teacher guidance and supervision, and they represent a constructivist view of learning.

ASK YOURSELF

Which view described in the text best reflects my experiences with computers? Which view, if any, would I advocate for working with young children?
. . . .

Computer programs for young children should be interesting and challenging, not boring and repetitive.

Another view held by some educators is that computers have no place in early childhood classrooms because they detract from the time children need to have concrete experiences with real materials while both working and playing. This view holds that computers are not developmentally appropriate for young children and have little to offer in the way of learning because they are too abstract and print dominated. Educators who hold this view want to protect children from experiences beyond their capabilities that may frustrate or confuse them. The idea behind this view is that children must learn through real objects and cannot think abstractly at the level required by most computer programs. The view that children learn only through hands-on activities is a misinterpretation of constructivism. A constructivist view holds that it is the thinking or reflective abstraction that occurs when children manipulate objects, including computers and computer programs, that is the key to learning and not the objects themselves. However, it is important that computer programs for young children be challenging but not overwhelming and that they be interesting and not just boring, repetitious busywork.

NAEYC has developed a position statement on technology and young children that emphasizes the responsibility early childhood teachers have to critically examine the benefits of technology to children. Computers can supplement but not replace appropriate early childhood activities such as art, blocks, and dramatic play. Teachers must find ways to integrate technology into the regular program to provide equitable access to all children, including those with special needs. Research shows the benefits of technology to children's learning when it is used in developmentally appropriate ways, including collaborative play, learning, and creation (Clements, Nastasi, & Swaminathan, 1993).

NAEYC POSITION STATEMENT ON TECHNOLOGY AND YOUNG CHILDREN

Major aspects of the position statement include the following:

1. In evaluating the appropriate use of technology, NAEYC applies principles of developmentally appropriate practice (Bredekamp, 1987) and appropriate curriculum and assessment (NAEYC & NAECS/SDE, 1992). In short, NAEYC believes that in any given situation, a professional judgment by the teacher is required to determine whether a specific use of technology is age appropriate, individually appropriate, and culturally appropriate.

2. Used appropriately, technology can enhance children's cognitive and social abilities.

3. Appropriate technology is integrated into the regular learning environment and used as one of many options to support children's learning.

4. Early childhood educators should promote equitable access to technology for all children and their families. Children with special needs should have increased access when this is helpful.

5. The power of technology to influence children's learning and development requires that attention be paid to eliminating stereotyping of any group and to eliminate exposure to violence, especially as a problem-solving strategy.

6. Teachers, in collaboration with parents, should advocate for more appropriate technology applications for all children.

7. The appropriate use of technology has many implications for early childhood professional development.

Source: NAEYC. (1996). "Position statement: Technology and young children—ages three through eight, adopted April 1996," *Young Children, 51* (6), pp. 11–16.

CONSTRUCTIONS

Interview

Ask three early childhood teachers at random whether they are familiar with the NAEYC Position Statement on Technology and Young Children. If they are, ask how that paper has influenced their work with children. Share your findings with your classmates.

Effects of Computers on Children

Research shows that computers can contribute to children's learning and enhance, not detract from, social interaction. Seymour Papert (1993), who studied at Piaget's Center for Genetic Epistemology in Geneva, Switzerland, developed the Logo computer language, in which children use the turtle cursor to give commands to the computer. Papert's idea was for children to create programs and take an active role in manipulating the computer rather than passively responding to it. Clements (1987) found that when given free choice of activities, young children spend about the same amount of time playing on the computer as they do in other play activities such as blocks. Computer play is interesting to young children, but it does not take time away from other activities. Furthermore, children prefer programs that give them a feeling of control over the computer. Using Logo to actively solve problems helps children develop a more sophisticated level of thinking. Clements (1994) found that children's creativity in noncomputer activities improved following Logo use. In addition, the teacher should continue to play an important role by encouraging and questioning children. Children who use computers as another tool in their play experiences are more likely to find ways of creatively using technology than children who merely respond to electronic drill and practice.

Children may benefit more from computer use that is child regulated.

Computers are also helpful to beginning writers by freeing them from the motoric aspects of handwriting. They are more willing to take risks, revise their work, and subsequently build a sense of competence (Clements, 1987). Wright (1994) found that computer experience prodded children to explore beyond their previous boundaries. Clements and Swaminathan (1995) claim that children experience benefits from computer use when activities are primarily child initiated and child regulated and involve open-ended projects coupled with appropriate noncomputer activities. In addition, Haugland (1995) found that children gain most from computer experiences if they are reinforced with specific concrete activities. Haugland (1998) has developed the Haugland Developmental Software Scale for evaluating how well software for young children meets their developmental needs. The scale consists

Assistive technology enables children with special needs to participate in classrooms. *(© Bob Daemmrich/Stock Boston)*

of ten criteria, each with characteristics used to assess the extent to which the software meets that criterion. The ten criteria include age appropriate, child in control, clear instructions, expanding complexity, independence, non-violence, process orientation, real world model, technical features, and transformations. The criterion of transformations includes characteristics such as people of diverse cultures and diverse family styles. For the complete scale, see Haugland (1998) or visit the Computers and Young Children Web site at **http://cstl.semo.edu/kidscomp**.

Equity and Technology

The availability of computers in programs and schools varies greatly depending on the community and its resources. The same holds true for their availability in homes. More affluent families are more likely to have computers. Less advantaged children have fewer computer experiences at home. To what extent can programs and schools provide equitable access to technology to all children, regardless of their families' economic conditions? It is in the best interest of our nation to give all children equitable access to technology. Technology and especially computers can make education more equal, or it can create a wider gap between rich and poor. In 1995, almost 42 percent of households with children had a personal computer (Milone & Salpeter, 1996). That means that the majority of homes do not have such technology.

Children need equal access to technology opportunities.

More disturbing than the inequities in computer access is the discrepancy in type of computer use in school by socioeconomic level. For example,

> ### COMPUTERS AND CHILDREN WITH SPECIAL NEEDS
>
> Young children with special needs can benefit from **assistive technology** devices that enable them to participate more actively in classrooms. Assistive technology devices for special needs children provide them with increased experiences, opportunities, independence, and participation in regular classrooms (Snider & Badgett, 1995). Assistive technology may be any item, either low or high tech, used to maintain or improve the functional abilities of children with disabilities. Examples include communication boards, voice recognition devices, and touch screens. Federal mandates require the use of such devices in educational programs serving children with special needs.

national surveys indicate that students in schools in low socioeconomic areas are about three times as likely to use computers for drill and practice as those in higher socioeconomic schools (Milone & Salpeter, 1996). Similarly, students in advantaged areas are three times more likely to be learning to program the computer (Milone & Salpeter, 1996).

In addition to socioeconomic inequities, there is some evidence of gender inequity as well. Milone and Salpeter (1996) report gender differences in attitudes toward computer use. Although males and females have about the same access to computers and score the same on computer performance measures, females are less likely to be exposed to out-of-school computer activities, less likely to participate in optional computer activities in school, and less likely to major in computer science in college.

Providing equity in technology will require sensitivity on the part of educators to potential inequities in terms of socioeconomic level, gender, and special needs. Teachers have an ethical and legal responsibility to ensure that all children receive equitable computer experiences. Programs offered to young children must be not only appropriate but also equitable in their use.

CONSTRUCTIONS

1. Research

Visit a local elementary school and study how computers are used in the early childhood grades (prekindergarten through third grade). Find out how many computers are available for each class, where they are located, and how accessible they are to children.

2. Analysis

If possible, observe in some primary classrooms and note how many girls use computers compared to how many boys and for how long.

COORDINATING MULTIPLE PERSPECTIVES

Now that you have explored some of the issues affecting early childhood education, you may wonder how a teacher ever finds her way through the maze of issues and multiple perspectives. A constructivist approach to issues involves considering all the relevant perspectives before coming to an informed decision. When you seek out information from credible sources, such as professional literature or more experienced teachers, you can coordinate these various perspectives with what you already know to make the best decision. Teachers who are knowledgeable about current research can articulate reasons for their perspectives. They know why they teach the way they do, and they are able to explain to others, providing a reliable and credible rationale for their practices. As has been discussed previously, autonomy is the ability to distinguish between appropriate and inappropriate actions on the basis of an internally constructed standard of behavior (Kamii, 1992).

Teacher autonomy (self-regulation) involves considering relevant variables in decision-making.

Autonomous teachers make decisions after carefully considering relevant variables. Autonomy is self-regulation—the ability to decide for oneself without having to be told by others. You develop professional autonomy when you have a chance to share your views with others and to hear and debate the views of others. Through exchanging perspectives, you come to a deeper understanding of where you stand on issues and develop an appreciation for other views. Listening to someone else's view does not mean you will adopt that view. It means considering the new view in relation to your own view. It may result in changing or modifying your view to a more adequate understanding of the issue.

In making decisions that affect children, autonomous teachers always consider what is in the best interests of children rather than what might benefit them professionally by winning favor with administrators or parents. Autonomous teachers consider how the decision might affect children's learning. Will it benefit children in some way? For example, an autonomous teacher who has studied the research on children and computers may decide that her class will not participate in electronic drill-and-practice programs because children have little to gain from such participation, but she will use the computer as a creative tool within the classroom. The teacher can provide an informed rationale based on scientific research to explain her decision to the principal and parents. She can show that her decision has been made out of consideration for what is most appropriate for the children.

Autonomous teachers promote autonomy in children.

Similarly, autonomous teachers can help children develop autonomy by providing child choice, child-initiated activity and decision-making, and the exchange of points of view among children. When children have opportunities to debate issues and exchange points of view, they learn to understand situations from more than just their own perspectives. They are encouraged to decenter their perspectives so that they can look at the situation from a different angle. This process encourages the rethinking of issues, which generally leads to greater understanding. For example, an abused child may have developed a self-view of being worthless and bad. Through exchanging views in the classroom, the child learns that the teacher views her as capable and competent and that other children view her as a friend and worthy of affection. While the teacher communicates respect for the child's view, she can also offer her own view and the views of other children to help the child rethink her view of self (DeVries & Zan, 1994). The teacher does not negate or deny the child's view, but instead presents a perception that may result in the child choosing to modify her view.

This chapter has presented multiple views on several issues affecting children, families, and teachers. The constructivist view on coordinating perspectives has been offered as a way of helping you think about these important issues as you develop a deeper understanding of what it means to teach young children.

SUMMARY

- An issue (1) has a high impact on children and teachers, (2) is enduring and has existed for quite some time, and (3) is something that a teacher must do something about.
- Major issues confronting children and families include violence, child abuse, homelessness, poverty, and technology.
- It is every citizen's, and especially every teacher's, responsibility to report (not prove) suspected child abuse.
- Early childhood programs can play a beneficial role in helping children and families deal with difficult issues by providing resource information, assistance, and a peaceful curriculum for children.
- The most important element for the recovery of a traumatized or distressed child is at least one caring adult in that child's life who provides emotional support and unconditional acceptance.

▸ Computers should supplement, not replace, good early childhood activities such as block building and art.

▸ All children in a program should have equal access to technology.

▸ Autonomous teachers are able to coordinate multiple perspectives, consider relevant variables, decide what is appropriate for children, and articulate their thinking to others (parents, teachers, and administrators).

CONSTRUCTIONS

1. Analysis

Discuss an issue with others in which you exchange points of view on the issue. Following are some issues to consider:

Segregating homeless children in separate classrooms

Reporting child abuse you have observed in the community

Use of corporal punishment in classrooms

Use of video games in classrooms

Following the discussion, reflect on your view of the issue. Has it changed?

2. Research

Surf the Internet looking for sites that are appropriate for young children.

3. Advocacy

Take a stand on an issue affecting children that you feel strongly about, such as media violence. Write a letter describing what you think should be done and send it to someone, such as a legislator, in a position to make changes.

RESOURCES

Children and Violence

Benard, B. (1991). *Fostering resiliency in kids: Protective factors in the family, school, and community.* San Francisco: Far West Laboratory for Educational Research and Development.

Resiliency is discussed and suggestions are given for fostering resiliency at home, at school, and in the community. Emphasis is put on meeting children's basic needs and on reciprocal caring relationships.

Bernat, V. (1993). Teaching peace. *Young Children, 48* (3), 36–39.

Suggestions are given for helping children learn how to create peace in their relationships with others.

Carlsson-Paige, N., & Levin, D. E. (1992). Making peace in violent times: A constructivist approach to conflict resolution. *Young Children, 48* (1),

4–13. Problem-solving approaches to conflict resolution focus on the importance of perspective taking and community building.

Castle, K., Beasley, L., & Skinner, L. (1996). Children of the heartland. *Childhood Education, 72* (4), 226–231.

Teachers' and children's reactions to the Oklahoma City bombing are described. The focus is on one second-grade classroom in which the teacher and children dealt with this violent event in an autonomous and healing manner.

Clark, R. (1995). Violence, young children, and the healing power of play. *Dimensions of Early Childhood, 23* (3), 28–31, 39.

This article describes how play can help children overcome the destructive effects of violence.

Craig, S. E. (1992, September). The educational needs of children living with violence. *Phi Delta Kappan, 74* (1), 67–71.

The author describes how constructivist approaches, such as engagement of children in their own learning, are important for children living with violence. The important role of teachers in children's cognitive development is discussed.

Demaree, M. A. (1995). Creating safe environments for children with posttraumatic stress disorder. *Dimensions of Early Childhood, 23,* 31–33, 40.

Many suggestions are given for providing a safe, predictable classroom environment for children suffering from trauma.

Dinwiddie, S. A. (1994). The saga of Sally, Sammy, and the red pen: Facilitating children's social problem solving. *Young Children, 49* (5), 13–19.

Problem-solving steps that actively engage children in resolving conflicts are given, with many examples of what teachers can do to promote constructive conflict resolution.

Farish, J. M.(1995). *When disaster strikes: Helping young children cope.* Washington, DC: NAEYC.

This brochure outlines the symptoms of stress in children and strategies teachers can use to help children cope. In addition, it provides tips for teachers and staff on how they can deal with their own feelings and stress when bad things happen.

Furman, R. A. (1995). Helping children cope with stress and deal with feelings. *Young Children,* 50 (2), 33–41.

The author provides many examples of what caring adults can do in working with children suffering from stress.

Garbarino, J., Dubrow, N., Kostelny, K., & Pardo, C. (1992). The healing role of play and art. In *Children in danger: Coping with the consequences of community violence* (pp. 202–222). San Francisco: Jossey-Bass.

The authors describe symptoms of posttraumatic stress disorder in children and point out that it is not just an inner-city problem. They emphasize the importance of providing healing play opportunities for traumatized children.

Head Start Bureau. (1994). ***Responding to young children under stress: A skill-based training guide for classroom teams.*** (DHHS Publication No. 515-032/03010). Washington, DC: Government Printing Office.

This publication takes a team approach to helping children who are suffering from stress. It has many practical suggestions for adults working with young children.

Kamii, C., Clark, F. B. & Dominick, A. (1995). Are violence-prevention curricula the answer? ***Dimensions of Early Education,*** *23* (3), 10–13.

The authors say that violence is complex and results from many factors schools can't control, including poverty, indifferent or violent parents, and television. They stress that teachers need to rethink their goals for children from a Piagetian perspective, emphasizing autonomy and constructivist approaches to conflict resolution.

Levin, D. E. (1994). Building a peaceable classroom: Helping young children feel safe in violent times. ***Childhood Education,*** *70* (5), 267–270.

The author gives many examples of how teachers can create a peaceful classroom.

PAVE: Partnership to Address Violence Through Education. PAVE is a joint project of the Center for Early Education and Development in the College of Education and Human Development, University of Minnesota; Minneapolis Technical College; and St. Paul Technical College. It offers materials, such as bibliographies, on the topic of young children and violence. For information, contact PAVE at **pave@tc.umn.edu** or visit the project's Web site at **http://www.umn.edu/mincava/pave/preview.htm**.

Wallach, L. B. (1993). Helping children cope with violence. ***Young Children,*** *48* (4), 4–11.

This article provides suggestions for adults in helping children learn to cope with the experience of violence in their lives.

Technology

ERIC/EECE. (1995). ***A to Z: The early childhood educator's guide to the Internet*** (ED 407178, Catalog #214, $10.00). Urbana, IL: ERIC Clearinghouse on Elementary and Early Childhood Education.

Available from ERIC/EECE: 805 W. Pennsylvania Avenue, Urbana, IL 61801-4897. This guide offers numerous tips on using the Internet and sites appropriate for early childhood education.

Kid Works Deluxe Software for Grades K-3. (1997). Davidson and Associates, P.O. Box 2961, Torrance, CA 90509.

Can be used by young children to write and illustrate their own stories. It has multimedia tools including the incorporation of graphics and sounds into stories children create plus the feature of reading back to children the stories they have written.

Rothenberg, D. (1995). *The Internet and early childhood educators: Some frequently asked questions* (Report No. EDO-PS-95-5). Urbana, IL: University of Illinois, Elementary and Early Childhood Education Clearinghouse.

This publication answers some of the most pressing questions that early childhood teachers have about using the Internet.

U.S. Department of Education (1998). *Parents' guide to the Internet.* This guide is designed to help parents, regardless of their technology expertise, use the Internet as an educational tool. It includes a basic overview of the Internet, plus listings of educational sites for children and families. It can be obtained from the department's home page at **http://www.ed.gov/** or from the U.S. Department of Education, Office of Educational Research and Improvement, Media and Information Services, 555 New Jersey Ave., NW, Washington, D.C. 20208-5570.

Web Sites for Children and Families

American Library Association **(http://www.ala.org/parents/index.html)**
For good books to read, including Newbery and Caldecott Award winners.
ERIC Clearinghouse on Disabilities and Gifted Education
(http://www.cec.sped.org/ericec.htm)
50+ Great Sites for Kids and Parents
(http://www.ssdesign.com/parentspage/greatsites/50.html)
A list from the American Library Association.
Franklin Institute Science Museum **(http://sln.fi.edu/)**
For on-line exhibits at the museum.
Great Sites: Amazing, Spectacular, Mysterious, Wonderful Web Sites for Kids and the Adults Who Care About Them
(http://www.ala.org/parentspage/greatsites/amazing.html)
Healthlinks **(http://www.mcet.edu/healthlinks/index.html)**
For educational materials on health issues.
Library of Congress **(http://www.loc.gov)**
For exhibit information.
Parents and Children Together Online
(http://www.indiana.edu/~eric_rec/fl/pcto/menu.html)
For stories to read.
Starbright **(http://www.starbright.org)**
Advanced technology for disabled children.

PART 3

Settings

*I*N *PART 3 WE shift focus from the children served in early childhood settings to an analysis of the types of settings and to the professionals who create and maintain those settings. The two chapters in this part will help you better understand the nature of the settings and the ways in which curriculum is developed relative to the needs of the children served. A key factor to consider in comprehending program settings and curriculum is how program goals come from theories held by those who plan curriculum.*

Chapter 7 provides an overview of the types of programs available for children from birth through age eight. This chapter explains how programs are funded and administered. The framework provided may help you extend or transform your current ideas about the types of programs available.

In Chapter 8, you will learn about curriculum in anticipation of your own role in planning curriculum in response to children's needs and interests. Our emphasis is on the child's construction of knowledge rather than on the teacher's transmission of content. Examining examples of curriculum emerging from children's purposes will help you further develop understanding of ways in which teachers encourage children to solve problems and to become more autonomous.

7

Professionals in Early Childhood Settings

• •

This chapter will help you develop knowledge about the various programs that are included in the broad category of early childhood education. You may have had experience in a child-care center or volunteered in a first-grade classroom helping children who are just learning to read. Before you enter the field as a professional, you'll need a more extensive view of the profession. Such a view will help you determine how the role you choose fits into the overall scheme of opportunities available for young children and their families. You also may decide to pursue options that you had not previously considered.

After reading this chapter you should be able to discuss the following topics:

▶ The many types of programs in which early childhood professional educators work with young children
▶ How early childhood programs vary in their purpose, the characteristics of the children served, and their sponsorship
▶ How early childhood programs are funded
▶ How early childhood programs are administered

INTRODUCTION

Most of the class members are seated in the classroom, conversing and waiting for the instructor. Amy, however, is standing in the hall by the classroom door as Eric approaches.

ERIC: Hey, Amy, what's up?

AMY: I'm just waiting for Dr. K. My sister Maggie called me last night in tears, and I want to see if I can help her out.

ERIC: Sounds serious.

AMY: Well, yeah, it is. Maggie's baby sitter just quit, and she doesn't have anyone to take care of her two-year-old. I feel awful that I can't do it because she *has* to work.

ERIC: Hey, maybe you could bring the kid to school with you—you know, we could study a real kid!

AMY: Get serious, Eric. Remember that day we observed two-year-olds? They were all over the place. And besides, someone has to be home when her son comes home from kindergarten. Maggie's really scared that she'll have to quit her job and they'll have to sell their house.

ERIC: Here comes Dr. K. now. Hope she can help you.

After hearing that Maggie's dilemma is fairly common, Amy agrees to share her sister's situation with the class. She describes the problem and nearly everyone has an opinion about what Maggie should do. Zenah volunteers to write the ideas on chart paper (see the box below).

When they are finished, Dr. K. gives her opinion.

DR. K.: These are good options, but there's one more that you may not know about. In our county, we have a **resource and referral agency** that helps people locate the child-care services they need. Their computerized system can be used to search by location, age of the child, cost, and type

ASK YOURSELF

What are some of the options that Amy's sister has? Do I think Amy is overreacting, or could this be a serious problem for a family with young children?

Finding good-quality childcare is a common dilemma.

POSSIBLE CHILD-CARE SOLUTIONS

Call her church or temple.

Ask her neighbors.

Check with her pediatrician.

Ask the kindergarten teacher or principal.

Get a night shift job so that her husband could be home with the children.

Quit her job and move. Then buy a house when the children are older and she can go back to work.

of care preferred. The service is free, and the parent also can obtain tips on what to look for in the setting. But it's up to the parent to decide whether the situation is right for a particular child. Some businesses work through our resource and referral—or R and R, as it is usually called—to provide enhanced services for their employees. The R and R then contacts several caregivers that the parent has selected from the computer search to see whether there are openings. The employer also provides an on-site counselor through R and R to talk with families about what to look for. I'll give Amy the phone number after class.

Amy looks relieved as the class moves on to their discussion of types of early childhood programs. We'll leave them now and turn to an opportunity for you to construct knowledge about use of early childhood programs in your area.

CONSTRUCTIONS

Research

Work with a partner to plan and complete two interviews.

- a. Select two families. Each family must have a child or children between the ages of birth and eight years. (Be sure to explain the purpose of your interview and how you will use the information you obtain.)
- b. Find out what type of child-care programs they use (if any).
- c. Find out why they made those child-care decisions.
- d. Inquire about the pros and cons of their decisions from their families' perspectives.
- e. Prepare a written report containing the information you have obtained. Include your reflections on the data.
- f. Be prepared to present your data orally to your classmates.
- g. As always, maintain confidentiality—and don't forget to thank the families.

In the episode about Amy's sister, you heard about two program options in which young children were being cared for by someone other than their families. The situations were home care (sometimes called baby sitting) and kindergarten. In this chapter, we discuss these options and many others. We also address the question of who participates in each type of program (children, staff, and decision-makers), how each program is funded, and the importance of cohesive theoretical tenets in creating a program.

TYPES OF EARLY CHILDHOOD PROGRAMS

Early childhood education encompasses all organized, regularly scheduled programs for children ages birth through eight years.

Early childhood education encompasses all organized, regularly scheduled programs for children ages birth through eight years. These programs have been created to serve a variety of purposes. You will learn about the history of these programs in Chapter 9, but in this chapter we review the types of programs that currently exist in the United States. (Although many young children participate in a range of classes and activities, such as dance, sports, and scouting, these programs are beyond the scope of this book.) In the following section, we discuss the various types of early childhood education programs and the clients they serve.

Childcare

Data describing the main child-care arrangements of all American children under five years of age indicate that parents provide primary childcare for less than half of these children. For more than half of the children under age five, the main childcare may be provided in a center, in the caregiver's home, or in the child's home by someone other than the parents (Phillips, 1995). These centers and homes care for children whose parents aren't available to care for them during the day because they are at work, going to school, or participating in a training program. In some cases, parents may need help because they are emotionally or physically incapable of caring for their children on a full-time basis.

Full-Day Care. Primarily designed for preschool-age children, full-day programs also serve infants and toddlers. You may think immediately of a child-care center. However, many parents prefer to have their infants and toddlers, as well as their preschoolers, with a family child-care provider in the child's own home or in the provider's home with a small group of children.

The guidance of a caring, consistent adult is a basic need in childcare.

In some places, childcare is available during the evening and even through the night. For example, in a factory that has round-the-clock shifts, the employer may find that some of the employees need night care for children. A hospital may provide a child-care center for its employees through 11:00 P.M. or midnight, when the second shift ends. Children have dinner at the center or in the caregiver's home, and at bedtime they change into their pajamas and sleep on cots. After work, the parents carry their sleepy (and often sleeping) children home to their own beds.

Regardless of the hours of operation, if a full-time program is of good quality, the children will have major amounts of time to participate in constructive play under the guidance of adults who recognize the relationship

In good-quality early childhood education programs, adults are always nearby to support children's activities. (© Elizabeth Crews)

of play and learning. As caregivers or teachers design the curriculum, environment, and adult-child interactions, a guiding principle is provision of many opportunities for children to be appropriately independent.

Child-Care Centers. Children in full-day care may participate in many more activities than might otherwise be available at home, such as cooking and going on field trips. Because the schedules of working parents may limit family opportunities for this type of enrichment, child-care centers assume the responsibility for them. Some children spend fifty hours a week at a center. Therefore, during a full-day program, many of the children's basic needs also are met. These include breakfast, lunch, snack, naptime, outdoor time, and opportunities for playing by oneself in a quiet, well-supervised area. Certainly, the companionship and guidance of a caring, consistent adult is a basic need that good-quality centers meet.

Some full-day child-care programs take the approach that their primary service is to ensure that the child is physically safe. Such programs provide what is often referred to as **custodial care**. This approach is considered inappropriate by early childhood educators, who are aware that children's needs in every area of development (physical, emotional, social, intellectual, and moral) must be met in an integrated way. Kagan (1994) points out that "pedagogically, the early care and education movement is challenging policy makers and consumers to overcome distinctions between care and education, suggesting that there is actually little difference." Koralek, Colker,

ASK YOURSELF

How would I feel about spending ten hours a day with the college students who are in the class you are taking now? What might it be like to be required to stay in the same room with the same teacher all day? What would be my probable reaction if the teacher were in charge of telling me when I could leave my seat, when I could use the restroom, and even when and what I could eat?

. . . .

and Dodge (1993) describe what is expected in quality early childhood programs. They spell out these expectations by explaining what you should see and why. In addition, they include warning signs that you can look for and comments on why certain practices may be occurring. For example, children should be able to choose their own activities for a large block of time instead of sitting and listening to the teacher for long periods. Seeing the latter should be a warning sign, indicating that the program is inappropriate and needs to be improved.

Also inappropriate are programs that require children to move en masse from activity to activity about every fifteen minutes. Art, music, story, sharing, snack, outdoor, and circle time come one right after another without allowing time for children to make choices and to become fully engaged in projects which they initiate. Koralek, Colker, and Dodge's standards for quality early childhood programs are shown in Table 7.1.

A number of full-day programs attempt a compromise. They place emphasis on offering an "educational" program in the morning and custodial care in the afternoon. Staff members who have better preparation for teaching are assigned to morning hours, while those with little or no specific preparation in early childhood education are assigned to provide afternoon custodial care, an unacceptable plan. Some child caregivers are called educarers to denote both roles, educating and providing care.

At some centers, staff members may plan the morning program and then leave the children to their own devices in the afternoon. Although staff are required to be physically present with the children at all times, in this latter type of arrangement they may be more focused on chatting with other adults or sitting back and supervising from the sidelines. Such behavior is unacceptable.

ASK YOURSELF

How does what I read in Chapter 4 about children as sense makers relate to who should be teaching young children? Does my understanding of children as sense makers have an effect on the type of curriculum and schedules children need?

· ·

TABLE 7.1 Standards of Quality

The program is based on an understanding of child development.

The program is individualized to meet the needs of every child.

The physical environment is safe and orderly, and it contains varied and stimulating toys and materials.

Children may select activities and materials that interest them, and they learn by being actively involved.

Parents feel respected and are encouraged to participate in the program.

Staff members have specialized training in early childhood development and education.

A clearly defined curriculum framework guides the daily program of activities.

Source: Adapted from *The what, why, and how of high-quality early childhood education: A guide for on-site supervision* (pp.1–6), by D. G. Koralek, L. J. Colker, and D. T. Dodge, 1993. Washington, DC: NAEYC.

In family childcare, the child is in a homelike situation with a few other children.
(© Bob Daemmrich/ Stock Boston)

Children's need for appropriate programming does not diminish after lunch.

Unfortunately, children may be relegated to watching television or videos on a regular basis, a practice early childhood educators strongly oppose. Because many TV programs and videos designed to appeal to children provide little or nothing to enhance their development, teachers must carefully preview what children are permitted to watch on special occasions. Teachers also must consider what children are missing when they are passively watching what someone else has created. Would it be better to read to a small group or to tell them a story? Could the teacher provide a special art activity or some puzzles or table blocks that are reserved for afternoon play? Children's need for appropriate programming does not diminish after lunch!

Home Care. Many children are cared for in someone else's home. The caregiver is usually referred to as a family daycare provider or **family child-care provider**. (The second term is more descriptive in that it explains what the caregiver actually does rather than when the care is provided.) The caregiver's home is referred to as a family child-care home. Specific, supervised spaces must be provided for the children's use, and, as much as possible, family uses should be separated from caregiving uses. In family childcare, the child is in a homelike situation with a few other children. (Some states permit no more than six children with one caregiver. The caregiver's own children are included in the group size.) Unlike at a center, where the children are usually grouped by age, in a home setting children of various ages play together. In some situations, children may not have a same-age playmate (for example, a caregiver may be serving two infants, two toddlers, and one four-year-old).

CONSTRUCTIONS

1. Research

    a. Find out the licensing and health department rules for sick-child care in your community.

    b. Ask two parents how they manage childcare when their children are sick.

2. Writing

Prepare a paper including the following points:

    a. An explanation of the current sick-child care situation in your community

    b. What you would do if you could improve this situation

    c. Perspectives on sick-child care from the points of view of the child, the parent, the caregiver, and the employer

In family child-care homes, the equipment will not be as extensive as that at child-care centers. At the same time, fewer children share the equipment. Children may have more opportunities to participate in family-style activities, such as preparing their own lunches under the caregiver's guidance.

Some families choose home care because the caregiver lives in their neighborhood or is a relative. Children may, therefore, be able to spend their days in a familiar environment and perhaps play with their neighborhood friends. This is especially important to young school-age children, who form strong friendship groups in school and may form equally strong friendship groups in the neighborhood. Trawick-Smith (1997) points out that during the primary grades, the peer group increases in importance, as do special friendships. At this age, children are less egocentric and more other-centered. Their developing intellectual and social abilities allow them to analyze and choose friends based on traits that appeal to them. Being with friends in a familiar setting may be a better choice for some school-age children than going to an after-school program at a child-care center, where a third peer group (neighborhood, school, and center) is created.

The likelihood of finding evening and weekend care is greater in a home than at a center. When parents' workdays begin very early, or when their hours vary from week to week, the flexibility offered by home-care providers is essential. Because the caregiver is attending to only a very small number of children, she also may be able to accommodate a mildly ill child. This support is crucial

The needs of the child must take precedence in childcare.

to many parents who simply cannot be absent from their jobs. Seriously ill children or children with highly contagious diseases would, of course, not be welcome. The challenge is to meet the needs of the child, the parent, the caregiver, and the employer. But the needs of the child should take precedence.

In some cases, a caregiver comes to the child's home on a regular basis to provide childcare. Unfortunately, many children in such situations are still being cared for by nonprofessionals, some of whom spend most of their time watching TV or chatting on the phone. Certainly, caring "babysitters" do provide childcare, but babysitters are typically pre-teens, teenagers, or adults who have received little, if any, training for their role. Usually babysitters are hired by a parent on an hourly basis. At any rate, their role, while not necessarily unprofessional, is nonprofessional and is beyond the scope of this text.

Sometimes a caregiver lives in the child's home and is employed by the family primarily to take care of the child or children. Such a caregiver is called a **nanny** or an au pair. These terms imply that the caregiver has had specific training for this role and will be able to attend to all the child's developmental needs, rather than simply "filling in" while the parent is away from home. Many au pairs are young women who come to the United States under the auspices of an agency that will place them with a family. Their salaries and duties vary widely, but generally their responsibilities for children are extensive.

Before- and After-School Care. More and more families require before- and after-school care for their children during parents' working hours. These programs are often held at the children's schools or at sites such as the YMCA. During before- and after-school hours, children have supervised opportunities for playing with peers, enjoying a snack, and completing homework—activities that some of you may recall doing at home when you were in the primary grades. In some ways, these programs are similar to the full-day care programs discussed earlier, but well-managed school-age programs allow children more freedom and more opportunities for planning their own activities in keeping with their developmental needs.

When these programs are held in childcare centers, school-age children may share space with preschoolers. In public school settings, these programs may take place in the gym or cafeteria. In both settings, children have limited opportunities for semiprivacy. Furthermore, equipment, materials, and supplies may be limited or inappropriate for an after-school program. Programs in dedicated space can allow children to start projects, and carry activities over from day to day without having to start all over. They may want to decorate the room with posters or their own art.

ASK YOURSELF

What challenges do I think an eighteen- or twenty-year-old woman might face upon coming to the United States and being placed in charge of several children in a home situation? What advantages might the children experience as a result of this type of care?

Well-managed school-age programs provide children with opportunities to develop their own activities.

After-school programs provide a variety of materials for children's use. *(© Elizabeth Crews)*

Preschool Programs

A second category of program is referred to as preschool or prekindergarten. Several decades ago, the term *nursery school* was used more frequently. This type of program for two- to five-year-olds is usually provided on a half-day basis, with children attending for two, three, four, or five days a week from September to June.

The general goal of such a program may be socialization, education, or a well-integrated developmental approach. Usually children attend because their families want them to have opportunities to socialize with peers in a group setting away from home. Other families expect their children to get an early start on their education during prekindergarten. Of course, early childhood educators recognize that preschool-age children have already been learning all their lives. Activities at preschools are similar to those in a good full-day care program except that in preschool, because of the shorter day, children usually do not receive meals or take a nap.

Head Start. One category of preschool programs designed for a particular population is referred to as **Head Start**, a federal program initiated in 1965. Children are admitted to local Head Start programs based primarily on financial need. Federal income criteria are set relative to poverty loads and the number of people in the family. For example, in 1997 a family of four with an income of no more than $16,050 was eligible for Head Start (Administration for Children and Families, 1997).

The program's services include a daily schedule designed to enhance children's social-emotional, cognitive, and physical-motor areas of development. In addition, each child receives free medical, dental, and mental health care, and the family receives needed social services. No fees may be assessed for any services, such as supplies, field trips, or baby-sitting during parent programs.

The goal of Head Start is to bring about a greater degree of social competence.

"The overall goal of the program [Head Start] is to bring about a greater degree of social competence in preschool children from low-income families. Social competence refers to the child's everyday effectiveness in dealing with both his or her present environment and later responsibilities in school and life" (Head Start Program, 1996, p. 57186). Reaching this goal through comprehensive services prepares children for full participation in school by the time they reach kindergarten. "The evidence is convincing that those who attend high-quality Head Start centers are ready when they get there [kindergarten]" (Zigler & Styfco, 1993, p. 17). Since it is obviously difficult for a homeless child or a child with inadequate clothing to succeed in school, Head Start coordinators help families find ways to meet those basic needs. Programs may be available to help parents obtain a **general equivalency diploma (GED)**, which is a high school equivalency program, or even learn to read. Some Head Start agencies offer job skills classes, while others teach homemaking skills such as budgeting, sewing, and shopping for nutritious foods.

The success of Head Start is due in part to ensuring that children enter kindergarten in good health and, as much as possible, with the same kinds of experiences that their classmates have had. Another major factor is the strong role that parents play. Although parents are not required to participate, they receive much encouragement and support from staff, including a parent coordinator whose role is specifically to assist parents. Special training is provided so that parents can develop the skills they need to voice an opinion effectively, to conduct a meeting, and to become comfortable with school personnel. Parents are taught how to advocate for their children now and in the future. Armed with these capabilities, parents are better able to see that their children's needs are met in later schooling situations.

Head Start parents learn how to advocate for their children.

Head Start is by design as much a social services program as an educational one. This federal program has been so well received that some states are beginning to fund additional Head Start programs with state tax dollars. Many communities are working out ways to use various funding sources to ensure that children who are eligible for Head Start programs but need full-day care can obtain funding from other sources for the parts of the day not covered by Head Start. This is sometimes called a **wraparound program**. In all cases, for

ASK YOURSELF

Should all children under kindergarten age be provided with full-day care at taxpayers expense? Why or why not?

· ·

a program to be considered a Head Start program, staff must follow **performance standards**, carefully delineated requirements that are closely monitored by regional and national Head Start staff on a regular basis.

Preschool Special Education. Until relatively recently, few provisions were made for educating children with special needs. When they were in school, all children with special needs were usually grouped together. Through the efforts of parents and other advocates, laws were passed requiring that services be provided to all children. In fact, Head Start standards in the early 1970s mandated that at least 10 percent of the enrollment be filled by children with handicapping conditions.

Although at first teachers may have felt unprepared to work with children with disabilities, many soon realized that collaboration with families, special educators, and other related professionals enabled them to recognize that most children with and without handicaps can be fully integrated. Today's teacher preparation programs are expected to prepare teachers to work with all children. Good teachers recognize that every class has children with a wide range of developmental abilities, learning styles, needs, and interests. These teachers create ways to support a child with a visual impairment or one who uses a wheelchair. In early childhood education, all children should be educated together without regard to ability. In most cases, this means that children with special needs will be included in the regular classroom.

Several laws have been particularly significant in enabling young children to receive the services they need. These include the following:

Laws have been created to allow all children, including those with disabilities, to receive an appropriate education.

▸ Public Law 90-538 (1968; Handicapped Children's Early Education Assistance Act, or HCEEAA). Under this program, federally funded centers developed new models for working with infants and young children with disabilities. Now we refer to this program as the Early Education Program for Children with Disabilities. Note that the revised name emphasizes the children rather than the disabilities. This emphasis affects attitudes and practices. It reminds all of us to think about the whole child first, then adjust for the disability as necessary.

▸ Public Law 94-142 (1975; Education of All Handicapped Children Act). This law guarantees the right to a free public education for all children up to age twenty-one. Incentives were provided to motivate the creation of programs for preschool children with special needs.

▸ Public Law 99-457 (1986; Education of the Handicapped Amendments). Here services for three- to five-year-olds with handicaps are mandated, while services for children younger than three years are encouraged.

▶ Public Law 101-336 (1990; Americans with Disabilities Act, or ADA). This act provided broad protection of equal rights for all people regardless of disability. One major focus is access—that is, the right to participate, as well as the facility to enable that to happen. For example, all people, regardless of handicapping conditions, should be able to get into a building to receive services, and there should be no barriers such as stairs, doors that are difficult or impossible for some people to open, or signs that cannot be read by persons with visual impairments. The law has many facets affecting everyone, not just educational institutions and educators.

States are required to provide free public education for children with disabilities.

Although early childhood education programs have usually welcomed all children, federal legislation has formalized service opportunities and requirements. In some cases, public schools may organize preschool classes specifically for children with disabilities. "Typically developing" children (those without disabilities) also are invited to enroll, allowing the classes to be inclusionary and giving families and children opportunities to know one another and to work together. States are required to provide free public education for children with disabilities, but preschool children who do not have a disability are usually required to pay tuition, since most states do not yet fund preschool education for these children. (A notable exception is the funding provided by some states for Head Start.) Public schools may provide itinerant teachers to work with children with disabilities in private preschools, or they may provide a special education team teacher (Rose & Smith, 1994). In some states, if parents prefer, the staff member will come to the home to work with the family and a very young child.

Each child with a disability must have a written **individualized education plan (IEP)**, or an **individualized family service plan (IFSP)** for children younger than three years and their families. The IEP or IFSP is based on appropriate assessment, followed by a team meeting including the child's family, the early childhood teacher(s), and other professionals who work with the child. Although the IEP is a formal document, it may be revised based on the child's needs. At least annually, each IEP must be formally reviewed by the team, including the family. Specific requirements for IEPs are included in Wolery and Wilbers, 1994.

CONSTRUCTIONS

Research

    a. Find out what the numbers attached to each piece of legislation, such as Public Law 94-142, mean.

    b. Examine a copy of the *Federal Register* and find out what it contains.

c. Investigate the process of creating a law.

d. Ask your Congressional representative or state legislator about any current legislation affecting children and families.

Kindergarten and Primary Education

Kindergarten is widely available in the United States and is typically designed for five-year-olds, although some families prefer to have their children wait until age six to attend. Some states require that children successfully complete kindergarten before entering the primary (first through third) grades.

Primary schooling is universal, compulsory, and available to every child, including those with special needs. You are surely well aware that in the United States, children must attend school beginning at about age six or seven, based on each state's laws.

Programs that meet compulsory schooling requirements are available in both public and private schools. The purpose of these programs is to educate children, and their emphasis is on academics, especially literacy. However, more and more educators recognize that children's needs for social, emotional, physical, and moral development must be integrated with their need to master content and with rich opportunities to advance their thinking. Developing the ability to solve problems, for example, may on the surface appear to be strictly an intellectual activity, but upon reflection you will recognize that all the other aspects of development come into play when children work to solve problems. One type of problem involves child-child interactions. One child may want to play with a particular truck that another child is already using. Instead of grabbing the truck, he can learn, with help from a teacher, to ask for a turn; suggest an activity involving trucks, such as building a garage; or offer to trade another interesting vehicle for the truck. As children develop motor skills, they also encounter problems. Perhaps a child is trying to slide down a pole on the playground. She sees other children doing it, but she can't figure it out. She might watch other children or ask another child to tell her how to do this. She also might keep trying various approaches to moving her body to the pole and letting her arms and legs slide her down. A child who is trying to write a friend's phone number but can't remember how to make the first number, a 5, might look around the classroom and find a calendar. Starting with one, he may count until he reaches five, then use that as a model. Additional information about this topic is found in Chapter 4.

A specialized type of private compulsory education is home schooling. More and more parents are assuming the responsibility for teaching their own children in their own homes. According to the U.S. Department of

Home schooling is a specialized type of compulsory education.

Some child-care centers provide kindergarten programs, but they may not be publicly funded.
(*© Elizabeth Crews*)

Education, 500,000 to 700,000 children are currently being taught at home, and the number is growing. The model is now legal in every state, but all states require performance standards and periodic review of home-schooling activities (Roorbach, 1997).

Table 7.2 lists all the types of early childhood programs we have discussed and organizes them by the type of service offered.

When Dr. K.'s class meets again, the students bring with them reports of interviews they have conducted. Each student has contacted two families to discuss the childcare they have chosen. As class starts, Zenah seems a little depressed. She asks if she can report first.

When a caregiver is sick or school is closed because of bad weather, many parents face a difficult problem.

ZENAH: The people I interviewed have their children in at least two different places a day. One child goes to a neighbor's before school, then the school bus picks him up, and after school the bus takes him to the YMCA for an after-school program. When the neighbor is sick or school is closed because of bad weather, that Mom is really stuck. She can't afford to be off work, and her little boy is too young to stay home alone.

(*Tillie interviewed two parents whose children attend the child-care center where she works.*)

TILLIE: It's easy. The parents drop them off at 7:00, the school bus picks them up at 8:30 and brings them back at 3:30, and the parents pick them

TABLE 7.2 Types of Early Childhood Education Programs

Service Offered	Available Programs
Full-day care	Child-care center Family child-care home Corporate program
Preschool	Church-sponsored program Privately sponsored program Head Start Corporate program Early childhood special education
Before- and after-school care	Child-care center Family child-care home Program in school building or agency
Kindergarten and primary grades	Public school Private school Charter school Home school

up at 5:00. Both of those families have younger kids, and they just stay at our center from 7:00 til 5:00.

DANIELLE: Ten hours in one place! Poor little things. I couldn't stand that.

(Tillie, of course, thinks that her center is a great place to be, and Eric, ever the peacemaker, jumps in and asks Amy what she has found out.)

AMY: One mother I talked with said she had decided not to work till her children went to first grade. So she takes the four-year-old to preschool every morning, and once a week she and her two-year-old go to a play group with three other two-year-olds and their moms. They take turns meeting at each other's houses. But life for the second family is a lot different. That mom could afford only one month off the job when her baby was born, and she doesn't have a car. She and the baby take the bus to a center near the restaurant where she works. She said at the center there are twelve babies in one room and two people to take care of them. She's worried that her baby isn't getting enough attention. She told me that before she went back to work, it took almost all of her time to take care of that one baby.

(Eric interviewed a third-grader's father.)

ERIC: His life is pretty much like when I was in school—the third-grader, I mean. He rides his bike to school every day and rides back home at three o'clock. He and another boy on his street go to the next door neighbor's, have a snack, and then they are back out riding their bikes. The only

Tuition for full-day childcare may cost seven thousand dollars or more annually.

thing they don't like is that they have to go in and do homework at 4:30. It sounds like a pretty good arrangement to me.

(Eric's second interview was with a grandmother who is raising her twin grandchildren.)

ERIC: Their parents are divorced, and their father works about ten hours a day. The grandmother takes them to a local nursery school. She told me that her parents had sent her to nursery school when she was a child, and she still remembers the joy of getting a turn on the big red tricycle—not the little ones. She always wanted the big one. She also told me, "Nursery school is really different now. In fact, they even changed the name to preschool. And the rooms look different from what I remember; they have wall charts and math games. One thing's the same, though. They still have big red tricycles." I tried to write down exactly what she said because she seemed so happy that I was asking her opinion.

ZENAH: Would it be okay to share my journal entry?

(Dr. K. is pleased to have a volunteer.)

ZENAH: *(reading)* I'm not sure I'd be in college today if it hadn't been for Head Start. I still remember Miss Mae. She made sure we had breakfast and lunch at school and that we paid attention at story time. Miss Mae had lots of paper and crayons and scissors for us—things Momma couldn't afford. I think Momma must have liked my Head Start class, too. She came to school a lot to help out.

(Zenah explains that she sends her son, Cory, to Head Start. Since Zenah is in college, she is also eligible for vouchers to help with childcare after Head Start is over for the day.)

ZENAH: Some parents at Cory's school aren't eligible for Head Start or vouchers. I saw the school brochure and found out that the full-day program costs seven thousand dollars per year per child. Imagine! Seven thousand dollars! Head Start has really been great for me and Cory, but when I graduate and get a good job, I'll be able to save for his college And maybe I'll have grandchildren. They won't need Head Start because Cory will have a good job, too.

DANIELLE: Grandchildren! I don't even want to think about it!

(Dr. K. uses this opportunity to turn the group's attention from life's transitions to their next assignment.)

DR. K.: So far I've heard that two of the interviews elicited memories of an adult's early childhood schooling experiences, and Zenah has been thinking about her own experiences. Tonight I'd like you all to work on this construction. *[See the accompanying box.]* And by the way, Zenah mentioned an annual child-care tuition figure of seven thousand dollars. Be thinking about whether that is realistic or way out of line.

CONSTRUCTIONS

Reflection and Journal Entry

Think about your own early childhood education. Record your memories in your journal.

   a. How old were you when you started in an early childhood education program?

   b. Where and when did you participate in this program?

   c. Why did your family enroll you in this particular program?

   d. What was the program like? Can you remember anything about the space? The surroundings? The teacher? The other children?

   e. What were the benefits of the program to you?

FUNDING EARLY CHILDHOOD EDUCATION

Funding in early childhood education is complex and depends in part on government regulations (see Table 7.3). Understanding the basics of early childhood education funding will help you make decisions about your professional role. In the future, you may also be responsible for obtaining funding for a program, or perhaps you will work for an organization that provides funding and be responsible for evaluating the programs that are to receive funds.

Funding Noncompulsory Programs

Understanding the basics of early childhood education funding will help you make decisions about your professional role.

Finding funds for programs for children younger than kindergarten age and for before- and after-school programs is quite challenging. Because these programs are not compulsory, they generally do not receive major portions of their budgets from tax revenues, as primary school programs do. Not-for-profit centers usually receive at least partial funding from tuition paid by parents. Government or other agencies may provide the balance of support, based primarily on client needs, although rarely are all child-care needs met. For example, a center may charge parents tuition on a sliding scale based on the parents' ability to pay, as determined by income and number of family members. The same center may also receive a United Way allocation, foundation support, and funds provided by state block grants. **Block grants** are funds that flow from the federal government to each state, to be used as the state sees fit within limits set by Congress. Public-service nonprofit organizations, such as the YMCA, also fund or operate centers. Other nonprofit corporations sometimes contribute limited

TABLE 7.3 **Funding Sources for Early Childhood Programs**

Service Offered	Taxes	Tuition	Grants
Full-day care	I	yes	NP
Part-day care	I	yes	NP
Before- and after-school	I	yes	NP
Kindergarten and primary grades	yes	Private	NP

I = based on income level or child with special needs;
NP = usually not-for-profit organizations only.

> Even low child-care staff salaries consume a major part of a center's budget.

funds for staff salaries and benefits to help maintain good-quality programs for children at an affordable cost. The net result of this fragmented funding system is that teacher salaries in child-care centers are often quite low. By far the largest item in child-care budgets is personnel. Thus the personnel budget is most seriously affected by limited funds.

As an illustration, let's assume that the Corner Child-Care Center serves 50 children in 4 classrooms for 10 hours a day year round. Each child's tuition is $5,000 ($100 per week, funded partially by Department of Human Services vouchers based on parents' income eligibility). The center's total yearly income is $5,000 × 50 children, or $250,000. Now let's assume that there are 7 full-time staff members, each earning $18,000 per year, or $126,000, and 6 part-time staff members, each earning $9,000 a year, or $54,000. Salaries thus cost $180,000 plus 30 percent for benefits for full-time staff members: $126,000 × .30 = $37,800. So far, the center's income and expenses are as shown in the accompanying box.

**SIMPLIFIED INCOME AND EXPENSE FIGURES
FOR A CHILD-CARE CENTER**

Income
$250,000 (50 children × $5,000 each)

Expenses
$126,000 Full-time staff salaries (7 full-time staff members × $18,000)
  54,000 Part-time staff salaries (6 part-time staff members × $9,000)
  37,800 Benefits ($126,000 × .30)
$217,800 Total

Note that we have not considered any benefits at all for part-time workers, although employers are required to pay half of their Social Security tax and should provide at least some benefits. Furthermore, we haven't included rent or mortgage payments; utilities; equipment and supplies for the classrooms, kitchen, office, and restrooms. Nor have we considered food, licensing fees, or insurance. Look back at the boxed illustration to determine how much money this center has left to provide these items.

Did you subtract the expenses from the income? If you did, you can see that the amount is less than $33,000—for rent, utilities, equipment and supplies, food, licensing, insurance, and so on.

You may be wondering whether seven full-time staff members are needed. Let's assume that the center enrollment looks like this:

  8 infants
10 toddlers
15 three-year-olds
17 four-year-olds
50 children total

The center will need at least two adults in each of the four classrooms (or eight adults). Remember that this is a child-care center. Therefore, it will be

---

RELATIONSHIP OF CHILD-CARE TUITION AND FAMILY INCOME

Jones Family

$14,560 Full-time employee (40 hours a week × 52 weeks at $7 per hour)
$ 5,000 Tuition for one child for one year
$ 9,560 Funds available for taxes, rent, utilities, food, clothing, medical care, transportation, and so on.

Hanover Family

$14,560 Full-time employee (40 hours a week × 52 weeks at $7 per hour)
$10,000 Tuition for two children for one year (2 × $5,000)
$ 4,560 Funds available for taxes, rent, utilities, food, clothing, medical care, transportation, and so on.

Sanders Family

$20,800 Full-time employee (40 hours a week × 52 weeks at $10 per hour)
$ 5,000 Tuition for one child for one year
$15,800 Funds available for taxes, rent, utilities, food, clothing, medical care, transportation, and so on.

A child-care center is a business that requires an effective manager as its leader.

open about ten hours a day. (In an administration class, you will learn how to schedule staff members' hours so that there are enough people to meet children's needs for a good-quality program without costing the center more than would be appropriate.) The center also will need a director, who will probably also serve as secretary/receptionist. Part-time staff members will be needed to do bookkeeping, cooking, cleaning, and maintenance. A center is a business that requires an effective manager as its leader, since no center can continue to serve children and families well with insufficient funds.

One important financial consideration involves the amount parents are able or willing to pay for childcare. The box on page 292 provides a sample of the effect of the hypothetical $5,000 tuition on the incomes of three families after child-care expenses. We will assume that each family has one employed adult and no other adult available to care for the child or children and that no tuition assistance is available.

Another critical financial consideration is the salary schedule to which professional teachers are entitled. Many teachers of children who are kindergarten age and older earn at least $24,300 for a nine-month teaching position, or $2,700 per month. If a preschool teacher earns $2,700 per month for 12 months, that teacher's salary would be $32,400. What effect would this have on tuition? (Note that according to the Web site of the American Federation of Teachers, **www.aft.org/research/reports/salarysv/ss97/index.htm**, the starting salary for primary education teachers nationwide was $22,171 in 1997. With 15 years of experience, teachers in 1997 were earning $34,213.)

Admittedly, this budget discussion has been oversimplified for illustrative purposes. You'll learn about the finer points of child-care center budgeting in an administration course, but this example provides a rudimentary understanding of the reason the personnel budget in a child-care center is seriously affected by limited funds.

ASK YOURSELF

The simplified budget shows full-time teachers earning $18,000 for their work as early childhood educators for twelve months, forty hours per week. Is this a fair salary based on the type of work early childhood educators do? Why or why not? Is this the salary I hope to earn when I complete my education?

CONSTRUCTIONS

1. Research

How does the tuition you are paying for your education compare with the $5,000 tuition figure in our hypothetical situation?

2. Research

In the example described earlier, seven full-time staff members were each to be paid $18,000 annually. What effect would paying all of them $32,400 per year have on the center's budget? What effect would this have on the Jones, Hanover, and Sanders families?

Tax Monies. The most readily available tax monies for preschool are those provided by the federal government for Head Start. Nonetheless, even Head Start programs have a limited amount of money available, and Head Start staff must spend many hours documenting how the funds are used.

Head Start staff must document how funds are used.

Another form of tax support is the voucher system, which provides eligible parents with vouchers to be used as payment at child-care centers and family child-care homes that agree to accept them. Currently, as part of the welfare reform program, some states are providing special child-care vouchers to parents. The welfare reform program was created in 1996 under Public Law 104-193, the Personal Responsibility and Work Opportunity Reconciliation Act. This law was created to move people from welfare to work. One provision of the law involves funding state block grants called Temporary Assistance to Needy Families (TANF).

The vouchers associated with TANF can be used for a child-care center, family child-care provider, or relative of the child. Generally in the past, relatives were not eligible to receive these vouchers, even though they were providing care essential to enable parents to support themselves and their families. Your community may be participating in this new program.

ASK YOURSELF

Should tax monies be used to pay a child-care provider who cares for children of relatives? Why or why not? Should relatives who provide childcare receive the same amount as non-relatives? Is my state participating in this program?

CONSTRUCTIONS

Research

Find out whether your state provides child-care vouchers for TANF recipients. If so, what are the eligibility requirements? Are all the funds being used?

Tuition. For-profit child-care centers, which frequently belong to national or regional chains, obtain funds from tuition paid by parents. Because the owners of the centers are in business to make a profit, these centers do not receive either tax revenues or nonprofit contributions.

An employer may subsidize childcare.

Employer Subsidy. An employer may subsidize childcare in some form, perhaps by providing space for a for-profit organization to conduct a full-day program on the premises. You may be surprised to know that the U.S. Army operates the largest employee-sponsored child-care program in the world (Koralek, Colker, & Dodge, 1993). Other employers offer a menu of benefits, including, as an option, funds for individual employees' child-care payments. A popular option is employer-sponsored resource and referral. In this plan, employees have access, through an on-site consultant or a direct phone line, to information about types of care, availability, costs, and programming. All of these employer-sponsored practices are designed to support parents who work for that employer. The employer benefits in terms of reduced absenteeism and higher staff morale.

Funding Compulsory Education

In colonial America, compulsory education and public funding began in the 1600s. By the early 1800s, state-aided education was available primarily for poor children. Later in that century, each state legislature gave communities permission to create school districts and to tax property to support the schools (Braun & Edwards, 1972). Today property tax funding of public education is hotly debated, since many people see it as leading to a disparity between education provided for rich children and that provided for poor children. This disparity occurs because some districts have valuable property that generates many tax dollars, while other districts to have low property values that generate limited tax monies. Wealthier districts may also be more willing to vote for additional taxes for schools. Verstegen (1994), in an article on reforming school finance, points out that to reach the goal of both "excellence and equity for all children and all schools" (p. 250), radical reform of school finance systems is needed.

Public Schools. Funding for public schools has certain peculiarities. Most of the funding for public schools (and, to a limited extent, private schools) comes from state and local taxes. Also, varying levels of federal support are available for specific purposes. This layered funding system is based historically on the principle of local control of education, which allows voters to have a partial voice in policies and funding. Many citizens and some courts find the system unfair, since wealthy communities and states regularly provide more money for schools than low-income districts or those with a small industrial tax base. Some affluent parent groups are able to raise large amounts of money for playground equipment, computers, library books, and other "extras"—benefits that parents in low-income areas may not be able to provide. Courts in some states have ordered sweeping changes in school funding, on the theory that their constitutions require equal treatment of all children. This phenomenon bears watching—and input—by all persons interested in education. A succinct account of school funding and related issues is provided by Ryan and Cooper (1995).

Private Schools. Funds for primary grades in private schools come from tuition and contributions from alumni, interested citizens, and various sources mentioned earlier. Often private schools sponsor fundraising events

---

Many citizens and some courts find the system of funding schools unfair.

ASK YOURSELF

How are public schools in my area funded? Should school funding in my area be changed? If yes, how? If no, why not?

and expect parents to volunteer as well as contribute money in addition to their tuition payments. Parents are willing to participate for several reasons.

▸ They wish to enhance the quality of their children's education.
▸ They chose a private program seeking certain qualities, such as religious education, smaller classes, or perceived overall quality.
▸ They wish to get to know the staff and become recognized as interested parents.

Although many people regard the practice as controversial, some tax monies are provided to private schools. In most states, legislation has been carefully drafted to cover only ancillary services such as transportation or library resources, thus avoiding constitutional challenges based on government support of private (particularly religious) activities.

A few experimental programs involving vouchers are being tried in various parts of the United States. Parents are offered vouchers to use at any school (public or private) that meets state requirements. Parents can use these vouchers to pay tuition at private schools if they so choose. The idea is controversial, since some families may choose to use the vouchers at schools that teach a particular religion. However, the goal is to give parents choices as to how their children are educated.

Charter Schools. A **charter school** is a school open to all and paid for by tax dollars. However, it differs from other public schools in that it is not managed by government bureaucracies. Rather, a charter school may be managed by a group of parents, an organization, or a for-profit business. The goal is to provide parents with choices in the education of their children and to reinvent public schooling in the United States by creating innovative solutions to public schooling. Yet charter schools are accountable to public authorities for student learning, nondiscrimination, and so forth. In 1991, Minnesota passed the nation's first charter law. By 1998, twenty-eight states had adopted charter laws, and about eight hundred such schools had been created (Manno, Finn, Bierlein, & Vanourek, 1998). Some citizens are concerned about using taxes to support schools that do not receive the same daily oversight as do noncharter public schools. Others feel that this is a fair way to give children and families choices that would otherwise not be affordable.

> One goal of charter schools is to reinvent public schooling through innovative programs.

CONSTRUCTIONS

1. Research

Select a school system or a program for children from birth to age eight. Find out how much the program costs per child per year and its source(s) of funding. (In consideration of school personnel, work out a plan with your classmates so that only one person is assigned to contact each school or program.)

2. Analysis

Compare your findings with those of your classmates. Prepare a graph to show the variations in costs.

3. Synthesis

Draw conclusions from the data.

4. Reflection

How do you feel about the findings from these data? Should changes be made in funding? Why or why not? If you recommend changes, what would they be?

Back in Dr. K.'s classroom, we notice Tillie, Amy, and Zenah at the front of the classroom. They are reporting on their visit to three sites. As you listen in on their presentation to the class, you may want to compare their findings with your own ideas about programs for children.

TILLIE: The first place we visited was a child-care center. We observed the infants and toddlers for a while, and then we had to leave for our interview with Mrs. Whitson, the director and owner. Amy really wanted to stay and play with the babies, but me, I wanted to get out of there! Even though there were two caregivers and eight babies, those women were busy every minute. But still they took time to talk to the babies, even when they were changing diapers and feeding them.

Anyway, when we talked with Mrs. Whitson, she said that it's very difficult to make decisions about staffing, because fewer children would mean either higher tuition or lower salaries. She said that if there was any way they could afford to change to a 3:1 infant:teacher ratio, they would do that. She explained that that would mean each caregiver would have three babies to look after instead of four. But most of their revenue comes from tuition. The parents pay $150 per week. That's over $7,500 a year. What if you had two children? You'd have to be a millionaire!

DR. K.: Well, maybe not a millionaire, but that is a lot of money for most young families. Tillie, what do you think the purpose of this program is? And please tell us what kind of service the center provides.

TILLIE: Mrs. Whitson said that the purpose of the program is to provide good-quality care for infants and toddlers while their parents work. That's why they are open from 6:30 A.M. until 6:00 P.M. So their main

Having fewer children in a child-care center usually means higher tuition or lower salaries.

service is full-day care. They also have programs for parents who want to come and learn more about child development. They also have a preschool in another part of the building.

AMY: Really, I'd call it a child-care center for preschoolers. It's very different from the preschool we visited. The children at the preschool were doing all kinds of fun things—but then I thought those babies and tods were having fun, too. Anyway, the preschoolers had made a bus out of a refrigerator box, and they wanted me to get in and go for a ride. I did! About 11:30, a lot of adults came into the room. I think they were parents or baby sitters. All the children went home, but Marcia, the director, told us that in an hour the afternoon classes would be there. Marcia said their program is sponsored by their church, although not all the children are members of the church. But the preschool doesn't have to pay rent because the church sees the program as part of its mission. The teachers don't teach religion, but the church board does administer the program. I think the program seemed pretty much like our campus lab school. Oh, I almost forgot. Marcia said they are NAEYC accredited, and they are really proud of that. I'll let Zenah describe our third-grade visit.

ZENAH: Preschool to third grade—it was a huge difference. To begin with, the children looked huge to me, but I guess I was comparing them with preschoolers. And they were so smart. You should hear them read. Oh, and one boy had made a pendulum, and he gave an amazing explanation. It's funny—we saw a pendulum in the preschool, and they were having a great time with it. And even the infant crib gym was sort of like a pendulum.

The principal, Mr. Abrams, said the third-grade teacher's most important job is to prepare the children for the fourth-grade proficiency test. I wondered why that was so important, but I thought it would be rude to ask. He said the school is funded with tax money, mostly from property taxes, but some from state income tax. He showed us a very complicated financial formula. Last year they had to eliminate school buses because the voters didn't pass a levy, and now the parents have to drive the children. Mr. Abrams said the school superintendent and the elected board of education are really in charge. I always thought the principal made all the decisions.

DR. K.: We'll have time for one more team to report, and then we'll finish the rest of the reports during the next class. After that, your assignment will be to analyze the information from all the groups.

We hope you'll complete these assignments, too. Check the following box for help with making your visits. We also wonder whether your thinking about the principal's role is similar to the idea Zenah expressed. The next section provides information on how program decisions are made.

TIPS FOR VISITING CHILD-CARE PROGRAMS AND SCHOOLS

To make your visit successful:

▶ Dress appropriately; wear comfortable and conservative clothes. Avoid jeans, shorts, clothing with messages, hats, and anything else that might distract from the learning environment. You will probably be sitting on a child-size chair or even on the floor.

▶ Avoid heavy makeup and jangling jewelry.

▶ Bring a small notebook and pen, but no book bags or other bag (if at all possible).

▶ Arrive a few minutes early and go immediately to the office to check in.

▶ Go to the assigned classroom and follow any instructions the director or principal may have given you. For example, you may be asked to sit in a particular place to observe, or you may be encouraged to participate with the children.

▶ As you depart, quickly and quietly thank the teacher, who will probably be quite busy.

To make your interview successful:

▶ Be prepared with appropriate questions and writing materials.

▶ Adhere to the schedule.

ADMINISTRATION OF EARLY CHILDHOOD EDUCATION PROGRAMS

A board of directors, school board, or individual center owner determines the policies of a school or center.

Technically, a board of directors, school board, or individual center owner determines the policies of a school or center. Procedures for implementing these policies are created by the director or principal or by the central administration of a group of schools or centers. For example, the board may state a policy that all staff members are to be evaluated annually. It is then the director's responsibility to see that procedures for accomplishing this requirement are put in place.

Underlying the decision-making process is the philosophy adopted by those responsible for the school. Whether or not the school's philosophy or theoretical stance has been made explicit, the beliefs of the school's decision-makers to a large degree influence what will be taught; what the expectations for children, staff, and families will be; how the environment will look; and how learners will progress and be assessed.

No matter which type of early childhood program you examine, you'll find that none operates completely independently. Several "external" participants must be involved. These include authorized standard-setting bodies, such as government agencies and funders. Equally important in determining whether a center will remain viable is the availability of appropriate staff. These are the people who will make the day-to-day, minute-by-minute decisions that affect the children directly.

Permission to Operate a Program

A school or center for young children must obtain a license or permit to operate from a public authority. Most states set minimum standards for preschools or child-care centers. Head Start programs and some family child-care home providers also are regulated. The state department of human services or the health department usually oversees the licensing inspections and ensures that rules created by the state for the health and safety of children are followed. Receiving a license to operate does not indicate that the center is of good quality. Consumers are, therefore, responsible for visiting the center, observing the program, and discussing policies with the director. They also must continue to monitor the program in terms of whether it meets their children's needs.

Some states register family child-care home providers, although individuals may care for a small number of children without being licensed. They must, however, follow other requirements set by the government, such as payment of Social Security and other federal, state, and local income taxes. If a family child-care provider has any employees, the appropriate taxes must be withheld and rendered to the taxing body at the required time. Although a family child-care provider may be viewed by a parent as "just a nice person who takes care of my children," each provider is, in fact, a small businessperson and must meet regulations and manage finances according to government requirements. Parents of children in a family child-care home also must monitor the program to ensure that their children receive the care that they need. Fortunately, most center staff members and home providers sincerely attempt to meet children's needs (a challenging job), but government regulation plays a minimal role in ensuring that that occurs.

Each state's department or office of education charters public and private schools. When preschools, child-care centers, and Head Start programs are operated by schools, they are usually authorized and overseen by the same office of education that works with the schools. Since having preschool children in schools is a relatively new practice, administrators and governing bodies are working together to provide appropriate settings for these younger children. For example, sending a preschooler down the hall to a restroom crowded with sixth-grade students is not safe. Expecting

ASK YOURSELF

What are other examples of situations in elementary schools that may be difficult for preschoolers or their teachers? Can I think of other benefits that might not be available at a separate site designed just for preschool?

Administrators and preschool staff are learning to work together to meet the needs of preschoolers and older children.

preschoolers to have lunch at cafeteria tables designed for older children is not comfortable and makes it difficult for small children to manage their meals. Sharing a playground with noisy older children may frighten many preschoolers. By contrast, preschool teachers may be able to take advantage of a well-stocked school library's collection of picture books, and parents may appreciate having their preschoolers in the same building as older siblings. Administrators and preschool staff are learning to work together to support the needs of both preschoolers and older children.

Teacher Qualifications

Preschools. When the department of education regulates preschools, they may require higher standards for teachers than those required by human services agencies. Some education departments, believing that preschool education is at least as important as education for older children, require that preschool teachers have a bachelor's degree and a preschool teaching certificate. Therefore, preschool teachers should be as well qualified as teachers working with older children. When preschool teachers meet the same requirements as other teachers, they expect the same salaries and benefits. Support from a teachers' union may lead to that outcome.

Human services departments, however, have been reluctant to require high standards for teachers. Typically, all preschool regulations are minimal, focusing primarily on basic health and safety. In part, this approach is related to the noncompulsory nature of education for young children. These regulations also reflect the limited tax support for children's education prior to kindergarten. Finally, programs for children under age five are viewed as caregiving rather than educating. Since caregiving is erroneously seen by many as a natural ability of adults, especially women, many people believe that no special preparation is needed. However, one of the most important policy changes recommended by the National Center for Early Development and Learning to improve the quality of child-care is to "find ways to recruit and retain more highly educated and skilled staff (National Center for Early Development and Learning, 1997, p. 3).

Your study of child development will help you understand the importance of going beyond custodial care. Keeping children fed, clean, dry, and warm is important. Helping them to develop intellectually, physically, socially, emotionally, and morally also is essential. Meeting all these needs with a group of children from various backgrounds requires understanding of child development (typical and atypical), parents' roles, cultural differences, early childhood curriculum, and regulations governing programs for

ASK YOURSELF

What are the differences between caring for one's own children and caring for a group of other people's children? How might these differences relate to preparation needed by the teacher or caregiver?

A charter school may be managed by a group of parents.
(© Elizabeth Crews)

children. Expecting someone with no preparation beyond high school to meet all these requirements is unreasonable.

CONSTRUCTIONS

1. Journal Entry

As you continue to develop your understanding of early childhood education, you will learn about the effects of minimal standards on children's development. What do you think they might be? Write your responses in your journal.

2. Research

Use your research skills to find out what professionals in the field have found to be marks of good-quality early childhood education.

Compulsory Schools. In contrast with standards in preschools, the standards most carefully enforced in compulsory schools seem to focus on teacher qualifications. Therefore, a program for four-year-olds will be closely monitored for health and safety, but minimal teacher qualifications, such as a high school diploma, may be required. However, when those children turn five and enter public school kindergarten, they will be taught by a certified teacher. Ironically, less attention may be placed on the condition of the kindergarten and primary school building. Another emphasis is on curriculum standards. In some districts, raises for teachers are based on how well they meet the standards as evidenced by students' scores on standardized tests.

Accrediting Organizations' Influence on Decisions

Accreditation may lead to increased parental interest, enhanced reputation, and attraction of better-qualified staff.

The purpose of accreditation is to demonstrate that the program meets higher than minimum standards and is, by implication, doing a good job. Accreditation may lead to increased parental interest, enhanced reputation, and attraction of better-qualified staff. Whether or not to seek accreditation is usually a choice made by a center or school administration. Some funders may require that a school or center be accredited to continue receiving financial support.

An example of an accrediting body is the National Academy of Early Childhood Programs, a division of NAEYC, which has developed the following process for accrediting programs (National Academy of Early Childhood Programs, 1991).

▶ A comprehensive self-study is completed by the staff.
▶ Results of the study are sent to the academy headquarters.
▶ A trained volunteer validator visits the center for a day or two to record observations of what happens, particularly with regard to staff-child and child-child interactions, to view the program "in action," and to examine record keeping and facilities. The validator's report is shared with the administrator, who is invited to add comments.
▶ The report is sent to academy headquarters.
▶ A panel of qualified volunteers uses all the available data to determine whether a center will be accredited or deferred until improvements can be made.

Some staff members resist the time-consuming, soul-searching process of completing a self-study. The process, to be valuable, must follow certain procedures. For example, when a center staff is considering NAEYC accreditation, NAEYC provides the center with its *Guide to Accreditation* and multiple copies of observation forms and questionnaires. At least the lead teacher and the director (or other appropriate person) observe and evaluate each classroom. The administrator evaluates administrative criteria, and each staff member uses the staff questionnaire to evaluate the program. Parents evaluate the program using the parent questionnaire. Centers also may have staff observe in each other's classrooms or ask parents to evaluate classes based on NAEYC criteria. Once data have been gathered, staff members decide on improvements they would like to make and then make those changes. They then decide whether to seek accreditation. This process usually takes at least several months, and even if accreditation is not sought, participating in the process ultimately benefits the entire staff and its clients.

Obviously a self-study must be accurate and must list weaknesses as well as strengths. Accrediting bodies are not looking for "perfect" programs, but rather for those that are committed to sound goals and objectives and that are making progress in working toward them.

Funders as Decision-Makers

Funders rightfully may expect to support only those programs whose philosophy is compatible with theirs. For example, one funder may want to provide money for a program that emphasizes the development of independent thinking, while another organization may support programs that emphasize teacher authority. In one community, a group of parents who were concerned that their children were not being given opportunities to make choices and to move forward at their own pace funded a school called the New School. They chose the director and made her responsible for employing teachers who would carry out that mission. Several of the parents and their successors served on the board of directors of the school. Other examples include schools organized and supported by various religious groups and their congregations.

Of course, taxpayers are funders. You may be aware of incidents in which taxpayers have become irate when a particular topic was included in (or removed from) a school's curriculum. For example, some families do not want their children to read stories that include witches. Others want children to learn a second language in primary school. Some call for "back to basics"; others feel that the arts are being neglected. Every taxpayer, whether the parent of a public school child or not, has a voice, particularly in voting on school issues such as tax levies and school board membership.

Parents who pay tuition want and deserve an accounting of what they are getting for their dollars. Usually they are quite close to the school situation both emotionally and physically. If they opt to do so, they can keep a close watch on school expenditures.

Government agencies and private foundations that provide grants expect that the funds will be used for agreed-upon purposes and that timely and accurate financial and programmatic reports will be filed. Citizens who pay taxes also want to know how their money is being spent. Any funder can de-

Parents who pay tuition want and deserve an accounting of what they are getting for their dollars.

cide to withdraw support or can refuse to make additional commitments. The link between program philosophy and funding is crucial to the viability of any program. Thus, when funders demand back-to-basics programs or some other change, schools may feel compelled to adjust the curriculum so that they can to continue to receive funds.

Staff as Decision-Makers

All teachers base their teaching on some sort of theory about how children learn. A teacher's theory may be one that she or he can articulate or one that is but a vague idea. Nonetheless, theory forms the basis for practice, and a teacher's theory forms the basis for her decisions regarding the basic curriculum model. Although a school system may have adopted a particular set of goals and standards, the way teachers implement those policies is based on their beliefs about how children learn. These beliefs typically include positions on the following issues:

▸ How children actually acquire knowledge and skills
▸ Ethics, morality, and how they should be manifested
▸ Teachers' roles vis-à-vis parents' roles
▸ Methods of measuring effectiveness

Obviously, a teacher's own background, personal values, education, research, and training will contribute to these beliefs.

In a very real sense, the staff is in charge of the program. Even though funders, government bodies, and agencies have a great amount of influence, what actually happens day to day is based on staff members' decision-making. Teachers, therefore, have a serious responsibility to understand each other's perspectives and philosophies and to work together to create a cohesive program for children and families.

Marcon (1992) studied the effects of three models on preschool children. Her comparison among the three groups indicated that "children in classrooms where teachers held strong beliefs about early education . . . did better on standardized measures of development than children whose teachers were torn between opposing models" (p. 527). Throughout this book, you are encouraged to develop your own clear understandings and beliefs about early education.

The proper balance of individual initiative and teamwork is essential.

When sufficient numbers of well-trained staff are available, and when they assume serious responsibility for fulfilling their roles, the program is likely to be effective. Naturally, administrative staff oversee program operations, but all staff members at all levels make major contributions to program management. When there are too few staff members or when staff members fail to work productively, low morale often results, a condition that can quickly decrease the effectiveness of the rest of the staff. The proper balance of individual initiative and teamwork should be the objective.

Decision-Making Based on Constructivist Theory

Despite the challenges to centers, schools, and teachers as they strive to create and maintain a cohesive philosophical approach, many centers succeed in providing effective early childhood education. In the most effective situations, the theoretical approach is described, and the staff is then employed to implement programs that flow from that theory. Since you are being encouraged to reflect on and develop an understanding of constructivist theory because of its scientific validity, you will probably find yourself most comfortable in schools that espouse teaching practices growing from that theory. A similar statement could readily be made for students who study Maria Montessori's ideas or those of the behaviorists. However, it is not our purpose in this book to discuss contrasting theories. Quite clearly, we subscribe to constructivist theory as the basis for sound educational practice, and therefore that theory forms the foundation of what we write and do.

Earlier in this chapter, you read about the many types of programs for children. Any program (childcare, primary grades, after-school care) can be based on any theory. Thus you will find constructivist primary grade classes, Head Start programs, and preschools, but you will also encounter programs that follow other theories about how children learn.

SUMMARY

- Noncompulsory programs included in early childhood education are childcare, preschool, Head Start, before- and after-school care, and kindergarten. Compulsory programs include public and private primary grade classes and, in some states, kindergarten.
- Funding for early childhood education programs comes from many sources, including taxes, tuition, and grants.
- A free public education must be provided for all children with disabilities who are at least three years old.
- The largest expense in every education budget is salaries.
- Government agencies regulate all educational programs.
- Programs may demonstrate better-than-minimum standards by participating in accreditation programs.
- The decision-making individual or body of an educational program is determined by the type of educational organization and by its funding.

CONSTRUCTIONS

1. Research
Form a group with one or two classmates and visit three children's programs, one serving infants and toddlers, one serving preschoolers, and one serving kindergarten and primary grade children. Your instructor may assign you to specific sites and times, or you may need to schedule your own appointments. Ask to spend at least a half hour observing in a classroom and to meet with someone who can provide information about the program. (See the box on page 299 for tips on visiting programs.)

2. Analysis
Consider what you observed. What do you think the teacher's goals were? How did she seem to be achieving those goals? Did you get an idea of her beliefs about how children learn? What do you think those beliefs are?

3. Reflection
Think about what the children were doing, such as painting, building with blocks, or reading. Reflect on what purposes these activities may have served for the children.

4. Writing
Prepare a report comparing and contrasting the three programs you visited. Consider population served, type of service available, source of funding, person or group responsible for administering the program, and other pertinent information gleaned from your interviews and observations.

5. Analysis
If your class has completed the same research on funding that Dr. K.'s class worked on, analyze the data your class produced. Were there similarities and differences among the groups' results? Were there similarities and differences across populations served? What do you think contributed to the results you obtained?

Note: When you report your data, keep in mind that you have surveyed only a few of the programs in your area. The results might be different if you were able to survey the entire United States. What would you predict the results would be if you compared U.S. programs with those in other countries?

6. Writing
Prepare a report on your analysis of the class findings. After your instructor reviews your report, you may want to place it in your portfolio.

7. Research
Read NAEYC's *Position Statement on Quality, Compensation, and Affordability, Revised 1995.* What can you do to help reach the three basic needs described in this document?

8. Journal Entry

Now that you have read about, visited, and heard about a variety of programs in early childhood education, reflect on which type of program seems most interesting to you in terms of your role in the profession. Has your thinking on this topic changed since you began this course? If so, what has led to the change?

RESOURCES

Arce, E-V. (1997). *Perspectives: Early childhood education.* Boulder, CO: Coursewise.

A reader that provides up-to-date information on early childhood education. Suggested Internet links are a valuable resource.

Bredekamp, S., & Willer, B. (Eds.). (1996). *NAEYC accreditation: A decade of learning and the years ahead.* Washington, DC: NAEYC.

This volume offers a collection of articles on accreditation, with an emphasis on reaching the goal of high-quality early childhood education.

Carver, J. (1997). *Boards that make a difference: A new design for leadership in nonprofit and public organizations* (2nd ed.). San Francisco: Jossey-Bass.

Provides a clear account of the principles and concepts of the Policy Governance model.

Lambert, L., Walker, D., Zimmerman, D. P., Cooper, J. F., Lambert, M. D., Gardner, M. E., & Slack, P. J. F. (1995). *The constructivist leader.* New York: Teachers College Press.

Adults employing a constructivist model need leaders who themselves are constructivists. Lambert et al. provide a wealth of information about such a leader's role.

Maternal and Child Health Bureau. (1992). *National health and safety performance standards: Guidelines for out-of-home child care programs.* Arlington, VA: National Center for Education in Maternal and Child Health.

A joint collaborative project of the American Public Health Association and the American Academy of Pediatrics, this book, available in loose-leaf format, contains detailed standards and rationales for each guideline. It encompasses every aspect of childcare, including program.

Mitchell, A., Stoney, L., & Dichter, H. (1997). *Financing child care in the United States: An illustrative catalog of current strategies.* The Ewing Marion Kauffman Foundation and the Pew Charitable Trusts.

The authors have gathered data on a wide range of strategies for financing childcare. They include programs related to government, business, and public-private partnerships.

National Education Goals Panel. (1996). *National education goals report: Building a nation of learners*. Washington, DC: U.S. Government Printing Office.

One of a series of annual reports on progress toward meeting the national educational goals. This sixth report emphasizes standards and assessment.

Sciarra, D. J., & Dorsey, A. G. (1999). *Developing and administering a child care center* (4th ed.). Albany, NY: Delmar.

A guide to administration of early childhood programs that emphasizes both program and people management.

Willer, B. (Ed.). (1990). *Reaching the full cost of quality in early childhood programs*. Washington, DC: NAEYC.

The dual meaning of *full cost* is described as including both the finances involved in providing high-quality childcare and the social cost incurred when that quality is not provided.

8

Creating Curriculum in Field Experiences

· ·

First Day of School

Today is the first day of school
I think it's going to be really cool,
With a teacher and classmates
And desks and chalkbords too,
I hope when I'll get to see you!
We will do reading and writing,
And centers with fun
I hope we will do everything
before the day is done,
I'll find somone to play with
And somone to see,
I hope they will do the
same with me! "Oh, boy" hear
I go, And I hope I get
first row!

By Brittany Moser, age 8½
Aspechilly To: Mrs. Pezzullo
One of my favorit teachers!

In Chapter 3, you were introduced to a variety of early childhood programs. In Chapter 7, you learned about how early childhood programs vary and are funded. By now you are probably aware of the great variety of programs for young children. This chapter focuses on the curriculum that exists in early childhood programs. You will follow our students into their various field placement sites, where they attempt to understand children's understanding of curriculum. Examples of curriculum are presented from a constructivist perspective of what curriculum means to children. This chapter will help you develop a deeper understanding of the following:

▶ The traditional view of curriculum as content
▶ Curriculum defined by the early childhood profession
▶ The constructivist view of curriculum as child sense making
▶ How constructivist curriculum is defined through children's choices, sense making, play, need to know, and interests.

INTRODUCTION

Dr. K. and the class members have invited the principal of a K–5 elementary school, Mrs. Shirley Lewis, to speak with them. The class is interviewing Mrs. Lewis about **field placement sites,** real early childhood classrooms where students are placed for extended periods of time to observe, participate, and get to know what it is like to be an early childhood teacher.

ZENAH: Mrs. Lewis, what is your job like? What do you do?

MRS. LEWIS: I do a lot of nuts-and-bolts kinds of things: playground duty, noon duty, lunchroom duty. One afternoon a week, I teach in a classroom to give teachers some planning time and keep my skills polished. I don't think people realize all the things a principal does: manage the office, put on Band-Aids, pass out bags of ice, call parents. The job description goes on and on. But it's something that I wake up every morning and look forward to.

AMY: What is a typical day like at your school?

MRS. LEWIS: *(Laughing.)* I don't think there is a typical day! Usually my day starts between 7:30 and 8:00. I go to the cafeteria and supervise free breakfast and make sure everybody gets to their classrooms and the day starts on a positive note. I also supervise lunchtime and generally make sure things are running as smoothly as they can. I'm usually open to students, teachers, and parents during the day.

ERIC: What is your view of curriculum?

MRS. LEWIS: I think what excites me the most are changes taking place in the curriculum. The research on how children learn is just fascinating—the thought process and critical thinking skills. I think we sometimes underestimate the potential of young learners. It's amazing what they know and how they can apply it. For example, we have several teachers who are implementing curriculum based on projects that emerge from children's interests. Others are integrating art across all areas of the curriculum, including social studies and science. Dr. Constance Kamii has consulted at our school. As a result, many teachers are using more games in mathematics and focusing more on children's sharing their strategies for solving problems and less on getting the correct answers.

TILLIE: What advice would you give us as we go to our field placements?

MRS. LEWIS: Don't have any preconceived notions about what a typical young child looks like or does or how that child behaves. Be open and receptive to all children's backgrounds, and be sensitive to them. Being a good listener is critical. Young children are so open and say what they feel. Sometimes we have to interpret that, but we should always listen and not blow off anything that's said. Nurturing—I think that is critical. We take for granted that young children are loved. But that's not always the case, or they don't always feel like they are. You have to look at each child individually. That's hard to do! The more we don't have any preconceived notions about where a child should be or needs to be, the better off we are.

DANIELLE: I know we're a long way from it, but what do you look for in teachers you hire?

MRS. LEWIS: Enthusiasm, willingness to grow, common sense, ability to apply not just their educational experiences but their life experiences to what they do in a classroom, and, of course, a sense of humor!

ASK YOURSELF

What do I want to know about early childhood curriculum?

WHAT IS CURRICULUM?

Traditional curriculum focuses on subject matter.

What do you think of when you hear the word *curriculum*? Do you think of a course of study, a set of specific courses, content areas, objectives, and competencies, or a written document? A common definition of **curriculum** is all the learning experiences for which the school takes responsibility. Some people claim that teachers are curriculum makers. Others say that curriculum comes from children. The traditional view of curriculum as subject matter relegates the child to the role of curriculum consumer, one who takes in what others have produced. The notion of curriculum as subject matter implies that what is worth knowing exists outside the child. The child consumes or internalizes that subject matter, and as a result the child will know what others know.

In this chapter, we present the view of curriculum as the sense a child makes of classroom experiences. Curriculum viewed this way becomes the child's meaning or understanding of the world and how it works. This understanding is derived from an active process of knowledge construction from the inside. The child actively seeks to understand the world better by putting things into relationships. When a child relates one thing to another (such as four legs and a tail mean dog) knowledge grows, resulting in greater understanding.

Curriculum as sense making means that children are actively engaged in the process of deciding their own learning objectives as well as how they will go about learning. In essence, the only objectives a child ever achieves are the ones he has chosen. What a child chooses to think about and relate to becomes the curriculum for that child. That's not to say that the teacher has no role in curriculum. To the contrary! The teacher plays an important role in planning meaningful learning experiences for the group as well as for individuals within the group. Such planning requires that teachers know both relevant content, such as mathematical relationships, and children—who they are and how they learn.

Constructivist curriculum focuses on sense making.

Teachers can support a child's construction of knowledge by attempting to understand the child's understanding. This can be done through careful listening and observing of the child's activities and asking just the right question at the right time to help the child make new connections to what she already knows. Teachers can create just the right settings for children to ask and answer their own questions. Teachers can create discrepant events that call for transforming previous ideas, and support children's knowledge construction in resolving discrepancies. In addition, teachers can reduce their adult authority and encourage child autonomy through giving choices and providing opportunities for children to make decisions. Teachers can encourage children to live cooperatively in a classroom community, having opportunities to share experiences and viewpoints on issues that are important to them. Through sharing perspectives, children learn to appreciate others' points of view. They are encouraged to clarify their own thinking when presenting their ideas to others. Curriculum involves constructing ideas about classroom community and what it means to be a contributing member to that community.

This chapter focuses on communities of children as well as communities of adults learning to work with children. As you enter each community, consider what curriculum means. Is it established in advance by the teacher? Does it emerge from children's interests? Does it result from negotiating between teacher and children? What does it mean to be a curriculum decision-maker?

As you learned in Chapter 2, early childhood professional organizations, such as NAEYC, provide information and guidelines to educators. During

> ### NAEYC's Definition of Curriculum
>
> Curriculum is an organized framework that delineates the content that children are to learn, the processes through which children achieve the identified curricular goals, what teachers do to help children achieve these goals, and the context in which teaching and learning occur. The early childhood profession defines curriculum in its broadest sense, encompassing prevailing theories, approaches, and models (Bredekamp & Rosegrant, 1992, p. 10).

Professional organizations have developed curriculum standards.

the past ten years, professional organizations have developed and adopted standards for practice. These professional standards address curriculum and assessments. The professional organizations mentioned in Chapter 2, such as NAEYC, ACEI, and Southern Early Childhood Education (SECA), have developed curriculum standards calling for developmentally and culturally appropriate practice in early childhood education. In addition to these groups, professional organizations representing content areas have also developed curriculum standards that impact early childhood education. Some of the most well-known content area standards come from the National Council of Teachers of Mathematics (NCTM) and the International Reading Association (IRA). Professional standards provide guidelines for curriculum planning, implementation, and assessment. Curriculum standards that have had the greatest impact on the field of early childhood education are the NAEYC guidelines for developmentally and culturally appropriate practice. These guidelines are mentioned throughout this book and represent a consensus view derived by early childhood professionals. The following box gives an overview of these guidelines. You may want to find and read the document of the NAEYC guidelines for a more comprehensive view of these guidelines for curriculum.

> ### NAEYC Curriculum Guidelines
>
> Developmentally appropriate practice results from the process of professionals making decisions about the well-being and education of children based on at least three important kinds of information or knowledge:
>
> 1. what is known about child development and learning: knowledge of age-related human characteristics that permits general predictions within an age range about what activities, materials, interactions, or experiences will be safe, healthy, interesting, achievable, and also challenging to children;

Curriculum includes developmentally appropriate practice.

2. what is known about the strengths, interests, and needs of each individual child in the group to be able to adapt for and be responsive to inevitable individual variation; and

3. knowledge of the social and cultural contexts in which children live to ensure that learning experiences are meaningful, relevant, and respectful for the participating children and their families.

Source: From *Developmentally appropriate practice in early childhood programs* (Rev. ed.), p.36, edited by Sue Bredekamp and Carol Copple, 1997. Washington, DC: NAEYC.

CONSTRUCTIONS

1. Research

Find an early childhood professional magazine or journal such as *Young Children* (at the library, in a teacher resource room, on the Internet, or from a friend) that contains an article on developmentally appropriate practice. Read and write a brief summary of the main points the author makes about developmentally appropriate practice. Record your summary, including bibliographic information, on an index card, in a computer file, or in a professional resource file for future reference.

2. Analyze

Obtain a copy of the NAEYC developmentally appropriate practice guidelines from the library, a teacher, or a friend. Select an age group, such as ages three through five, and read the guidelines for that age group. Analyze the major points made in the document for planning curriculum for this age group. Report your results to classmates.

FIELD EXPERIENCES

A desire to work with young children may come from previous experiences working with children, baby-sitting, or having children of your own. Early childhood programs provide *field experiences*, sometimes called *practica* or *internships*, in secure settings in which students can learn to plan for and interact with children in appropriate ways under the close supervision of experienced teachers called **cooperating, supervising, mentoring, head,**

Children benefit from making choices among available opportunities. *(© Elizabeth Crews)*

Student teachers, co-operating teachers, and university supervisors collaborate in field experiences.

or lead teachers. Connection to the student's teacher education program usually occurs through the **college or university supervisor,** who visits students in field placements and assists them and their cooperating teachers with the successful completion of the field experience.

Field experiences in early childhood classrooms are meant to be learning experiences in which students formulate, try out, and revise their theories of teaching young children. Using the strategies described in Chapter 1 (for example, observing, questioning, and reflecting) in your communications with your cooperating and supervising teachers should help you to expand your knowledge of what it means to teach young children. We, the authors of this book, began as students, made mistakes, had successful experiences, and reformulated our theories of teaching. Today we continue to construct knowledge of what it means to teach children and those preparing to teach children. Learning really is a lifelong process!

We will rejoin the students as they enter their field experiences in real classroom settings. Each student has been placed in a different classroom with children of different ages. To get them started, the district-level early childhood director, Dr. Kay Grant, meets with all the students in a group to introduce them to the community and to the various programs where they will be working for a few months.

MULTIPLE PERSPECTIVES

From the Field

Dr. Kay Grant is director of early childhood education in the Muskogee, Oklahoma, public schools.

Welcome to the early childhood programs in Muskogee! I am very pleased that you have chosen to do your field experiences here. We offer a variety of early childhood programs, including multiage preschool, Head Start, Even Start, four-year-old programs, kindergarten, and before- and after-school care. I think we have some of the best and most talented teachers around. I can assure you they are all looking forward to working with you. I would like to mention a couple of points before you enter your classrooms.

For my first point, I will use the analogy of teaching as offering children good nutrition. Children can subsist on Twinkies and Fruit Loops, but do those things maximize growth and potential? No. Children make sense of their world by connecting what they know to what they don't know and constructing various incorrect associations and explanations along the way. To do that, they need real things and genuine experiences.

Good, bad, or ugly, children's home environments are real, and we have got to provide the bridge for them to connect those experiences to school and, more importantly, for them to see some relation between what we do in school to the world around them. So a crudely written invitation to come visit the classroom may be more meaningful than perfectly copying the spelling words off the board. Ask a kindergartner what they want to learn, and they will tell you to tie their shoes and blow a bubble with bubble gum or maybe to whistle. Those are the real things that have value and use in their world. Exposing children to books that have wonderful stories or information about something they are interested in, as well as encouraging them to express thoughts, feelings, and emotions in writing, helps them to see how those things might be useful in their world, too.

Confidentiality of information gained in field experiences is a sign of professional ethics.

For my second point, I will mention that professional ethics is very important and should never be taken for granted. Set the tone early so that you do not "trash talk" your students, their families, or your coworkers in or out of the workplace. You will lose out on a few juicy pieces of gossip from the lounge lizards, but it will be worth it. Parents will come to respect that if they talk to you about a concern, it will not be shared in the lounge at break. Fellow teachers and your administrator will view you as a professional. There is a big difference between being friendly and a part of the team and participating in unprofessional behavior. Besides being unprofessional, it is also highly illegal.

Seek out those with whom you can share your successes and get advice about your concerns. Include your administrator in the circle periodically. Sharing a success on one day makes asking for help the next much easier. Treat the cooks, secretaries, bus drivers, and custodians as your partners in education. Again, extend that mutual respect. Treat them as you would like to be treated, and you will be modeling for students as well as improving your school's climate and raising everyone's performance a notch. Maybe have your students send a note of thanks or recognition to the favorite friendly food service worker who starts everyone's day with a smile or the bus driver who waited patiently for the child to retrieve the papers he dropped. Learn to look for the positive, to observe, to listen, and not to be afraid to ask questions when you don't understand. Be a model for how to deal with frustration and creatively solve problems. It is what we hope for our students, but how can they do it if they have never seen it done?

I hope you all have some wonderful learning experiences in our classrooms.

• •

Following Dr. Grant's welcome, the students are to go to their individual classroom assignments.

TILLIE: Where do we go now?

AMY: I think she said we can go to our classrooms. Let's meet on Friday afternoon and compare notes.

DANIELLE: I just hope I can remember all the things our instructor told us to look for. What's a lounge lizard?

ERIC: Something we're not supposed to be. See you later!

In the remainder of this chapter, we will introduce various aspects of curriculum within the contexts of programs for young children in which our students find themselves placed for field experiences.

Children's Choices

Zenah has been placed in a classroom for two- and three-year-old children. For the past two weeks, she has been observing and assisting her cooperating teacher, Ms. Brown, who functions as a lead teacher. Zenah has noticed that each day in this classroom, children have many choices of activities. They can choose to build with blocks, explore materials at the water table, engage in dramatic play with props such as clothing and dolls, play with Play-Doh, or do other activities the teacher and her assistant have planned. Zenah has observed that the teachers do not *make* the children do any of the activities, but rather encourage them by inviting their interest and playing with them on the floor. Zenah has been wondering whether so much choice is good for children. She recalls her own childhood experiences in which her mother and other adults told her what she could and couldn't do or play with. Zenah has wondered how children will know what is appropriate for them to do if adults don't tell them. She is concerned that children who are allowed to choose might choose the wrong thing to do or do nothing at all.

Ms. Brown has asked Zenah to take a group of five children to the library to choose books to bring back to their classroom. The children are excited about getting books and head straight for the picture book section. Let's join Zenah and the children as they make their book selections.

MARK: *Caps for Sale! Caps for Sale!* Teacher, *Caps for Sale!*

ZENAH: It looks like you found a book you like, Mark.

MARK: Read, teacher, read!

ZENAH: Let's read it back in our room. Can you help Rachel find a book?

(Zenah watches as Chris moves from the picture book section to the next set of shelves containing books with more words.)

ZENAH: Chris, come back here and pick one of these books. Those books are too hard for you!

(Chris persists until he pulls one of the more difficult books off the shelf. The book he has selected is much smaller than the picture books and has pages loaded with small print.)

CHRIS: Dis one. Want dis one.

ZENAH: Chris, I found a good book for you. Look at this one. It's called *Where's Spot?*

CHRIS: Want dis one. Want dis book.

ZENAH: You won't like that one, Chris. It has too many words. Let's take the Spot book.

CHRIS: No! Want dis one!

(Zenah reluctantly agrees to allow Chris to take the book he has selected, even though she thinks he is making a mistake. She helps the other children with their selections and takes the Spot book as a backup for Chris.)

That afternoon, after the children have gone for the day, Zenah describes the library trip to Ms. Brown.

ZENAH: I tried to tell Chris the book he wanted was too hard for him, but he wouldn't listen to me. He insisted on choosing a book with too many words.

MS. BROWN: That's okay, Zenah. It's more important for him to be able to choose the book he wants, even if it is too difficult. Young children often choose books for reasons that don't occur to us. He may have chosen it for its smell or color. My guess is he chose it because of its small size. The smallness is a novelty to him, and he likes being able to hold the whole thing in his hands. I read the book to him today and noticed how much he enjoyed holding it and turning it around in his hands. He wasn't all

Children construct knowledge in play.
(© Elizabeth Crews)

Children need choices to learn.

that interested in the story, but I did notice he carried it around with him for quite a while.

ZENAH: I never thought that children choose books for such different reasons. I've noticed that children have a lot of choice in your room. Do you think all children can handle that much choice? Some children seem overwhelmed and don't know what to choose. Don't we need to tell them sometimes?

MS. BROWN: I'm glad you noticed that children do have many choices in my room, because I think children learn to make good choices by having opportunities to choose. If we always tell them, they will grow to depend on us and won't learn to make their own decisions. But if you notice a child who seems overwhelmed by the choices, it is okay to guide that child. You could give the child a choice between two or three things. Or you could invite the child to do an activity with you. Then, when it's time to move on, encourage the child to choose the next activity. Once children learn that the activities will be available tomorrow, they tend to relax with the choices. I try to always include some of their favorite activities, such as the water table, each day if possible.

When you get here tomorrow, why don't you discuss with Chris the book he chose and try to understand why he chose that book? Understanding how children make choices helps us learn their interests and individual personalities. We can make better curriculum planning decisions when we know the individual interests of children.

The next day, Zenah speaks with Chris about his book choice.

ZENAH: Chris, I can tell you really like this book from the library. Can you tell me what you like about it?

CHRIS: I like it! Big brother has little books!

ZENAH: So your big brother has little books like this one?

CHRIS: Yeah. He reads me. He's BIG BROTHER!

ZENAH: You like your big brother to read little books to you!

CHRIS: Yeah!

CONSTRUCTIONS

Journal Entry

Write a brief journal entry in which you describe what might have happened if Zenah had not allowed Chris to choose his own book. In what ways might his future choices be affected?

ASK YOURSELF

What choices did I make today? How would I feel if someone made those choices for me and expected me to like them? What do I think Zenah learned about Chris and how he makes choices? In what ways will this knowledge help Zenah in planning activities in this classroom? Can I think of an activity I could plan based on what I know about Chris's interests?

CHOICES ARE IMPORTANT

Why Choice?

We are most likely to become enthusiastic about what we are doing—and all else being equal, to do it well—when we are free to make decisions about the way we carry out a task. (Kohn, 1993a, p. 192)

The responsibility to choose does not have to be thought of as turned over to students **or** kept by the teacher: some choices can be negotiated together. The emphasis here is on shared responsibility for deciding what gets learned and how the learning takes place. That negotiation can become a lesson in itself—an opportunity to make arguments, solve problems, anticipate consequences, and take other people's needs into account—as well as a powerful contribution to motivation. (Kohn, 1993a, p. 224)

From *Punished by Rewards* by Alfie Kohn, 1993, New York: Houghton Mifflin.

We cannot expect children to accept ready-made values and truths all the way through school, and then suddenly make choices in adulthood. Likewise, we cannot expect them to be manipulated with reward and punishment in school, and to have the courage of a Martin Luther King in adulthood. (Kamii, 1991, p. 387)

From "Toward autonomy: The importance of critical thinking and choice making" by C. Kamii, 1991, *School Psychology Review, 20* (3).

Children learn to make good choices by having choices.

Benefits of Choice

▸ Positive effects on general well-being, physical health, and survival
▸ Increased emotional adjustment
▸ Greater feeling of academic competence
▸ Increased responsible participation and self-regulation
▸ More enthusiasm for learning, resulting in greater academic success
▸ Creativity is enhanced
▸ Higher levels of reasoning and problem solving
▸ Increased respect
▸ Greater initiative and independence
▸ Democracy is learned through living it

Giving Choices

▸ Movement around the classroom
▸ Choice in materials, centers, activities, and playmates
▸ Choice of what to learn, why to learn, how to learn, and where to learn
▸ Choice of whether and how to share work products
▸ Choice of what and how to assess progress

From "Choices for children: Why and how to let students decide," by A. Kohn (1993, September), *Phi Delta Kappan, 75* (1).

Making Sense

Tillie has been placed in a classroom of four-year-olds, even though she wanted to be with older children. Tillie grudgingly agreed to work with this group. She wasn't quite prepared for the high level of physical activity and noise she found in the classroom. She has found it difficult not to reprimand these children for being too noisy and impolite.

Mrs. Conway, the teacher, has encouraged Tillie to interact more with the children. She asked Tillie to lead the daily morning group time. Tillie was afraid at first but gradually has grown to look forward to the experience. During one morning group time, while Tillie is leading the children in a discussion of the weather, an unexpected event occurs. A name card from the helper chart, situated behind Tillie and in front of the children, falls to the floor. Without pausing, Tillie picks it up and reattaches it to the chart while continuing the discussion. The card falls off again, and Tillie reattaches it

Group times provide opportunities for shared experiences.
(© Elizabeth Crews)

again. The third time it falls, Tillie decides to use the event as a **teachable moment,** an opportunity for teaching and learning about a spontaneous event.

TILLIE: Let's see if we can figure out why the card won't stay on the chart. Does anyone have any ideas?

LISA: Teacher! Teacher! I know!

TILLIE: Tell us, Lisa.

LISA: It's because the red chart doesn't like the blue nametag!

TILLIE: Does anyone else have an idea? Mitchell?

MITCHELL: I don't know.

TILLIE: Does anyone think they might know why? Jennifer?

JENNIFER: Is it because the tape isn't sticky?

TILLIE: It might be, except there isn't any tape on the card. What might be another idea? Lisa, you seem eager to share again.

LISA: *(Speaks forcefully in a very loud voice this time, almost yelling to make her point.)* IT'S BECAUSE THE RED CHART DOESN'T LIKE THE BLUE NAMETAG!

TILLIE: *(Looking exasperated and ready to move on.)* No, Lisa. It's because the card is too heavy for the chart and because gravity pulls it down!

Later that day at lunch, Tillie remarks to Mrs. Conway that some of the children must have poor family lives, because they like to mouth off to adults. She asks Mrs. Conway what to do when this happens.

MRS. CONWAY: I'm not exactly sure what you mean, Tillie. I noticed during group this morning that you seemed a bit frustrated by Lisa's comments. She was waving her arm like crazy to get your attention, and when she finally did, she restated her idea in such a loud voice perhaps because she thought you didn't hear her the first time.

TILLIE: That's just what I mean! Lisa was mouthing off and acting silly to distract the group. What should I do about that?

MRS. CONWAY: Are you sure she was mouthing off? The impression I had was that she was very eager to share her idea with you, and when you ignored her, she became even more determined to get your attention. Another interpretation of what happened is that she is thinking about the problem and is eager to share her ideas with the group. Her response about the chart not liking the name card might have more to do with her current level of understanding of physical objects than it does with being disrespectful. If you ignore, reject, or correct a child's thinking, they may stop thinking and be reluctant to discuss ideas with others. I'm taking a graduate course this semester on Piaget's research on children's thinking. Lisa's comment just might be an example of what Piaget called animistic thinking, when young children attribute human characteristics and intentions to inanimate objects. I can give you some reading about this.

Meanwhile, you might want to think more about children's thinking in terms of their level of understanding. When children are at different levels, group time is a great opportunity for them to share and listen to different perspectives. Considering a problem from a variety of perspectives helps children learn that their perspective isn't the only one. This perspective sharing helps them rethink the problem and create solutions they wouldn't have thought of otherwise. During group time tomorrow, why don't you think about children's thinking by listening carefully to their comments? You can ask them to clarify their ideas or ask whether everyone agrees. Then let's talk about your interpretations of their thinking.

Children show they are thinking in what they say and do.

You may recall from Chapter 4 that young children construct knowledge based on what they already know about object relationships. In constructing causality relationships, young children move from thinking they cause events to happen to realizing that other things, such as objects or people outside themselves, may cause things to happen. In addition, they often attribute human intentions to objects, such as thinking that the moon follows them as they move from one place to another (Piaget, 1932/1965). When children think, even though their thinking does not yet reflect adult causality, it shows they are actively making relationships. Children's thinking at any point in time may be misconstrued by adults who view it as cute or, even worse, as misbehavior.

CONSTRUCTIONS

ASK YOURSELF

Analyze these comments from four-year-olds, which may seem cute or odd to adult ears. What does each comment imply about the child's thinking? What would my adult response be to each comment?

"My foots hurt."

"I brang my bear."

"She thinked it in her head."

"The moon is following me."

"If you break the cookie in two pieces, you have twice as much."

"You want it, but I want it badder."

1. Research

Interview a toddler teacher, a kindergarten teacher, and a second-grade teacher. Ask each one for guidelines they use to plan curriculum. Share your findings with other students.

2. Research

Individually interview three children ages three, four, and five. Sit across the table from each child during the interview. Show the child a piece of paper with a picture of a clown on one side and an elephant on the other side. Hold the paper in the middle of the table so that the picture of the elephant faces you. Ask the child to tell you what picture you (the adult) see. Compare the children's responses. What do you conclude about their thinking?

Children's Play

Danielle is doing her first practicum in kindergarten with five- and six-year-old children. She is in Mr. McGuffey's classroom, which has a variety of activity centers and large blocks of time in which children can choose activities. Mr. McGuffey has encouraged Danielle to observe children at play to determine what they are learning. Danielle has seen children construct buildings with blocks, paint at the easel, write their names and other words on paper and at the marker board, make volcanoes at the sand table, play store, and invent and make games. She thinks it is easy to see that children writing their names on their artwork have learned to form letters and to express themselves, but she wonders whether children playing with dinosaur puppets are really learning anything. Danielle views play as separate from learning. However, she continues to remain open to the idea that children learn through play. Lately, as she has spent more time in this room, her observations of children's play have shifted from focusing on a specific activity, such as easel painting and what it has to offer, to looking for patterns in children's play across time.

As we join Danielle, she is observing two boys who are playing a teacher-made bingo-type game. Each child has a board divided into boxes with a picture of an animal in each box. They take turns spinning a spinner and covering the picture of the animal on their game board that the spinner points to.

Children learn through play.

Children construct rule knowledge through playing games. *(© Patrick Watson/The Image Works)*

JUSTIN: *(Takes the spinner from Matt and places it on a specific animal that he needs to cover.)* I want to win! I want to win!

(When it is Matt's turn, he spins the spinner the way an adult playing the game would do.)

MATT: Here goes! Oh, I got a bear again. I don't need a bear! Your turn.

(Danielle wonders why Mr. McGuffey doesn't tell Justin that he is not playing fairly by the rules. Why does he let Justin continue to cheat to win? Also, why doesn't Matt protest the cheating? Why does he go along with Justin and not cheat himself?)

JUSTIN: *(Continuing to "cheat.")* Look! I got a tiger! I win! I win! Let's play again, and this time you win!

MATT: *(Takes the spinner and clears his card.)* Okay. Let's go.

Danielle continues to observe the boys, who play another game. She feels the urge to intervene and explain to them the fair way to play. She decides to continue observing and question Mr. McGuffey about this behavior later.

DANIELLE: Mr. McGuffey, did you see the way Justin and Matt were playing that spinner game?

MR. McGUFFEY: Good observation, Danielle! I did see what Justin did. In my view, the boys were cooperating in their play and playing the game according to their understanding of the rules. As long as they both agreed and no one got upset, the game continued as they negotiated the play together. Their play appeared to me to be much more cooperative than competitive. Sometimes I see children play out of turn or take two turns. As long as no one protests, they do not perceive a problem. When I join them in a game, I sometimes point out when someone plays out of turn, and I ask if that is okay. Playing as an equal game partner allows me to question their understanding without asserting my adult authority. I'm just an equal player in the game.

Did you notice their interest in the game was more on playing together than on the outcome of winning? Sometimes I think teachers make too big a deal out of winning and getting rewards.

What do you think would have happened if you or I had interrupted their game to enforce the rules?

Children learn negotiation through game playing.

CONSTRUCTIONS

Interview

Play a game with a five-year-old child. Ask the child to explain how to play. Ask the child what *rule* means, then ask her to tell you a specific rule for the game you are playing. As you play the game, observe to

ASK YOURSELF

What do I think would have happened if Mr. McGuffey had enforced the rules? What might Justin and Matt have done? (Reflect on playing games with children.) What do I know about the way children play games that I didn't know before? How will this knowledge help me as a teacher?

what extent the child plays by the rules. If the child departs from the rules, ask if it is okay if you do that, too. Write a brief summary of your conclusions.

Children construct rule knowledge through game playing and creating classroom rules.

CHILDREN AND RULES

Children's Ideas About Rules

What Is a Rule?

Stuff you gotta do and stuff you don't gotta do.
Can'ts and don'ts.
What you 'posed to do, or you get in trouble.
Don't hit. Don't bite.
Do it or else!

Who Makes Rules?

Parents.
Grownups.
Teachers.
God.
We do.

Can Rules Be Changed?

No.
Never.
A rule is the rule, and you can't change it.
Grownups can change a rule.
You can if everyone agrees.

What Children Gain from Creating Their Own Rules

Active involvement.
Reflection on their own experiences.
Making meaningful connections of how rules relate to behaviors.
Respect for rules.
Sense of classroom community.
Problem solving through negotiation.
Cooperation.
Inductive thinking.
Ownership of rules and the classroom.

Source: From "Rule-creating in a constructivist classroom community," by K. Castle and K. Rogers, 1993, *Childhood Education, 70* (2), pp. 77–80.

Need to Know

Eric is placed in first grade with Mrs. Richards, who engages the children in planning topics of study. Eric observes Mrs. Richards do a brainstorming session with the children to see what they might come up with in planning a topic of study based on their interests.

Mrs. Richards gathers the children in a group and asks them what they would like to know about. They suggest several ideas, including bugs, the solar system, tornadoes, and eagles. They settle on a study of tornadoes because most of the children are fascinated by that topic, possibly because they live in an area prone to tornadoes and two children have actually lived through one. Eric can tell by her gestures and comments that Mrs. Richards is somewhat apprehensive about the topic because the study of tornadoes might distress the children, especially those who have been in a tornado. However, she agrees to the topic because of the children's high level of interest in it.

Mrs. Richards continues the discussion of what the children already know about tornadoes. The children give much information related to the strong wind, noise, and destructive nature of tornadoes. Several tell stories about what happened when a tornado came to their community and how it affected people, animals, and property. Mrs. Richards then asks the children what they would like to learn about tornadoes and how they might pursue questions of interest to them.

UDAY: Maybe we could learn how to know when a tornado is coming.

MELISSA: Or we could study where you should go to be safe.

JORDAN: I want to know how the tornado sirens work and who makes them go.

ALEX: How about if we get the TV weatherman to come to class?

CHANDRA: Let's study how to keep safe in a tornado. I've been in one, and my mommy took us into the bathtub!

MRS. RICHARDS: You are all coming up with some great questions! What would be some things we could do to answer them?

SHANNON: We could get some books from the library.

SAM: We could make a tornado!

MRS. RICHARDS: How could we do that, Sam?

SAM: Maybe get a giant fan to stir things up. We could turn it on full blast and see what happens in our room.

MANDY: My sister made one in a bottle. Could we do that? You just shake it up and watch it swirl!

JOEL: We could pretend to be storm watchers and warn people it's coming!

LOREN: We could ask people who know to come here and tell us how to be safe.

MRS. RICHARDS: Who might know, Loren?

LOREN: Maybe people who have been in one and lived, or a person who knows about weather.

BRIAN: My uncle goes out and chases storms in his truck. Maybe he could come, or we could go with him to see a storm!

MRS. RICHARDS: I think we have lots of ideas to explore now. Maybe we should start with what is available in our library, like books and videos. Do we have volunteers for that?

The children came up with the list of questions in the accompanying box. The teacher and children worked together to make a conceptual web that illustrates the connection between the topic of tornadoes and the different aspects of studying tornadoes of interest to the children (see Figure 8.1). In addition, the children created a list of activities they could do to learn more about the aspects of tornadoes each child chose to explore. This is an example of how children, with a teacher's help, create curriculum.

Over the course of the next two weeks, the children engaged in a flurry of activities pursuing their questions about being safe in a tornado. They read books, saw tornadoes on videos, and heard speakers, including individuals who had lived through tornadoes, a weatherman from the local TV station, and a civil defense worker who answered their questions about tornado

Learning comes from a need to know.

QUESTIONS THE CHILDREN ASKED ABOUT TORNADOES

How do animals get lost in a tornado?

How can you protect yourself from a tornado?

How do tornadoes twist?

How do tornadoes destroy buildings?

How do tornadoes get smaller?

Figure 8.1
Tornado Conceptual Web

> ### CHILDREN'S IDEAS FOR TORNADO ACTIVITIES
>
> 1. Watch videos
> 2. Ask what to do
> 3. Make tornadoes
> 4. Make up game
> 5. Read tornado story
> 6. Someone tell about them
> 7. Timed test on how long it takes us to take cover

warnings and sirens. Eric supplied the "weather watcher" dramatic play area with civil defense props, instruments to measure wind velocity, weather maps, and microphone equipment for broadcasting weather information, all of which he obtained from his university. The children produced a newsletter, complete with graphics, on their classroom computer. The newsletter was filled with interviews about living through a tornado and being prepared, as well as tornado poems and stories. They shared their newsletter with the rest of the school. They invited the other first-grade class to their room to share tornado safety tips they had learned, including what they could do at school if a tornado was in the area.

ERIC: Mrs. Richards, do the children always do so much and learn so much while studying a topic?

MRS. RICHARDS: Eric, I cannot believe how much these children have learned about tornadoes! They have been studying this topic for two weeks now, and their interest is still very high. You know, at first I was reluctant to study tornadoes because of the topic's potential to scare the children. But I think the opposite has occurred. Now that they know so much more about tornadoes, they feel confident in their ideas on how to be prepared for one. It's as if their knowledge has helped them feel capable in knowing what to do. Mrs. Jackson could not believe how much our children knew and were able to share with her class! This study has been a wonderful example of how capable young children are when they have a need to know something. It will be interesting to see if their confidence and autonomy continue as we begin new topics of study.

ERIC: I think the most amazing thing I learned from this was that even though the children knew and talked about how tornadoes sometimes take lives, they remained focused on what they can do to save lives and to be prepared. They thought a lot about how to protect their pets, too.

ASK YOURSELF

How many different types of knowledge can I find in the tornado study? In how many different ways did the children express what they were learning about tornadoes? How many examples can I find of different curriculum areas—such as mathematics, reading, language arts, science, and art—integrated around one topic?

Children learn when they
are interested and ask
their own questions.
(© Elizabeth Crews)

Their energy was focused on what they could do rather than on being afraid. Children are amazing!

Knowledge that children create when they have a need to know can mean more to them because they have raised their own questions that spark interest and stimulate their thinking. Teachers can expand on children's curriculum activities with just the right question at just the right time to stretch children's thinking (Duckworth, 1996). The list in the box below presents some thought-provoking questions teachers can use to promote children's thinking.

QUESTIONS THAT PROMOTE THOUGHT

What do you think?
Why do you think that?
How do you know?
How do you know what you know is true?
What are some reasons for your thinking that?
How does your idea compare to (another child's idea)?
What if you . . . ?
Would it make a difference if you . . . ?
What might happen if you . . . ?
Does anything surprise you about . . . ?
Can you explain your idea to (another child)?

Children's Interests

Amy's field experience is in a program for three- and four-year-old children. Amy has spent the last two weeks getting to know the children as individuals. She has interacted with them, played outdoors with them, and read stories to them. She has been particularly interested in how her teacher, Ms. Davis, plans for the three special needs children in this group. Amy has spent a lot of time with Shawn, who has been identified as moderately mentally retarded. Shawn likes to hold Amy's hand and stay close to her.

Amy has noticed that when other children try to talk to Shawn or draw him into an activity, he tends to withdraw and tries to hide behind Amy. She hopes she will be able to help Shawn interact more with the other children. She has tried engaging another child in an activity that Shawn likes, such as nesting a set of wooden chickens and eggs, in hopes that Shawn will join them. Sometimes he comes close and watches without saying much. Amy will put a toy in his hand and talk about it. Then she will take a toy and offer it to the other child, modeling how Shawn might make a friend.

The children in this program have shown an interest in horses, beginning when one child brought her horse to school to show everyone. Ms. Davis set up a "cowpoke" dramatic play area complete with cowpoke hats, boots, ropes to lasso a bale of hay, and stick horses to ride the range. Although the other children have enjoyed playing with the cowpoke props, Amy has noticed that Shawn hasn't spent much time on that activity. Then one day Shawn bursts into the area from outside and begins to grab all the ropes he can.

ASK YOURSELF

What is an interest of mine that I could share with young children? Fred Rogers of *Mister Rogers' Neighborhood* (1994) says that when we love something and share that interest with children, we offer them a special gift. What gifts can I offer children? Playing an instrument? Potting clay? Sewing? Gardening? Have a special collection that I could share with children?

KERRY: Stop, Shawn! We are playing with the ropes!

DREW: Shawn, you can play with us, but you can't take our ropes. Come here. You can be a cowpoke. Ride this horse. (*Tries to hand over a stick horse to Shawn, who rejects it.*)

SHAWN: (*Hanging on tightly to the ropes.*) No play! No! Go outside. Make 'pider home.

AMY: Shawn, the children are trying to tell you that they need the ropes for their play. You can have them when they are through.

SHAWN: No! Now! Make 'pider home! Go outside. (*Pulls away and heads for the door.*)

AMY: Maybe we should follow Shawn and see what he is trying to do with the ropes. Then maybe we can encourage him to give them back.

(*Amy is reluctant to make an issue of the ropes because this is the first time she has observed such a high level of interest in Shawn. Luckily, the other children are curious to see what Shawn is up to, and they all head outside to the play area. Shawn runs to a wooden climbing structure that has horizontal and vertical boards that make a square similar to a frame.*)

SHAWN: 'Pider home! 'Pider home! 'Pider come to home! *(Is busy draping the ropes over the boards and weaving them together.)*
AMY: Shawn, what are you making with the ropes?
SHAWN: 'Pider home for 'piders!

(Everyone watches as Shawn carefully works the ropes so that they form an irregular web attached to the wooden frame.)

JOEL: He's making a spider web! A spider web!
MELISSA: Can we do it, too, Shawn? Can we help you with the spider home?
SHAWN: *(Offers a piece of rope to Melissa.)* Okay. You help make 'pider home.

Interest fuels active learning.

Amy was amazed at how quickly the other children were able to figure out what Shawn was doing and saying and how eagerly they offered to help. She was even more pleased that Shawn had finally begun to make some friends. But she was most impressed that Shawn had come up with a perfectly wonderful idea for making a spider web out of ropes! Amy began to look for even more ways to promote interaction in this classroom full of inventors.

CONSTRUCTIONS

Planning

Take the interest you just identified in Ask Yourself (page 333) and plan one activity for children around it. Include a description of the interest and the activity; materials, including books, you would need; questions you might ask children to help initiate interest; and how you would know what children had learned from the activity. Include a photo or two of the interest or activity to put with your written description, and include these in your own professional resource file.

FIELD EXPERIENCE SEMINAR WITH DR. K.

The students attend a regular seminar to discuss field experiences conducted by their university supervisor, Dr. K. To initiate the discussion, Dr. K. has asked the students to think about the theories they are developing as they work with children in classrooms and to share examples of the strategies they have used to formulate their ideas on teaching young children. You probably recall from Chapter 1 that these strategies include questioning, interviewing, observing, analyzing and synthesizing through discussing, researching, reflecting, writing, and documenting through portfolios. Her intent is to encourage the students to integrate their learning in class with what they experience in the field sites.

DR. K.: Has anyone been surprised by what they have learned about working with young children?

TILLIE: Well, I was surprised that children who seem to me to be troublemakers may actually just be thinking according to what they know about a situation. I have found that when I listen more to children and try to understand their understanding, I don't have to get on them as much, and I work with them better.

DANIELLE: But how can you do that when all the other children are trying to get your attention?

AMY: If you don't listen carefully to children, you won't know why they do what they do or what interests them the most. I spent a lot of time at first getting to know individual children. I thought a lot about what motivates them and why. I can now anticipate how they might respond to what I have planned and prevent some problems by accommodating individual differences.

ERIC: The thing that surprised me the most is how capable young children are. If they are interested in a topic, there is no limit to what they will learn and do. When they have a need to know something, they will pursue it until they are satisfied. My kids learned things about tornadoes that even I didn't know!

TILLIE: I also learned that if you aren't careful, you can really turn kids' thinking off. If you don't let them make some decisions about what they want to learn, children will constantly ask you what you want them to learn. I planned two different activities on two different days. One activity gave them choices among alternatives. The other one did not. The difference was amazing! When children get to choose, they are more interested and stay with an activity longer. They get more out of it.

DR. K.: Zenah, you're very quiet today. What have you learned about encouraging children to make decisions?

ZENAH: I agree that it's important. Children can make good choices, but sometimes they need guidance. The thing that surprised me the most is how much I am applying what I have learned to my own children! I've been trying to give them more choices so that they'll learn to make good decisions. The other day my son, who eats junk food most of the time, got to decide what we would have for dinner. I couldn't believe how much effort he put into thinking about what would make a balanced meal! I'm going to do that more often.

DR. K.: Did anyone bring an activity they have done with children to share with the group?

AMY: I brought something I did for my portfolio on sharing an interest with children. I love to garden, so I brought in some gardening tools, soil, and plants, and we made a small classroom garden. The children loved it! Here is a picture of Shawn looking for spiders around the plants. The children learned that spiders eat insects that harm plants. I have to be careful now when I see a spider in the room not to step on it!

ZENAH: It seems to me that play is so important to learning. In play, children make decisions, have choices, and share perspectives. I'm wondering whether children who don't get opportunities to play are actually hindered in their learning. I think when I go back to my classroom, I will focus on helping children expand their play interests. Does anyone have any ideas about this?

Our students are well on their way to becoming early childhood professionals. They will continue to work with children in the creation of meaningful curriculum. By sharing their insights from their experiences with one another, they will continue to construct their own theories of what it means to teach young children. Some of them may construct basic tenets of curriculum from a constructivist perspective. The box below presents assumptions underlying a constructivist perspective of curriculum. These assumptions

ASK YOURSELF

How many examples of different strategies for formulating teaching theories applied by the students to their classrooms can I identify from their seminar discussion? What can I conclude about the meaning of curriculum from the students' classroom situations? How does this compare with my initial view of curriculum?

CONSTRUCTIVIST CURRICULUM ASSUMPTIONS

- ▸ Children are sense makers.
- ▸ Children actively construct knowledge.
- ▸ Children learn to make decisions about their learning by having opportunities to choose among activities and materials.
- ▸ Children make sense out of learning experiences even when they make errors that seem cute or silly to adults.
- ▸ Through understanding children's understanding, teachers improve their ability to plan meaningful programs for all children.
- ▸ Play is a child's natural means of understanding the world and how it works.
- ▸ When children share their perspectives with each other, they come to learn that other perspectives exist, and to learn to coordinate their perspectives with others' perspectives.
- ▸ Interest drives children's questioning and pursuit of understanding.

have been represented in examples of the field experiences described in this chapter.

Teaching theories are constructed and reconstructed.

Now that you have had a glimpse of the experiences of beginning early childhood teachers, you may be wondering how these experiences fit into the field as a whole. Next we will show you some additional views of professionals and how they came to develop their ideas and practices.

SUMMARY

▸ Early childhood education students are placed in field sites consisting of early childhood programs to learn about curriculum.

▸ Cooperating, supervising, lead, or head teachers work with early childhood education students in field experiences.

▸ Traditionally, curriculum has been viewed as content.

▸ Early childhood professional organizations, for example, NAEYC, have defined curriculum and developed curriculum standards for early childhood practice.

▸ NAEYC advocates for developmentally and culturally appropriate curriculum and assessment.

▸ A constructivist view of curriculum focuses on child sense making.

▸ Teachers support children's knowledge construction by attempting to understand children's understanding and planning programs that help transform children's thinking.

▸ Early childhood teachers plan curriculum with children's choices, interests, decision-making, need to know, and play in mind.

▸ Children derive many benefits from having opportunities to make choices in their learning.

▸ Children's sense of things may appear cute or as misbehavior to some adults who do not attempt to understand children's understanding.

▸ Play in the curriculum can help children share their own perspectives and grow to understand the perspectives of others.

▸ Children's ideas of rules are constructed through playing games and creating classroom rules they agree to live by.

▸ Children become more interested in learning when they have a need to know.

▸ Teachers can promote interest in children by sharing an interest or hobby with children.

▸ Early childhood students construct theories about children's learning from working in early childhood programs, and closely observing and reflecting on what they experience in these programs.

▶ Early childhood students' theories change as they reconcile previous ideas with new experiences and as they share perspectives with other students and teachers.

CONSTRUCTIONS

1. Analysis

Have a conversation with a five-year-old child. Analyze the child's thinking using what you have learned from this chapter and Chapter 4.

2. Research

Find one early childhood professional journal article that gives examples of how young children create curriculum. Add the article to your resource file.

3. Interview

Interview a six- and an eight-year-old on what they like to learn in school. Compare their ideas and draw conclusions about their sense making, interests, need to know, and need for choices.

4. Journal Entry

Write about what you think a classroom for four-year-olds would look like to promote sense making, choices, interests, and the children's creation of the curriculum.

5. Observation

Visit an early childhood classroom that actively engages children in creating the curriculum.

RESOURCES

Castle, K. (1990). Children's invented games. *Childhood Education*, *67* (2), 82–85.

Castle gives examples of how children integrate curriculum through creating games from beautiful junk.

Chaille, C., & Britain, L. (1997). *The young child as scientist* (2nd ed.). New York: Longman.

This book gives many examples of children raising and exploring their own questions in an attempt to better understand the world and how it works.

Edwards, C., Gandini, L., & Forman, G. (1993). *The hundred languages of children*. Greenwich, CT: Ablex/JAI Press.

The authors explore how children construct their knowledge and provide examples of children's sense making through the exploration of different materials.

Forman, G., & Hill, F. (1980/1984). *Constructive play: Applying Piaget in the preschool*. Menlo Park, CA: Addison-Wesley.

The authors illustrate with photographs and text the stages of children's thinking as they explore objects, solve problems, and attempt to answer their own questions about objects in developing physical and logico-mathematical knowledge.

Hendrick, J. (1997). *First steps toward teaching the Reggio way*. Columbus, OH: Merrill, Prentice-Hall.

Hendrick describes a project approach to curriculum with examples from the Italian Reggio Emilia schools.

Isenberg, J. P., & Jalongo, M. R. (Eds.). (1997). *Major trends and issues in early childhood education*. New York: Teachers College Press.

This book covers recent trends and issues in early childhood curriculum, including developmentally, individually, and culturally appropriate practice.

Kamii, C. (1991). *Early literacy: A constructivist foundation for whole language*. Washington, DC: National Education Association.

This book gives a rationale for how children make sense of print and how teachers can facilitate children's construction of literacy.

Kamii, C., & DeClark, G. (1985). *Young children reinvent arithmetic*. New York: Teachers College Press.

The authors provide research evidence and classroom examples of how children actively construct their knowledge of arithmetic.

Kamii, C., & DeVries, R. (1980). *Group games in early education: Implications of Piaget's theory*. Washington DC: NAEYC.

This book defines physical knowledge and gives suggestions for facilitating the construction of physical knowledge through group games. It is full of examples of games teachers can do in classrooms.

Murphy, D., & Goffin, S. (1992). *Project construct.* Jefferson City, MO: Department of Elementary and Secondary Education.

The authors describe the state of Missouri's efforts to move toward a constructivist curriculum in early childhood. They also give a constructivist rationale for curriculum.

Surbeck, E., & Glover, M. K. (1992). Seal revenge: Ecology games invented by children. *Childhood Education,* 68 (5), 275–281.

Surbeck and Glover describe a games project in which primary-aged children created ecology games that integrated all aspects of the curriculum.

PART 4

Professionalism

*P*ART 4 CONTAINS *three chapters that focus attention on professional development and the perspectives of past and present professionals. Constructivist theory suggests that cognitive conflict, cooperation, and social reciprocity inherent in interactions with peers and other teachers enhance individual growth in the field. These three chapters encourage you to think about the process of becoming a teacher.*

Chapter 9 introduces many of the early childhood educators who have paved the way for our work today, and you will meet the people whose efforts developed and refined the roles of contemporary early childhood educators. Chapter 9 will help you juxtapose historical events and current practice in early childhood education. In Chapter 10, you will meet a number of early childhood education professionals from around the country. Through their words and ideas, you will be able to view the many positions available to you as well as to consider issues in the field. Finally, Chapter 11 encourages you to think about your own development as a professional. In this chapter, you will revisit the idea of autonomy and its importance in a constructivist approach to teaching.

9

Views of Professionals Over Time

• •

Throughout this book, you have met contemporary early childhood professionals and learned about some of the opportunities available in the field today. The aim of this chapter is to invite you to visit the professionals who pioneered and helped develop the field of early childhood education. We want you to use the information presented here to expand and transform what you currently know so that you can construct a more complete understanding of the field of early childhood education. This backward journey should help you find historical figures with whom you can identify and help you learn about significant events that changed the field. To facilitate your journey into the past, we offer the perspectives of contemporary and past professionals through their writings and interviews. We present snippets of information about selected individuals to help you know the early leaders through their deeds and the social and political contexts in which they worked. These encounters will not be an exhaustive presentation, but rather a slice of the history of early childhood education. Through this chapter, you will learn more about the following:

- ❱ How teachers have changed over time
- ❱ The factors that have influenced that change
- ❱ The leaders in the field and their significant contributions
- ❱ The way the field has changed over time
- ❱ The factors that have influenced that change

INTRODUCTION

ASK YOURSELF

Do any of the students' comments reflect my initial reaction to a chapter on the history of the field? What images and feelings do I get when I think about studying the history of early childhood education? What do I already know about it from other classes? Was it presented as dry, boring details and dates to be memorized? Or did I think and talk about events that have played a significant role in who and what I am today?

The students in Dr. K.'s class have arrived a little early and are discussing the assigned reading—a chapter on the history of early childhood education.

DANIELLE: Has anyone read this history chapter yet?

AMY: If you want to know the truth, no. I just hate history. I know it's important, but it's boring.

TILLIE: Yeah, I don't like going all the way back to B.C. Recent history is one thing, but back then they had no technology at all, and I don't think that we would ever be faced with the problems they were faced with then. I feel like I should be learning more about teaching than about things that happened in B.C.

ZENAH: It doesn't help my teaching to study that far back. The world is completely different now.

ERIC: I read it, and I liked it. Knowing what went on in the past gives me an appreciation for today, and it allows me to carry on intellectual conversations. You know, it makes you well-rounded.

AMY: Well, maybe the history of early childhood will be more interesting than world history because it's a field I'm interested in.

DANIELLE: I don't think history makes me well-rounded. I think I get that from my English and speech classes.

A CONSTRUCTIVIST VIEW OF HISTORY

Our feelings and ideas about the history of any topic and its value in our lives are closely linked to our experiences with the topic. Whereas some of you may hypothesize that history has little relation to your lives or your teaching career, others may hypothesize that learning about significant events in the lives of others in the field builds connections between past and present.

A constructivist perspective holds that you have to start with what you know to advance your knowledge on any topic. When you think of the history of early childhood education, you might start with your own memories of your early schooling. You can reflect on your own experiences and then trace those experiences backward by reflecting on the experiences of others who are significant to you, such as your parents and grandparents. This backward look should help you identify many of the **perturbations** that have significantly changed your life, the lives of others, and the field itself. Remember that perturbations are those annoyances that irritate you to the point that you are forced to do something about them, like the grain

The history of the field is a record of perturbations and how they have led to reform.

of sand in an oyster shell that forces the oyster to produce a pearl. Although they are irritations or annoyances at the time, these perturbations bring about change. The attempt to eliminate perturbations is what makes our knowledge about teaching and learning advance. The history of the field is a record of perturbations that have challenged traditional ways of looking at education and how the resolution of those issues led to educational reform.

When you begin to search your own educational experiences and those of your immediate family, you usually start out with some hypotheses that you want to test or questions that you want to answer. Additionally, you will want to relate these experiences to your current understanding of the field.

MULTIPLE PERSPECTIVES

From a Student

Betsy Dean, an early childhood student at Auburn University, interviewed her sister, her mother, and her grandmother to compare and contrast their early educational experiences.

I conducted interviews with my grandmother [born in 1912], my mother [born in 1941], and my sister [born in 1973]. The early educational experiences that I uncovered were distinctly different yet remarkably similar. Even though the experiences occurred over a sixty-year time span, the interviews revealed common ties that bound the three together.

Before I carried out the three interviews, I hypothesized that I would find more differences than similarities. However, my findings did not support this hypothesis, since the similarities far outweighed the differences. For all three interviewed, their fondest memory of school centered around the social interaction that occurred during the school day and the overall excitement of simply going to school and learning something new.

The teachers at the three different schools were females. The "favorite" teacher was remembered not just for what she did but [for] how she established the classroom environment, whether it was in an "orderly" manner, as my mom described, or in a "fun" fashion, as my sister discussed. Another similarity among all three of my relatives was that their education helped to prepare them for their later occupations: Social Security worker, piano teacher, and speech pathologist.

The classroom layout, along with the daily schedule, had many commonalties across the three generations. In all three classrooms, the teacher's desk was at the

Parents and grandparents recall early classrooms that had desks nailed to the floor in straight rows. *(© Culver Pictures, Inc.)*

front of the room. Basically, the same subjects were taught [reading, writing, arithmetic, spelling, and social studies], but no emphasis was placed on science. The children, for the most part, were only allowed to play at one time during the day [which began as recess and "evolved" into physical education]. There was no "free play" allowed in any of the classrooms described. The overall method of instruction was transmission of knowledge, whether it came in the early form of lecturing or the latter form of worksheets. During the "eight-to-three" day, throughout the months of September through May, all three of my relatives spoke of the heavy emphasis placed upon learning the alphabet and the numbers.

Even though there were numerous similarities across the generations, there were also some obvious differences. Most of the notable changes occurred between the time my mom and my sister were in elementary school, somewhere between 1947 and 1980. In other words, my grandmother's and my mother's interviews were very similar, while my sister's was quite different. However, there were a couple of exceptions. My grandmother attended school in a two-room schoolhouse, and my mother's school had a room for each grade. Also, my mother spoke of being able to start school in the middle of the year, which was not the case in the earlier or later generations.

In the years between 1947 and 1980, the layout of the classroom changed from having the children sit in rows to having them sit in clusters. Although children in the earlier classrooms may have hung their pictures up in the classroom, the idea of displaying children's work did not seem to have a big impact until the 1980s. The arts [which include music, theater, dance, and visual arts] were not emphasized until this time also. In both of my grandmother and mother's schools, the principal was male, but in my sister's elementary school, the principal was female. Finally, because of the advances in technology, the transportation to and from school changed from walking to riding in a car.

When I analyzed each interview closely, I found some exciting implications. For instance, my grandmother's earliest classroom [in 1918] was comprised of grades one through four. In other words, my grandmother had the opportunity to construct knowledge in a multiaged classroom, a method that is becoming popular now. I feel quite sure that even though my grandmother saw the circumstance as a burden, she was actually fortunate because she was able to learn not only from her teacher, but also from her older peers.

When my mom spoke of the beautiful artwork that was displayed close to the ceiling in her early classroom in 1947, I could not help but make a connection to the Reggio Emilia preschools. She was only six years old, and even today she can remember the prints that hung in her classroom. The bird prints may not have been drawn or painted by a famous artist, but this memory speaks for itself about the power and the message portrayed by truly good art.

As for my sister, her first memory of learning dated back to when she was three or four years of age, when my dad helped her learn to read *The Teeny, Tiny Woman*. Because she was introduced to reading at an early age and shown how much fun it can be, she has within herself a lifelong love of reading. This reminded me of early intervention services: If you can reach a child at an early age, the difference you can make in his life is truly remarkable.

I feel that the knowledge that I acquired through conducting these interviews is extremely valuable. As Isenberg and Jalongo (1997) state: "Early childhood education can never be decontextualized or occur in isolation. Rather, our work on behalf of young children is deeply woven into the social, political, and historical fabric of our lives, children's lives, and their families' lives both in and out of school" (p. 11). Speaking with my grandmother, mother, and sister helped me to personalize this statement, noting how all of these aspects not only need to be recognized but also appreciated. I also personalized the interviews by placing myself in the teacher's shoes in each of the three classrooms. For example, in both of my mom's and my sister's classroom, one wall was lined with windows. After reading *Inquiry at the Window*, I wanted to go back in time and place a bird feeder outside those windows and basically just utilize the windows as a connection to the outside world.

These interviews have helped bring to the surface the good and the bad of the early childhood classroom teacher and environment, along with how far we have come and what we have had to go through to get to where we are today. However, they have also shown me how much further we need to go in educating the young children of today. Because of this realization, I feel more than ready to have a classroom of my own. I plan on utilizing the knowledge I have constructed with these interviews in order to be that favorite teacher, to create that memorable classroom environment full of children's work, and to make that all-important difference in children's lives.

• •

Notice how Betsy's hypothesis was similar to Tillie and Zenah's beliefs that historical reality is significantly different from today. However, as Betsy reflected on the information, she found that this hypothesis did not hold to be true, and there were more similarities than differences. We invite you to test your own hypotheses about how early childhood education was in the past.

CONSTRUCTIONS

1. Interview

Conduct an oral interview on the early educational experiences of individuals from three distinctly different age groups to compare and contrast these experiences over three different eras (grandparent, parent, and child). Tape-record and transcribe all three interviews and analyze them to find similarities and differences related to what was taught; how it was taught; how it was evaluated; what they liked and disliked about school; and pertinent issues, attitudes, and expectations for schooling they discussed.

2. Synthesis

Synthesize your findings into a two-to-three-page paper and be prepared to discuss your findings in class.

WHY STUDY EARLY CHILDHOOD HISTORY?

Today's new ideas are coordinations and transformations of past experiences.

Remember that a constructivist perspective holds that we always start with what we know and that learning is the expansion and transformation of that knowledge. You started with what you knew about early childhood education and are expanding it as you conduct your interviews. Now you are ready to move back further in time to become acquainted with the writings, lives, and accomplishments of the many courageous professionals who have contributed to the field of early childhood education. Realize that today's new ideas are coordinations and transformations of past experiences. As you enter the field, you must implement, shape, and build your ideas based on earlier ones.

Another reason we study the past is that by acknowledging our past, we gain a perspective that empowers us. This perspective allows us to clarify who we are, how our philosophies and theories fit into the whole educational scheme, and who inspired us. Based on our awareness of the roles our early mentors played in helping us shape our theories, we begin to better understand what we can do. For example, a group of early childhood educators helped us by conceiving of and then writing the 1987 handbook *Developmentally Appropriate Practice in Early Childhood Programs Serving Children From Birth Through Age 8*. We may not agree with the entire handbook, but we do know that it has been a major factor in how early childhood teachers implement classroom practices that consider children's development and their uniqueness.

Another purpose for studying the past is that we can identify issues, trends, and perturbations for early childhood education and see how those have developed over time. For example, an administrative chain of command has become a major issue in education. Michael Katz (1971) maintains that this **bureaucracy** was created to make education more efficient, centralized, and standardized. However, it resulted in a distribution of power that put the teacher and the child at the bottom of the hierarchy. It also resulted in graded systems in schools. For example, the one-room school concept, which included multiage grouping, was abandoned and replaced with same-age grade levels. This in turn caused the rigid organization of subject matter and the isolation of children who were not progressing as the curriculum deemed appropriate. On the other hand, this bureaucracy played a major role in showing individuals that they needed powerful national organizations and certification to speak out for what they and their colleagues viewed as important for young children.

Yet another reason for studying the history of early childhood education is that when examining our past and the kinds of curricula and programs earlier educators designed and used, we can answer questions about today's early childhood education curricula and programs. We can identify the source of the problems, see what has been done to solve them, and examine how they have changed over the years.

The most important reason for studying history is to see what has happened to the child—the learner. We can see how various events, programs, and theories have helped or hindered children in becoming all that they are capable of being.

ASK YOURSELF

Why start the educational process so early? Why institutionalize the very young child? Wouldn't it be better if all young children stayed at home until age seven?

CONSTRUCTIONS

Journal Entry

Think about all the reasons for studying the history of early childhood education. Write down those that are the most convincing to you. Analyze the motivation behind your choices. Are they based on your interest in what has happened to the learner in the past? Are they based on your desire to better understand your own education and how it differed from what is happening today?

JUSTIFICATION FOR THE FIELD OF EARLY CHILDHOOD EDUCATION

Nationally, early childhood education is defined as the education of children from birth through age eight. It is not the lower end of elementary education, but a distinct field that addresses the specific needs of the young child. According to Marvin Lazerson (1972), three major themes justify the need for the field of early childhood education. Each of these themes emerged as a result of many perturbations within society relating to the welfare, study, and education of young children.

Social Reform

Many people believed that early education would solve social and educational problems, while others held that childhood is a unique period of life.

The first theme was the belief that early childhood education could produce social reform. It was thought that we could change and better society by educating and providing for the health and welfare of all children, particularly the children of the poor. Parent education, a strong component of most early childhood programs, was one avenue for this kind of reform. Another avenue was the effect early education programs had indirectly on younger siblings in the home. Educational programs were designed to help children learn behaviors that would make them more socially acceptable, such as how to share, how to make friends, and how to solve problems. Early education was thought to be the cure for most of society's ills. Notice how society's poor and undereducated were the perturbation for the need for social reform.

Uniqueness of Childhood

The second theme focused on the fact that young children are not just miniature adults, but are developmentally unique intellectually, socially, physically, and linguistically. Schools for young children needed to provide for the nature of childhood by giving children experiences appropriate to their developmental levels. Young children do not learn in the same ways that adults learn, and they need to have opportunities to play, to choose, to make mistakes, and to receive special attention and guidance. Notice that knowledge about the nature of the learner created the perturbation for practices that conformed more to the developmental needs of the young child.

Educational Reform

Throughout history, early childhood teachers and philosophers have been highly critical of the common educational practices of their times. Early in our history educators looked to early childhood practices to reform what they considered to be bad practices in the schools. Many preschool and kindergarten teachers criticized the overuse of worksheets and rote memorization in the primary grades, while many primary teachers criticized kindergarten teachers for children's lack of proper handwriting skills. Each group hoped to influence the other. Notice that this problem is the perturbation for how to improve education in general.

As we study more about the history of early childhood education, we can see at what point each of the three themes first became prominent. We can also see the current importance of each theme and the balance among them. We can make predictions about the movement of the field. For example, we can offer the hypothesis that we have moved from hope to disillusionment to recovery through partnership, collaboration, and networking. We can offer the perturbation that we are in a period of transition as we try to understand and create a seamless society, a society without arbitrary divisions. History chronicles our earlier attempts to decide who should be educated and how. As you begin to look at the history of the field, try to relate it to these three themes as well as to current issues that perturb you today.

CONSTRUCTIONS

Journal Entry

Write a brief journal entry in which you describe the themes that are important to you today. Explain how they are similar to or different from the three historical themes identified by Lazerson (1972). Tell what has influenced your thinking about these themes.

PIONEERS IN EARLY CHILDHOOD EDUCATION

Many dauntless men and women pioneered the field of early childhood education, and their ideas still influence us today. Many of the issues that they confronted are issues that we continue to confront today.

Ancient Influences

Dauntless men and women who pioneered the field of early childhood education still influence us today.

Throughout the world, ancient societies had influential people whose ideas regarding the education of young children were a reflection of the society's culture, values, and traditions. Many of these ideas and traditions, such as educating only upper-class males, are out-of-date and irrelevant today. However, some ideas regarding what should be taught and how it should be taught are as current now as they were then.

ASK YOURSELF

What do I know about the early pioneers in early childhood education? What issues did they have to address? Were their issues similar to the ones addressed today?
....

Confucius (c. 551–479 B.C.). Confucius was one of the earliest educators in Chinese history, and his influence is still significant today. He is known as a man of wisdom and a great educator. For Confucius, the goal of education was to help humans become moral and charitable. His philosophy emphasized that education was to serve the needs of the individual. Poetry, rites and rituals, writing, and music were the subject areas that he emphasized in his curriculum. He was an advocate of a developmental approach to learning, and he held that teachers should consider the individual needs of each learner. He advocated education for those who were most qualified and used a test to determine the qualifications. Through this avenue, common people were allowed to be educated (Smith, 1991).

Plato's educational goal was to produce a strong state.

Plato (427?–347? B.C.). When we think of influential leaders of early childhood education, we must include Plato. He advocated a system of educating Greek leaders of the ruling class. His educational goal was to produce a society that was harmonious and just, a strong state. His objectives included the development of wisdom, temperance, and justice. His philosophy differed from that of Confucius in that his interest was not in the individual, but in how that individual could be educated to best serve the state.

In *The Republic* and *The Laws,* Plato suggested that children from two to six years of age be placed in an educational nursery and that games be used to facilitate their mental and physical growth. For children six to eighteen, he recommended a curriculum that included reading, writing, music, literature, science, and physical education (Morris, 1992). These lessons were to be taught through the use of concrete objects and games. Plato did not believe in **corporal punishment,** but he did hold that many materials needed to be censored, as children should be exposed only to things of high moral value. Additionally, Plato held that education should be for both males and females. Although these ideas were considered **utopian** by many, Plato's work gave rise to the following ideas:

- State control of schools
- Education of the masses
- Early learning through play and active experience
- Use of concrete experiences in learning

Aristotle (384–322 B.C.). Aristotle, another Greek philosopher, also supported education for children before six years of age (Osborn, 1991) but held that they should be nurtured at home by the mother or wet nurse and be provided a tutor to ensure that the education was liberal and moral. He differed from Plato in that to him the purpose of education was to bring out specific abilities and talents of the individual child (Osborn). His guiding principle was that children learn by doing. Consequently, habit formation was the way by which children could learn to be model citizens (Morris, 1992). Another of Aristotle's major contributions to early childhood education was his belief in the liberating power of education. He held that through education, the individual is freed from ignorance.

Quintilian (A.D. c. 35–c. 100). During this period of Roman history, there were many opportunities for people to rise to positions of power in the senate and other government institutions if they were well educated in public speaking. Quintilian, a rhetorician and educator, held that the goal of education was to produce good orators who would be of service to the state. In his book *Institutio Oratorio*, he suggested a system of education that included four distinct periods in a student's life. Those of interest to early childhood professionals are the first and second periods. The first period included children from one to six years of age. During this time, Quintilian suggested, children should be around people who are of high moral character and should not be exposed to people of bad character or to any kind of evil. The curriculum was to help children learn Greek and Latin. (Did you think parent involvement in early childhood education, modeling, and learning more than one language were new ideas?)

The second period included children from six to fourteen years of age. During this time, children should have a teacher whose moral character is flawless, and learning to read and write should be very agreeable, with games and interesting pursuits and no physical punishment.

St. Augustine (A.D. 354–430). After the fall of the Roman Empire, the Catholic Church took control of the state. St. Augustine was instrumental in the development of Christian thought, which became the educational doctrine of the time. St. Augustine held that the main purpose of education was to convert the child to Christianity and that the church should control the educational policies of the schools. Although he supported a curriculum that included grammar, music, mathematics, and astronomy, he thought that all children should have a strong foundation in the teachings of the church. He believed that all children are blessed with divine wisdom, which enables them to interpret what they hear and to learn.

CONSTRUCTIONS

Research

Compare and contrast the philosophies of ancient education pioneers in terms of their views of the purpose of education, whom should be taught and why, and how they should be taught. Identify the oppositions in their views that created the perturbations that brought about changes.

The Middle Ages and the Renaissance

During the Middle Ages, schools were controlled by the church.

During the early part of the Middle Ages, education was religious in nature, and the Catholic Church controlled most of the schools. Students learned the liberal arts, and the Bible was studied continually. During the latter part of the Middle Ages, two initiatives reflected a breaking away from the religious education of the earlier Middle Ages. The guild system, an initiative for training young men for commercial endeavors, was established. In this system, a male child started as an apprentice, moved up to a journeyman, and ended as a master craftsman in the endeavor in which he was being trained. The order of the knighthood, an initiative for educating the elite male, consisted of three stages: page, squire, and knight. Despite these two initiatives, the education of the Middle Ages was primarily religious.

During the Renaissance, education was once again controlled by the state, and its primary emphasis was on man the individual. This period saw the rise of the middle class, the glorification of wealth, and the perturbation between religion and science as a means for understanding the world. Two influential pioneers, whose ideas had significant implications for early childhood education, emerged during this time.

Desiderius Erasmus (1466?–1536). Erasmus felt the perturbation between church and state control of education. He believed that the purpose of education was to allow the individual to make independent judgments about what he held to be true and right. Erasmus was a resolute Christian who believed that the child should be at the center of the educational endeavor. This child-centered belief was the beginning of the humanist movement, a movement defined as a deep concern or love for humankind. Erasmus thought that teachers should love their children, and through this love each child's innate abilities will mature.

ASK YOURSELF

What ideas from Erasmus and Luther are still current today? Do I feel some of the same tensions between church and state in education? If so, in what ways do these tensions manifest themselves?
....

Martin Luther (1483–1546). Martin Luther was a religious reformer who was perturbed by the ideas that the pope was superior to other men and was the only one who could interpret the Bible. Luther held that the goal of education should be for all men to be able to understand God by studying and interpreting the Bible. Although his goal was a religious one, he strongly believed that each individual had the right to read and interpret the Bible for himself. Therefore, he thought that the schools should be state controlled to provide for the education of the masses. He translated the Bible into the **vernacular** language of the German people so that they could read it. This translation became the Germans' primary textbook.

The Early Modern Period

During the early modern period, there was renewed enthusiasm for learning.

During the early modern period, there was renewed enthusiasm for learning, and philosophers and theorists began to speak of a child-centered approach to early education. These early thinkers were instrumental in advancing educational thought.

John Amos Comenius (1592–1670). Comenius, a Moravian bishop, moved educational thought into the early modern period. He believed that all children should be educated and that learning, morality, and piety were essential to a good life (Braun & Edwards, 1972). Comenius suggested that teaching should appeal to the interests of the learner, that the school day should be divided into subject areas, and that teachers should teach in a manner congruent with children's development. He recommended a curriculum for children at four different age levels, two of which are appropriate to early childhood. The first curriculum, for children one through six years of age, was the school at the mother's knee. Comenius believed that the family was responsible for early learning, which consisted of the native language, social behaviors, religion, music, and art. The second curriculum was called the vernacular school, suggesting that children would no longer have to use the Latin language for learning but could continue to learn using their native language. In this school, children used picture books and real materials to learn science, math, art, and religion. Comenius designed the first children's picture book, *Orbis Sensualium Pictus* (The Visible World in Pictures).

John Locke (1632–1704).

John Locke was a teacher, a doctor, a theorist, and a religious critic. He believed that individuals acquire knowledge as a result of their experience. He thought that the child's mind is a blank slate (tabula rasa) on which the learner's experience is written. Like many other early scholars, Locke placed an emphasis on natural education and play. In fact, many people maintain that his views and writings opened the door for sensory education. Some of his other educational beliefs included the use of reason rather than corporal punishment, the use of experience rather than textbooks, the integration of physical and intellectual development, and the teacher as one who loves his students.

Charles Perrault (1628–1703).

Charles Perrault was the author of some of the most beloved collections of stories for children. He is best known for his *Contes de Ma Mère l'Oye,* which appeared in France around 1697. This collection included "Little Red Riding Hood," "Cinderella," "Sleeping Beauty," and "Puss in Boots." Later, these beloved stories were translated into the English *Mother Goose Tales.* The significance of Perrault's contribution is twofold. First, he recognized the need for children to have quality literature. Second, he realized that children love to read good stories and that there was a market for children's books.

Giambattista Vico (1668–1744).

Vico was "the pioneer of constructivism at the beginning of the 18th century" (von Glasersfeld, 1995, p.6). His contribution to early childhood education arose out of a strong perturbation regarding how Western philosophers defined knowledge. He challenged the traditional idea that the knowledge of the individual should be considered true only if it correctly reflects the real world that exists independent of the knower (von Glasersfeld, p. 6).

Vico held that knowledge exists within the knower and that it comes into existence as the knower experiences the physical and social worlds. He published these ideas in *The New Science* (1725), which he rewrote and published as a second edition in 1730. In this book, Vico shows how thought and action are related to imagination and reason.

Vico held that history, as a record of human thought and action, can provide a more reliable understanding about humanity than natural science. He held that humans are historical entities and that the nature of human thought and action changes over time. He believed that the art, philosophy, economics, and religion of a culture are interrelated and that the expression

ASK YOURSELF

How do Vico's ideas re-
late to constructivism?
Can I find similarities
between Vico's explana-
tions of thought and
what I learned about the
early thought process of
young children in Chap-
ters 3 and 4?
• •

of those ideas through myth, art, and poetry is the means by which knowledge is transmitted and understood.

Vico hypothesized a cyclical development of thought that parallels the
cyclical development of humans from birth to death and of societies from
rise to fall. This development proceeded through three ages. The first age is
characterized as thought that results from a stimulus-response—type link
between loud noises (like thunder) and fear. He referred to this kind of
thought as common sense.

During the second age a logical link is made between two observable
ideas, and in the third age these links become organized into structures for
the perception of reality. To Vico, thought was the process of abstraction
that allows the things one can see, touch, smell, taste, and hear to be recalled through images that are separate from the things themselves.

Jean Jacques Rousseau (1712–1778). Rousseau is best known for
Émile, a novel in which he laid out his ideas for a form of education that
would protect children from the evils of society until they reached man-

---

ROUSSEAU'S RECAPITULATION THEORY

Human's Growth and Development	Civilization's Growth and Development
Infancy (birth to 5)	Animal stage

This stage is for the physical development of the body, in which the
child develops his motoric abilities and his sense perceptions. The
child should be kept free of restraint and allowed to harden by nature's methods.

Childhood (5 to 12)	Savage stage

During this stage, the child must learn from experience because he
cannot reason. Learning takes place through necessity. That is, the
child will learn to read when he feels the necessity to read.

Age of reason (12 to 15)	Rational stage

At this stage, reason emerges, and the child can be educated to use
his own ability to reason. Here curiosity and utility are the factors
that motivate learning.

Social stage (15 to 20)	Social stage

At this stage, the social urge emerges. The student yearns for human relationships and begins to develop a sense of morality and an
appreciation of beauty.

hood. (Note that Rousseau, like most early philosophers, considered the education of men, not of all people.) He called for education that would preserve each child's natural goodness until he was old enough to protect himself. Interestingly, he focused on the health of the child, the use of firsthand experience with objects, using the senses to acquire knowledge, and the teacher as tutor. He changed the face of education with his radical ideas that childhood was a stage of life and that development from childhood to adulthood **recapitulated** the development of civilization. The box on page 357 shows how, in Rousseau's theory, the stages of human growth and development parallel the stages of civilization.

The Modern Period

By the early part of the nineteenth century, many of the themes of modern educational reform had been developed in theoretical and philosophical writings throughout Europe. Those themes included more **child-centered** methods of teaching, education for the masses, education for females, and state responsibility for providing financial support of schools. Many public and private schools, colleges, and technical schools were established during this time. Although these ideas had been advocated earlier, it took the work of two of the most influential pioneers of this period to put the ideas into practice in Switzerland and Germany.

To Pestalozzi, the goal of education was social reform.

Johann Heinrich Pestalozzi (1746–1827). Pestalozzi was a Swiss educator who developed a method for educating young children based on the ideas of Plato, Comenius, and Rousseau. He put this method into practice at his school for orphans and children of poor farmers in Yverdon, Switzerland. Unlike Rousseau, he did not glorify the natural state of man. To Pestalozzi, the goal of education was social reform, in that through education man could become a responsible citizen. He is best known through his writings, which include *Leonard and Gertrude* (1781), and *How Gertrude Teaches Her Children* (1801), an educational classic (Osborn, 1991). His observations of Gertrude, a country woman whose naturally warm ways of working with children changed a village, were the basis for these two texts. Through these writings, Pestalozzi developed his thinking about how young children should be educated.

Pestalozzi was interested in developing a method of teaching that was consistent with the laws of human nature. He advocated the education of the whole child, with an appropriate balance between the education of the head, the hand, and the heart. He devised object lessons for children's intellectual development (the head), basing these lessons on children's direct observations of things in the natural world. Children could observe by touching, smelling, seeing, and hearing natural objects. These sensory experiences were thought to heighten their awareness and lead children's thoughts from the simple to the complex and from the concrete to the abstract. Children were part of the labor force of the school and farm, and Pestalozzi referred to this active manual training as the education of the hand. Operating a farm, housekeeping, spinning, and weaving were all part of the curriculum. The education of the heart referred to the teaching of moral and religious values. According to Pestalozzi, education of the head, hand, and heart had to be integrated for a child to develop harmoniously. Additionally, he thought that love should be continuously present in the classroom and that the classroom should be homelike.

Friedrich Froebel (1782–1852).

Froebel, an educational innovator of the early nineteenth century, is known as the father of the kindergarten. He founded the first kindergarten for children under age seven in Blankenburg, Germany, in 1837. He spent the rest of his life refining the principles and methods on which it was based and training young women as kindergarten instructors.

Froebel's philosophy was based on the eternal unity of all things stemming from God and encompassing the laws of physical nature and the human spirit. He believed that the aim of life is to discover and unfold this divine unity. The inner nature of man is designed for this purpose and is characterized by a striving self-activity. This activity is the process of taking in the outer world through the senses and outwardly expressing one's inner nature, the synthesis of which leads to the revelation of the divine unity. Within this philosophy, Froebel included two laws—the law of opposites and the law of connections. He held that everything that exists has an opposite, such as man and woman, spirit and matter, and that the fundamental opposite in learning is the inner self and the outer world. The law of connection is the complement of the first law and functions to bring together two opposites by a mediating force or object. This joining of opposites is the divine unity of Froebel's philosophy.

Education, according to Froebel, is a growth process that begins at birth and should follow the natural development of the child. However, in the continuity of development, there are stages that should be fully developed before proceeding to the next stage. Froebel held that adults have to give the child time to develop and that teachers must follow the child's natural instincts. The box on page 360 outlines Froebel's stage theory.

Froebel held that the curriculum of the kindergarten should be representative of society and that play is the self-activity by which children learn. He designed a curriculum around a set of ten gifts (materials) with which children

Froebel's kindergarten curriculum provided opportunities for children to construct the necessary concepts for geometry through play.
(© Corbis/Bettmann)

FROEBEL'S STAGES OF DEVELOPMENT

Infancy (birth to 3). This stage consists of sensory development through self-activity. The mother is the most important teacher at this stage. She provides for exercising of the limbs, as well as for maintaining the proper environment for self-activity.

Childhood (3 to 6). This stage begins with the appearance of language. The child begins to express the inner self outwardly. The activity of the child is play, and play should bring joy to the child. The emphasis of education during this stage is on the process of development rather than the product.

Boyhood (7 to 10). This stage reverses the prior stage; its aim is to make the external internal. Play becomes purposeful work, and the emphasis is on the product rather that the process. Instruction is a feature of this stage, and the curriculum includes religion, natural science, language, and art.

could play and occupations (activities) in which they could engage. Froebel called these materials "gifts of God," because they were used not only for object lessons but also to represent the concepts of unity and diversity. The presentation of the gifts was systematic, with each gift foreshadowing the

Froebel made a significant contribution to the field through his invention of blocks as instructional materials for young children. Note the block constructions on the table. (© *Carondolet Historical Society, St. Louis*)

following one and the simple leading to the complex. Each gift represented a form of life, love, and light. The gifts led to discovery and included solids, surfaces, lines, points, and reconstructions.

The first ten gifts were made primarily of wood, although the first gift, the ball, was also made of worsted wool or yarn for infants. The ball is the symbol of the simplest form of unity. The second gift—a cube, a ball, and a cylinder—symbolized Froebel's laws of opposites and connections. The cube is opposite the ball in that the ball is continuously in motion, while the cube is continuously at rest, and the ball has no sides, while the cube is many-sided. The cylinder is symbolic of the connection between the two opposites, in that a cylinder can be at rest or continuously in motion, and it can be sided yet in part has no sides. The next four gifts were forms of blocks, with the third gift being the simplest set of building blocks ever invented. It was one solid cube divided into eight smaller cubes that could be used to create a variety of different things. Through playing with these four gifts of blocks, children began to discover part-to-whole relationships. The seventh gift was blocks that were flat planes rather than cubes, and the eighth gift was blocks that were flat sticks or geometric lines. The ninth gift was rings of copper or metal wire, and the tenth gift was a point, represented by natural objects such as peas, pebbles, or seeds. Froebel's gifts moved from solids to planes to lines to points, the basic concepts of geometry.

Froebel's occupations were craftlike in nature and allowed for creative activity, such as clay modeling, paper folding, weaving, and paper perforating. Froebel's curriculum also included arithmetic, nature study, language study, gardening, the care of pets, and games and songs. In 1844, he wrote *Mother-Play and Nursery Songs,* a book of more than fifty simple games and songs for mothers to use with their children. He used this book to train mothers in bringing the learning of the kindergarten into the home.

CONSTRUCTIONS

1. Journal Entry

As you read about these pioneers in the field, reflect and write about what might have happened to children and the early childhood profession (including yourself) had certain leaders not been able to complete or implement their ideas. Additionally, think about the three themes mentioned at the beginning of the chapter, then trace these themes through a time line.

2. Research

Research the life of one of these early theorists and learn more about the period in which he lived, including the Zeitgeist, what was happening in the lives of young children, and how the theorist's ideas were interpreted during his lifetime.

The students in Dr. K.'s class have just completed their research projects on the lives of some of the early childhood theorists and practitioners and are eagerly sharing their findings before class begins.

DANIELLE: Well, I did my research on Rousseau, and he really did influence the field with his ideas of play and natural development. But let me tell you! In real life he was not a nice man! Did you know that he abandoned his own ten children?

ZENAH: Wow, that seems strange considering all he wrote about children, but I guess we have to remember what we learned earlier in this class about abandonment and how it was viewed differently back then.

AMY: That's right, Zenah. You know when Dr. K. assigned these research projects I was dreading it because I thought it would be so boring, but now I'm really into history. I did Plato and I can't believe that play was an important part of the curriculum way back then. I thought it was something radical and new.

DANIELLE: Yeah, I didn't even think we should be studying history, and now I want to go on a crusade to put play back into the kindergarten.

ERIC: I can see the headlines now—Danielle, a dauntless crusader for play in the kindergarten classroom.

ZENAH: Well, I do think she has a point. When I was in kindergarten we never got to play. All we got to do was be quiet and fill in those worksheets.

TILLIE: Me too, Zenah! But I thought that was what early childhood teachers were supposed to do. This history chapter is really making me rethink my ideas about that.

ERIC: I really got into Froebel's gifts and occupations and how he thought children would learn those abstract ideas like unity and diversity by playing with them. I'm not sure that constructivists would agree with those ideas. Guess I could ask Dr. K. about that. But even if children don't learn all those abstract ideas from those gifts, I still think that many of them could be used in today's early childhood classrooms. I loved all of the different kinds of building blocks and the perforated cards.

TILLIE: I did Froebel too, and one of the things I found out was that he started and ended the day with the children in a circle. I think this was related to those ideas of unity and diversity too, because he would have them sing about unity while holding hands. Hmm, I wonder if that is how circle time got started.

ERIC: You may be onto something Tillie, and it looks like we have lots of questions for Dr. K. Don't you wonder if these early ideas influenced early childhood education in America?

THE KINDERGARTEN MOVEMENT IN AMERICA

Until this point in the chapter, you have learned about early pioneers who created theories and philosophies for early childhood practice. Although some were practitioners as well, their primary role was in establishing the ideas related to early childhood education. The next pioneers were Americans who are remembered because of their contributions to early childhood practice.

In colonial America, the goal of education during the seventeenth century was basically religious. In Massachusetts and Connecticut, schools were quite European, with Latin grammar schools for educating young men and dame schools for teaching poor children to read and write. In the

South, tutors educated wealthy boys and charity schools taught poor children how to read, write, and solve math problems.

> During the eighteenth century, the interest in education for religious and intellectual purposes began to wane.

During the eighteenth century, the interest in education for religious and intellectual purposes began to wane, as Americans began to view commerce as the way to advance. Toward the end of the eighteenth century, the church lost its control of the schools, and after the Revolutionary War, the state began to assume more responsibility for educating the masses.

With the Industrial Revolution in the early part of the nineteenth century, "two fifths of all persons employed in New England factories were children between the ages of seven and sixteen" (Braun & Edwards, 1972, p. 87). These children were spending up to sixteen hours a day, six days a week, at work. Consequently, there were few schools in operation, and few children were attending them. The schools were highly dogmatic and authoritarian, with schoolmasters who subscribed to the notion that sparing the rod spoiled the child.

The kindergarten movement of the late 1800s was a push to educate children ages three to seven or eight outside the home. Today this is generally referred to as early childhood education. This movement was significant in that it started outside public educational institutions, and it is still separate from traditional elementary school education in many ways. The methods used in the education of young children were a radical departure from the methods being used in traditional elementary schools. Early American public and private kindergartens followed Froebel's curriculum of songs, games, nature study, and play. The teachers exemplified Froebel's idea that they should serve as guides to children's development and should love the children.

Private Kindergartens

The first kindergartens in America were private and German-speaking. They were started by people who had learned Froebel's method before coming to America. As these private schools emerged, their philosophies found acceptance and fit in the Zeitgeist of post–Civil War America.

Margarethe Schurz (1833–1876). Carl and Margarethe Schurz moved to America in 1852 and established the first American kindergarten in Watertown, Wisconsin, in 1856. This kindergarten was a private German-speaking program based on Froebel's method. Margarethe had been a student of Froebel's in Germany. A number of educators in other parts of the United States heard about this kindergarten and visited it. By 1870, there were at least ten private German-speaking kindergartens in the United States.

Elizabeth Peabody (1804–1894). Elizabeth Peabody was one of the first and most influential people to visit the Schurz kindergarten. Peabody had heard Carl Schurz on one of his speaking tours and had become interested in kindergarten programs. She opened the first English-speaking American kindergarten, a private program, in Boston in 1860. She helped spread the word about kindergartens with her writing and lectures and later studied in Europe after hearing about Froebel's work. Peabody was invaluable in helping to start the first public kindergarten in St. Louis, Missouri.

Henry Barnard (1811–1900). Many people at all levels of society are needed to further a cause. Henry Barnard, the first U.S. Commissioner of Education, went to London to observe a Froebelian program. One of Barnard's writings, *Kindergarten and Child Culture Papers* (1880), helped popularize the kindergarten movement. Just as Froebel became known as the father of kindergarten, Barnard became known as the father of the American kindergarten (Osborn, 1991).

Public Kindergartens

During the post–Civil War years, a new appreciation of education and the arts began to emerge in the United States. Americans developed a new concern for others and a passion for social work. Many educators suggested that education should include more than the basics. Under the influence of Horace Mann, the first compulsory attendance law was passed in 1852, and the first public taxation for schools was passed in 1874. By the end of the century, graded elementary schools had been established, and the first public school kindergarten was started in 1873.

Susan Blow (1843–1916). Susan Blow was another important leader of the kindergarten movement. She began her work in St. Louis in the 1870s. With the help of William T. Harris, superintendent of the St. Louis public schools, she became the director of the first public school kindergarten in 1873. Blow was a strict Froebelian in her teaching approach, and she trained her teachers in the use of Froebelian methods. As she expanded her notions about early childhood education, she instituted home visits and mother's meetings, as well as field trips and nature studies. Blow moved to New York City and taught at Columbia University from 1896 to 1909. She was also active in one of the first early childhood professional organizations, the International Kindergarten Union. In 1930, the union's membership was extended to include the elementary grades, and the name

As a strict Froebelian, Blow included gardening as part of the nature study of the kindergarten curriculum. (© *Carondolet Historical Society, St. Louis*)

of the organization was changed to the Association for Childhood Education. Today it includes members from many countries and, as you read in Chapter 2, is the Association for Childhood Education International (ACEI).

Patty Smith Hill (1868–1946).   Another pioneer in the kindergarten movement was Patty Smith Hill. She received her early teacher training at the Louisville Kindergarten Training School, where she learned Froebel's methods. Hill broke from the Froebelian tradition, however, and added her own ideas, such as closely observing children and following their lead. She also expanded her interests to include nursery school education. Like Blow, she was active in the International Kindergarten Union and she taught at Columbia University from 1906 to 1931.

While Blow and Hill were teaching at Columbia, their legends were made. Many books and articles have been written about their disagreements over whether the Froebelian approach should be followed rigidly or other materials and activities based on the work of John Dewey and G. Stanley Hall should be included in the curriculum. It is reported that even though they held decidedly different points of view and were adamant about them neither ever said an unkind word to the other.

Hill introduced many new materials into kindergartens. She developed Patty Hill blocks, the forerunner of today's large hollow blocks, and Hill-Hart chairs, with accompanying sets of wheels, rods, and bars to make wagons and carts. The curriculum was determined according to the children's interests and included nature study, literature, music, games, dolls, art, and blocks. Hill is also known for writing the lyrics to the song, *"Happy Birthday to You,"* which was composed by her sister Mildred Smith.

African-American Kindergartens

The post–Civil War years marked the strict separation of black and white children in public schools and child-care facilities. Had it not been for leaders such as Lucy Laney and free schools such as Butler School on the campus of Hampton Institute, education for young black children would have been almost nonexistent.

Lucy Craft Laney (1854–1933). Lucy Craft Laney was born in Macon, Georgia, to slave parents who were able to purchase their family's freedom. She was a member of the first class to graduate from Hampton Institute, a black university founded in Virginia in 1868, and later from Atlanta University, a black graduate school founded in 1865. In 1883, she started a nursery and day school for African-American children that came to be known as the Haines Normal and Industrial Institute in Augusta, Georgia. The school's purpose was to provide an enrichment program for children. The program lasted for only four years (Osborn, 1991), and Laney's interest shifted to the education of older children. Laney was one of many people who established nursery schools, kindergartens, and daycare centers for African-American children because they were excluded from public programs.

Haydee Campbell, Mary Church Terrell, and Josephine Yates. The black kindergarten movement grew out of the National Association of Colored Women (NACW), an organization established in 1896. Mary Church Terrell (1863–1954), the first president of this organization, established a kindergarten section within the NACW, and Haydee Campbell served as the first head of this section. It is thought that Campbell studied under Susan Blow (Cunningham & Osborn, 1979). One of the goals of the kindergarten section of the NACW was to establish kindergartens throughout the South. According to Hunton (1908), there were at least fifteen black kindergartens in eight southern states by the turn of the century. Many of the major black

Through the work of Lucy Laney and others, the black kindergarten movement provided early educational experiences for young African American children. (© *Lucy Craft Laney Museum, Augusta, GA*)

universities also had kindergarten programs and offered academic courses in early childhood education.

Josephine Yates, president of the NACW in 1906 and professor of English at Lincoln Institute, was an influential leader in the black kindergarten movement. Her column in *Colored American Magazine* chronicled the development of the early black kindergarten movement (Osborn, 1991). In 1905, she wrote a plan outlining the role of the NACW in establishing black kindergartens throughout the South. This plan included committees to visit families where children were not in school, to find clothing for poor families, to repair and make clothing for children when none was available, and to aid young homemakers and the elderly. In this article, she concluded:

> The thoughts included in this plan show that colored mothers, teachers, and club women generally are alive to the best interest of the race; and through kindergartens, mothers' clubs and all other forms of its work, the National Association of Colored Women hopes to be a valuable instrument in the task of "Lifting as we climb." (Yates, 1905, p. 311)

As a follower of Froebel, Yates recognized the value of play in the curriculum and served as a balance against the attack on play by many other black kindergarten leaders. She spent considerable time translating Froebel's work into English so that others could come to appreciate the value of play.

After the 1880s, kindergartens began to be set up across the United States at a rapid rate. Although early on they did little to influence the education of young children in elementary schools, they were more influential after the 1890s.

CONSTRUCTIONS

Reflections

Now that you've read about the kindergarten movement, reflect on the observations you have made. What surprised you? What new information did you learn? What issues were important to these leaders? Draw a picture that could serve as a symbol for one of the pioneer's work. Explain your symbol to the class.

THE CHILD STUDY MOVEMENT

Another key movement that influenced early childhood education was the child study movement. Some early researchers, biologists, and doctors, such as Dieterich Tiedemann in 1787, Charles Darwin in 1840, and C. Feldman in 1833, produced written observations of their own children's or their patients' growth and development (Osborn, 1991). After the turn of the century, the child study movement formalized the use of university-based research in early childhood education to establish normative data about young children's growth and development.

University Researchers

From the turn of the century through the 1940s, philosophers, physicians, social workers, and researchers played crucial roles in early childhood education. G. Stanley Hall, John Dewey, Maria Montessori, Arnold Gesell, and Jean Piaget were all leaders in the child study movement. Although their viewpoints differed, they all affected the development of kindergartens, the primary grades, childcare, and nursery schools.

G. Stanley Hall is known as the founder of child psychology and the child development movement.

G. Stanley Hall (1844–1924). Hall is known as the founder of American child psychology and the child study movement. Through the use of a new research method, the questionnaire, he conducted systematic studies of large groups of children at Clark University. His findings opened the way for teachers to reconsider the Froebelian method and to base their instruction on child psychology. Hall was interested in supporting kindergartens and nursery schools with interdisciplinary teams of doctors, psychologists, and educators. He believed that this **multidisciplinary** approach to early childhood education was in the best interest of the child. Hall emphasized the recapitulation concept of development, theorizing that in a short time children go through the same developmental process as the species goes through over a long period of time. This concept gave rise to the idea of *readiness,* the notion that each step in a child's development is natural, that the next step cannot be taken until the child is ready to take it, and that no one should interfere with that development process.

John Dewey (1859–1952).

Dewey was one of the most influential leaders of the child-centered **progressive movement** in kindergarten and the primary grades. He established an experimental school at the University of Chicago, where he tested his ideas about education. To Dewey, education was the continuous reconstruction of experience. He advocated a problem-solving method to be used in teaching young children, but he felt that the need to know had to come from within the child. Like John Locke, he believed that people learn by doing, and he suggested that school does not prepare us for life but rather *is* life. One of the outcomes of Dewey's ideas was the **project approach** to education. This approach integrates all subject matter around children's real-life experiences and encourages them to engage in projects of their choosing. As you learned in Chapter 8, Dewey's ideas influenced educational practice in many educational fields.

One of the outcomes of the progressive education movement was the merging of kindergarten and the primary grades, starting around 1929. As a result of this merger, kindergarten programs moved into public school settings, and kindergarten teachers were forced to confront philosophical, academic, and program perturbations. Their primary goals were not the same as the elementary teachers' goals. Often the kindergarten teachers would compromise by allowing some of the children's time to be devoted to "reading readiness" and other such "transitional" skills. They did away with project work and replaced it with learning centers. The progressive movement peaked and began to decline in the 1930s. As the movement ebbed, the cost of the merger with elementary education became apparent to early childhood educators.

Maria Montessori (1870–1952).

Montessori, an Italian doctor, developed an educational method for teaching children from birth to age six. This method was based on the belief that all children have similar needs regardless of their social status or intellectual abilities. Furthermore, she viewed mental retardation as an educational rather than a medical problem.

Montessori became interested in the education of young children while she was serving as an intern in the psychiatric clinic of the University of Rome. She assumed the directorship of a school for children with mental handicaps, and while working at this school, she designed and used materials that enabled the children to pass local school exams. Her next teaching assignment was to establish a school for poor children living in a crowded

---

During the progressive education movement, kindergarten and the primary grades merged.

ASK YOURSELF

What do I know about the early research on young children? Have I heard people describe children's behavior in terms of norms? What kinds of studies have been conducted with children?

tenement house who went unsupervised for long periods of time. In this tenement, she worked with "fifty to sixty children between the ages of two-and-a-half to seven years" (Braun & Edwards, 1972, p. 111). She was a social reformer in that she devised a scheme whereby part of the parents' rent resulted in collective ownership of the school. Her views emphasized the importance of cooperation between home and school.

Based on her research with these tenement children, Montessori created learning environments and materials for training the senses that were appropriate for all children. She maintained that children must develop in all areas—physical, intellectual, linguistic, and social. She held that perceptual learning, which trains the senses through the handling and moving of materials, is one way to help children develop the ability to think. Influenced by Edouard Seguin's teaching materials and methods for mentally retarded children, she developed a number of learning materials that children could manipulate. To Montessori, the materials had to be simple, inherently interesting, and self-correcting (Braun & Edwards, 1972).

Along with the use of these sensory materials, the Montessori curriculum included exercises in practical life, muscular development, and the teaching of academic skills. Today Montessori's method is still very popular, and teacher training facilities are located throughout the United States.

Arnold Gesell (1880–1961). Gesell studied under G. Stanley Hall at Johns Hopkins University. He used photography to record the behavior of young children at each stage of development. As a result of many years of study, he compiled **normative data** based on sampling the growth and development of large numbers of young children. Although Gesell did not consider norms to be rigid time lines for "normal" development, his studies did lead to the notion that young children develop certain behaviors at certain ages. Gesell viewed nursery schools as vital because of their ability to support the readiness concept. He held that children will learn certain concepts only when they are ready, and to try to teach these concepts before then is not only a waste of time but also harmful to the child's development.

Jean Piaget (1896–1980). The work of Jean Piaget had a strong impact on the American early childhood movement. As we saw in Chapter 4, Piaget started his career as a biologist and did some of his first research on mollusks. Because of his background in biology, Piaget offers a unique theoretical perspective that integrates biological, physical, and intellectual development.

Piaget became a **genetic epistemologist** because he was highly interested in the origins of knowledge. He studied children so that he could discover how knowledge develops in a child's mind. His research supports the idea that children construct knowledge from within their minds. Additionally, he found that action is the source of all knowledge for young children.

Piaget's earliest and best-known work suggests that children's thoughts are qualitatively different at different stages of development (see Chapter 3). This aspect of Piaget's theory seems to support the notion of readiness as put forth by other developmental theorists. His later work on the functional side of knowing, which you learned about in Chapter 4, has become more popular in recent years in that it is more useful in educational settings.

MULTIPLE PERSPECTIVES

From an Early Childhood Researcher

Hermina Sinclair was a colleague of Jean Piaget.

I do want to say something about the danger of many developmental theories, including Piaget, when one doesn't read the author carefully. I think there is a danger to read into these accounts of cognitive development the notion that at this level the child cannot do this or that, or at this level such a concept is still developing. I think readiness is a very dangerous issue if it is defined as a prerequisite for learning to do something else. To give an example of such a possible misconception, I will use one that fits nicely into some other experiments and seems to be understandable without knowing any of Piaget's theory.

You have a child of four, and this child can already count. We will ask him, "Would you count?" and usually they already start at the left if the chips are put on the table in a line from left to right. So he counts one, two, three, four, five, six, and seven. You ask him, "Would you start counting on the other side?" For the four-year-old, it is not at all obvious that the answer has to be seven again. So he will count it again and will be quite happy to say seven again. And if you ask before he counts, "Can you tell me what it will be when you start counting there?" he will say, "Well, no," and then start counting. In other words, *seven* to this four-year-old child has a very different meaning from *seven* to an older child, who, when asked the same question, just shrugs and says, "Seven, and also seven the other way. Why ask such utterly silly questions?"

There are two ideas that at the age of four are not yet developed in the child's number concept. One is the feeling of necessity. For the older child, there is no question: Counting one way or the other way gives necessarily the same answer. That idea is absent in the thinking of the four-year-old. The second idea is the notion that the **spatial** order of the action of counting determines the product, so that if you are asked to choose a different spatial order, you cannot be sure of the product. There is still a close link between the spatial order of the action of counting and of the position of the objects counted. The link between the subject's action and his product is too close, and it comes out as if only one specific action will have that specific result: too close a spatial link and not enough feeling of necessity.

These are negatives that might make us forget that being able to put your counting words into one-to-one correspondence with each chip and not counting one twice or skipping one is already a great achievement. We must remember that the one-to-one careful correspondence of word to object is a basic ingredient of any kind of number concept. It is a very important achievement. Now, the other important achievement is knowing the number words. That achievement you can only learn from someone else. The one-to-one correspondence children can work out for themselves, but knowing the words is a typical social acquisition.

What I want to underline is that it is all right to look for things that are missing at a certain level, but what one should not forget is to look for what is already there that is a cognitive achievement. So when you read certain books that describe what a child has not yet mastered, never forget it is just as important to always look for what is already there. In fact, one of Piaget's recommendations when interviewing children was if the child does not give what you think is the right answer to the question, ask yourself to what question the child's answer would be the right answer. It's a very difficult task. The child says something that you feel is totally wrong. Now you wonder to what question would that be a right answer. It is an excellent exercise for psychologists who are dealing with cognitive development and perhaps for constructivist educators.

● ●

CONSTRUCTIONS

1. Research

Try interviewing a child using one of Piaget's clinical interview tasks. Listen for answers that you think are totally wrong. Write those answers down.

2. Analysis

Take each of those answers and try to determine the question you think the child was trying to answer. Then give the child's wrong answers to a partner and have him determine the question he thinks the child was trying to answer. Compare your answers and share your work. Were there some that were easy? Difficult?

University Laboratory Schools

During the early 1900s, as the idea of child study became an accepted and valued practice at major universities, researchers felt a need to have samples of children close at hand to study. Lawrence Frank recognized that **laboratory schools** had to be established to conduct systematic and complete studies of children's growth and development. Through his work with the Rockefeller Foundation, he was able to raise sufficient grant money to set up institutes of child study at Columbia University and at the University of Minnesota (Osborn, 1991). Frank served as a catalyst to change the emphasis from child study to child development and is considered the key leader of the child development movement. He pioneered the idea that child development should be researched through an **interdisciplinary** approach to understand the whole child. The findings from a multitude of different disciplines, such as biology, medicine, anthropology, and education, should be integrated into one whole interpretation. Frank also helped establish child study centers in schools of home economics as a support for the family.

Lucy Sprague Mitchell and Caroline Pratt were two more of the dauntless women in early childhood education who played a major role in developing university laboratory schools. In 1914, they opened the Play School in New York City. Funded by the Rockefeller Foundation, this school later became the laboratory school for the Bureau of Educational Experiments (now Bank Street College of Education). At the request of the children, Mitchell and Pratt changed the name of the school to the City and Country School in 1919. They adopted a new philosophy developed by John Dewey and did not implement Froebel's ideas per se. For Mitchell and Pratt, the role of an early childhood teacher was to guide the children and manage the classroom activity.

Mitchell and Pratt viewed university laboratory schools as a way to model exemplary educational programs, provide data for research, and educate parents about the implications of research. One of Pratt's major contributions was the invention of unit blocks, a series of blocks in which one size is a unit and the others are fractions and multiples of that unit. She based her design on Froebel's four building "gifts" (Cartwright, 1988).

Because Mitchell was a follower of Dewey, she valued children's interactions with their environments. She noted that the only stories available for children were nursery rhymes and classical literature. One of her major contributions was to write realistic stories called "The Here and Now Stories," which told about contemporary children's activities and used language appropriate for children.

The unit blocks invented by Pratt are the kind most used in today's preschools and kindergartens. (© *City and Country School Archive, New York*)

CONSTRUCTIONS

1. Exploration

Find a Web site of a laboratory school that was not mentioned in this chapter.

2. Research

What is the history of that laboratory school? When did it begin? Who was its pioneer? What research findings have come from that school?

3. Report

Record your findings and share them with a classmate.

THE NURSERY SCHOOL AND CHILD-CARE MOVEMENT

Although the child study movement advocated nursery schools and elevated them to a new level of importance, the nursery school movement, which advocates providing a healthy and safe environment for children, has been a vital force in the education of young children for years.

Nursery School Leaders

The nursery school movement has been a vital force in the education of young children for years.

Robert Owen (1771–1858). Robert Owen is credited with establishing the first infant school in England in 1816. He received children from the time they could walk to ten years of age, when they were eligible to work in the mills. From his early work with infant schools, the idea grew and spread throughout England. In 1822, Owen came to America and established an infant school and daycare center in Indiana. Along with providing for the care of the children, Owen provided a curriculum that included play, music, and physical activity.

Margaret McMillan (1860–1931) and Rachel McMillan (1859–1917). Margaret and Rachel McMillan were pioneers in health services for children and were the first to use the term **nursery school.** They were interested in the total child and wanted programs that provided a healthy environment that included lots of sunshine, play space, and attention to children's medical needs. Their 1908 nursery school, the Deptford School, became the first open-air nursery school in England. Margaret established a daily health inspection for all children in the nursery school, and they became resistant to illness in a neighborhood prone to epidemics and deficiency diseases. When more than seven hundred children between the ages one and five died of measles, there was not one fatal case at the Deptford School in London. In one report to the school's electors, McMillan claimed that the average number of delicate and diseased children entering elementary school at the age of five was 30 to 40 percent, while the average of the open-air nursery was 7 percent (Braun & Edwards, 1972).

Abigail Adams Eliot (1892–1992). Abigail Adams Eliot studied with Margaret McMillan in 1921 and is considered the pioneer of the nursery school movement in the United States. Eliot had been trained as a social worker but decided that she was more interested in the education of the young child. In 1922, she founded the Ruggles Street Nursery School Training Center in Boston. The school was free, and many of the children's parents were poor and uneducated. Eliot became interested in working with both the children and their parents, a new idea in education. She held that educating the parents about their children improved the children's physical and mental lives. By 1933, there were seven hundred nursery schools throughout the country, and Eliot determined that teachers needed a college education to understand their work. In 1951, the training center became the Nursery Training School of Boston, a professional school in the College of Special Studies.

Harriet Merrill Johnson (1867–1934). Harriet Merrill Johnson set up a nursery school at the City and Country School of the Bureau of Educational Experiments (now Bank Street College of Education) in New York City in 1919 (Braun & Edwards, 1972). In *Children in the Nursery School* (1928), Johnson suggested that the school should foster children's personal development. Strongly influenced by the writings of Sigmund Freud, she was a proponent of play in nursery schools, as she believed that play was a means by which children could resolve conflicts. She also held that observations of children engaged in play could provide information about their emotional urges.

Patty Smith Hill (1868–1946). Although more often linked with the kindergarten movement (see page 366), Hill started a laboratory nursery school at Columbia University's Teachers College in 1921. Because of her keen interest in nursery education, she was helpful in sending Abigail Eliot to England to study with Margaret McMillan. In 1925, Hill organized the Committee on Nursery Schools, with a membership of twenty-five. Later this became the National Association for Nursery Education and, in 1964, the National Association for the Education of Young Children (NAEYC).

African-American Nursery Schools

Dorothy Howard established the first black nursery school in Washington, D.C., in 1927 and operated it for more than fifty years. Phyllis Jones Tilly opened a black laboratory nursery school at Hampton Institute two years later, in 1929. A second laboratory nursery school, under the direction of Pearlie Reed, was established at Spelman College in 1930, and a third one, under the direction of Flemmie Kittrell, opened at Bennett College in 1931. These three schools emphasized a curriculum based on a child development approach using a program of work that focused on the whole child (Osborn, 1991).

Works Progress Administration Nurseries

During the Great Depression and World War II, women joined the work force in great numbers. To address the problem of care for children whose mothers worked, federal money was used to establish and fund Works Progress Administration nurseries and war nurseries. The nurseries had two major purposes: (1) to provide employment for previously unemployed teachers and (2) to provide a place for working mothers to leave their children. The war nurseries also were known as Lanham Act Nurseries, after the 1942 Lanham Act, passed to provide funds for war-impacted communities.

Head Start Program

No history of the nursery and child-care movement would be complete without looking at President Lyndon B. Johnson's Great Society and War on Poverty, which addressed children's needs through government programs. Johnson, like Plato, thought that he could build a strong country through education. In the 1960s, nearly 1 million children from low-income families entered school each year for the first time. Many of these children had little self-confidence and many different health problems. Many children either dropped out of school at an early age or made grades that added to their low self-esteem. Johnson wanted a program that would give these children a better start by providing them with health care and the early education they needed to be successful in school. In his view, society had to recognize that good education begins with very young children and that society is responsible for providing that education if the parents are unable to do so.

> Head Start addressed children's needs through a government-funded program.

Head Start, the first government early intervention program to address the total health, education, and social needs of very young children, was launched as an eight-week summer program in 1965. It was designed to offset the cyclical nature of poverty by giving preschool children from low-income families a quality early childhood program that would meet their personal, social, nutritional, educational, and psychological needs. It became an established year-round program in August 1965 and was well received throughout the United States. In response to Johnson's request for an evaluation of Head Start in 1965, the Westinghouse Learning Corporation and Ohio University were contracted to evaluate former Head Start children. Their findings suggested that the summer program was totally ineffective and the year-round program was only marginally effective (Brown, 1985). Although this study met with severe criticism because of the way it was conducted, the result was that all summer programs were given the option of shifting to year-round programs. By 1971, however, there was concern that Head Start would be phased out altogether. Head Start parents and staff fought vigorously for continuation and won. (Refer back to Chapter 7.)

Planned Intervention

The Westinghouse report on Head Start caused many educators to question the effectiveness of the traditional nursery model being used in this program. They began to develop innovative follow-through approaches that they thought would sustain the Head Start children's initial gains. These approaches fell into four categories (Spodek & Brown, 1993), based on the theoretical or philosophical explanations of learning that the researchers thought held the greatest potential for success: behavioral, constructivist, Montessori, and open education. Research efforts in these areas were pooled, and the results were used to revamp Head Start. This planned intervention had lasting effects in improving school success, students' achievement, and children's attitudes and had an overall positive impact on Head Start families.

CONSTRUCTIONS

1. Research

Select, research, and analyze one of the planned variation models described above.

2. Analysis

Examine how consistently the theory or philosophy of the model determined the components included in program and the manner in which they were implemented and evaluated.

3. Report

Present your analysis to the class as an **advocate** for the use of this program and show how you would demonstrate accountability through evaluation of the outcomes of the program.

LAWS AND GOVERNMENT STANDARDS

In addition to the many pioneers we've mentioned, hundreds of others have helped shape the field of early childhood education. These are the unnamed people who were part of or behind various movements, inventions, and laws. This section presents some of the laws and standards that have had major effects on early childhood education.

The Industrial Revolution led to dramatic changes in child rearing and education in both England and the United States. Prior to the Industrial Revolution, very few children went to school. They had little need to learn to read and write or were taught these basics at home. The family made most of the goods and products they needed. Children's lives were devoted to farming or serving as apprentices to learn a trade. They could learn all they needed to know from their parents or the people to whom they were apprenticed.

The Industrial Revolution moved families from work on the land to work in the factories and from the country to the city, where they could no longer produce all the goods they needed to live. Additionally, this new kind of employment separated people's work from the home and parents from their children. According to Osborn (1991), children in the United States as young as "five or six years of age worked in factories for as long as sixteen hours a day" (p. 33). This gave rise to a major social problem—regulating child labor.

Industrialization created another problem that had to be addressed. There was a need for more skilled and educated workers than there had been in the past, and thus a need for better means by which to educate children. Following the Civil War, the kindergarten movement began to spread throughout England and the United States (see pages 363–368), and people were beginning to realize the educational and commercial benefits of educating children. By the early 1900s, America had a system of education that was supported by federal and state governments and provided free elementary and secondary schooling to all white children. As people involved in the education of children grew in their understanding of how children learned and of what kinds of programs served the best interests of children, a need for professional standards arose.

Child Labor Laws

Early in American history, there were no child labor laws. Children were considered to be part of the family's labor force as soon as they were able to work. Massachusetts passed the first child labor law in 1836, and although there was a decrease in the number of children employed between 1836 and 1838, this act was never really enforced. In 1904, a national committee was formed to investigate problems relating to the hiring of children under age fourteen, the number of hours children worked, and night work for young children. This committee produced legislation in 1906, but Congress did not pass it. In 1916, the Keating-Owen Act limited the number of hours children could work and the age at which children could be employed. Two years later, this law was declared unconstitutional. Not until 1938 did the Fair Labor Standards Act set up the first standards for the use of minor children in the labor force. This act prohibited the employment of children until age sixteen and was found to be constitutional by the Supreme Court. It is still in effect today.

Child laborers were finally protected in 1938 by the Fair Labor Standards Act.

School Attendance Laws

The Massachusetts child labor law of 1836 was also the first school attendance law in that it ruled that children could not work in factories unless they had attended school for at least three months during the previous year. As noted above, this law was rarely enforced. By 1860, seven states had passed similar school attendance requirements, varying only in the number of months of attendance they required. Even though the states did not strictly enforce these laws, they were important because they signaled the transfer of responsibility for education from parents to schools.

Unfortunately, these laws covered white children only. In fact, white society actually had laws *against* the early formal education of black children. Because of this, African-Americans had to devise their own means of educating children. Sabbath schools and later clandestine schools, secretly held in the basements of churches or homes, helped educate some black children. Not until 1954 did the U.S. Supreme Court rule that all schools must be integrated. In 1964, the Court ruled that schools could no longer deny the constitutional right of a black child to attend an integrated school. Today most states have compulsory attendance laws and are fully integrated.

Laws for Special Children

Laws require that all children, including those with disabilities, receive an education.

The first law guaranteeing an education to all children regardless of their exceptionalities was Public Law 94-142, passed in 1975. This law states that free and adequate public education in the least restrictive environment should be provided to all children, including those with disabilities. It also notes that due process should be provided in the screening of these children and that materials used for screening and testing children should not be racially or culturally biased. Two other laws, Public Law 95-49 in 1977 and Public Law 99-457 in 1986, were passed to provide incentives for states to extend these services to younger groups of children and to designate federal funds to support these programs. In 1997 Public Law 105-17 provided an amendment to the Individuals with Disabilities Education Act to extend the right of parents to be active participants in the special education process.

PROFESSIONAL STANDARDS

Although several major early childhood events occurred during the 1980s, we want to focus on two. First, in 1986, under the direction of Sue Bredekamp, NAEYC defined and later published what its membership considered to be developmentally appropriate practices for the education of young children. This handbook (Bredekamp, 1987), revised in 1997 (Bredekamp & Copple, 1997), has served to define what early childhood professionals value for young children and the standards by which programs can be evaluated.

The NAEYC handbook provides specific examples of appropriate and inappropriate practices for children at each level of development—infants, toddlers, preschoolers, and children in the primary grades. For example, in the area of curriculum for three- to five-year olds, an appropriate practice is that "curriculum content from various disciplines, such as math, science, or social studies, is integrated through themes, projects, play, and other learning experiences, so children develop an understanding of concepts and make connections across disciplines" (Bredekamp & Copple, 1997, p. 130). An inappropriate practice would be that "children's learning and cognitive development are seen as occurring in separate content areas, and times are set aside to teach each subject without integration" (Bredekamp & Copple, 1997, p. 130). Along with the NAEYC standards, many professional subject matter organizations, such as the National Council for Teachers of Mathematics, the International Reading Association, and the National Council for Teachers of English, have published standards that support and extend the NAEYC standards in their curriculum areas.

The second major movement that began in the 1980s and expanded in the 1990s is the push for even more professionalism in the field of early childhood education. This can be observed with the emergence of a number of professional research journals, such as *Early Childhood Research Quarterly, Research in Childhood Education,* and the *Journal of Early Childhood Teacher Education.* It can also be seen in the establishment of the National Academy of Early Childhood Programs, a national accreditation system for early childhood centers and schools. Finally, it can be seen in professional organizations' role in obtaining state certification for early childhood education teachers in public school settings and in expanding the educational and training components of credentials such as the Child Development Associate (CDA), based on field training and multiple experiences with young children.

CONSTRUCTIONS

1. Research

Read one section of the NAEYC handbook *Developmentally Appropriate Practice in Early Childhood Programs* (Bredekamp & Copple, 1997).

2. Analysis

Compare what is being advocated for children today with your own early childhood experiences. In what ways are they similar to what is advocated, and in what ways are they different?

3. Report

Present your findings to the class.

A FORWARD LOOK

Now that you have learned about the field of early childhood education and the pioneers and events that have made it what it is today, it is time for you to consider how all of this relates to you as a prospective early childhood professional. What is it like to be an early childhood educator today? First, you will have the support of NAEYC, an organization that has more than 100,000 members. Its accreditation project provides high standards by accrediting and then monitoring the quality child-care centers in which you might work. Head Start continues to thrive and offers many career opportunities for teachers. Other teaching possibilities can be found in new programs like Even Start, which has a strong parent component, so that services are expanded to a larger population. Corporate childcare is expanding because of the need for quality childcare for working women. Programs such as those found in Reggio Emilia and Pistoia, Italy, may influence you, and you may want to learn other new approaches for helping young children.

What will the children be like? Although some children's living conditions are better than in the past, many children still live below the poverty level, don't have adequate medical care, and don't receive any educational experiences prior to formal schooling. Violence has become a major problem for children. You may have children who bring weapons to school or who think they have to have a weapon to protect themselves at home and at school. Another problem you may encounter is alcohol and drug use. Additionally, like the children in Maria Montessori's tenement house, you may have a number of children who go home to an empty house because their parents work and can't afford childcare. Your classrooms will be more diverse due to the emphasis on inclusion and cultural diversity.

Consider how Betsy Dean was surprised when she found that many of the ideas of the past are still current or being revisited today (see pages 345–348). The belief that early childhood education leads to educational and social reform is still with us, as is an appreciation for the uniqueness of childhood. The role of play as the avenue by which young children learn has been supported throughout history. The idea that the curriculum should be child centered and based on what we learn from the study of children has been upheld throughout history. You can use these and other ideas from the past to help you decide what kind of teacher you want to be. Similarly, some of the early pioneers might be models to help you address perturbations that arise through the course of *your* history in the field. We hope that this journey through the history of early childhood education has filled you with a sense of pride that you are part of such a respected and challenging field.

This chapter has presented a wealth of information about the history of the field you plan to enter. Your constructions and experiences in revisiting this history and your own past provide the foundation on which you can begin to build your professional life. We wonder what contributions you might make to the field.

SUMMARY

▸ A constructivist perspective holds that you have to start with what you know.

▸ We study our history to empower our present; to identify issues, perturbations, and trends of the field; and to predict our future.

▸ Early childhood is justified as a field in that it is a way to reform society and education and it is a unique and special time of life.

▸ Many dauntless women and men have pioneered the field of early childhood education.

▸ The kindergarten movement, the child study movement, and the nursery school movement have become integrated into what is now known as early childhood education.

▸ Laws and professional standards have been developed and enacted over time to improve the quality of the lives and education of young children.

▸ There have been many perturbations throughout history that continue to raise questions about early childhood programs. These perturbations include the conflict between church and state control of education, whether education should serve the interests of the individual or the state, the conflict over which curriculum is most appropriate, the conflict over the methods that should be used, and the question of who should be educated.

▸ Many ideas that have remained constant throughout the history of early childhood education support important contemporary ideas. These include the role of active experience in the learning process; the education of the whole child, integrating physical, mental, and psychological well-being; the role of play in the learning process; the idea that learning is most effective when it builds on the interests of the learner; the idea that we learn from careful observation of the child; and the idea that education should be based on child development.

CONSTRUCTIONS

1. Analysis

Select a present-day issue and trace it from its beginning in the history of early childhood education. Determine how long the issue has persisted and how it has been approached differently throughout history.

2. Documentary

Prepare a documentary using a computer program or video to tell about a significant historical figure or time period. The documentary should include references to the Zeitgeist of the person or period, influences affecting the person or period, the philosophical or theoretical basis of the person or period, and the person or period's impact on early childhood education today.

3. Reflections

Early childhood education grew from the integration of ideas from three different fields: education, child health and welfare, and child study. Go back through the chapter and identify how and when these three areas merged into one field.

RESOURCES

Books

Brosterman, N. (1997). *Inventing kindergarten.* New York: Abrams.
 In this beautiful book, Brosterman attributes the success of the modern era to Froebel's kindergarten. Froebel's gifts are beautifully photographed and explained in this delightful text. The modern art of Georges Braque and Juan Gris and the architecture of Frank Lloyd Wright follow the section on Froebel's gifts and show how they were influenced by them.

Paciorek, K., & Munro, J. (1999). *Sources: Notable selections in early childhood education* (2nd ed.). Guilford, CT: Dushkin/McGraw-Hill.
 A book of the original writings of many of the early childhood historical pioneers. These writings have been organized around contemporary early childhood topics.

Web Sites

The Annenberg/CPB Project Exhibits Collection
 (http://www.learner.org/exhibits/renaissance/)
 This site provides an introduction to the Renaissance. Students can choose from a menu to learn about different aspects of the period.

City and Country School Home Page **(http://www.ccs.pvt.k12.ny.us/)**
 Parts of this site are still under construction, but it includes a biography of Caroline Pratt, displays of children's projects, and information on the school.

Giambattista Vico Home Page **(http://www.connis.com/~gapinton)**
 This site is linked with Amazon.com and provides a biography of Vico and his writings.

Informal Education **(http://www.infed.org/thinkers/)**
This site includes a brief outline of the contributions of many of the pioneers discussed in this chapter, along with some examples of their writing, details of their lives, and links to other Web sites. Pioneers included are Plato, Aristotle, Froebel, Owen, Rousseau, Dewey, Montessori, and Pestalozzi.

The Jean Piaget Archives **(http://www.unige.ch/piaget/presentg.html)**
Here you can travel to the Piagetian archives in Geneva, where you will learn about the activities of the archives and read a wonderful biography of Piaget.

Margaret McMillan
(http://www.spartacus.schoolnet.co.uk/Wmcmillan.htm)
This site provides photos and a complete biography of the McMillan sisters.

Robert Owen **(http://midwales.com/peopleplaces/rowen/)**
You can learn about Robert Owen's life and social reform philosophy. The graphics are particularly interesting.

Welcome to Bank Street College **(http://www.bnkst.edu)**
Here you can find current information about Bank Street College of Education, the School for Children and Families, and some of today's Bank Street experts in the field of early childhood education.

10

Meeting Today's Early Childhood Professionals

· ·

In this chapter, you will meet early childhood professionals whose roles vary widely, yet each of them contributes significantly to the well-being of young children. As you read about these women and men, you will be able to consider how their responsibilities and challenges meet the expectations you now hold for your own role in the profession. Perhaps, too, you will consider a role that you had not thought about previously. You will learn about these issues:

▶ Opportunities for professionals in the field of early childhood education
▶ What various early childhood professionals do in their jobs
▶ Pros and cons of each type of position
▶ Prerequisites for entering a particular role

INTRODUCTION

Once again, the students are gathering for Dr. K.'s class.

TILLIE: Gosh, it's almost the end of this course. Dr. K. sure has taught us a lot!

DANIELLE: Well, we've taught ourselves pretty much, too. I learned more by going to observe in various teachers' classrooms than I did in class.

AMY: I think I figured things out when we had discussions. If I had a different idea than someone else, I used to just disagree. Now I try to explain my idea. That's not always easy for me.

TILLIE: I didn't see any of the teachers we observed talking about all these theories.

ERIC: But they were *using* their theories.

TILLIE: Mostly they were reading stories and figuring out how to solve problems.

AMY: So?

ERIC: Maybe we could ask Dr. K. to bring some early childhood educators to class so we could ask them what their jobs are really like.

Like the students in Dr. K.'s class, you are probably thinking about the choices you'll make. When you are ready to enter the early childhood field professionally, you will be asking yourself several questions:

▸ With what ages of children do I work most effectively?

▸ In which types of settings do I prefer to work?

▸ Do I want to work directly with children on a regular basis, or do I prefer to be in a supportive role for children or families?

Throughout this book, you have read about the range of ages included in early childhood (birth through age eight), and you have visited a variety of settings personally or through the pages of this book. Now we consider the roles early childhood educators play in each of these settings. One approach we use is to present interviews with people who have chosen a variety of roles in the field. Our goal is to give you as much background as possible to support your decision about your entry into the field. Of course, we expect that over time you may change roles several times.

ASK YOURSELF

What are some of the questions I have now regarding the role of early childhood education professionals? What else do I want to know before I make some decisions about working with children?

Our goal is to give you as much background as possible to support your decisions about entry into the field.

TEACHING

Probably most of you will work directly with children in a classroom setting. Perhaps you have been planning for this role for many years, and you are truly looking forward to it. Having your own classroom and children, arranging the setting, planning the curriculum—all these facets of teaching appeal to you. Let's take a closer look at opportunities in this area and at what a real teacher's day is like.

Infant and Toddler Classrooms

Let's begin at the beginning of a child's life with settings for the youngest infants and toddlers. You will find that the number of caregivers/teachers and their assistants entering this aspect of our profession is growing rapidly. This growth seems to be occurring because more families are choosing center care for their very young children. Another factor is the high turnover rate in the field because the job is so demanding. Keep in mind that direct care encompasses playing with and conversing with children, as well as feeding, changing, and comforting them, while maintaining a safe, healthy, supportive environment. In performing all these varied functions, caregivers meet children's cognitive, emotional, social, and physical needs, facilitating their development rather than pushing them to reach some predetermined standard. Adults in this type of situation must be able to recognize and appreciate very young children's needs and accomplishments. When young children's needs are met, the children are comfortable. When they are comfortable, they are free to explore and learn (Gonzalez-Mena & Eyer, 1997).

> Caregivers facilitate each child's development rather than pushing the child.

Because of the varying needs and schedules of very young children, each child's day is usually planned on an individual basis. That means the teachers plan materials that will be available throughout the day and provide many opportunities for the children to explore. But the time for caregiving activities (such as feeding and diapering) and for play are to a large extent determined by the children's own rhythms. As children move into toddlerhood, their needs and schedules become more predictable, and many of them will participate in routines together, usually beginning with lunch as a social situation. However, free play is the norm. According to the widely accepted developmentally appropriate practice document (Bredekamp & Copple, 1997), *inappropriate practice* includes the following: . . . Adults impose "grouptime" on toddlers, forcing a large group to listen or watch an activity without providing opportunities for children to participate. (p. 84). Bredekamp and Copple contrast that with *appropriate practice* as follows: "Adults frequently read to toddlers, one individually on a caregiver's lap or in groups of two or three. Caregivers sing with toddlers" (p. 84). Chapter 3 provides more detailed information on this topic. NAEYC (1991) has recommended child-staff ratios as shown in Table 10.1.

Look at this table to determine how many toddlers one primary caregiver should be responsible for if there are eight toddlers in the group. What about eight infants? Have you read about or known any family with triplets

The knowledgeable caregiver sees feeding as a time to provide emotional and social support to infants. *(© Susan L. Ruggles/ The Picture Cube)*

ASK YOURSELF

Do I really think working with infants and toddlers requires a professional early childhood education? Why or why not?
····················

or quadruplets? If so, you may have noticed that caring for three or four babies is more than a full-time job for one person. Yet in child-care situations, caregivers routinely care for three or four babies for eight hours a day. In many states, higher ratios are legal and quite common. People who work with infants and toddlers must be knowledgeable and skilled, but it is essential that they be expected to care for no more than the number of children recommended by most knowledgeable educators. You will need to be sure of the expectations for caregivers when you are considering employment in an infant or toddler classroom so that you will be able to provide the kind of caring and teaching that you know is needed.

TABLE 10.1 Recommended Child:Staff Ratios for Infant and Toddler Groups

	Group Size			
Age	*6*	*8*	*10*	*12*
Infants (birth to 12 months)	1:3	1:4		
Toddlers (12 to 24 months)	1:3	1:4	1:5	1:4
2-year-olds (24 to 30 months)		1:4	1:5	1:6
2½-year-olds (30 to 36 months)			1:5	1:6

Source: From *Accreditation criteria and procedures of the National Academy of Early Childhood Programs* (Rev. ed.) (p. 41), by NAEYC, 1991. Washington, DC: NAEYC.

The best approach to meeting the needs of infants and toddlers is to assign primary caregivers.

Primary Caregivers.

The best approach to meeting the needs of infants and toddlers is to assign **primary caregivers.** This plan allows a child to become attached to a specific caregiver, who attends to no more than two or three other infants. One adult can work with a slightly larger number of toddlers, but their needs for caregiving are still great. Although a primary caregiver is assigned, when that person is not immediately available (perhaps feeding another baby), the partner caregiver in the group will assist as needed. Keep in mind that the partner also is responsible as primary caregiver for a comparable number of babies. Thus two adults in infant and toddler programs must work together well as a team.

The lead caregiver's partner may be a teacher or an associate or assistant. Despite the fact that one adult is usually given primary responsibility for the management of the overall setting, each adult must be equally respected and valued by the other. When the relationship between the **lead caregiver** and the associate or assistant is positive, the focus remains on meeting the children's needs. In such situations, adults who enjoy very young children will feel rewarded at the end of the day, even if that day has been strenuous physically, mentally, and emotionally. The satisfactions in which a good teacher delights more than compensate for the challenges.

CONSTRUCTIONS

1. Reflection

As you have observed in classrooms, you have probably seen two adults working together. What were the differences in their roles? How did the children seem to respond to each of them?

2. Research

Read about the roles of teachers and assistants from one or two sources. Use that information and your own observations and experiences to design job descriptions for a teacher and an assistant.

Early Intervention.

If you enjoy working with infants and toddlers, you may want to consider an **early intervention program (EIP).** Our expectation is that children with special needs will be included in groups of typically developing children. Most infant/toddler programs are full-day programs for working parents, but some parents of children with special needs prefer part-day early intervention programs. Therefore, groups have been created especially to provide these services. Families whose children have been identified as having special needs are entitled to the services,

When the level of frustration appears overwhelming, a teacher steps in to offer enough support to enable the children to manage. *(© Elizabeth Crews)*

which are sometimes delivered in group settings and sometimes in the child's home. Keep in mind that for families who prefer it, full-day programs are also an option. Whether children with special needs are included in general programs or are in special programs, each child has her own written plan that the parents, teachers, and specialists work out together.

All teachers are expected to be prepared to work with children with and without special needs. However, some teachers who are especially interested in addressing handicapping conditions may choose to work primarily with children with special needs. These teachers' educational programs will consist of regular early childhood education, with additional course work and practicum experiences in special situations. For example, such a teacher may work with children whose disabilities warrant their being in a small group in a learning setting for part of the day. Such a placement is appropriate only when the child's individualized education plan (IEP) team makes this determination. Recall from Chapter 7 that an IEP team must include the child's family and that the family must participate in and approve the plan rather than merely signing something prepared by a professional educator.

Another role that teachers who specialize in early childhood special education may play is that of serving as a consultant and model for classroom teachers. They may help classroom teachers modify the environment or schedule, as well as help plan appropriate activities for individual children

Early intervention specialists may serve as consultants to classroom teachers.

with disabilities. Specialists may model teaching approaches or may work directly with a child, providing the additional support that child needs. For example, in a second-grade classroom, a specialist may work with a child with a visual impairment, developing ways in which that child can independently manage the same assignments that the rest of the class is doing. The specialist may then move to a first-grade classroom to support a child with a behavioral disorder as that child struggles to maintain appropriate behavior in the group setting. Some routine special supports can be provided by assistants who have been trained, but when there is a wide range of situations, each requiring specialized knowledge, the early childhood special educator is an important addition to the school team.

Let's look in on Dr. K.'s class again. Eric has obtained a new job as an assistant teacher in a toddler classroom, and Dr. K. has asked him if he'll tell the class what being with ten toddlers for four hours a day is like. Eric is eager to give some examples of his experiences.

ERIC: At first the children seemed afraid of me, but I remembered that I should let them approach me. Dr. K. has told us that over and over. Now when I arrive, one little boy always rushes up to me chanting, "Eric, Eric, play, play." I think he really needs attention, but the teacher said I need to interact with other children, too. Even though there are two of us and ten children, we are still busy every minute and could use about three more people to help, especially when it's time to go outside on a cold day.

Yesterday Maggie, who is about a year and a half old, brought me a board book and plopped down on my lap, saying, "Book." There was a picture of an animal on each page. She could say either the animal's name or the sound it makes for about half of them. Her favorite is "baaaaa." When she didn't know a name or a sound, she turned to face me, looking right into my eyes as though she knew I'd know. She's another one that's hard to resist.

Oh, and then there's José. Every day he has added at least one new word. Today he identified the color of a car he was playing with—"lellow." He really beamed when I said, "Yes, your car is yellow." I was proud of myself, too, because my teacher had reminded me twice not to quiz toddlers with "What color is it?" She told me to observe each child, and I'd soon learn what each one's interest is at that moment. It's true, too. I was about to make a sound like a car, and then I found out he was really concentrating on the color.

DANIELLE: Well, how do you know what to do or what to say to a little kid?

TILLIE: Oh, for heaven's sakes, Danielle. Just say whatever you feel like. Those kids don't really know what you're talking about.

Observe each child to find out what she is interested in.

ASK YOURSELF

Should caregivers have to focus on the children all the time? Or should they be expected to talk with other adults, rather than the children, as they go about the routine care of young children? Would the latter approach make the job more appealing to people?

ERIC: Well, they don't understand everything yet, of course. But you'd be surprised how much they do know. They just can't explain it all in words yet. I've found out that I don't have to be talking all the time. Toddlers can tell when I'm interested. I'm surprised at how interested I am in such little children, but I like knowing how important their early development is.

ZENAH: Does it bother you when your friends who are studying business and engineering ask what you're studying?

ERIC: Yeah, kind of. One guy asked me how anyone could stand to feed and change kids all day. I think if that really was the way I saw it, I wouldn't stick with it. But now I understand where all that feeding and changing and helping with snowsuits fits in. Besides, half of the toddlers in my class don't need to be changed anymore. They're becoming quite independent, and I think I've helped with that. And most of them manage all their own eating, even though there's a lot of cleanup to do afterward. It's funny, but they love to help with that, too.

One thing I have learned is how important consistency is. When I missed a day because I had to go out of town with the soccer team, they all wanted to know where I was. They seem to know about when it's time to go outside or have lunch or a nap. If we're too far off schedule, the toddlers let us know one way or another.

I really do want to give these children the best I can. Dr. K. and a couple of the other profs have made it clear that these early years are so important in development. We really can make a difference. I've been wondering how I could keep working there when I graduate. What if I had a family? The salaries are really low.

Dr. K. promised that they would discuss that topic further at another session.

MULTIPLE PERSPECTIVES

From the Field

Following is part of an interview with Florine Fuqua, infant teacher, at the UAW Chrysler Day Care, Huntsville, Alabama.

INTERVIEWER: Thank you for meeting with me after a busy day with infants.

MS. FUQUA: It *has* been a rough day. Two of the babies had colic, and they cried a lot. I said to myself, "Oh, Flo, do you want to do this?" But I do. I like giving love to babies, holding them. I like being able to send them off to the next class seeing that I have worked so hard and they are ready to move on to the next age.

ASK YOURSELF

Reread Ms. Fuqua's interview. Think about whether I would be able to enjoy and support babies when they are loving and fun as well as when they are crying incessantly.

· · · · · · · · · · · · · · · · · · · ·

INTERVIEWER: Let's go back to the beginning. How did you get into this field?

MS. FUQUA: I'm from Chicago, and I went to college there and got a degree in social work and child development. I took a teaching job and liked it.

INTERVIEWER: Have you ever thought of getting out of this field?

MS. FUQUA: No, never. I love the children.

INTERVIEWER: What is a day like in your program?

MS. FUQUA: Hectic! We have good days, and there are wild days. A lot depends on the children and how they are feeling, but no matter what, I'm busy every minute.

· ·

Preschool Classrooms

Usually one person is responsible for overall planning for the center.

Programs for preschoolers (ages three to five years) employ educational coordinators, lead or head teachers, teachers, associate teachers, assistants, and aides. All of these people have day-to-day roles in the classroom. Each center organizes its own staffing plan, but usually one person, the **educational coordinator,** is responsible for overall planning for the center, while each classroom has one person, the **lead, classroom,** or **head teacher,** who assumes the responsibility for that classroom. Within each classroom, there must be sufficient numbers of teachers and assistants to meet state licensing requirements. Moreover, good-quality programs employ enough staff members to meet children's needs. That number often exceeds the mandated number.

With preschoolers, as with infants and toddlers, teachers and assistants focus mainly on helping children progress in all areas of development. The goal is not to accelerate development, but to make the child's current life beneficial in terms of enjoyment; development of dispositions and interests; learning in emotional, social, cognitive, and physical areas; and appreciation of his role of in the world.

We have established that it is certainly not appropriate for infants and toddlers to be expected to attend to the teacher in a whole-group activity. Even in preschool, the teacher's role is not to gather children around to instruct them as a group. Whole-group time is short and generally includes child participation such as singing. Rather, the adult role is to set up an environment that is rich in possibilities, to observe children, and to add to or subtract from the environment according to their needs. Teachers spend much of their time observing and reminding themselves to let children "do it on their own" whenever possible. At the same time, they watch to ensure that the level of frustration doesn't become overwhelming. If that appears

Teachers develop curriculum by listening to children and learning about what the children know and are interested in. *(© Elizabeth Crews)*

to be about to happen, good teachers step in and offer enough support to enable children to manage.

Social Development. Another major role is helping children develop an understanding about how to relate to one another. Some children seem to do this quite naturally. Others seem constantly to be pushing, pulling, hitting, crying, and becoming less and less friendly to other children. The teacher must step in and break the cycle before it becomes an ingrained pattern (see Figure 10.1). Of course, it is expected that most children (and adults) will sometimes be irritated, frustrated, unfriendly, and irritating, as

Figure 10.1

All children occasionally display hostile behavior. The teacher's job is to prevent this from becoming a pattern by helping children learn ways to handle situations that anger, frighten, or upset them.

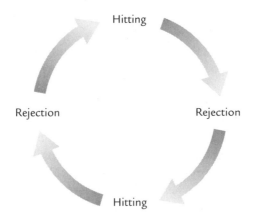

Hitting

Rejection

Rejection

Hitting

well as happy, approachable, friendly, and agreeable. Denying so-called negative feelings may lead a child to feel ashamed of these feelings. Instead, the teacher should recognize the feelings and help the child learn to manage behaviors related to the feelings.

Even joy can get out of hand. Young children may be so excited that they cannot manage their own behavior. Again, the teacher can point out that they really are delighted to be going to the zoo or having a birthday party and can help them channel the excitement into acceptable behaviors, such as making decorations for the party.

Good teachers comment, question, and instruct judiciously. Teachers are in classrooms to facilitate children's exploration of materials and ideas rather than to entertain them or keep them busy.

Meeting a Variety of Needs.   Meeting basic needs for safety and health (including room temperature, nutritious foods, cleanliness, daily outdoor play, and so forth) is essential. Teachers model basic health practices (for example, hand washing). Often we forget that mental health, fostered by appropriate attention and interaction with children, adults, and objects, is equally essential. In fact, some programs organize classes across age groups (two to five years, for example) so that children can be in the same class for three years. This is called the **multiage model.** Others choose **looping.** In this configuration, a teacher works with a group of a particular age, let's say three-year-olds. The following year, the group stays intact and the teacher moves up to be a teacher of four-year-olds, the same children she worked with the previous year. The third year, the teacher starts over with a new group of three-year-olds. In both models, children spend less time adjusting to new children and adults and to different teaching styles and procedures (Katz & McClellan, 1997).

Even joy can get out of hand.

CONSTRUCTIONS

1. Research

Look for research on the multiage model and on looping. Are there strong data to support either of these organizational approaches?

2. Interview

Talk with two teachers about the effects multiage groups or looping have on professionals in the field.

After the class discussed teaching in infant, toddler, and preschool classes, Dr. K. presented the following scenario.

Fifteen three-year-olds were comfortably seated at little tables in their classroom. Karen, their assistant teacher, entered with the lunch tray sent by the cafeteria. (Because the class meets in a public school, the children are served the same type and quantity of food as is served to the elementary school children.) She began to serve each child a whole hot dog in a bun, a whole dill pickle, and a canned peach half. Meanwhile, the teacher, Juanita, was opening the half-pint milk cartons that each child received. Suddenly disaster struck.

Ramon had been holding his hot dog bun tightly and had just taken a bite. As he did, the hot dog squirted out the other end of the bun and landed on the floor. Almost at the same instant, Tina, trying desperately to break a piece off the slippery peach half, pressed the small plastic spoon hard, broke it in half, and watched in dismay as the peach slithered off her plate and onto the floor right next to Ramon's hot dog.

Such excitement! Every child stood up to see—some excited, some delighted, some anxious about what would happen next. One thing they had all learned was that food from the floor wasn't clean and was not to be eaten. Karen and Juanita also knew that the cafeteria sent one and only one serving for each child and teacher. What now?

Dr. K. asked the class to discuss what the teacher, Juanita, might have done. What were the issues? What were possible immediate and long-term solutions?

TILLIE: She should just tell Ramon and Tina that she had told them to ask for help if they needed it.

AMY: But, Tillie, Ramon didn't know he needed help, and Tina was trying to do it on her own.

ERIC: And besides, we already know that hot dogs are just the diameter to choke a child. The cafeteria staff should have cut them in half lengthwise.

DANIELLE: When was the last time you were in a cafeteria? If it's anything like my grade school, it's chaos. They'd never have time to be cutting up children's food.

TILLIE: I sure don't think the teacher should give up her lunch. She won't have anything to eat until dinner. She needs her energy, too.

AMY: Maybe just this once, she could ask the cafeteria for one extra lunch.

DANIELLE: Or she could ask the children if anyone wanted to share.

AMY: But if the food is already on each child's plate—I don't know what the health inspector would say about that.

DR. K.: You've generated lots of ideas. As it happens, I was in the classroom when that happened. Those aren't the teachers' real names, but the situation really did occur. Here's what Juanita did.

Juanita had not yet been served, so she told Karen to give her hot dog to Ramon and her peach to Tina, but to cut each food item into several pieces first. She then began cutting each child's hot dog in half lengthwise as well as crosswise. The children were delighted, saying that each now had four hot dogs. She did the same with the pickles and peaches. It was a little hectic. Children were calling, "Do mine, do mine," and both teachers knew that they couldn't expect the children to wait until all the cutting had been finished.

Juanita also made a mental note to visit the cafeteria director. She was concerned about the nutritional value of the food, as well as about the amount of time it would take to cut up the food and open the milk cartons daily. Still, she was grateful that the cafeteria staff had agreed to put the food on trays, even if Karen did have to carry them up a flight of stairs. She certainly didn't want to go back to the original plan of having three-year-olds eating in the school cafeteria. The tables and chairs were way too big, and the noise and commotion typical of an elementary school cafeteria would be overwhelming to her young children. Juanita knew she'd have to work hard to convince the staff of the particular needs of preschoolers.

The lead teacher must ensure that other adults in the classroom know what is expected of them.

Working with and Supporting Team Members. The lead or head teacher must ensure that other adults assigned to the class, whether paid staff or volunteers, know what is expected of them. The leader also must see that they actually do what is expected and guide them when they make mistakes. Strong interpersonal skills are needed. A recent college graduate assigned to a head teaching role may feel overwhelmed if the assistant teacher is much older, has been an assistant for ten years, and has several grown children of her own. However, the teacher's up-to-date professional knowledge can be joined with the assistant's experience and procedural knowledge to create an excellent team.

Together, the teacher and assistant plan opportunities for the children; acquire and arrange materials, equipment, and furnishings; and ensure that the environment is attractive and ready for the children each day. The lead teacher is ultimately responsible for planning and implementation, but generally this is difficult or impossible to accomplish without the support of one or more assistants. Furthermore, the teacher is responsible for major communication with parents, even though the assistant will greet and converse with them. Keep in mind that, based on staff members' assigned hours, some parents may come to know a particular assistant far better than they know the teacher. Perhaps the child arrives in a carpool, and the teacher is scheduled to leave before the parents arrive to pick up the child. Some centers alleviate this situation by scheduling alternating shifts, but teachers who prefer to work from 6:30 A.M. to 3:00 P.M. so that they can be home when their own children get out of school may find alternating shifts difficult. Creative planning is needed to ensure that everyone's needs are met.

Some programs for preschoolers operate on a half-day basis. In that case, staff may work with both morning and afternoon groups five days a week or as little as two half-days per week. The flexibility of such scheduling enables some teachers who do not need full-time work or who are employed part-time elsewhere to follow a variety of interests. This type of scheduling may be important to you in some situations, such as when you are beginning graduate school.

ASK YOURSELF

Which of the three age groups discussed in the preceding section (infants, toddlers, or preschoolers) seems to present the most challenges for teachers? What are the benefits and drawbacks of working with each of these groups?

Becoming an Assistant Teacher. Programs for children ages five years and under often welcome candidates for teaching positions who have earned a **Child Development Associate (CDA)** credential or an associate's degree in childcare or early childhood education. These candidates may have more **practicum,** or student teaching, experiences with young age groups than candidates with a bachelor's degree. At the same time, candidates with a CDA, associate's degree, or bachelor's degree may prefer to enter the field as assistants, working under the guidance of an experienced teacher until they build up their confidence. Assistant teachers make valuable contributions to children's development. In a well-run center, assistants have many of the same responsibilities as teachers. This fact leads to a satisfying career for many.

Kindergarten and Primary School Classrooms

Teaching in kindergarten and the primary grades is often quite different from teaching younger children. Certainly, the children have grown and developed, and they have different needs. Nonetheless, their need for support and guidance in all areas of development remains. As you surely are aware, school attendance is compulsory, and in some states children are required to attend kindergarten before entering first grade.

In planning and implementing instruction, teachers consider their beliefs about how children learn.

Another factor that differentiates K–3 from earlier education is the curriculum. Teachers are responsible for following a curriculum that may be provided by the school district or some other body. **Accountability** is related to the children's scores on **standardized tests.** Both these factors influence the way teachers teach. In planning and implementing instruction, teachers consider their beliefs about how children learn; their knowledge of the curriculum, the assigned textbooks, and state regulations (such as number of minutes per subject per week); and parental input. They juggle all these factors to create daily, weekly, and annual plans.

Routines and Schedules.   Many of you may be working in child-care centers while you are in college. Therefore, you are familiar with those types of programs from an adult perspective. Even though you have experienced elementary school as a pupil, you may be surprised when you enter a first-, second-, or third-grade classroom—or even a kindergarten—because you may be using a "preschool lens." That is, when you walk into a preschool classroom that is managed appropriately, you expect to see the children making choices during most of the day. Certainly there are routines—set times to have lunch, rest or nap, and to gather for group time. Snack time, using the restroom, arrival, and dismissal often occur on each child's schedule rather than as a group. Using that lens, you may be expecting older children's programs to be similar.

By contrast, you may be expecting something quite different when you arrive at a primary school. You may recall a very structured classroom from your own childhood. The teacher would usually be at the front of the room, where her desk was located. In your mind's eye, you may see children quietly bent over stacks of worksheets, with an occasional child surreptitiously releasing a paper wad or a note to a classmate. What could be worse than having the teacher catch you in the act of passing the note on, especially if you didn't write it? The picture you remember is the picture you'll still see in many of our schools.

MULTIPLE PERSPECTIVES

From the University

Joan Moyer, a member of the Arizona State University early childhood education faculty, is a professor devoted to preparing teachers. Here is her perspective on what sets early childhood education apart from programs for older children.

The emphasis in early
childhood education
is on the child.

The emphasis in early childhood is much more on the child—how the child learns, how the child grows and develops, and how you use that information in terms of setting up a program, an environment, the curriculum. By comparison, in elementary education, the emphasis tends to be more on the content areas—how to teach science, how to teach math, how to teach social studies—without a whole lot of regard for the individual child in that situation.

• •

Daily schedules for children in most kindergartens and primary classrooms differ from those in most preschools. Children arrive and leave at specific scheduled times. They may stand in line to enter and leave the classroom several times a day—for arrival, bathroom break, water fountain, lunch, recess, going to and from other activities (art, music, physical education, assemblies), and finally for dismissal. In between, they may be assigned to desks or tables and expected to remain there unless given permission to move. Specific tasks are to be completed by specific times. Talking may be allowed only when children raise their hands and are called on by the teacher.

When someone becomes a teacher, it is almost always after having experienced at least sixteen years as a pupil. Thus both positive and negative experiences shape the way teachers teach. Many have the attitude, "It was good enough for me, so I'll just do what I already know. Look at me; I'm a success." These same people may not be so quick to support old ideas in medicine, engineering, technology, and so forth. Yet for them, the old way in education must be continued. Others may say, "I hated school. I want to be a teacher to make sure children will never have to go through what I did."

The teaching profession continues to grow, and we must use what we have learned about children, families, curriculum, teaching, learning, and the school environment. Teachers who understand this seek out and implement ways of teaching that are more in concert with the ways children learn. They focus on the children's needs as they exist in the present, while keeping an eye on the world the children will live in as adults. The pace of change makes it impossible to know exactly what that world will be like, but teachers know they must help children learn to find information for themselves, solve problems, and make reasoned decisions.

The Teacher's Role. The teacher's role varies greatly in the two types of classrooms described and in the many variations that fall in between them. In the first situation, the teacher is very much the director, deciding to the minute what will occur when. Teachers who use this approach may use curricula created by textbook manufacturers or packaged programs, or they may create their own activities. Children complete assignments in short time frames, with frequent whole-group transitions. Teachers are responsible for management of the transitions, for management of materials, and for management of time. Many sincere teachers use this approach. If you recall classrooms just like this, you may remember waiting for direction, waiting for order, waiting for a turn. You may also remember waiting for everyone else to catch up with you or never being able to catch up with the rest of the class.

You will still find many classrooms across the country and around the world in which the teacher is seen as the knower and dispenser of information. The children are seen as receivers of that information, and they are expected to commit it to memory so that they will be able to return it to the

ASK YOURSELF

What was my experience when I was in early childhood education as a child? How might that influence my teaching?

Teachers must help children find information for themselves and become problem solvers.

teacher on command. This strong statement does not imply that children should never memorize or that teachers don't know more about some things than children. Rather, it is a reminder that the teacher's role goes far beyond dispensing information.

In the second type of teaching, children are more autonomous and hence take more responsibility for their learning. They decide, within limits, when they need to use the restroom, when an assigned task is complete, and when and how to obtain help from a peer or the teacher. Children may work on proj-ects over an extended period of several weeks or months. They document their work for themselves, their teachers, and their families. The content of the curriculum is integrated rather than being addressed during subject-specific time periods. In addition to having more responsibility for learning, children have more responsibility for their own behavior. To conduct a classroom this way, teachers must be flexible. They must be willing to listen to children's ideas and to let them assume some of the leadership.

Teachers are responsible for building positive relationships with each child and for helping the children develop a classroom community. Teachers accomplish this via their own behavior, through their responses to children and their behavior, and through guidance as situations arrive. They encourage children who behave appropriately and support those who are having difficulty by guiding them to more appropriate ways to act.

Teaching involves hundreds of decisions daily. Because many schools and school systems are large and depersonalized, it is easy for teachers to become impersonal, rationalizing that they have no say, that they must just do what they are told. Although mutiny is not necessarily the answer, hiding behind "They make me do it this way" is not the mark of a committed teacher. William Ayers (1995) points out:

> These rationalizations *become* an expression of your values: following orders *over* taking this kid's needs seriously; using the boring teachers' guidelines *above* engaging kids in a project that grabs and propels them. To teach takes commitment, strength, struggle, a willingness to grow and develop. It is certainly not for the faint of heart. Becoming a teacher is hard work. (p. 3)

Teachers do have a wide range of responsibilities. They must be familiar with the expectations of the district and of the school in which they are teaching. Usually detailed objectives for each grade level have been delineated by the district, the state, or both. Although recognizing that not every child will be able to meet every objective and that some children may already be well beyond accomplishing some of the objectives, the teacher is responsible for addressing the prescribed curriculum. If the requirements are rigid and the teacher does not support the objectives or the methodology,

Teaching is a highly personal set of hundreds of decisions each teacher makes daily.

ASK YOURSELF

What are my values in terms of balancing administrative expectations and children's needs? What thought have I given to my beliefs?

she must be able to explain to administrators and parents what is being done in the classroom and why. If a reasonable agreement cannot be reached, a teacher who supports particular values will usually need to find a district that is more compatible with her understanding of the teaching/ learning process.

CONSTRUCTIONS

Journal Entry

Is William Ayers right? Is becoming a teacher hard work? Do you think *being* a teacher is as difficult as becoming a teacher? Why or why not?

Tillie and Zenah went to visit a nearby primary school. After this visit, they agreed that being a teacher is hard work and challenging. Back in Dr. K.'s class, they give the following report.

TILLIE: Jean Simmons, a third-grade teacher, invited us to visit her class. As we entered, we immediately noted that there seemed to be children *everywhere*! Some were seated at tables, others were lounging on large floor pillows, Josie was rocking in the teacher's rocking chair, and we even spotted two boys, Daryl and Alex, under one of the tables. It was easy to learn their names because Ms. Simmons called them by name frequently. Ms. Simmons, seated on the carpet, was listening to Sally read and recording observational notes. She told us later that she uses these notes to keep track of Sally's progress and does the same for each of her twenty-seven pupils. As Sally finished, Ms. Simmons thanked her and said rather quietly, "Girls and boys, in a few minutes we'll be going to the computer lab to work on our local history time lines. When I call your group, please put your books away, gather your time line notes, and join me in a line at the door. You have all worked well this morning, and I appreciate the way most of you have been reading quietly. After lunch, we'll have time to hear from a few of you who have finished a book and want to recommend it. Then we'll hang your time lines in the hall."

ZENAH: As Ms. Simmons gave these directions, most of the children were looking at her and appeared to be listening. Patty, however, was busy playing with her bracelet and showing it to the girl next to her. Ms. Simmons paused and looked directly at Patty, who quickly put the bracelet in her pocket and looked at the floor.

She then organized the transition. "Maureen's group, Ted's *(pause)*, Martin's, and Rita's group." A burst of activity, and in a minute or two the children were following Ms. Simmons to the computer room. Later Ms. Simmons told us that their time lines will be the culmination of their study of the founding of their city—its people, geography, economy, and government. Over the past six weeks, they have heard speakers, gone on field trips, and read from many sources, including their computers. The children compared prices of food and clothing over time. Art, music, nutrition, and health were part of their study, and they talked with family members and neighbors about their city. A guest speaker who has lived in the city for a long time showed slides of the area taken over many years. Ms. Simmons has taken many opportunities to integrate many of her district's curriculum goals and to find ways to interest each child.

Teachers integrate their districts' curriculum goals.

TILLIE: As the children settled in to work on the computers and help each other, Ms. Simmons had a few moments to speak with us. She pointed out that, because her students span a five-year academic range (even though they are all third-graders), she helps each of them find opportunities to learn and grow. She explained that some of her students can barely read a beginning first-grade book, while others easily handle books meant for sixth-graders. Some children have very strong mathematical understanding, while others are just beginning to develop number sense. The differences are also pronounced in writing, with some of her third-graders creating stories with several chapters and others struggling with a sentence or two.

We asked about the children's study of the city. As we suspected, the project has involved much work on Ms. Simmons's part, much more than the way she originally taught—following each subject page by page in textbooks. We looked around at the children—some frustrated at their attempts to create a time line, others amazed or delighted at what was happening on the screen, but all quite involved.

ZENAH: Since we both had class back on campus, we thanked Ms. Simmons and went to the office to sign out. We left thinking that we could readily understand what Ms. Simmons meant when she told us, "These children are really their own teachers. I'll never go back to the old way."

CONSTRUCTIONS

Journal Entry

Reread the report that Tillie and Zenah gave about their observation of Ms. Simmons. Then write your responses to the following questions in your journal. Discuss your thinking with one or more of your peers.

a. What responsibilities does Ms. Simmons have?

b. What approaches does she use to help children behave appropriately?

c. How does she handle inappropriate behavior?

d. What evidence is there that she assesses the children's progress?

e. Is Ms. Simmons's curriculum integrated? What is the basis for your response?

f. Does Ms. Simmons encourage autonomy? If so, how?

g. Is this the kind of role you envision for yourself? Why or why not?

As you have learned, researchers have contributed a great deal to our developing understanding of schools and schooling, of how children learn, and of what the teacher's role should be to support that learning. Teachers sometimes feel constrained by administrators, school boards, and citizens who do not want to allow any changes in response to new knowledge about children's learning styles, curriculum, and classroom management. Nonetheless, thinking teachers use what they know, consider new information, and take into account the children they are assigned to teach. They refuse to accept blindly and in a lock-step manner a curriculum imposed from above. These teachers work to help their children learn and develop in all areas. They value the pupils' creation of a classroom community, and they reflect on the needs of each individual child.

Good teachers help children learn. They help them understand that learning isn't always fun or exciting. Often learning involves hard work, mistakes, and rethinking. Good teachers focus on the immediate goal of helping children accomplish at their own levels and on the long-term goal of a lifetime of continued learning and satisfaction. Although the reality of preparing for the world of work is important, the more significant reality of preparing for life in a community is essential. Teachers in kindergarten and the primary grades attend to social development while helping children learn to read, write, and solve problems in mathematics. Similar problem-solving skills, attitudes, and dispositions enable children to develop socially and cognitively and to operate autonomously while taking into account the needs and interests of others.

Helping children prepare for life in a community is essential.

Additional Roles for Teachers. You may have heard the old refrain that teachers don't have time to teach. They are too busy being nurse, psychologist, manager, coach, and social worker. Certainly teachers understand that although they do have to empathize with the child who falls and hurts his knee, their role is limited, for the teacher's protection as well as the child's.

However, teachers also know that there won't be a nurse in every school, at least not every day. Learning what should and should not be the teacher's role is partly learning to be a teacher and partly learning the culture of a particular school building and district.

Teachers spend hours before school starts and after sessions are under way arranging and maintaining the classroom. Children can learn to take on much of this responsibility, but the teacher has the ultimate job. Teachers also gather materials and arrange for them to be distributed in ways that do not distract the children from their work or cause them to wait for the tools they need.

To teachers fall the jobs of collecting money for special events, sending announcements and messages home, and receiving and responding to communications from families. Teachers plan and implement field trips, prepare children for schoolwide activities, and supervise volunteers and assistants. They write reports to parents, hold conferences, and keep the principal informed of the children's accomplishments and of any challenges they encounter with parents or other community members. Although myriad additional tasks could be listed, each teacher's real goal is helping children develop fully.

Rewards for teachers vary. Some teachers are fairly compensated; others are not. Many teachers work to fix these inequities. One reward that almost all teachers experience is the pleasure of seeing children make progress.

Dr. K.'s class has just finished reading Eleanor Duckworth's *The Having of Wonderful Ideas and Other Essays on Teaching and Learning* (1996). Each of them was supposed to think of a wonderful idea for a project for the week. Amy opted to interview several kindergartners to learn how they responded to conservation tasks. Dr. K. said that she'd also have to learn about being a researcher, getting appropriate permissions, collecting accurate data, and maintaining confidentiality. She agreed that this project would benefit Amy and encouraged her to continue to pursue this type of research when she has her own classroom.

Teachers have to learn to be researchers.

Eric decided to find out about the author of a poem Duckworth mentions since no one in the class was familiar with the poet. Dr. K. noted that Eric was engaged in another type of research that teachers must frequently employ.

Tillie decided to interview a Head Start teacher. Dr. K. was delighted, because the teacher Tillie selected had been in her classes a few years before. Dr. K. has just asked Tillie to report on her interview.

TILLIE: The teacher I interviewed, Kendra, decided to go back to college after her children were beginning to be pretty independent. She earned her degree and teaching certificate. Because her preschool practicum had been her favorite experience, she interviewed for preschool jobs and accepted a position in a rural area. Kendra told me that from her earliest schooling experiences, she disliked teaching directly by the teacher, with no opportunities for children to give their ideas. "Children should be active," she said, "both mentally and physically."

AMY: She sounds like a good teacher, but did you ask her how she comes up with wonderful ideas for her classroom? That's what I'm worried about.

TILLIE: Actually, I did ask. Kendra said that at first she was worried that she wouldn't be able to think of things that would appeal to the children. She just started collecting stuff—her whole basement is full of keys, bottle caps, ribbons, and other collage material, as well as books. She has hundreds of books. She brings things to class, arranges them in baskets or on trays, and lets the children decide what to do with them. The classroom was pretty well equipped when she started teaching there, but the children seem to prefer the stuff that we might call junk.

DR. K.: Perhaps Kendra would welcome some of you as observers. I'll give her a call, and maybe I'll drop by her classroom again myself. One of the biggest satisfactions in *my* teaching is seeing my students become really good teachers, and Kendra is a fine example of that.

Zenah and Danielle had interviewed Martha, a K–1 teacher. Martha told them that she gets most of her ideas from teacher's books and magazines.

DANIELLE: Martha told us that as soon as her magazines arrive, she looks through them for ideas. She brings them to school and tries them out right away.

ZENAH: I wondered how they fit with what the children are working on, but Martha told me you just have to read through the district objectives, and you can always check one off with any activity. Then before you know it, you will have covered all the objectives.

DANIELLE: That seems backward to me. Shouldn't you be thinking about what the children are interested in and what they are learning, then plan with them how they could accomplish that?

Children should be active both mentally and physically.

ASK YOURSELF

What do I know about how teachers plan and why they use the approach they use? Based on what I have studied about how children learn and the roles of teachers, what are some of the factors I believe are important in teachers' planning?

CONSTRUCTIONS

Research

Check two or three issues of one of the widely available teacher's magazines and decide whether they could be valuable to an early childhood educator. How would you use them? If you do not find them valuable, what are your reasons?

ADMINISTRATION

Administrators can maintain contact with children while assuming a leadership role.

Many teachers decide to move to the role of administrator in an early childhood education program after a number of years in the classroom. They can then enjoy being in contact with the children while taking a leadership role with staff and parents.

Child-care Administration

In childcare, administrators, usually called directors, may not be required to have additional preparation for their new responsibilities. Nonetheless, studying fiscal and human resource management will contribute to the ease with which new leaders perform their jobs. Currently, a movement to create a certificate for directors is gaining momentum. The child-care center administrator also may be assigned to half-time teaching or to substitute for whoever is absent, be it teacher, cook, or janitor. Often a center administrator does the grocery shopping, fixes stopped-up toilets, and takes out the garbage. The director may be the only one available to answer the phone, greet visitors, take applications and tuition payments, and conduct visitors around the center.

Public School Administration

A significant responsibility of the principal is to establish a positive, productive climate.

In public schools, administrators are required to be properly certified for the roles they seek, whether principal, curriculum supervisor, or superintendent. They also learn about both program and people management. Some of a school principal's tasks are hiring, supervising, and evaluating teachers; providing curriculum leadership; managing the school budget; and assuming responsibility for the physical plant. Discipline issues often consume much of a principal's day, and conversations and meetings with parents, school board members, and other citizens also are important. In public schools, it is likely that the principal's role will be limited by the district's union contract. In small schools within small districts, the principal may perform many of the roles that the child-care center director assumes. But in larger schools, even elementary school principals frequently have assistant principals, who may handle discipline issues. A significant responsibility of the principal is to establish a positive, productive climate in the school building. To accomplish this, principals must respect both faculty and students, while maintaining a commitment to an excellent education program.

Many professionals work in jobs only peripherally related to early childhood education. Judges and attorneys need an understanding of child development to work effectively with child witnesses. *(© Jim Pickerell/Stock Boston)*

MULTIPLE PERSPECTIVES

From the Field

Following are excerpts from an interview with Dr. Linda Winters, an elementary school principal.

INTERVIEWER: Dr. Winters, you had been teaching quite successfully. What led to your switch to administration?

DR. WINTERS: A love of teaching really is where it started. I looked at the whole scope of the educational process, and early in my career I started kind of narrowing my focus into the supervisor role. I went back to school and obtained degrees in administration.

INTERVIEWER: What do you look forward to in your work?

DR. WINTERS: Being with the children. When you come to our building you may see me out there in the halls, and there's a lot of hugging going on. That's good, solid contact with the kids, and they know I care about them.

INTERVIEWER: What is a typical day like?

DR. WINTERS: Fractured! Some days I can walk around the school to see what is going on. But a lot of my work is on the telephone, often with parents who want something addressed immediately. I see a lot of children, too, sometimes for discipline. I have a very positive approach to working with children. I require good behavior, but I always approach it positively with them. Yesterday was a good example of a fractured day. I had appointments scheduled back to back from 7:30 A.M. until evening because we were evaluating teachers. Three major discipline situations came up, and two irate parents arrived. Somehow I handled it all, but I really felt the stress by the end of the day.

INTERVIEWER: Have you thought about changing jobs?

DR. WINTERS: This is where I want to be, in the school building, on the frontline of education. I wouldn't change my job.

• •

MULTIPLE PERSPECTIVES

From the Field

A director of a child-care center has to make sure parents understand all the policies and procedures the center follows.

Following is an excerpt from an interview with Martha Ginn, director of Chrysler Corporate Child Development Center, Huntsville, Alabama.

INTERVIEWER: Ms. Ginn, please tell me about your role as director in this corporate center.

MS. GINN: I am responsible for managing this facility for a corporate child-care management company. We service a lot of big corporations.

INTERVIEWER: Is there a typical day for you?

MS. GINN: Not really. For example, yesterday I led a tour for a group of high school students who were in a parenting class. Then I had another tour for a company that was considering starting a center for its employees. Three parent conferences came next. All of them were about their children moving up to the next age group. I also conducted an informational interview with parents whose children will start in the center soon. I have to make sure they understand all the policies and procedures we follow.

INTERVIEWER: Sounds like a pretty challenging day! Let's talk about your greatest success.

MS. GINN: Oh, just getting this place up and running. It was already built when we came in, and it's huge—over thirty-four-thousand square feet—and it cost $4.5 million. We started with just nine children, and now we are full with over two hundred.

ASK YOURSELF

Have I ever thought of being an administrator someday? From my perspective, what are the pros and cons?

• •

CONSTRUCTIONS

Research

Using the Internet and other resources available to you, find out as much as you can about corporate childcare.

   a. Why do corporations create child-care initiatives?
   b. What models do they use: Resource and referral? On-site center? Others?
   c. What are the pros and cons of corporate child-care programs for children, families, child-care staff, and the corporation?

Include this information in your portfolio.

AUXILIARY PERSONNEL

Working with Children

Although being a teacher may be your goal, you may find interesting options in other fields. School librarians and media specialists have contact with many children and staff. They support children and teachers by providing interesting books, software, and other media and by creating an inviting atmosphere in the center where materials are housed.

Reading specialists guide children as they work to create their own understanding of the reading process. Given the opportunities to work with individuals or small groups of children, these specialists can provide the support that reluctant or unsuccessful readers may need. Both of these roles may require additional training. Some colleges and universities offer a master of library science (M.L.S.). They also may provide graduate degrees in literacy or special programs in teaching reading. Some states have specific certificates or licenses for each of these roles (school librarian, media specialist, reading specialist) as well as others. Outside the school setting, adults work with children in physicians' offices, hospitals, museums, parks, recreation centers, camps, social service agencies, and many other places.

MULTIPLE PERSPECTIVES

From the Field

Gail Klayman is the assistant director of the child life program at a children's hospital. She is a **certified child life specialist**, a certification granted to persons with a child development background who have

Some early childhood professionals work in child life departments in hospitals, helping children retain contact with their interests while they recover. (© *George Bellerosi/ Stock Boston*)

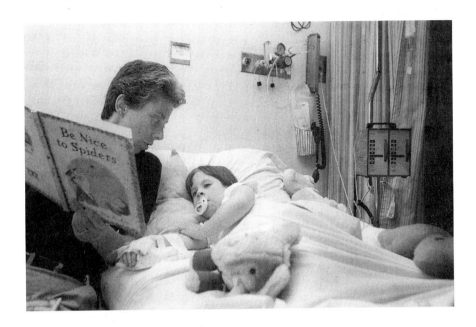

Child life specialists work with children who are hospitalized.

worked with hospitalized children for a specified period of time. Another requirement for this certification is an internship under the guidance of a certified child life specialist. Gail spent several years working in a playroom setting at the hospital with patients who were well enough to leave their rooms on foot or on a transport cart, and she often wheeled children who couldn't get out of bed down to the playroom. Currently assigned to the intensive care unit, Gail provides normalizing activities for patients—that is, she tries to make their time in the hospital as similar to their at-home lives as possible, within the constraints of their medical condition.

MS. KLAYMAN: With the children, I do a lot of **therapeutic play.** If a child has been brought to the hospital via medical helicopter, that child may wake up in a hospital room and have no idea how he got here. I use photos of the helicopter and talk with him about the people who helped transport him. To prepare myself, I made a trip with the transport team.

INTERVIEWER: How did you get this job?

MS. KLAYMAN: I had a hospital practicum in college, and I began working here as soon as I graduated. Eventually, I became a specialist in death and dying because of the population to which I have been assigned. To find out more about the needs of the terminally ill, I worked with a hospice, where I volunteered and participated in training. Along the way, I developed a death education curriculum as the required project for my master's degree.

● ●

Working in Related Fields

People who design appropriate clothes, toys, and media for children help them develop.

Some educators decide that they are interested in children but they just don't want to be with them every single day. Their choices may involve roles that support children's growth and development in other ways. For instance, people who design appropriate clothes, toys, and media for children make worthwhile contributions. The designers and architects who plan environments for young children, the judges who rule in cases involving children, the reporters who cover children's issues, and the advocates who contact legislators to let them know what is important for children and why all play significant roles in helping children grow and develop.

Following are several brief excerpts from interviews with people who work in fields related to early childhood.

MULTIPLE PERSPECTIVES

From the Field

JoAnn Mazza, social worker in a human resources agency: Our agency takes calls from people who are concerned about children who they believe have been mistreated. We evaluate the information they provide, and, if appropriate, we send an investigative worker into the field to talk to the families and children and to find out what they need to be able to protect their children. I enjoy working with children, trying to help them feel comfortable so that they can discuss problems with me. But I also like helping parents who don't know how to be parents. Actually, I think that teachers are more important than social workers in a child's life. Teachers see a child every day, and they can be a great influence on each child. Even though we are responsible for making decisions about children's lives, they don't look upon us as role models. Teachers can be those models for children.

Dwight Faye, district court judge: We have essentially three types of children that come before the juvenile court:

1. Dependent children whose needs for food, clothing, and shelter are not being met

2. Children who need supervision because of some type of truancy—running away from home
3. Delinquent children who are charged with offenses that would be crimes if they were adults

Our job is to protect children and to help them modify their behavior if they are delinquent. Today's children really skip from infancy to young adulthood—they don't have a childhood. They face a proliferation of drugs and the distortion of reality presented by TV. They believe that every problem should be solved in thirty minutes minus commercials, and they expect to have a nice house and everything they want without really having to work for it.

> When children don't know how to behave, the schools must step in.

Parents, churches, and synagogues used to teach children how to behave. When that doesn't happen, the schools must step in, because by the time you have the teenagers, it is really hard with peer pressure to modify their behavior. If we start out early enough with kids, maybe we can make a difference.

Mary Wathey, child development specialist with Cigna Health Plan, a large health maintenance organization (HMO): I work directly with patients as part of our well-child care program. We do a developmental screening when the child is nine months old and again at two years of age. If we pick up potential problems, we are responsible for following up.

I started out as a teacher, took time off to have a family, and then one day in the pediatrician's office, I became interested in the screening that he was doing. Before I knew what was happening, I had talked myself into a job in the medical field. Since then I've taken courses, attended conferences, and grown with this relatively new and expanding field. I love it!

The focus of pediatrics is broadening to include a lot more development issues, a lot more behavioral kinds of things. Some HMOs are employing child development specialists to be temperament counselors, providing parenting classes and temperament counseling for parents whose infants have difficult temperaments. I think this really is a growing field.

Eileen Cooper-Reed, advocate with the Children's Defense Fund: My staff and I do research on children's issues and then mobilize the community to help reach whatever solutions are needed. Children have always been my focus, even though I have worked in a variety of specialties, such as urban regional planning, social work, and recently as a juvenile court referee.

As a **child advocate,** I understand that there has to be a continuum of care and that the very first piece of the continuum is so important. The child's first caregivers set the tone. Schools have to pick up on that and help *every* child love learning.

Everyone in the community is responsible for our children. As advocates, we work to help people understand this. Parents are the first source of a nurturing, caring environment, but if they can't or won't provide it, someone needs to help. That means one of the issues we advocate for is good schools and good teachers for every child. We advocate for programs for children before and after school and for funding for childcare so that every child has good care.

The issues are constantly changing in one sense. Yet we see many of the same issues still facing us. One of my roles is to educate people about how they can become advocates. I work to help them understand the legislative process and their roles in it.

Dr. Shirley Raines, dean of education at the University of Kentucky: I started as a nursery school teacher and then taught kindergarten. My major professor for my master's thesis was on the Head Start board, so when there was an opening for staff development coordinator for Knox County in Tennessee, she recommended me. Three months later, I became director of fourteen Head Start centers. Next came directorship of a community college child center. I've been in higher education since 1978, but credit for taking me to teacher education goes to Head Start, because the job in staff development let me know that I could work with adults.

• •

CONSTRUCTIONS

1. Political Action

Select an issue that affects children and write to your congressional representative, state legislator, or city council member expressing your opinion. Tell the legislator what action you would like to see taken and why. Your letter should be one page if possible. Take a positive approach. For example, you may be interested in the issue of before- and after-school care for children. Is more oversight at the state level needed for these programs, or should local groups be responsible for them? Another possibility is your concern about standardized tests. Should standardized tests be given to first-graders, or should they be delayed until second grade or later?

> Everyone in the community is responsible for our children.

2. Site Visit

Visit a well-baby or well-child clinic in your area. What do you think it is like to be a child in the waiting room? What are the roles of the adults who work there? Are they doing anything to make this time manageable and worthwhile for parent and child? Are additional staff members needed to accomplish this goal?

ADVICE FROM PROFESSIONALS

The professionals from whom you have heard in this chapter and others often had some suggestions for future teachers. Some of those are included here. As you read them, reflect on whether their advice might apply to you. Chapter 11 provides more in-depth advice and suggestions for people entering the profession.

> You have to adjust to the attitude and personality of each child.

WILLIE MAE PARKS, INSTRUCTOR AT ALABAMA A&M CHILD DEVELOPMENT RESOURCE CENTER. "You have to be able to understand that each child is different. And then you have to adjust to the attitude and personality of that child."

LEILA P. JADEN, ASSISTANT PROFESSOR. "Create a system so that you can schedule your days and weeks. It's not fair to walk into the classroom unprepared."

DORIS OUTLAW, THIRD-GRADE TEACHER. "Think positive! These are children, and you are in charge. Children will direct their attention to you. You'll need to watch the way you speak—yes, even to using correct grammar—the way you dress, and the way you treat the children: 'No screaming, please.' And keep the lines of communication open between you and the parents even if it seems as though they don't want to hear from you."

LINDA WINTERS, PRINCIPAL. "Get as much experience as possible while you are in college. Take advantage of volunteer opportunities. Get a good grounding in the areas you'll be teaching, but keep in mind that you are not through learning when you get that degree."

MARTIN VAN SHERRILL, PEDIATRICIAN. "Don't get into teaching unless you are a committed person. The person who is committed is someone who enjoys the profession and wants to do it even though it sometimes interferes with other life goals."

JOANN MAZZA, SOCIAL WORKER. "Seek out a teacher whom you really admire, who has been working for a while. Find out how that teacher got started."

DWIGHT FAYE, DISTRICT COURT JUDGE. "Treat children with care. Realize that many of them leave you every day to return to very difficult conditions at home."

EILEEN COOPER-REED, ADVOCATE WITH THE CHILDREN'S DEFENSE FUND. "Ask yourself if you love what you do. If you don't, you shouldn't be in the classroom."

MARY WATHEY, CHILD DEVELOPMENT SPECIALIST. "Be a risk taker."

JUDY COLLINS, STATE LICENSING SPECIALIST. "Accept people where they are. Take them by the hand and walk with them. It's important to have ideals and standards. Even more important is being able to share that information without putting people down."

CONSTRUCTIONS

Journal Entry

You have read advice from many people who play various roles in early childhood education. Select one of the suggestions and develop a plan to carry it out. Include your plan in your journal.

SUMMARY

▸ People play various roles in early childhood education. Each role is important and in some way related to children's well-being and development.

▸ Whereas some jobs confine the early childhood educator to one place, perhaps a rather isolated situation, others keep the individual in the public eye.

▸ In some roles, the professional has extensive autonomy, while in others the expectations and procedures are quite specific.

CONSTRUCTIONS

1. Journal Entry

Think of a teacher who helped you in some way. Write a journal entry describing what that teacher did that you valued. Now describe what a typical week was like in his or her classroom.

2. Journal Entry

Think of a teacher of whom you were afraid or one you just didn't seem to relate to. Write a journal entry describing how you felt and what you think led to those feelings. Describe a typical week in his or her classroom.

3. Analysis

Compare what the weeks were like in the two situations you described above. What were the similarities and differences? What conclusions can you draw?

4. Journal Entry

Enter in your journal your ideas about how your own classroom might look as a result of your own experiences.

5. Research

Look for projections on numbers of people currently in teaching positions who are expected to retire or resign in the near future. What are some of the reasons teachers give for remaining in or leaving the teaching field?

6. Interview

Select one of the professional roles described in this chapter (teacher, administrator, auxiliary professions). Interview a person who is filling that role now and find out what a day is like in that position.

7. Research

Gather data about one of the auxiliary roles described in this chapter. What current job opportunities are available in this area? Does this position require additional education?

RESOURCES

Books

Jones, E. (Ed.). (1993). *Growing teachers: Partnerships in staff development.* Washington, DC: NAEYC.

Using true stories, mentors describe teacher growth. Examples include staff members involved in CDA programs, Head Start, primary schools, and other programs.

Marzano, R. (1992). *A different kind of classroom: Teaching with dimensions of learning.* Alexandria, VA: Association for Supervision and Curriculum Development.

In considering restructuring and reforming schools, this author focuses on how teachers teach and how children learn.

Nash, R. J. (1996). *"Real world" ethics: Frameworks for educators and human service professionals.* New York: Teachers College Press.

Written for teachers and everyone else, Professor Nash's book contains thought-provoking material. The goal is not to give solutions to ethical dilemmas, but, as the title suggests, to offer a framework.

Spafford, C., Pesce, A., & Grosser, G. (1998). *The cyclopedic education dictionary.* Albany, NY: Delmar.

An up-to-date resource that provides definitions for all facets of education. Six appendices include information such as federal legislation related to education and a sample individualized education plan.

Web Sites

Association for Childhood Education International (ACEI) **(http://www.udel.edu/bateman/acei/)**

This site provides information relating to children's programs for a broader range than early childhood. It is a good source of information about the early childhood profession.

National Child Care Information Center **(http://nccic.org/)**

This site includes information about licensing of child-care centers and a wide range of child-care issues.

11

Personal Development as a Professional

· ·

The aim of this chapter is to guide you as you explore career opportunities among the many choices the early childhood profession offers. To assist you in making informed choices, we share a variety of perspectives about being an early childhood teacher. The perspectives include positive and negative opinions, and they come from children as well as from adults who are both internal and external to the field. We investigate teacher roles and characteristics of successful early childhood professionals. Further, we examine career paths, both your own and those of others. We also examine the importance of autonomy as it contributes to sound decision-making. After reading this chapter, you should be able to discuss these issues:

▶ Perspectives of others about the early childhood teaching profession
▶ Personal characteristics that are critical for success in teaching
▶ The importance of autonomy in the process of charting a career
▶ Personal career options in the early childhood field

You are the architect of your future in the early childhood profession.

It has been said that the future predicts the present. This sounds contradictory, but as you chart your options for career paths in early childhood education (your visions of the future), you will also be reexamining your motivation to enter this field (your experiences from the past) to help you determine what you do now. YOU are the architect of your future in the early childhood profession.

421

INTRODUCTION

Dr. K.'s students are walking out of one of the last classes they will have before the term ends.

AMY: Gee, I'm really going to miss this class. I feel like I've learned so much. It makes me want to just know more! I'm excited about the next course on curriculum! I love it so much, I want to go on to a big university, then teach—and maybe even get that master's degree someday.

TILLIE: Well, finishing this class makes *me* just want to find a full-time job. In fact, I have to. I've used up the money I saved, and working part-time doesn't pay enough. Besides, I already know what I need to do to get started in a teaching position. I knew a lot of it before I took the class.

DANIELLE: Get off it, Tillie. You didn't know all that stuff about constructivism and how to teach in a way that respects children and families. You were a control freak!

TILLIE: Thanks a lot, Danielle! But, yeah, you're right. I still think that children need a lot of adult direction in the classroom. Maybe it's a cultural thing with me. I think African-American families want more direct teaching of their children. Anyway, I'm going to apply for the position of a teacher's aide at one of the back-to-basics charter schools. I think I might fit in there.

AMY: I can't believe that you want to do that! I mean, I understand that you need to make money to live—but after all we learned about autonomy and heteronomy? I can't believe you forgot that!

TILLIE: *(Laughing.)* No, I didn't forget. In fact, I'm exercising my autonomy and choosing something I think is right for me. I have to try out what I think is best. You can't argue with that! It sure would be right for me financially.

AMY: I guess you're right, Tillie. Danielle, what are you going to do? Will I see you in the next class?

DANIELLE: Oh, I'm staying in school, but Daddy says I need to work part-time. That may really interfere with my social life! I think maybe I'll see about being a nanny for the Nelsons. They asked me before if I would consider it. That might give me some real-life practice. I have a lot of stuff to try out on those kids now. I bet Eric will do just what he said at the start of the class: Go on through school, teach, and then become a principal.

TILLIE: Now you're being sexist, Danielle! Why do you think he'll be a principal? Just because he's a guy? I think *I* would be a great principal.

DANIELLE: You probably would, but I wouldn't want to work for you! Won't you need more school for that? *(Laughs)*. And maybe an advanced class in heteronomy?

> ### CHANGED WITH THE SEASONS
>
> #### By Jessica, age 7
>
> Everyone changes
> like the seasons.
> You don't stay the same.
> You change every second.
> Everything around you changes.
> You change like a leaf.
> It will be green and
> then it will fall
> and turn brown.
> Everything in the world
> changes.
> When you change
> you grow wiser too.
> We all change!

CONSIDERING THE FUTURE

Isn't it interesting that seven-year-old Jessica already has an intuitive sense that we are constantly evolving and that, as we change, we become wiser? Jessica seems to think that it happens automatically with the passage of time, but as the dialogue between the students indicates, there are other factors to consider, too. Change doesn't always come easily. As you may have learned in your human development course, there are developmental tasks that adults typically encounter with age. These include finding a meaningful relationship, having children, and making career decisions.

One developmental task in adulthood is to decide on a career.

One of the developmental tasks for adults is to decide on a career or direction for their lifework (Havighurst, 1972). Look back at your journal entry from Chapter 7, where you were asked to reflect on the position in early childhood that sounded the best to you (see page 273). Have you changed your mind, or do you agree with what you wrote then? Which direction will you chart for the future? Consider the career paths or routes that individuals in early childhood education have taken to reach their current positions. Think back to the way professionals interviewed in this book came to the positions they now have. How will *you* start? Do you already have a beginning by virtue of the job you have now or one you have held in the past?

As you saw in their dialogue, our students are embarking on different career routes. As in their cases, your perspective, as well as your individual abilities, needs, and interests, will influence your career decisions. In our

A job you held in the past may provide a key to your future career. *(© Ann Chwatsky/The Picture Cube)*

Many factors determine individual career paths.

students' cases, finances and personal beliefs have influenced each of them to choose a particular path at a specific time. Those aren't the only influences, however. Like our students, you may be considering various career paths in light of a mixture of your desires, needs, beliefs, interests, past experiences, personal circumstances, timing, and finances.

CONSTRUCTIONS

Journal Entry

In your journal, describe your current career projections. Describe several different possibilities, recording questions about each option. Keep both an open mind and your responses in mind as you read through this chapter.

PERSONAL REASONS FOR A CAREER IN EARLY CHILDHOOD EDUCATION

In previous chapters, you have read about the diversity of positions in the field of early childhood education, and how different individuals reached their current positions. Look back at the listing of career options in Chapter 7 (see Table 7.2 on page 288). Are there other positions in the field that are not listed there? What are they? Some of them might focus more on serving families than children. Think about who usually fills positions in early childhood education and childcare. One of the things that you may have noticed is that women dominate early childhood settings today. Why do you think this is the case, and is that positive or negative? What does that mean for men who choose this field? What are the different paths by which individuals enter the early childhood field today?

The experience of working with children often leads women to consider a career in early childhood education.

As you have read in Chapter 10, people in this field may start with volunteering or with a job. They may or may not think about that job as a first step in a career. As you have seen from the interviews and biographies in other chapters, women in early childhood often take nontraditional routes to a career. This occurs in part as they deliberately build their careers around the complex needs of their own children and families. In past decades and in other fields, a nontraditional path has been seen as a drawback to career development, but in this field the experience of working with children often strengthens women's resolve to continue to work with young children and families. Men also have found nontraditional paths into the field. For example, some men volunteered as Big Brothers and decided they enjoyed working with young children. Regardless of your gender, why are *you* considering becoming an early childhood professional?

CONSTRUCTIONS

Journal Entry

Explain why you are considering going into this field. After you have listed as many reasons as you can, underline the three or four strongest reasons. Analyze the motivation behind these reasons. Is your motivation based on self-fulfillment or on improving conditions for children? Is it based on interest in how children learn? What needs would you meet for yourself by entering early childhood education? What else motivates you to enter this field?

Becoming a Teacher

Most often, our students tell us that they choose to become teachers or teacher's aides because they love children. Is that something you wrote? What does it mean to love children? Is that enough to make you a good teacher? Some students claim that their motivation comes from "seeing the light come on" in children's eyes when they understand something for the first time. Other students say that they want to be teachers because

ASK YOURSELF

Where am I going in early childhood education? Do I have what it takes to work with children and families? Will it be a wise career choice for me? What are the opportunities and concerns related to each position?

If this course or my past experience with children has already convinced me that this field is where I belong, what is the best choice for me in the field, both immediately and long term? Why do I think so? How do my personal goals fit with my career choices?

· · · · · · · · · · · · · · · · · · · ·

Your motivation for becoming a teacher of young children requires examination.

A constructivist approach focuses on learning.

they had a particular teacher who recognized their talents or who encouraged them and gave them affection and attention. They want to be that person in another child's life. By contrast, some students claim that they had such bad teachers that they want to prevent children from having a similar experience. Some of our students have parents who are teachers, who encouraged their children to visit their classrooms as the children grew up. They found that they liked being there. Still others wound up in education after trying something else first, deciding instead that they really wanted to work with children and families. Some male students want to be role models for children being raised in single-parent homes where the parent is female.

Some of these feelings reflect a romanticized view of teaching children. Yes, as you saw in Chapters 3 and 4, there are significant intangible rewards for working with children and families, but teaching also has been described as the hardest job anyone can have. It is a frustrating fact that, as you saw in Chapter 7, salaries in this field are not comparable to those in other professions that require a similar amount of college preparation. Did you realize that? If money is a strong motivation for you in choosing a career, you may want to think about the amount of time it will probably take for you to be paid well in this field. Perhaps you should even consider other career options. If you are a person motivated more by a desire to work with children and families than by money, you are probably pursuing the right career. If you are intrigued by what you learned in Chapters 3, 4, and 8 about the way children learn and the interesting and sometimes curious ideas they share, you may want to become a constructivist teacher. As Tillie indicated, however, this approach may not be right for everyone who decides to become a teacher.

Becoming a Constructivist Teacher

Educators who prepare future teachers to take a constructivist approach (the authors of this book, along with Catherine Fosnot, George Forman, Eleanor Duckworth, Constance Kamii, Rheta DeVries, Marjorie Fields, Christine Chaille, and others) believe that such an approach focuses much more on learning than on teaching in the traditional sense. Constructivist publications promote the idea that the role of a teacher is to encourage learners to create and answer questions of importance to them, and to act as collaborators who both encourage and challenge children to take their thinking further. As you saw in Chaper 8, we believe that being a constructivist teacher is much more demanding than being a traditional teacher. If you want to be a teacher who takes a constructivist approach, you must "start where children are" in their understanding. As you learned in Chap-

ter 1, constructivist teachers themselves use many tools to learn, and they are not passive recipients of knowledge. Constructivist teachers engage in, and also encourage children to engage in, active learning, and to use previous experiences, reflective analysis, and collective research to learn. A constructivist teacher must continue to study the way children think and learn, to build knowledge about individual children and families, as well as understand the central concepts of the academic disciplines. Do you have the desire to be that active learner and to really understand children and families? Does finding creative ways to engage learners in content appeal to you at a deep level? To answer these questions, consider other aspects of what constructivist teachers do.

ROLES OF CONSTRUCTIVIST TEACHERS

- The teacher is a *presenter*. The teacher must present activities to groups of children, present options to individual children, present ideas to children engaged in ongoing activities. Presenting is different from transmitting because it implies that what is presented is available for children to take or leave.
- The teacher is an *observer*. In order to present good, facilitative options, to interact appropriately, and to understand the children's interests and knowledge, the teacher must be a constant observer in both informal and formal ways.
- The teacher is a *question asker and problem poser*. The teacher must be able to ask questions and pose problems that stimulate theory building without being disruptive to the child. The ability to do this stems from the observation of children, as well as understanding them.
- The teacher is an *environment organizer*. The environment must be carefully and clearly organized so that children know what to do. Organizing the environment from the child's perspective is an important part of encouraging self-direction.
- The teacher is a *public relations manager*. The understanding and support of many people is critical for the success of any educational effort. Because of the nature of the constructivist classroom, the teacher must clearly and consciously articulate what is going on and why.
- The teacher is a *documenter* of children's learning. Meaningful documentation of what children do and what they learn is an important aspect of today's classroom. As we move to more complex

---

curricular goals, simple, quantitative measurements will not capture what children are doing and learning.

▸ The teacher is a *contributor to the classroom culture*. From the types of questions the teacher asks to the physical room arrangement to the tone in the teacher's voice, the teacher contributes to the culture and values of the classroom. The creation of this culture can happen explicitly as well as implicitly.

▸ The teacher is a *theory builder*. In order to be responsive to children, teachers must cultivate their own understanding and interests and maintain their enthusiasm. Nurturing your own capabilities and preventing burnout is important and often overlooked. Just like children, teachers need environments and support for building, growing, experiencing conflict, changing their ideas, and always being open and interested when ideas don't work as anticipated.

Source: From *The young child as scientist: A constructivist approach to early childhood education* (2nd ed.) (pp. 54–55), by C. Chaille and L. Britain, 1997. New York: Longman.

You may be wondering why we are talking about teachers' roles under the category of personal reasons for entering the field. We believe that taking a constructivist approach with children is quite demanding and calls for special characteristics. These characteristics are personal, and they affect how you interact with children, families, and peers in professional settings. The phrase "professional use of self" captures the idea that a teacher's intrapersonal and interpersonal characteristics and knowledge are woven inextricably into who she is as a professional.

CONSTRUCTIONS

1. Reflection

Look over the roles listed in the box. What personal characteristics are necessary for an individual to be successful in performing these roles? What skills and knowledge would an individual need to have to embody these roles?

2. Analysis

Which of these characteristics do you have? Which do you need to develop? Do you believe they can be learned if an individual does not have them? Do you believe teachers are born, or can a person be taught to be a good teacher?

With-it-ness is an important quality for early childhood teachers.
(© Elizabeth Crews)

As part of a class discussion, Dr. K. asked small groups of students to talk about the characteristics they think teachers of young children should display. Join Zenah, Eric, and Amy as they share their ideas with each other.

ZENAH: I know that Dr. K. hates this idea, but I think one of the most important things is for a teacher to have fun with kids in the classroom. In this case, it means someone would have to be playful, maybe even silly at times, in order to be a teacher that the kids like.

ERIC: I'm curious. Why does Dr. K. have trouble with that? I have trouble with it because just being popular with kids doesn't mean that the parents will like you! I don't agree that teachers should be silly. We aren't there to entertain children; we're there to help them learn something. I think that maybe a really important characteristic is to be curious about all kinds of things. Being curious can lead to having interesting and even fun activities while children learn.

ZENAH: Eric, you're no fun! But I can see what you mean. I guess I don't really mean a teacher should be silly, but it seems to me that school can be kind of like a prison. I was visiting a classroom the other day, and the teacher was just a drill sergeant. I couldn't wait to get out of there, so just imagine how the kids must feel! What I'm trying to say is that school should be a happy, inviting place where kids learn, and they should also like what they're doing—

Amy: *(Interrupting.)* Yeah, Zenah, and the personal characteristics of teachers would be that they are tuned in to kids and know what is enjoyable and interesting to them. I think that relates back to the idea of "with-it-ness" that Dr. K. talked about when she gave an example the other day. I think that means that you have to really listen to kids and to hear what's behind their words. You also have to be able to talk to them in a personal way—you know, be sensitive to their feelings *and* their ideas.

Eric: I agree, Amy. The problem I have in thinking about that is how to know each child—and even their families—when you might have twenty-five of them! I think good teachers have those characteristics, but how do they do it? I wish I could just be a clone of Ms. Mason. She does all that so easily.

> Each individual must determine his or her own path to being a good teacher.

Perhaps you also wonder how some teachers can be so in touch with children and how they make learning in the classroom enjoyable and exciting. If a magic answer exists, we don't know it! Each person must find his or her own path to being a good teacher. You are learning many helpful techniques and strategies from observing, working with other teachers, and listening to advice, but only you can build your own teaching theory. To get started, let's listen to other perspectives about what it takes to be a successful teacher and about being a teacher in general.

WHAT IS A GOOD TEACHER?

Children's Perspectives

First we will listen to the voices of children. To capture some of the different ideas that children have both at a young age and as they get older, we include an interview with a five-year-old boy and a discussion held in a multi-age classroom of second- and third-graders.

MULTIPLE PERSPECTIVES

From a Young Child

A student (Karen) who was completing an assignment in one of her first classes in early childhood education conducted this interview with a young child (Robert). The setting was a public school kindergarten classroom. This is part of a longer interview. To ensure confidentiality, the names of the individuals involved have been changed.

Karen: Hi, my name is Karen. I was wondering if you could help me with some schoolwork that I have.

Robert: Uh-huh.

ASK YOURSELF

Why did Robert, at age five, give the responses that he did? What can I learn from Robert? What themes can I identify in his responses? Did he say anything that surprised me?

. . . .

Young children have their own ideas about good teachers.

KAREN: What is your name, and how old are you?

ROBERT: My name is Robert Warren Knowles, and I am five years old. . . .

KAREN: Have you ever had a really good teacher?

ROBERT: Yeah, Mrs. Lunt. She teaches me all sorts of things right now. Mom tells me to call her Mrs. Lunt, but her real name is Suzanne.

KAREN: What makes her a good teacher?

ROBERT: How she learned stuff when she was a kid. She teaches us that. We play on the playground, and one time we made a puppet fireman.

KAREN: Are there things that bad teachers do?

ROBERT: Teach kids to be bad. They only do a little bit of things in school. All they can do is tell kids to write *dog* and then go home. That's all, because they don't like to teach.

KAREN: What would I need to do to be a good teacher?

ROBERT: Take glitter and glue and have the kids make a fireman with glitter all over it and real wheels that go around. Teach them how to put glass into windows. *(Whispers.)* Guess what? I'm telling you a lot better things than Mrs. Lunt can teach. *(Back to normal.)* Take them out to play and show them how to make a rock fireman.

KAREN: Okay. Thank you. That was just what I needed. We're all done now.

ROBERT: Okay. But if you're ever here again and I'm here, maybe I can help you with your schoolwork again!

• •

MULTIPLE PERSPECTIVES

From School-Age Children

This is a multiage classroom in a private school. There are twenty-one second- and third-grade children in the class.

ASK YOURSELF

What themes did this group of children discuss? Were there similarities to what Robert said? Did they say anything that surprised me? What can I learn from these older children about their perceptions of what it takes to be a good teacher?

. . . .

INTERVIEWER: What makes a teacher a *good* teacher?

CHILD 1: I really think being a good teacher means being nice to everybody. Like when somebody gets mad at somebody, they help them solve the problem together and help you feel okay.

CHILD 2: I kind of think a good teacher is caring about their students, because most of the time there are teachers who just let students do whatever they want, like walk around the room and just fiddle around, and I know that our teacher doesn't take that kind of thing

INTERVIEWER: What does she do that lets you know that she cares about you?

CHILD 3: I know a lot of things that she does, but I'll just say one. Well, like when we're working on a project, she watches us and she tells us to focus on certain things.

Second- and third-grade students have strong opinions about teacher characteristics.

CHILD 4: Yes, she tries to teach us as much as possible, and she does everything she can to help us learn.

CHILD 5: She lets us have privileges, but not always. We can lose some because she cares about us, but if we're fooling around, she can't give us those privileges because it's not really fair to the rest of the class.

INTERVIEWER: So there are consequences—

CHILD 5: Some people lose computer time.

INTERVIEWER: *(Looking at another child.)* And what do you think?

CHILD 6: Mary [teacher] has been really respectful the whole year so far.

INTERVIEWER: How does she show that she's respectful? How do you know?

CHILD 7: She always teaches us hard things.

INTERVIEWER: She challenges you sometimes to think harder and better?

CHILD 8: Well, um, what I think, well, I can't read too good, and, like, she knows how to help me do better, but she knows I'm really good in building in the garden. I think that's beautiful.

CHILD 7: She respects our feelings. She doesn't make us just go say we're sorry. She helps us solve the problem. Like if we're sad, she'll just stay and help that person instead of wandering off.

CHILD 6: When we have math problems, when we stress out sometimes and we can't really get 'em, she doesn't just tell us to just do them ourselves; she explains stuff to us.

INTERVIEWER: It sounds to me like the teachers here really pay attention to you—as people.

CHORUS: Yes.

INTERVIEWER: And are respectful of you, and that's important to you.

CHORUS: Yes, yes.

CHILD 6: They don't treat us like toy bears and stuff. They treat us more like humans.

INTERVIEWER: And that's really good, I think. *(Everyone laughs.)*

CHILD 9: The teachers here just keep getting gooder and gooder, um, better, and there are way too many good teachers here. I don't want to leave this school.

INTERVIEWER: I can understand how you feel. *(Pauses.)* Let's talk for a minute about the other side. What is it that teachers sometimes do that you don't like? What should we tell people who want to become teachers *not* to do, because it really bothers you?

CHILD 10: If they put our feelings down really bad and aren't nice to us.

CHILD 11: Sometimes teachers get angry when kids don't behave, and that's okay. But it really hurts my feelings when teachers won't let all of the kids do anything. Everyone has to stay at our desks and do boring things.

ASK YOURSELF

If the interpersonal relationship is important to children, does it mean I should be friends with children and not enforce consequences of violations of classroom rules? Could a teacher accomplish both? What parameters should teachers set in their interactions with children? In terms of content, should children just be kept busy with activities, or should they do in-depth projects? What is the difference?

CHILD 12: If you're having an argument and you go like "No, it was mine," then the teacher just walks over and says, "Okay, break it up. You go to time-out for five hours; you go to time-out for fifteen minutes." 'Cause she likes one person better than the other, um, and that's not being a good teacher. Teachers should respect *everybody*.

● ●

You must have noticed that children pay special attention to how they are treated. The interpersonal relationship set by the actions and tone of the teacher is what children notice first and remember longest. It has often been said that young children remember who you are (as a person) and how you treat them much longer than they remember the content you taught. As Robert and the older children both told us, however, being engaged in projects that are active and of interest to them is also important.

Early Childhood Professionals' Perspectives

Besides children, we asked a variety of individuals in early childhood education to share their thoughts about personal and professional characteristics of good teachers. A child-care provider, public school teachers, a child-care administrator, a public school early childhood director, and a teacher educator responded to questions about what beginning teachers need to be successful in the classroom. In many cases, they offered advice. As you read, see if you think their advice is helpful. One of the workplaces mentioned is the Family Literacy program. (Family Literacy is a holistic, family-focused approach that targets at-risk parents and children. The children attend preschool while parents receive educational services on site. This is a program that has been implemented in various locations in the United States.)

MULTIPLE PERSPECTIVES

From the Field

People working in the field provide the wisdom of practice.

Practitioners in the field are voices of experience and wisdom. We have selected segments of interviews from a variety of individuals whose careers are representative of the field. Some quotes come from individuals you have met earlier in the text.

Florine Fuqua, Infant Teacher, UAW, Chrysler Day Care Center, Huntsville, Alabama: This is going to be a challenging field. If you don't have the patience, don't do it. Because there's gonna be days when you're going to question whether you are in the right career. You have to really have a lot of love, and you have to want to make a difference in someone's life. If you don't want to make a difference, don't go into this field, because our children need so much given to them nowadays, more than in years before. It's a lot of hard work, and you have to say it's not just the glory of looking at it and seeing the money. The money is good depending on where you get hired. But it's more difficult than you think, and if you are coming in looking [at it] from the outside and not looking at it from the inside, you're gonna really be surprised. Because it's hard; it's really hard. It's difficult, and I wouldn't ever fib to someone that it's not, because it is. Either you are born with this talent or you are not. And everyone is not born to work with children. I don't care how much they say, "I want to be a teacher to help children." They say that statement so loosely. Then when they get in there, they go, "Well, I just thought I could do it." But you can't play with people's lives like that, okay? Our children need a lot of work, and if you feel like it is too much, then you need to step down and be an adult about it and say, "Listen, this isn't what I thought it was gonna be. Let me step down." Because you can do more harm to the child than you really realize.

Martha Ginn, Director of Chrysler Corporate Child Development Center, Huntsville, Alabama: Get as much training as possible. Really stop and ask yourself a question: "Do I really want to be here? Do I really love children?" Because if you are looking for the tangible rewards, money, there are none. It is truly a love for children. If you do have that desire, you want to equip yourself with the right tools. That comes down to getting as much education as you can. Try to focus in on the school that would offer a good early childhood program. Try to get hired in an accredited center. There are more and more corporations that are providing corporate childcare. You want to be hired by one that offers training. Our teachers are paid very well. They have paid benefits. Of course, that is very difficult for a child-care facility that is not subsidized by a corporation. Obviously, you have to eat. That would be what I would try to do if I were starting all over again.

Kristi Dickey, First-Grade Teacher, Public School: Teaching is one of the most important things you can do. That's scary! I did not realize how important it was until those first children walked in my room and I thought "I have them for a whole year! Eight hours a day for a whole year!" They spend more time with me than they spend with their families. You have a lot of power to make it a really good experience or a horrible experience. I'm not sure we always realize the impact we have on children.

Don't take the first job you're offered. Try to figure out whether your philosophy is close to the principal's you would be working with. At my school, we have some very traditional teachers and some developmental teachers. We have begun to realize we are not going to change each other's thinking, and we have begun to accept each other. Never go in with the attitude that "my way is best," because you will change every year. Always be open-minded and never judge just by what you see. Do some interviewing yourself if you can. Try to visit the schools and even do some volunteering in some of the schools you want to work in. I loved the school where I did my student teaching and wanted to work there. But even that job became very different when I was actually working there. Try to find out as much as you can about the school.

Vicky Gordon, Preschool Teacher, Family Literacy Program, Public School: I think it's important that they [prospective teachers] really love learning and that they have curiosity and a sense of adventure to experiment and try things, and [they are] not somebody who just wants to impart all their knowledge to someone, but not to be afraid to kind of sit with their hands back and let somebody fumble through and explore on their own. That's what I think is important, and that's what I try to do. And sometimes it's really hard, not only working with kids but with parents, too. When they're [parents] learning to use the computer, you just want to put their hand on the mouse, you know, and do it. But literally, sometimes, you have to just sit on your hands and let them figure it out for themselves. I think that's one of the most important qualities a teacher can have. I think teachers need to be intelligent, too, to be able to understand concepts or the way things work. Not just to have a factual knowledge, but to understand learning and to observe, to be really good observers. That's important.

Irene Williams, Preschool Teacher, Family Literacy Program, Public School: I have been on hiring committees before, and when my assistant was hired, I was on that committee. What I wanted most of all, at that time, was a dependable person—someone that would show up every day. Because when one is missing, you know, if you're working with a team—and that's how we work here—if one of us is not here, it's extremely difficult for the other person. I would look for someone that would show some initiative because this job, sometimes, it's spontaneous. You know, it's whatever has to be done, you better do it. And you cannot plan every minute of the day. A lot of things come up, and you have to go with the flow, so you need to be spontaneous. And I would look for someone

Forming relationships with parents enhances good communication between school and home. *(© Elizabeth Crews)*

that would treat the parents the way I want them to be treated and to treat the children with respect. Yet, at the same time, you have to have a sense of humor. Things go wrong, and you have to be able to roll with it. Every day is different. We plan, but sometimes our plans don't work out, so you have to have an alternate plan and just go with that. My assistant and I work very well together. We kind of anticipate what the other one needs, and the children cannot tell who is in charge. We are a team.

Marilyn Davis, Early Childhood Program Coordinator, Public School District: What do I look for in prospective teachers that makes them successful? Well, there are two pieces to my response. First, when I'm hiring an early childhood teacher, there's a whole piece of the knowledge of child development and constructivism and the understanding of developmental differences in children and whose responsibility it is to meet those differences. I ask people in interviews about constructivism, and I'm stunned by how many people don't know what that means. In fact, I had one talk about buildings, as in, you know, constructing things! I look for teachers who see children's strengths and understand about building on those. So that's kind of a basic level of understanding (Blasi, 1998).

For Family Literacy in particular, there's another whole piece. They have to be able to articulate. It's not good enough to do good things with children; they have to be able to articulate *why* they do those things. So much of their role is working with parents, and in order to help parents understand why it's important, for example, to let the child lead the play, you really have to be knowledgeable about what that means for kids and why it's important. That's something we don't see all the time. I have some very good preschool teachers who couldn't be good family literacy teachers because they don't know why they do what they do. Some of them do it intuitively and are very good with kids and are excellent in the classroom. They teach in programs where their contact with parents might be twice-a-year home visits or an occasional conference, and they're great in that environment. So the folks in family literacy have to be good early childhood instructors and good adult educators. To me, it is unusual to find a fairly new teacher who has the confidence and the knowledge to be okay talking to the parents. And they don't have to have tons of knowledge; they just have to know where to get the information and know how to communicate, to listen. They can't be scared of parents. They have to be willing to sit in there every day and talk with them.

ASK YOURSELF

Did I agree with everything that was said? If I disagree with something that was said, can I create a hypothetical response to the individual? What advice has given me the most food for thought?

Joan Isenberg, Teacher Educator, George Mason University, Virginia: First, know who you are and what you believe. Look in the mirror and ask yourself why you are going into this field. Always come back to what you believe is right for children and families and then test those beliefs against your practices. Secondly, be reflective about your teaching. Think about your responses to children and colleagues and decide if those are the responses that you really want to give. Thirdly, get involved early on in a professional association that offers you opportunity for professional growth and development and lifelong learning. Be an activist for your profession, and you'll stay in it!

Not all advice from the field is appropriate for constructivist teachers.

Those who are currently working in the field have a wealth of knowledge to offer those who are entering the profession. However, not all advice is appropriate for each individual, and sometimes what teachers pass on contradicts constructivist practice. For example, as a novice I was told by a veteran teacher, "Never smile before Thanksgiving. That way, children will know you mean business, and you won't have discipline problems." What problems might that philosophy cause? Think back to what the children told us that good teachers do. If you practice the habit of reflection and clear thinking about children and families, as Dr. Isenberg suggests, you will sort out constructivist advice from that which is more teacher centered.

CONSTRUCTIONS

1. Research

Write down a quotation from one of the professionals that you find interesting. Create some questions about that perspective.

2. Interview

Share a copy of the quotation with a practicing professional. Ask him if he agrees with the quotation. Using some of the questions you posed, converse with the professional about the quotation. Ask him what he considers crucial for success as a novice in the field.

The Community's Perspectives

Let's rejoin the students. They were asked to interview individuals in the community to sample opinions about teaching, teachers, and early childhood education.

ERIC: Wow! I was really surprised at the response I got when I questioned some people at the grocery store about early childhood. Do you know they think early childhood just means it applies to kids under five years old? One guy asked me why I wanted to work with little kids. It seems like he was implying that I'm a pervert. I was surprised by that comment.

ZENAH: Well, Eric, you *are* sort of strange. *(Laughs.)*

ERIC: Is it fair that men who want to be good role models and who really like children are judged like that? It makes me really wonder if people will assume that I'm gay.

AMY: Of course it isn't fair! You're not the only one that got some flack. Listen to this! One lady I talked to said that because I'm white, I couldn't possibly have the background to teach her kids, because they're black! I really didn't know what to say. Later, I thought of *lots* of things to say, but they wouldn't have been professional. I'm still thinking about what I should have said!

ZENAH: I wonder if white parents in the community would feel that way about a black teacher.

DANIELLE: I went to a park, and there were a couple of families having a picnic. They seemed to be having a good time, so I went over and talked to them, asked them about their children's schools, and what they thought of the teachers. They said they thought teachers work really hard, and they were happy with the teachers their kids have this year. But they all thought I was crazy to want to be a teacher because the pay is so low. They said I should get into the area of computers, and make big bucks. Does it pay better if you teach kids about computers?
(Everyone laughs.)

ZENAH: The parents I talked to said they want their kids to be taught phonics and basic "readin', writin', and 'rithmetic." They said the new state tests are going to finally shape up the education system.

TILLIE: That stuff about basic skills and tests sure doesn't fit with what we've learned here!

AMY: Don't get carried away. Remember what Dr. K. said about curriculum? We *will* know how to teach skills, content, all that stuff, but not by making kids use workbooks. Children are going to understand more the way I'll teach.

DANIELLE: Well, I just want to know who's right. What are we supposed to do? We have to listen to the parents and people in the community. I can't wait to see what Dr. K. says about all this community feedback!

Community members have varied beliefs about teachers and education.

This discussion reveals some fairly typical perspectives held by people in the general population. Because many individuals have gone through the public school system, they assume that they know what it takes to be a teacher and what should be taught. Although a variety of opinions helps make a democracy strong, it can present prospective teachers with problems. As Danielle indicated, public opinion cannot be ignored. How will you respond if someone says these things to you? As you ponder that, let's hear a sampling of voices from a community in Alabama.

MULTIPLE PERSPECTIVES

From the Community

People living in Huntsville, Alabama, were asked their opinions about teaching and education. Because tax revenues fund public schools, schools and districts are increasingly moving toward forming partnerships with parents and communities. Due to this trend, the opinions and beliefs of people living in the community must be understood and addressed. These individuals may have opinions that differ greatly from your own perspective. Have you heard others in your own community share opinions similar to these?

Jeff Carr, General Engineer

INTERVIEWER: How do you view the field of teaching and education today?

MR. CARR: It's sufficient for a motivated kid. If children have a lack of personal motivation, self-esteem, or do not have a supportive family, teachers may have a hard time reaching them. I think teachers are having a hard time getting those kids to do their homework and the lessons that they need. I think that overall the opportunity is there for the kids who do have a supportive family. It is sufficient for those types of kids.

INTERVIEWER: What could be changed about education to help children even more?

MR. CARR: Try to teach children on their level, and for younger kids, put it in a game format. I'm sure they do that today, but try to understand what the kid is going through at that stage and just try to reach them at their level.

Gene Davis, Test Operator, Telephone Company

INTERVIEWER: How do you view the field of teaching and education today?

MR. DAVIS: Overall, I don't think it's good—I mean, too good. I've been all over the country. The reason I say that is because when you look from state to state, each state has different curricula. One state is better than the other in the different ways they do things. Being here in Alabama, I see things that aren't too good.

INTERVIEWER: What advice would you have for beginning teachers?

MR. DAVIS: I guess really just to be more aware of the things that are going on in the world. I'd say the reason why teachers should be more aware of things is because if they are, they can help that child better. For example, if you take a child from a poor neighborhood, from the projects, a lot of times he, in a sense, is worse or harder to teach than a child who was brought up in a well-organized home. So I think teachers need to be aware of that. You can't teach every child the same way.

INTERVIEWER: What could be changed about education to help children more?

MR. DAVIS: I'll compare Alabama to what I saw in Colorado. Colorado is up there [in education rankings] and they have excellent programs.

The reason why is what they teach. They teach at a more advanced rate. I'm not saying the teachers are different. It's the *rate* of what is being taught. A child can learn things quick. They have that [absorbing] mind, as opposed to an adult.

INTERVIEWER: So the subject matter should be more advanced?

MR. DAVIS: I believe so. I really do believe it should be more advanced, because a lot of times parents say—people in general say—some subjects are too hard. I don't think it's hard enough. If you look at us as a nation, at the children coming up in school, it's like we are getting more unintelligent. I think it should be harder.

Jennifer Price, Stay-at-Home Mother

INTERVIEWER: How do you view the field of teaching and education today?

MS. PRICE: There are too many kids in a classroom. I view the system as good as far as teaching and things.

INTERVIEWER: What advice would you have for beginning teachers?

MS. PRICE: Patience would be the most important thing. And making each child feel that he is important, because some children may get more attention at school than they do at home.

INTERVIEWER: What could be changed about education to help children even more?

MS. PRICE: More one-on-one teaching. Having more time with each student. It's very hard, I know. I know at Riverton School [the local school], some teachers have thirty in a classroom.

Don Lambert, Administrator, Automobile Workers Training Center

INTERVIEWER: How do you view the field of teaching and education today?

MR. LAMBERT: I think it's the same as it has been for the past thirty years, and it appears to me that some changes are needed. Not having studied it, I don't know what the changes should be, but things change over time in education.

INTERVIEWER: What advice would you have for beginning teachers?

MR. LAMBERT: Be patient.

INTERVIEWER: What could be changed in education to help children more?

MR. LAMBERT: I'm not one that believes in year-round schooling. I think that children need free time, especially in the early years, the formative years. And I think that they need to be with other children. Learn to play in groups, learn to give and take, and learn that sometimes when they are hurt, they can't run to Mommy. They'll just have to get over it and keep playing. I think that way they learn a little bit of independence.

Annette Muniz, Secretary

INTERVIEWER: How do you view the field of teaching and education today?

MS. MUNIZ: I think it is difficult. I think there is more that should be done. The children need more; the teachers need more. They need more supplies; they need more of everything. And I guess if they had what they needed, besides discipline problems, it could be a lot better. The teacher has to be willing to be there—not just physically, but prepared to be there to deal with the children. If you really want to be there, you'll do a good job. It's not just being a teacher and "it's a job." It's not a job like a secretary, where you can go in and mess up. You can't mess up as a teacher. It's the kids who don't get the right education if you do. It's different than any other type of job. You're influencing the next generation, so it's not just a basic job. It's more important than just any job. It's a challenge in itself.

Martin Van Sherrill, Pediatrician

INTERVIEWER: How do you view the field of teaching and education today?

DR. VAN SHERRILL: Well, I think education today is much better than it was when I was in school. Some of the things kids do now we didn't do until we were older. They are doing things now that we *still* have not done! But I also feel that teachers today aren't as devoted as teachers were in the past. A teacher who has a child who is a little unruly today, who cannot make him learn, the first thing she wants to do is put him on some medication: "He has an attention deficit problem." Well, you might try to get his attention. He's a little bit different than Johnny or Jimmy, but you do need to get his attention. As opposed to asking the doctor to put him on medication, to smother him down so much that he is not tuned in to what is going on in the classroom. Then he's not even in tune with himself. He is just there. He is a zombie. And the class goes on. Everybody else learns. He goes on either with his medication, or he graduates to some other medication or some other type of street drug, because he knows what it's like to feel good and not in touch with reality. That's what the institutions are coming to now. I have too many kids on Ritalin. I know I have too many kids on Ritalin. But when the school says you've got to do something about this kid.... They have him shipped off to the psychologist or the psychiatrist. The psychiatrist says, "Hey, this kid is wild. You're going to have to do something about him." I don't think that's meeting the needs.

INTERVIEWER: What advice would you have for beginning teachers?

DR. VAN SHERRILL: Don't get into it unless you are a committed person. The person who is committed is someone who does what they do even if it interferes with their lifestyle; they still want to do it.

Dwight Faye, District Court Judge

INTERVIEWER: How do you view the field of teaching and education today?

MR. FAYE: I was, at one time, a classroom teacher myself. I taught chemistry and English in a high school in Florida before I went in the navy. It has changed so much. I was right out of college and taught school down there. I didn't have any discipline problems. The only discipline problems I encountered was a child chewing gum or one who didn't say yes sir and no sir. I go to schools now, and people there are trying to teach children and are not only having to teach the academic courses but deal with very severe discipline problems. They have horrible problems. It would be very difficult for me to teach nowadays. I think the teachers are trying very hard. I think it is a very honorable profession. Essentially, all the teachers are involved and trying to make a difference. And their efforts are being hampered by the climate that we have in America today. When a child talks about "I can't go to college because I don't have any money," refer him to the story of Booker T. Washington—how he got his college education and how he overcame all the obstacles. Or read the story of Martin Luther King in the Birmingham jail. Or go back to the classical thinkers who sustained Admiral Jim Stoffell, who was in prison with serious wounds in Vietnam for seven years. The only thing that got him through that was reflecting on the lessons he learned as a youth from the classics. I think that we, as of yesterday, need to be started down that path in this country. We have to make changes now to get back to absolute values that don't waver.

INTERVIEWER: What advice would you have for a beginning teacher?

MR. FAYE: Have a lot of patience and be careful. Realize that a lot of the children who are coming to you are going back into horrible conditions. We live in a reasonably affluent community here, and we still have children who don't know where they are going to sleep tonight, or will they be molested tonight, or will they have anything to eat tonight. At one time, I would go to Blossomwood Elementary School and jog early in the morning. Children would start filtering in well before time for school to start. I remember one little fellow loved to talk about football. I remember in the cold days of winter, he didn't have a coat. I think teachers need to be aware of children such as that in society. When I was growing up, I lived in a small county in south Alabama. At the time, we were the tenth poorest county in the nation. We had a very small rural school, and people all the way from bankers' sons to children of sharecroppers went to our school. We didn't have any real recognition of class distinction—at least I didn't. Things were tough, and everybody was trying to make it through. Now with the factor of TV, you'll see an old shack with a color TV coming from inside. That goes back to what I

was saying earlier. I think we have a problem trying to teach these kids about reality and [that] very few people live like the ones they see on TV. And another thing with television that I worry about is the recognition that violence is just a way of life. I think this has a bad influence on kids, numbing them. We really don't live in a society like that. And just common decency. People are not polite to people anymore. People don't treat their elders with respect. They don't smile and greet people. They are very rude and suspicious. This is something we need to work on as a nation.

• •

As you can see, people have some very strong opinions about education and what needs to be done to improve it. Do you agree with one or more of them? Do you think some of these people have some misperceptions, or do you? As a teacher, you will surely encounter such individuals. It is not our intent to frighten you by sharing the reality of how the general public views education. There is a great deal to be learned by hearing their positions, particularly if your values and ideas about education are in conflict with theirs.

All teachers should articulate reasons for teaching decisions and strategies.

As a teacher, you will need good communication skills, both in speaking and listening, as well as conflict negotiation skills. In particular, you will need to hone the skill of active listening and to develop the ability to articulate your position on an issue without becoming defensive. You also must understand what constitutes "good practice in early childhood education" to be articulate. Marilyn Davis, the early childhood program coordinator quoted on pages 436–437, indicated that family literacy personnel must be able to provide a rationale for the strategies they implement with children. We believe that this is something that *all* teachers must provide.

Let's turn to the examination of the knowledge base for early childhood education and the basic competencies required of early childhood personnel. As you read, note that this information comes from published sources rather than opinion.

PROFESSIONALISM IN EARLY CHILDHOOD EDUCATION

As you learned in Chapters 5 and 9, early childhood education has a long history. Part of what makes this professional area separate from elementary or secondary education is the age of the children served. NAEYC has specified additional criteria that define the field of early childhood education. They include a commitment to working with families and other adults on behalf of children, adherence to a code of ethics, and a desire to understand and implement guidelines specifying appropriate practice in early childhood education.

The early childhood education profession monitors and regulates the field, providing standards of practice.

The information in the next section differs from the opinions you have heard previously. The perspective that follows comes from the vision of leaders in the profession, as well as from the wisdom of practitioners. It includes standards, principles, and the ideals of professionalism. Standards and principles are based on theory and current research, as well as the consensus of thousands of early childhood professionals. A profession must set the parameters for quality practice and monitor the admittance to and practice of people working in the field to ensure that the standards are met. This includes the responsibility to provide goals for the preparation of those who strive to become professionals in the field (Bergen, 1992). These goals include the knowledge, skills, and dispositions necessary for the title of a professional in early childhood education. Think about why the tone of the information here is quite different from what you have already read.

National and State Guidelines

After years of work to establish a consensus within the field and with other professional organizations and accrediting bodies, NAEYC published and revised guidelines for the establishment and continuation of high-quality early childhood programs (NAEYC, 1996). This document provides the knowledge base for early childhood teachers. To implement the national guidelines, many states have subsequently put similar guidelines into place to create a professional development system. Although state requirements vary, these systems often include the tests and performance criteria

---

COLORADO'S CORE KNOWLEDGE AND STANDARDS: A GUIDE FOR EARLY CHILDHOOD PROFESSIONAL DEVELOPMENT

Practitioners at any level must have knowledge of the following content.
1. Child growth and development
2. Health, nutrition, and safety
3. Developmentally appropriate practices
4. Guidance (of children)
5. Family and community relationships
6. Cultural and individual diversity
7. Professionalism
8. Administration and supervision

Source: From *Creating and using core knowledge/competencies* (p. 4), by S. L. Azer, 1997. Boston: Center for Career Development in Early Care and Education, Wheelock College.

GEORGIA'S PROFESSIONAL DEVELOPMENT COMPETENCIES: EARLY CARE AND EDUCATION PROFESSIONALS

Practitioners are expected to:

1. Understand the principles of child growth and development
2. Establish and maintain a safe, healthy learning environment
3. Advance physical and intellectual competence
4. Support social and emotional development and provide positive guidance
5. Establish positive and productive relationships with families
6. Ensure a well-run, purposeful program responsive to individual children's needs
7. Maintain a commitment to professionalism

Source: From *Creating and using core knowledge/competencies* (p. 4), by S. L. Azer, 1997. Boston: Center for Career Development in Early Care and Education, Wheelock College.

---

you must meet to be certified or licensed in those states. As an example, look at the topics of core knowledge and competencies listed by two states, Colorado and Georgia (see the accompanying boxes). What similar topics do they address?

Each of the topics listed has many subtopics, as well as performance indicators or competencies on which candidates for professional development are evaluated. The accompanying box contains an example of how core knowledge and performance skills in the state of Texas interrelate. Note that these are samples from a much larger list, and that they match knowledge and skills.

TEXAS CORE KNOWLEDGE AND SKILLS FOR EARLY CARE AND EDUCATION PRACTITIONERS IN EARLY CARE AND EDUCATION

Core Knowledge Area One: Child Growth and Development
The candidate:

1a. Understands the processes of child growth and development from prenatal to young adulthood, including physical, social, emotional, and cognitive domains
1b. Understands the major theoretical approaches and theorists in child growth and development

1c. Understands the major methods of current child development study and research

Performance Skill One: Child Growth and Development
The candidate:

1a. Demonstrates a general knowledge of developmental processes and milestones for prenatal to young adulthood with special emphasis on prenatal to age three

1b. Applies developmentally appropriate practices to major child development theories and practice

1c. Applies developmentally appropriate practices to current methods of child development study and research

Core Knowledge Area Two: Health and Safety
The candidate:

2a. Understands the components that create safe and healthy indoor and outdoor environments that enhance growth and development

2b. Understands the nutritional needs of children, including special dietary or cultural needs

2c. Understands emergency medical and first aid procedures

2d. Recognizes the signs of child abuse and neglect and knows state statutes regarding the reporting of child abuse and neglect

2e. Understands the symptoms of common childhood diseases and reporting requirements

2f. Understands universal health precautions that help prevent the spread of infection

Performance Skill Two: Health and Safety
The candidate:

2a. Demonstrates planning for indoor and outdoor space that is safe, age appropriate, child centered, and balanced for active and quiet activities

2b. Develops menus that meet the nutritional needs of children, giving attention to special dietary or cultural requirements

2c. Demonstrates appropriate use of emergency medical procedures, first aid, and cardiopulmonary resuscitation for ages infants through adults

2d. Demonstrates recognition of the subtle and overt indicators of child abuse and neglect

2e. Demonstrates appropriate procedures for referral and reporting of child abuse and neglect

2f. Demonstrates procedures for recognizing and reporting common childhood diseases

2g. Demonstrates use of universal health precautions

Source: From *Report to the Texas legislature in response to House Bill 1863, section 7.05,* by Texas Core Knowledge and Skills in Early Care and Education. Texas Early Care and Education Career Development System Initiative, 1998.

Performance Assessment

A performance assessment of teacher candidates requires individual assessment.

As indicated in the Texas documents, new standards in states and the voluntary new national standards for beginning teachers will require that prospective teachers demonstrate that they can do particular things. Let's look more closely at some of the subtopics of typical competencies that you will need to exhibit and document. Since this chapter focuses on personal and professional growth, we examine competencies for that area. The accompanying box includes a section of a self-assessment instrument for some of the professional competencies developed in the state of Montana.

MONTANA EARLY CARE AND EDUCATION KNOWLEDGE BASE

Professionalism Assessment Key: Rate Yourself

1. Not yet aware
2. Developing an understanding
3. Beginning to apply
4. Frequently applies
5. Consistently applies
6. Thorough knowledge, ability to modify, evaluate, and synthesize
7. Fosters growth, exercises leadership, and advocates

Criteria

_____ Displays professional work habits, including dependability, time management, independence, teamwork, and responsibility

_____ Exhibits a commitment to the profession by advocating for quality programs and services for young children and their families

_____ Articulates a personal philosophy of early care and education that includes active learning, developmentally appropriate practice and assessment strategies, and inclusionary practices

_____ Supports linguistic and cultural diversity and developmental diversity through actions and attitudes

_____ Exhibits knowledge of other disciplines, which provide related services for young children and their families

_____ Exhibits knowledge and ability to access and work with multiple resources in meeting developmental needs of young children and their families

_____ Continually reflects upon practices and makes changes as a result

Source: From *Professionalism in Montana early care and education knowledge base,* by Montana Early Care and Education Career Development, 1998, pp. 23–25.

ASK YOURSELF

(Reread the self-assessment sample for the state of Montana. Rate yourself on this checklist.) Are there some areas that I have already begun to demonstrate? Are there some that I need to continue to develop? Which area is the *least* emphasized in my own development?

All of this may seem a bit overwhelming. There is much to know and learn about being a teacher, especially a constructivist teacher. The challenge of this book is to assist you as you *begin* in the field. We believe that we have given you many tools that can enhance your development. The best time to choose a career direction is now. The decision-making strategy of gathering information and thinking through future implications will benefit you in the long run. Even though you are just beginning your career journey, it is not too early to find out the requirements for the first position you hope to obtain. Finding out the name of the agency in your state that governs childcare and teacher certification, as well as the requirements for these and other positions, will provide you with advance information as you continue on your journey.

Career Ladders

Making wise choices about a career means gathering information now.

In many states, early childhood **career ladders** provide information about the various avenues for entering and advancing in the field. Listen to Danielle and Eric as they discuss the concept of career ladders.

DANIELLE: Eric, what does your home state require? It sounds like this state has just created a career ladder system. I like the image that gives me, but I'm not sure how you use one.

ERIC: My home state doesn't have anything like that yet. The idea I got from Dr. K. was that there are different levels in the profession and that you can advance from one level to another by climbing the rungs—or jumping through the hoops that the state department of education sets.

DANIELLE: Is this for P.E.? I thought it was for early childhood education.

ERIC: Oh, Danielle, I'm kidding! What I meant was that you advance from one position to the next depending on the additional training you get or

Your first step on a career ladder may or may not be your first full-time teaching position.
(© Elizabeth Crews)

ASK YOURSELF

Where would I be on a career ladder now? Am I at a higher beginning level than I first anticipated? What do I need to do to reach the next level? Compare where I am with where Danielle and Eric would be on the Texas ladder. Where would they be on the South Carolina ladder? What will they need to do to reach the next level?

· · · · · · · · · · · · · · · · ·

the degree you obtain. It's like getting promoted from assistant teacher to teacher. It just depends on what you have to do to get to the next level.

DANIELLE: Oh, I get it. Let's look at the handout she gave us to see if we're even on the ladder. Maybe we're at ground zero!

Danielle and Eric are beginning to understand what may seem like a complex system at first glance. Career ladders in early childhood education emerged from the application of a systems approach. This vision for professional development has several dimensions:

▸ A career development system is a coordinated, articulated system that is available and accessible for individuals seeking to advance in any of the variety of positions in the field.

▸ A career system will function to provide quality and consistency of preparation and is linked to best practice in the field.

▸ A career system offers many avenues for entering and advancing in the field.

Career ladders provide a system for advancing in the field of early childhood education.

▸ A career system seeks to ensure that compensation and responsibilities, qualifications and competence are in line.

▸ A career system will encourage links between systems that license child-care workers and centers and those that certify teachers in that state.

▸ A career system will enhance the notion that good *care* of children is embedded in good *education* of young children and vice versa. (Bredekamp, 1991; Bredekamp & Willer, 1992).

Let's look at two examples of career ladders that have been implemented in South Carolina and Texas (see Figures 11.1 and 11.2).

Figure 11.1

Early Care and Education Career Path: South Carolina

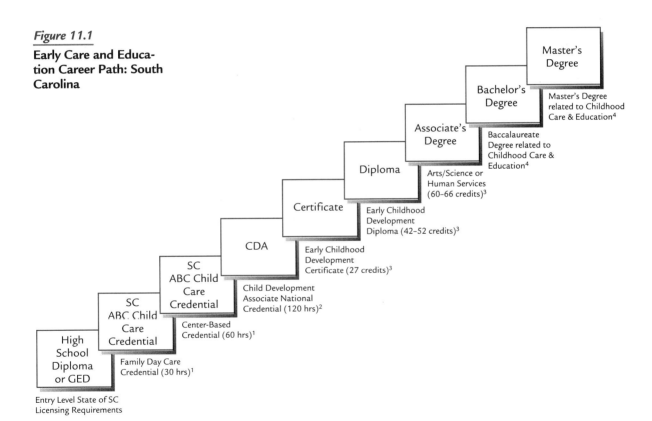

Master's Degree
Master's Degree related to Childhood Care & Education[4]

Bachelor's Degree
Baccalaureate Degree related to Childhood Care & Education[4]

Associate's Degree
Arts/Science or Human Services (60–66 credits)[3]

Diploma
Early Childhood Development Diploma (42–52 credits)[3]

Certificate
Early Childhood Development Certificate (27 credits)[3]

CDA
Child Development Associate National Credential (120 hrs)[2]

SC ABC Child Care Credential
Center-Based Credential (60 hrs)[1]

SC ABC Child Care Credential
Family Day Care Credential (30 hrs)[1]

High School Diploma or GED
Entry Level State of SC Licensing Requirements

[1]Entry level for SC Department HHS.
[2]Administered by Child Development Associate National Credentialing Program.
[3]Awarded by SC State Technical Colleges.
[4]Administered by 4-year private and public institutions.

Source: South Carolina's Early Care and Education Credentialing and Professional Development System. (1997). Center for Child Care Career Development. Greenville, SC. Reprinted with permission.

Figure 11.2 **Career Path of the Early Care and Education Practitioner: Texas**

Rationale: Training at each level needs to be articulated with the next level to enable participants to build a portfolio of credits as they progress in the career development system.

Participants may enter at any competency level depending on the ability to meet the stated requirements.

Training received by the participants must be based on the Texas Early Care and Education Core Knowledge and Competency Goals and conducted by a registered Early Care and Education Trainer or faculty and staff which meet the requirements of local institutions of higher education.

Competency Levels	*Requirements*
Level One	▶ Have a minimum of 8 hours of Texas Department of Protective and Regulatory Services–approved pre-service training, and ▶ be 16 years of age, and ▶ be working on a GED or high school diploma, and ▶ be enrolled in a training program approved by the TDPRS Child Care Licensing Division. *or* ▶ Complete a minimum of 8 hours of TDPRS-approved pre-service training, and ▶ have a high school diploma or GED, and ▶ be at least 18 years of age, and ▶ be participating in a training program which addresses the Texas Core Knowledge and Skills for Early Care and Education.
Level Two	▶ Meet all requirements for Level One, *plus* ▶ complete a minimum of 60 clock-hours of training which address the Texas Core Knowledge and Skills for Early Care and Education *or* ▶ complete a three-hour semester credit course which addresses the Texas Core Knowledge and Skills for Early Care and Education from a community college, trade school, or vocational education school.
Level Three	▶ Hold a Child Development Associate's Credential or its equivalent.
Level Four	▶ Hold a Texas child development early childhood certificate from a community college, trade school, or vocational education school.
Level Five	▶ Hold an Associate's Degree in Early Childhood or Child Development.
Level Six	▶ Holds a Bachelor's Degree in Child Development/Early Childhood Education *or* hold a Bachelor's Degree in a related field with 12 college credits in Early Childhood Education/Child Development and a state endorsement in Early Childhood.
Level Seven	▶ Hold a Master's Degree in Child Development/Early Childhood Education *or* hold a Master's Degree in a related field with 24 college credits in Early Childhood Education/Child Development.
Level Eight	▶ Hold a Doctorate in Child Development/Early Childhood Education *or* hold a Doctorate in a related field with 30 college credits in Early Childhood Education/Child Development.

Source: Texas Core Knowledge and Skills in Early Care and Education, Application Packet, Texas Early Care and Education Career Development System Initiative, Texas Head Start Collaboration Office, Charles A. Dana Center at the University of Texas at Austin, 1998, pages 21–27.

To find out more about how progress on a career ladder occurs, read the accompanying interview with Barbara Mezzio. As you read, mark her professional path on the Texas career ladder (Figure 11.2). Be sure to note where and how she entered the field of early childhood education, the steps she took to progress, and where she is now.

MULTIPLE PERSPECTIVES

From the Field

Following is an interview with Barbara Mezzio, director of the Children's Center at Mesa Community College (MCC) in Mesa, Arizona.

INTERVIEWER: Tell me who you are and where you work.

MS. MEZZIO: I'm Barbara Mezzio, and I'm the director of the Mesa Community College Children's Center, which is located on the campus of a community college. We serve students' and employees' needs for childcare.

INTERVIEWER: How long have you been there?

MS. MEZZIO: I've been with Maricopa County Community Colleges for ten, almost eleven, years.

INTERVIEWER: Always at Mesa?

MS. MEZZIO: Seven years at Mesa.

INTERVIEWER: Did you go there as the director of that center?

MS. MEZZIO: No, I started here as a lead teacher.

INTERVIEWER: What does that mean—a lead teacher?

MS. MEZZIO: What it meant was in addition to working with children and developing the program for the children, I was also responsible for supervision of what happened in the classroom as far as the arrangement of work-study students and other teachers in the classroom. I had these additional responsibilities. Someone else was the director, but I assisted her. So that was the difference—there was another teacher in the classroom.

INTERVIEWER: Now, in your current position, do you have any day-to-day planned time with the children, or are you mostly an administrator?

MS. MEZZIO: I'm mostly an administrator now. And that's happened slowly over the seven years. There used to be a time when I was still very much involved with the children and in the summer program. When it first began, I would work with the children. Now I teach only if one of my staff calls in sick or if we need another adult—if it's out of ratio.

INTERVIEWER: How do you feel about that gradual change?

Ms. Mezzio: *(Long pause.)* I had a choice just recently to go back to work with children, working the same amount, same position, different campus, but I would be directly working with children, and I chose not to do [that] because I feel that I—that isn't something I want to do anymore.

Interviewer: So you've changed?

Ms. Mezzio: I've changed. I've changed. I've grown, and I've changed. In fact, somebody was doing a lesson plan today, and it was interesting because I looked at it and realized that I haven't written a lesson plan in close to six years. I thought, "Wow, could I even write a lesson plan anymore?" But at the same time, I have learned other skills, new skills, and I like using new skills. I like empowering other teachers and causing them to think, to think about their work with children.

Interviewer: How did you specifically enter a nonpublic-school-based program, having a degree or background in early childhood education? How do you think other people might enter non-school-based programs?

Ms. Mezzio: I began teaching preschool because I got a degree [A.A.] in early childhood education in New York. Then I chose to get married instead of going on to get my B.A. My husband was in the service, so we moved to Sierra Vista [a small community near a military base in southern Arizona], and there weren't very many opportunities in early childhood education. An A.A. degree doesn't really allow you to go into the public schools, so I went to work at a for-profit child-care center.

Interviewer: Because you've said that, how did it measure up to what you thought quality settings should be?

Ms Mezzio: *(Laughs.)* Well, I'll step back a little bit. The first job I actually got was at the military base working in their preschool, which was part of their child-care program. Their director had absolutely no background, and it was a horrible program. I had just come from this incredible A.A. program in upstate New York that taught us everything, with a child development lab school that was just phenomenal. And I called up my professor in tears, saying, "I can't believe this." I mean, this place was awful, and he said to get out of there. So then, this next place that I went to was this for-profit child-care center. It was a hundred percent better, believe it or not, than the program at the military base at that time. So it didn't measure up to my lab experience, but as my professor had said, they had given me the ideal, because they wanted us to see what *should* be. So then I thought that [lab] was what was the norm. Looking back, it [the for-profit center] was not a good program, but the woman that ran it taught me a great deal about childcare and the function of childcare and how to implement the child's daily routines into the program so that *learning* takes place.

Interviewer: Using routines as a basis for learning?

Ms. Mezzio: Absolutely. We had to do everything, because the program operated in a church. We literally had to set out tables on a daily basis. After lunch, we had to break down the tables to change it into a nap room. We had to go grocery shopping. I mean, everything. And children were a part of that—that whole daily routine. So that's how originally I got into childcare, when the notion was just to take care of the children, not to teach them anything. When I finally got the opportunity to go back to school, I wondered if I should go back to get a B.A. in early childhood education, because that would get me certified, but I never wanted to teach in the public schools.

Interviewer: Why?

Ms. Mezzio: That's a good question. Originally, I thought I wanted to be a special education teacher. *(Sighs.)* I'm not real sure. I think that maybe what bothered me was the structure of the schools. I found I really loved early childhood, and at that time, when I was exploring that, I didn't have people like the mentor I have now, who could show me that good early childhood education practices could be implemented in public school classrooms. I think I always saw public schools as separate from early childhood education.

Interviewer: I was just thinking, maybe public schools didn't offer you freedom for creativity.

Ms. Mezzio: *(Laughs.)* Yes.

Interviewer: And a nonschool setting can provide that.

Ms. Mezzio: Right. I think that that was it. One of my experiences in my A.A. program was that we had to go into the public schools for eight weeks. And I taught in a special needs class, a class for children with mental retardation in an elementary school. As part of our A.A. program, I also had to give up two weeks of Christmas vacation to go work someplace in our hometown, so I spent two weeks full-time in the public school, in the kindergarten class there, in my hometown. So I think that's why. I just thought, "I don't really want to go and do dittos!" That's what the public school teachers did then, and it just didn't compare to what I saw at the lab school.

Interviewer: So how did you get from this for-profit center to working for Maricopa County Community Colleges and thus to where you are now?

Ms. Mezzio: We left the service, and we went back to New York. I was a waitress and actually was on my way to becoming a machinist's apprentice.

Interviewer: Wow!

Ms. Mezzio: I know—it's amazing. I think that I was exhausted from the work in childcare. I mean, in that program I had no equipment, with twenty-five children all by myself. I was totally exhausted. I was tired of going home on the weekends and doing my work for the center and getting paid very little.

INTERVIEWER: And subsidizing the program.

MS. MEZZIO: And subsidizing the program on top of it. So, after a full year of doing that, I was thinking, "I don't know if this is what I want to do." It was during that time that we moved back to Arizona. Once we got out here, I needed to work, so I went to work for a national child-care chain, which was okay. Then I became the assistant director there, and then I went to their main office as their special needs consultant, with only an A.A. degree.

INTERVIEWER: Did you feel a little out of your depth?

MS. MEZZIO: Oh, absolutely. There was no doubt about it. But I was told not to worry, because the person that was running it would teach me. She had a master's degree in special education.

INTERVIEWER: Did that happen?

MS. MEZZIO: No, absolutely not. They felt that because I was such a good, creative teacher, that I could handle the consultant position. I was to go into other classes and help teachers make the adjustment for children with special needs that were mainstreamed into their class. Well, I didn't realize what I'd be taking on. I thought all teachers knew how to teach, but they didn't have any background. I mean, none of them even had A.A. degrees. And so I started from the beginning, and, you know, I was up against directors that were mad because I'd go in and tell their teachers that what they were doing was inappropriate for children. But there were some great people to work with, too. For example, there was a speech pathologist and an occupational therapist that were wonderful. They were there to help me if I had questions. It took me about a year, and I finally decided "This place is not a good place for me to be working."

INTERVIEWER: But you had worked there as a teacher quite successfully?

MS. MEZZIO: Yes, because in addition to being the consultant, I was in the center and I was the teacher, and I had control of my room, and people were impressed with what I did with children.

INTERVIEWER: But you didn't have the "big picture," or the quality of position you really wanted?

MS. MEZZIO: Right. Even though I was being paid a low wage, I was told during my training in college that [the] pay would be low. But that was also what stopped me from going on to get my degree. I thought, "Why am I going to get a B.A. and get paid minimum wage?" And during some of that time, I started back at Mesa Community College taking business classes. I thought maybe, you know, once again, "Should I get out of this field, or should I stay with it?"

INTERVIEWER: Why did you [stay with it]?

MS. MEZZIO: The special education consultant job opened up opportunities for me. I started to go to the Network Breakfast [a local early childhood organization], and through getting information about conferences and activities, I started going to many early childhood events and meeting people. I saw that there was a whole other world in this field that I hadn't had access to before.

INTERVIEWER: Right.

MS. MEZZIO: And once I started seeing that, I thought, "Gee, there are other places to work." So that gave me that realization, and then a job opened at Phoenix Community College for the evening lead teacher position. I got the job and saw what it really was. I was there for four years, and actually I taught them that childcare can be quality, the same as any preschool program. It was after that that I got hired as the lead teacher here. Then I completed my B.A. degree in early childhood education.

INTERVIEWER: What happened after that?

MS. MEZZIO: That takes us back to where we started. Now I'm in this wonderful place—the Children's Center at MCC. It's a great school. The staff is paid ten dollars an hour, eleven dollars an hour—they've been with me forever. They are excited about coming to work. They want to learn more. They feel like they're professionals. I think that's the other part of it—people have to feel like they're professionals. They need to be treated like professionals.

INTERVIEWER: Just based on that, what advice would you give to somebody who would like to do what you do now, but also to someone who is thinking about entering the field?

MS. MEZZIO: Be patient and persistent; go the way that you feel. If you have a love and a passion for the field, you can just stick through thick and thin. And I think that we as early childhood people *continue* throughout our careers to *constantly* look at what we want from the profession and what we can give the profession, too. We can always go back to become the machinist apprentice, the—

INTERVIEWER: Air traffic controller?

MS. MEZZIO: *(Laughs.)* Right. I just finished working through that. My last career decision, I was going for a master's degree in business administration. I wasn't going for a master's in early childhood education. Of course, I just finished my M.A. in early childhood education. I guess I made the right decision, since I did win a national award for being the outstanding director of a campus-based child-care program.

INTERVIEWER: That is a pretty incredible achievement! I'm wondering, do you think things have changed appreciably since you got into the field?

Career paths in early childhood education are enhanced by reflection and new challenges as teachers develop.

MS. MEZZIO: Absolutely. For the better—yes, I do. It's been eighteen years now for me, and I remember when I first got out of college with my A.A., child-care conditions were terrible. Nobody cared. We didn't hear a lot on TV or in the news about early childhood. I think we have a long way to go in being treated as respected professionals, but I think there's been a lot of progress.

CONSTRUCTIONS

1. Analysis

Where did Barbara Mezzio begin on the Texas career ladder? What level had she reached by the time of the interview? What were some of the factors that influenced her decisions as she progressed in her career development? What questions would you like to ask her about her decisions?

2. Research

Interview a local well-known professional in your community. See if you can chart that person's career path on one of the career ladders.

3. Comparision

How are the two individuals different and similar? What are your thoughts about the pros and cons of starting at different points on the Texas career ladder? What do you think the challenges would be in each case?

4. Analysis

Chart a career path that you can project as a possibility for yourself. What will your next step be? What questions do you have about the requirements to reach the next level?

DEVELOPING AUTONOMY

You have just heard what many people—children, parents, and professionals both in the field and outside it—think about teachers and teaching. How can you, as an individual, respond to the ideas and opinions you have heard? What will be the right approach for you as a teacher, assistant teacher, administrator, or family advocate? Only you can answer that question. Your answer must be based on current knowledge and the professional skills advocated as the best practice, but it must also be based on your own teaching theory and experience with children and families. Do you recall Danielle's desire in Chapter 2 to have someone tell her everything to do as a teacher (see page 40)? Do you have similar feelings? Do you feel that such a book would be helpful, or are you ready to be more in control of your own direction? Remember, too, Tillie's statements earlier in this chapter about doing what is right for her own circumstance. She referred to this as autonomy.

We've discussed that concept several times in this book. With what you understand now, what does it mean to be an autonomous teacher? Why is that important? Constructivists Jean Piaget, Constance Kamii, and Rheta DeVries have written about the importance of autonomy. As defined in previous chapters, *autonomy* is the ability to know what is fair and true, both morally and intellectually. Autonomous teachers possess the professional knowledge that enables them to determine what is educationally appropriate for children and to articulate their reasoning to others. An autonomous person takes into consideration the perspectives of others and then decides what action to take, regardless of how popular that action may be. Autonomy is different from independence. When individuals act autonomously, they consider what is true and fair for *all*. One may act independently and yet not act autonomously.

Kamii (1985) says that "autonomous professionals can set their own goals from day to day and can plan their own activities based on scientific knowledge about how children learn." Similarly, DeVries and Kohlberg (1987) say that "autonomous teachers do not just accept uncritically what curriculum specialists give them. They *think about* whether they agree with what is suggested. They take responsibility for the education they are offering children" (p. 380). By this point, you should be beginning to feel comfortable stating a philosophy of how you will teach. Your ability to take a position based on your knowledge about how children learn sets you apart from the general public. You have begun to construct specialized, professional knowledge that you will be challenged to implement in your work with children. It will be honed as you live in classrooms or groups of children and as you encounter individuals who question or disagree with you. These encounters will be the very opportunities that will encourage you to learn more.

Developing autonomy is critical to professional growth.

ASK YOURSELF

(Reread information on autonomy on page 265. Then reread the conversation among Amy, Tillie, and Danielle at the beginning of this chapter.) Do I think Tillie was accurate in her response that she would be acting autonomously? Why or why not?

Disagreement with others provides opportunities to articulate your knowledge and beliefs.

TRANSITIONS

The process of reflecting—of thinking about a problem and analyzing different solutions to reach a hypothesis to test—is a critical habit to form as a foundation for continued, even lifelong, learning and growth. Throughout this book, we have suggested many activities to engage you in this process.

Appreciate your accomplishments and growth.

You know that contemplating events, whether by yourself or with a peer, often leads you further in your thinking.

As you read in Chapter 1, *reflection* includes the process of looking back and looking forward. Do that now and recognize how much you have learned since you first opened this book. We hope that you are more eager than before to be in this field. We expect that you realize that you still have much to learn as you move into creating curriculum and community with children. Take stock of the hard work and the thinking that you have done to reach this point. You have embarked on the journey that the Velveteen Rabbit described—that of becoming real. A real teacher can leave an enduring mark through the children and families she touches.

SUMMARY

▸ Personal development in a profession requires reflection on the past and projections into the future.

▸ Career paths emerge from an individual's interests, beliefs, needs, personal circumstances, finances, and personal decisions, as well as from past experiences.

▸ A realistic consideration of job demands and rewards will help you to re-examine your motivation to teach.

▸ A constructivist approach to teaching is based on the study of how children learn. It may not be the best approach for every teacher candidate.

▸ Children include personal and professional attributes in descriptions of good teachers, but special emphasis is given to the way teachers treat children.

▸ Current teachers' advice for becoming a good teacher will vary based on the experiences and teaching theory of each teacher.

▸ The perspectives of parents and community members often reflect their own schooling experiences and beliefs rather than a knowledge of how children learn.

▸ NAEYC has specified guidelines and standards for the best practice in early childhood education.

▸ A profession sets parameters for quality practice and provides standards for assessment of those in the field.

▸ Performance assessment requires that a teacher candidate demonstrate the application of knowledge.

▸ Career ladders in early childhood care and education provide a means of advancing professionally, taking into account the diversity within the field.

> ▸ Autonomy is the key to being an articulate, knowledgeable practitioner. It develops with knowledge of how children learn and multiple opportunities to respond to the challenges of those who do not understand a constructivist approach to education.

CONSTRUCTIONS

The Community

1. Research

Interview several individuals in your community, asking them the same questions that were posed in our interviews conducted in the community (see pages 439–444).

2. Analysis

Compare their answers with the thoughts of the people in Huntsville, Alabama. Are there some similarities? How did you respond to the individuals' comments, both outwardly and inwardly?

3. Synthesis

What did you learn by confronting various opinions about early childhood education and teaching?

The State

1. Research

Find answers to the following questions. What are the guidelines for professional development in your state? What are the requirements for working with children under the age of five? For working with children older than five? Does your state require certification or licensure? Will you have to take an exam or meet performance standards to qualify for certification? Does your state require that you create a portfolio for the position you hope to obtain?

2. Documentation

Write down the name of the agency that governs certification and or licensure. Include the agency's telephone numbers and the name of the individual who oversees the agency. If you are planning to work in another state, use the Internet to obtain this information for that state as well.

RESOURCES

Ayers, W. (1993). *To teach: The journey of a teacher.* New York: Teachers College Press.
This book provides insiders' knowledgeable and perceptive accounts of the processes involved in teaching and learning. It offers a very readable and insightful look at children, teaching, curriculum, and evaluation.

Ayers, W. (Ed). (1995). *To become a teacher: Making a difference in children's lives.* New York: Teachers College Press.

This book contains a collection of writing by good teachers. Their stories and perspectives remind readers that a primary reason for being a teacher is to live joyfully with schoolchildren and to attend to the wisdom of children. The interpersonal aspects of classroom life, traditionally ignored in the interest of content, are the focus of the many thoughtful essays.

Johnson, J., & McCracken, J. B. (Eds.) (1994). *Early childhood career lattice: Perspectives on professional development.* Washington DC: NAEYC.

This booklet contains seminal thinking about a career system for early childhood education and care. The essays are written by leaders in the field and provide detailed information about career paths, core content for professional development, strategies leading to professional development of staff, and a vision for a professional development system.

Lipka, R., & Brinthaupt, T. (Eds.) (1999). *The role of self in teacher development.* Ithaca, NY: SUNY Press.

The theme of balancing personal and professional development runs through all the essays in this book. The book focuses explicitly on transition points in the process of becoming a teacher.

Zehm, S., & Kottler, J. (1993). *On being a teacher: The human dimension.* Newbury Park, CA: Corwin.

This book speaks to the importance of teachers taking care of themselves, the idea that students can take care of themselves and each other, the importance of cultural and individual differences, and the key role of communication in education. Advocating a constructivist approach, the authors confront obstacles that make a teaching career challenging.

ABANDONMENT Forsaking or deserting; surrendering one's claim or right to something.

ACCOMMODATION One component of adaptation, within the functional aspects of cognitive development. Accommodation happens if the incoming information doesn't fit the existing structures. It is the actual change or modification of a mental structure to manage the incoming information.

ACCOUNTABILITY Responsibility assumed by educators to behave in a professional manner and to be able to explain actions taken in the educational process. Also, responsibility to use funds according to the purpose for which they were intended.

ACTION PLAN A formalized plan aimed at answering a question or moving forward on an agenda.

ADVOCATE One who speaks out for a cause; one who defends the cause.

AFFECTIVE DEVELOPMENT Development relating to the feelings of the individual.

AFFECTIVITY Pertaining to or resulting from emotions or feelings rather than from thought.

AMBIVALENCE The existence of mutually conflicting feelings or thoughts, such as love and hate together, with regard to some person, object, or idea.

ANALYZING Finding patterns in information or data that help you identify motives or causes, find evidence, and draw conclusions.

APPLIANCES The devices people use to access, send, and receive content via the World Wide Web.

ASSIMILATION A component of adaptation within the functional aspects of cognitive development. This is the internal process a child uses to take something in and interpret it on the basis of existing cognitive structures—in other words, to put new information into an existing schemata so that it can be used.

ASSISTIVE TECHNOLOGY Any low- or high-tech item used to maintain or improve the functional abilities of children with disabilities.

AUTONOMY (1) Self-regulation; the ability to distinguish between appropriate and inappropriate actions on the basis of an internally constructed standard for behavior. (2) According to Piaget, the ability to make decisions about what is true in the intellectual realm and what is right in the moral realm without being swayed by popular opinion.

BABBLING Sounds babies make by combining consonantal and vocalic sounds and repeating them (for example, ba-ba-ba).

BEHAVIORAL Relating to behavior. A behavioral teaching approach defines learning as a change in behavior and uses positive rewards and negative punishments to change inappropriate behavior and to continue appropriate behavior.

BLOCK GRANT Money provided by the federal government to state or local government. The federal government provides general regulations related to the purpose of the money, while recipients decide on specific projects.

BUREAUCRACY A government system marked by the diffusion of authority among numerous offices and the adherence to inflexible rules of operation.

CAREER LADDER An incentive plan that specifies hierarchical levels of professionalism. Steps up a career ladder involve additional training, experience, and documentation of performance that meet specific criteria.

CAUSALITY In infants, the idea that they see themselves as causing all events or activities. As the child's reasoning advances, she begins to realize that objects or events other than self can cause certain actions.

CENTRATION A child's tendency to focus on one attribute of an object to the exclusion of other attributes.

CEPHALOCAUDAL Directionally from the head to the foot.

CERTIFIED CHILD LIFE SPECIALIST A person who is qualified to work in a hospital setting by virtue of specialized training and internship. Duties include supporting children emotionally, socially, and intellectually during hospitalization, while working in concert with hospital staff and family members.

CHARTER SCHOOL A school that is licensed by the state or local school board to operate for a specified period of time. These schools are given a fair amount of autonomy and are expected to be innovative.

CHILD ABUSE AND NEGLECT Any action or inaction by someone responsible for a child that results in the harm or potential risk of harm to the child. It may include physical or sexual abuse, physical neglect, emotional abuse, or emotional neglect.

CHILD ADVOCATE A person who seeks support for children's issues.

CHILD DEVELOPMENT ASSOCIATE (CDA) A credential awarded to a person who has had some training and experience in a preschool or infant/toddler setting and who has passed a competency test.

CHILD-CENTERED Used to describe a curriculum that fosters the development of the child, appeals to the interests of the child, and views the child as different from an adult.

CLASSIFICATION The ability to mentally group objects according to similarities, differences, and part-whole relationships.

COGNITIVE DEVELOPMENT Development relating to the intelligence and thought of the individual. *Cognitive* comes from a Latin word meaning "thinking."

COLLEGE OR UNIVERSITY SUPERVISOR A higher education faculty member responsible for supervising early childhood student teachers' field experiences.

CONCRETE OPERATIONAL The Piagetian stage at which children's reasoning no longer relies on perception but uses logic in concrete situations.

CONSERVATION A child's ability to understand and conceptualize that the amount or quality of matter stays the same regardless of any changes. For example, you have the same amount of clay regardless of whether you make it into a sausage or a pancake.

CONTENT What children know. It is observable behavior and varies from child to child and age to age.

COOPERATING, SUPERVISING, MENTORING, HEAD, OR LEAD TEACHER An early childhood teacher who is responsible for working with early childhood student teachers in their field experiences.

CORPORAL PUNISHMENT Physical punishment administered to an offender, such as spanking with a board.

CORRESPONDENCES Comparisons that do not create transformations or modifications. A one-to-one correspondence is an example of a correspondence that a child between the ages of four and six makes.

CURRICULUM (1) The course of study or programming for a child-care or school program. (2) The framework may be standards set by a governing body, while the day-to-day curriculum is designed by the teacher. (3) An organized framework that delineates the content that children are to learn, the processes through which children achieve the identified curriculum goals, what teachers do to help children achieve these goals, and the context in which teaching and learning occur. (4) In a constructivist classroom, the sense that children make of classroom experiences. (5) All the learning experiences for which the school takes responsibility.

CUSTODIAL CARE Usually refers to childcare provided by caregivers who have little or no training and who focus primarily on children's physical needs.

DEFERRED IMITATION An external form of a representational competence in which an infant responds to others by imitating their actions, which were observed at an earlier time.

DIPHTHONG A complex speech sound beginning with one vowel sound and moving to another vowel or semivowel position within the same syllable, such as *oy* in *boy*.

DISEQUILIBRATION A mental sense of imbalance that occurs when incoming information does not fit into the individual's existing cognitive structures.

EARLY INTERVENTION PROGRAM Services for children ages birth to three or four years who have an identified disability or are at risk.

EDUCATIONAL COORDINATOR A person who guides the educational program of a center or school, usually in early childhood education.

EGOCENTRISM In a child, the belief that everyone thinks as he thinks and knows what he knows. At this stage of development, the child is unable to differentiate his thoughts from the thoughts of others.

EQUILIBRATION (1) The process of continuous balance between assimilation and accommodation. If an organism experiences disequilibration, it experiences a form of cognitive conflict or cognitive imbalance that results in a new process of balance or equilibration. Assimilation and accommodation are the mechanisms that control equilibration. (2) A sense of continuous balance between incoming information and existing cognitive structures; a mental state that all individuals strive to attain.

ETHOS A disposition, character, or attitude that distinguishes one group of people from other groups.

FAMILY CHILD-CARE PROVIDER A person who provides childcare in her own home for someone else's children.

FIELD PLACEMENT SITES Also called practica or internship sites. Early childhood programs in which early childhood students are placed to observe, participate, and learn about teaching and learning.

FOOT BINDING An old process whereby a young girl's feet were tightly bound with strips of cloth, restricting growth and thus resulting in small feet, thought to be beautiful in centuries past. This was a painful and (over a lifetime) disabling practice.

FORMAL OPERATIONAL THOUGHT Thought that allows you to understand, reason, coordinate, and draw conclusions using abstract notions as well as reality. Formal operational thinkers use not only facts from the real world but also deductive reasoning, possibilities, probabilities, and combinations.

FUNCTION An aspect of thought relating to the characteristics of intellectual development. Assimilation, accommodation, adaptation, coordination, transformation, and continuity play a role in the function of thought.

GENERAL EQIVALENCY DIPLOMA (GED) A diploma granted to persons who did not complete high school and who have passed an eqivalency test. May substitute for a high school diploma.

GENETIC EPISTEMOLOGIST One who studies the origins and nature of knowledge.

HEAD START A federally funded program designed to deliver health, educational, nutritional, and social services to economically disadvantaged preschoolers and their families.

HETERONOMY Being governed by others.

INCEST Sexual union between persons who are so closely related that marriage is illegal or forbidden by custom.

INDIVIDUALIZED EDUCATION PLAN (IEP) A written plan for an individual child with special needs. The plan is designed by a team including the parents and is required by Public Law 94-142.

INDIVIDUALIZED FAMILY SERVICES PLAN (IFSP) Similar to an IEP, but for younger children.

INFANTICIDE The killing of an infant; a person who kills an infant.

INFORMATION SUPERHIGHWAY A collection of interconnecting communication networks by which people create and send content, using appliances to access it.

INTENTIONALITY When a child initiates behavior that is directed toward certain ends or goals for some purpose.

INTERDISCIPLINARY Across two disciplines, such as psychology and language combined into psycholinguistics

INTERVIEW A series of questions that helps you gather information about someone's thinking, beliefs, ideas, and preferences on a given topic.

INTRUSIVE Forcing oneself on another person without his consent.

INVENTION The ability to solve new problems through new means.

ISSUE A problem or concern, such as child abuse, that (1) has a high impact on children and teachers, (2) is enduring and has existed for quite some time, and (3) requires that a teacher do something about it, such as reporting suspected child abuse.

LABORATORY SCHOOL A school associated with a university that serves as a laboratory for the study of teaching, learning, and child development.

LEAD CAREGIVER A person assigned to oversee the operation of a classroom for infants or toddlers, while also serving as one of the child caregivers.

LEAD, CLASSROOM, OR HEAD TEACHER A person assigned to oversee the operation of a classroom for children ages three and up, while also serving as a teacher in that classroom.

LOGICO-MATHEMATICAL KNOWLEDGE An understanding of internal relationships and the coordination of those relationships—for example, the relationships of same/different, some/all, and part/whole.

LOOPING An organizational plan involving assigning a teacher to a group of children for two or three years. The teacher stays with the children as they progress to the next level, rather than staying at one level or grade.

MENTAL IMAGES Internal representations of past experiences that are not exact replications of things observed but have some resemblance to them.

MORAL FEELINGS An outgrowth of affective and cognitive development in which a person does what is necessary rather than what he would like to do. Also called moral reasoning.

MOTORIC Relating to both small and large muscle skills or motor skills.

MOTORIC REFINEMENT The development and perfection of motor skills.

MULTIAGE MODEL An organizational plan in which children of a two- or three-year age span are grouped together in a class. As the oldest or most advanced group moves on to the next level, additional younger children are added to the group.

MULTIDISCIPLINARY Across many disciplines, such as medicine, psychology, and education.

NANNY An individual who cares for a family's children, usually in the children's home. Nannies may perform light housekeeping chores, live in the home, and be on call most of the time.

NATURALISM The doctrine that all religious truths are derived from nature and natural causes and not from revelation.

NETWORKS The pipelines that transport the content between appliances.

NORMATIVE DATA Data based on averages that imply a standard, such as what an average three-year-old should be able to say.

NUCLEAR FAMILY A self-contained family unit consisting of a mother, a father, and their children.

NURSERY SCHOOL A term coined by Margaret McMillan to refer to an educational setting for preschool children between the ages of three and five. The emphasis is on education, with children enjoying their play experiences and exploration of objects.

OBJECT CONCEPT A child's ability to use spatial constructions (shape and size) and form relationships to establish some continuation and organization with regard to the objects she recognizes.

OBJECT PERMANENCE The ability to know that an object still exists even when it is not visible.

OBSERVATION The gathering of information by noting facts or events. Observation is more than merely looking.

OPERATION An internally constructed system of actions that allows thoughts to be mobile, free from a dependence on perception, and logical.

PERFORMANCE STANDARDS Criteria that an agency is expected to meet based on funders' expectations. May also apply to criteria that students are expected to meet.

PERSONIFICATION A rhetorical figure of speech in which inanimate objects or abstractions are endowed with human qualities or are represented as possessing human form.

PERTURBATION The condition of being disturbed, perplexed, or confused.

PHYSICAL KNOWLEDGE Knowledge of objects in external reality. Physical knowledge is constructed through observation and acting on the object, because the ultimate source of physical knowledge is partly in the object itself.

PIAGETIAN TASKS Tasks designed by Piaget to help him understand children's thinking as a result of what they say and do in the task—for example, a conservation task to understand children's thinking about quantity.

PORTFOLIO A physical means of documenting your professional growth and your study of knowledge.

POST-TRAUMATIC STRESS SYNDROME/DISORDER A reaction to experiencing or witnessing violence in which an individual becomes sad, aggressive, apathetic, and/or preoccupied, with little energy for activities such as academic tasks.

PRACTICUM Experience for preservice teachers, providing them with opportunities to work with children, usually prior to student teaching or internship.

PREOPERATIONAL STAGE The Piagetian stage at which children's reasoning relies on representation and perception and is prelogical.

PRIMARY CAREGIVER A person assigned to a small group of children within a larger group in a child-care center classroom.

PRIMORDIAL Being or happening first in time.

PROGRESSIVE MOVEMENT Started by John Dewey, who held that learning progresses as the learner participates in activities in his social world.

PROJECT APPROACH An approach to learning that involves students in projects requiring them to study, explore, interact, and produce a product related to the project.

PROXIMODISTAL Directionally from the center of the body to the outer appendages.

QUESTIONING A spontaneous search for information, a way to build understandings and to figure out causes, origins, or rules. Questions can be both social and introspective.

REASONING The process of reflecting on actions, objects, and ideas, constructing and coordinating relationships across events and objects.

RECAPITULATE To repeat in the same way; to summarize.

REFLECTION The ability to think about the past, present, and future so that you gain new awareness.

REFLECTIVE ABSTRACTION An internal thought or reflection based on what is known. It is a process used in logico-mathematical reasoning.

REFLEX ACTION An inborn, involuntary action in response to some stimulus.

RESEARCH A dynamic process that allows you to become an inquirer, and even at times a collaborator, within the process of searching for answers.

RESOURCE AND REFERRAL AGENCY An organization that provides information to families and employers on topics such as the source and availability of childcare.

REVERSIBILITY A child's ability to reverse his or her thoughts back to the starting point.

SCHEMA A Piagetian term used to define an action or idea that, together with other actions and ideas, structures the mind.

SCHEMATA The plural of schema.

SENSORIMOTOR STAGE The Piagetian stage at which children's thoughts are the thoughts of action and sensory input.

SERIATION The mental ordering of objects according to physical characteristics, such as differences in size, weight, and length.

SIMULTANEITY Happening a the same time.

SMALL KINSHIP GROUP A small, tightly knit familial group that shares communal responsibilities.

SOCIAL FEELINGS When a child begins to have feelings for and about others.

SOCIAL INTERACTION The exchange of ideas among people.

SOCIAL KNOWLEDGE Knowledge of culture, its values, and its conventions. Holidays, written and spoken language, moral codes, and rules of conduct (holding the door for an older person or sending a thank-you note when you receive a gift) are examples of social knowledge.

SOCIOCENTRISM The point in a child's development when he can coordinate others' perspectives so that he functions as a social being.

SPATIAL Pertaining to, involving, or having the nature of space.

STANDARDIZED TEST An instrument prepared by a commercial organization and administered to children to determine achievement or aptitude. This type of test is administered according to specific procedures, and results must be carefully interpreted.

STRUCTURES The internal organizational properties or schemata that children have that explain their capacity for thought at given ages.

SWADDLING Wrapping or binding in bandages, swathing, or restraining and restricting.

SYMBOLIC FUNCTION A function that allows infants to begin internally representing objects and events and to begin solving problems. In other words, the symbolic function separates thought from action. Also called semiotic function.

SYMBOLIC PLAY A form of play in which a child takes an object and uses it to represent something else

SYNTHESIZING Putting the pieces of the analysis together to make predictions, solve problems, or create new hypotheses.

TEACHABLE MOMENT An opportunity for teaching and learning during a spontaneous event.

TEMPERAMENT A person's characteristic or generalized ways of functioning or responding.

THERAPEUTIC PLAY Play designed to facilitate the emotional and physical recovery of children who are hospitalized or who have experienced some disease or disorder. Typically, the facilitator is a specialist.

UNCONDITIONAL POSITIVE REGARD The display of care for someone without regard to their behavior, which tells the person that she is worthy of care, trust, and support: "You are a good person, and I care about you. I may not always like your behavior, but I like *you*."

UTOPIAN Excellent or ideal, but existing only in visionary or impractical thought or theory.

VERNACULAR The standard native language of a country or locality.

WET-NURSING The suckling of another woman's child.

WRAPAROUND PROGRAM A program designed to provide services to children during the hours when their primary program does not operate. For example, when a community offers half-day Head Start, a child-care center may provide services early in the morning and all afternoon, during the times when many parents are working.

REFERENCES

Abrahamse, D. (1979). Images of childhood in early Byzantine hagiography. *Journal of Psychohistory, 6* (4), 497–517.

ACEI. (1996, Summer). ACEI membership benefits guide. *Childhood Education, 72* (5).

Administration for Children and Families. (1997, March 17). *The 1997 family income guidelines* (Information Memorandum. Log No. ACYF-IM-HS-97.) Washington, DC: Originating office: Head Start Bureau.

American Telephone and Telegraph. (1998). Home page: Technology terms. In *Learning Network community guide,* p. 29. AT&T Learning Network and Scholastic, Inc.

American Telephone and Telegraph. (1998). Road map. In *Learning Network community guide,* pp. 5–6. AT&T Learning Network and Scholastic, Inc.

Aries, P. (1962). *Centuries of childhood: A social history of family life.* New York: Knopf.

Association for Constructivist Teaching. (1995). A.C.T. is . . . . *The Constructivist, 10* (4), 3.

Ayers, W. (Ed.). (1995). *To become a teacher: Making a difference in children's lives.* New York: Teachers College Press.

Azer, S. L. (1997). *Creating and using core knowledge/competencies.* The Center for Career Development in Early Care and Education. Boston: Wheelock College.

Barclay, W. (1959). *Train up a child: Educational ideals in the ancient world.* Philadelphia: Westminster Press.

Bar-Ilan, M. (1996). The emergence of childhood: A criteria from antiquity [On-line]. Abstract at **http://faculty.biu.ac.il/~barilm/absyaldu.html**.

Barnes, D. (1992). Influences of Ancient Greeks. In L. R. Williams & D. P. Fromberg (Eds.), *Encyclopedia of early childhood education,* pp. 16–18. New York: Garland.

Bergen, D. (1992). Defining a profession and developing professionals. *Journal of Early Childhood Teacher Education, 42* (13), 3.

Berthoff, A. E. (1978). *Forming/thinking/writing: The composing imagination.* Portsmouth, NH: Boynton/Cook.

Blasi, M. J. (1998). Preparing preservice teachers to work with children and families of promise. Unpublished doctoral dissertation, Arizona State University, Tempe, AZ.

Branscombe, N., & Taylor, J. (1988). I wanna write jes like in dat book: Talk and its role in the shared journal experience. In M. Lightfoot & N. Martin (Eds.), *The word for teaching is learning.* Portsmouth, NH: Heinemann.

Braun, S. J., & Edwards, E. P. (1972). *History and theory of early childhood education.* Belmont, CA: Wadsworth.

Brazelton, T. (1974). *Toddlers and parents: A declaration of independence.* New York: Dell.

Bredekamp, S. (Ed). (1987). *Developmentally appropriate practice in early childhood programs serving children from birth through age 8.* (Expanded ed.). Washington, DC: NAEYC.

Bredekamp, S. (1991a). *Guide to accreditation.* Washington, DC.: National Academy of Early Childhood Programs.

Bredekamp, S. (1991b). A vision for early childhood professional development. *Young Children, 47* (1), 35–37.

Bredekamp, S., & Copple, C. (Eds.). (1997). *Developmentally appropriate practice in early childhood programs* (Rev. ed.). Washington, DC: NAEYC.

Bredekamp, S., & Rosegrant, T. (Eds.). (1992). *Reaching potentials: Appropriate curriculum and assessment for young children* (Vol. 1). Washington, DC: NAEYC.

Bredekamp, S., & Willer, B. (1992). Of ladders and lattices, cores and cones: Conceptualizing an early childhood professional development system. *Young Children, 47* (3), 47–50.

Brown, B. (1985). Head Start: How research changed public policy. *Young Children, 40* (5), 9–13.

Cartwright, S. (1988). Play can be the building blocks of learning. *Young Children, 43,* 44–46.

Castle, K., & Rogers, K. (1993/94). Rule-creating in a constructivist classroom community. *Childhood Education, 70* (2), 77–80.

Center for Establishing Dialogue in Teaching and Learning. (nd). Membership application, p. 1.

Chaille, C., & Britain, L. (1997). *The young child as scientist: A constructivist approach to early childhood science education* (2nd ed.). New York: Longman, an imprint of McGraw-Hill.

Chaille, C., & Silvern, S. (1996). Understanding through play. *Childhood Education, 72* (5), 274–277.

Children's Defense Fund. (1998). *The state of America's children yearbook.* Washington, DC: Children's Defense Fund.

Christine, C. M. (1991). Network: The history of SMILE and CED. *The whole language umbrella catalogue.* New York: Addison Wesley Longman.

Classroom Connect. (1998). *Internet education catalog.* Torrance, CA: Classroom Connect.

Clement, R. (1991). *Counting on Frank.* Milwaukee: Gareth Stevens.

Clements, D. H. (1987). Computers and young children: A review of the research. *Young Children, 43* (1), 34–44.

Clements, D. H. (1994). The uniqueness of the computer as a learning tool: Insights from research and practice. In J. L. Wright & D. D. Shade (Eds.), *Young children: Active learners in a technological age* (pp. 31–50). Washington, DC: NAEYC.

Clements, D. H., Nastasi, B. K., & Swaminathan, S. (1993). Young children and computers: Crossroads and directions from research, *Young Children, 48* (2), 56–64.

Clements, D. H., & Swaminathan, S. (1995). Technology and school change: New lamps for old? *Childhood Education, 71* (5), 275–281.

Craig, S. E. (1992, September). The educational needs of children living with violence. *Phi Delta Kappan, 74* (1), 67–71.

Cunningham, C., & Osborn, D. (1979). A historical examination of blacks in early childhood education. *Young Children, 34* (3), 20–29.

Delpit, L. (1995) *Other people's children: Cultural conflict in the classroom.* New York: The New Press.

deMause, L. (1982). *Foundations of psychohistory.* New York: Creative Roots.

deMause, L. (1999a). Childhood and cultural evolution. *Journal of Psychohistory, 26* (3), 642–723.

deMause, L. (1999b). Woman and children at the cutting edge of historical change. **http://www.bconnex.net/~cspec/crime prevention/cutting.htm**.

DeVries, R., & Kohlberg, L. (1987). *Programs of early childhood.* New York: Longman.

DeVries, R., & Zan, B. (1994). *Moral classrooms, moral children.* New York: Teachers College Press.

Duckworth, E. (1987). *The having of wonderful ideas and other essays on teaching and learning.* New York: Teachers College Press.

Edwards, C. P. (1986). *Promoting social and moral development in young children.* New York: Teachers College Press.

Feeney, S., & Kipnis, K. (1992). *Code of ethical conduct and statement of commitment.* Washington, DC: NAEYC.

Fuerst, J. S., & Petty, R. (1996, June). The best use of federal funds for early childhood education. *Phi Delta Kappan, 77* (10), 676–678.

Fulwiler, T. (Ed.). (1987). *The journal book.* Portsmouth, NH: Heinemann.

Garbarino, J. (1992). *Children in danger: Coping with the consequences of community violence.* San Francisco: Jossey-Bass.

Gonzalez-Mena, J., & Eyer, D. (1997). *Infants, toddlers, and caregivers* (4th ed.). Mountain View, CA: Mayfield.

Gruber, H. E., & Voneche, J. J. (Eds.). (1995). *The essential Piaget.* Northvale, NJ: Aronson.

Gutek, G. (1972). *History of the Western educational experience* (Paul Nash, consulting ed.). New York: Random House.

Haugland, S. (1995). Classroom activities provide important support to children's computer experiences. *Early Childhood Education Journal, 23* (2), 99–100.

Haugland, S. W., & Shade, D. D. (1990). *Developmental evaluations of software for young children.* New York: Delmar.

Haugland, S. (1998). The best developmental software for young children. *Early Childhood Education, 25* (4), 247–254.

Havighurst, R. J. (1972). *Developmental tasks and education* (3rd ed.). New York: McKay.

Head Start Program; Final Rule, 61 Fed. Reg. 215 (1996) (45 C.F.R. Part 1301).

Heath, S. B. (1983). *Ways with words: Language, life, and work in communities and classrooms.* New York: Cambridge University Press.

Hilliard, A. (1992). African influences. In L. R. Williams & D. P. Fromberg (Eds.), *Encyclopedia of early childhood education.* New York: Garland.

Hunton, A. (1908). The NACW: Its real significance. *Colored American Magazine, 14* (7), 417–422.

Inhelder, B., de Caprona, D., & Cornu-Wells, A. (1987). *Piaget today.* Hillsdale, NJ: Erlbaum.

International Society for Technology in Education. (1999). *Educational software preview guide.* Eugene: University of Oregon.

Isenberg, J. P., & Jalongo, M. R. (Eds.). (1997). *Major trends and issues in early childhood education: Challenges, controversies, and insights.* New York: Teachers College Press.

Isenberg, J., & Quisenberry, N. (1988). *Play: A necessity for all children.* Wheaton, MD: ACEI.

Johnson, G. D. (1990, Spring). A multidimensional theory of early modern Western childhood. *Journal of Comparative Family Studies, 21* (1), 1–11.

Jung, C. G., & Kerenyi, C. (1963). *Essays on a science of mythology.* Princeton, NJ: Princeton University Press.

Kagan, S. L. (1994, November). Readying schools for young children: Polemics and priorities. *Phi Delta Kappan, 76* (3), 226–233.

Kamii, C. (1985, November 14). Turning out autonomous teachers in a heteronomous world. Keynote address at the annual conference of the National Association of Early Childhood Teacher Education, New Orleans, LA.

Kamii, C. (1986). *Number in preschool and kindergarten.* Washington, DC: NAEYC.

Kamii, C. (1991). Toward autonomy: The importance of critical thinking and choice making. *School Psychology Review, 20* (3) 382–388.

Kamii, C. (1992). Autonomy as the aim of constructivist education: How can it be fostered? In D. G. Murphy & S. G. Goffin (Eds.), *Project Construct, a curriculum guide: Understanding the possibilities,* pp. 9–14. Jefferson City, MO: Department of Elementary and Secondary Education.

Kamii, C., & DeClark, G. (1985). *Young children reinvent arithmetic.* New York: Teachers College Press.

Kamii, C., & Ewing, J. K. (1996). Basing teaching on Piaget's constructivism. *Childhood Education, 72* (5), 260–264.

Katz, L. G., & McClellan, D. E. (1997). *Fostering children's social competencies: The teacher's role.* Washington, DC: NAEYC.

Katz, M. (1971). *Class, bureaucracy, and schools: The illusion of educational change in America.* New York: Praeger.

Katz, P. (1983). Developmental foundations of gender and racial attitudes. In R. L. Leahy (Ed.), *The child's construction of social inequity.* New York: Academic Press.

Kohn, A. (1993). *Punished by rewards.* New York: Houghton Mifflin.

Koralek, D. G., Colker, L. J., & Dodge, D. T. (1993). *The what, why, and how of high-quality early childhood education: A guide for on-site supervision.* Washington, DC: NAEYC.

Kroll, J. (1977). The concept of childhood in the middle ages. *Journal of the History of the Behavioral Sciences, 13,* 384–393.

Langer, W. (1974). Infanticide: A historical survey. *History of Childhood Quarterly: The Journal of Psychohistory, 1* (2), 353–365.

Lazerson, M. (1972). The historical antecedents of early childhood education. In *National Society for the Study of Education, 71st Yearbook, Part II.* Excerpts published in *The Encyclopedia of Education* (Macmillan, 1971).

Lee, G. (1982). *Family structure and interaction: A comparative analysis.* (2nd rev. ed.). Minneapolis: University of Minnesota Press.

Manno, B., Finn, C., Jr., Bierlein, L., & Vanourek, G. (1998, March). How charter schools are different: Lessons and implications from a national study. *Phi Delta Kappan, 79* (7), 489–498.

Marcon, R. (1992, December). Differential effects of three preschool models on inner-city 4-year-olds. *Early Childhood Research Quarterly, 7* (4), 513–530.

McLerran, A. (1991). *Roxaboxen.* New York: Morrow.

Meddlin, B. J., & Rosen, A. L. (1986). Child abuse and neglect. *Young Children, 41* (4), 182–184.

Milone, M. N., Jr., & Salpeter, J. (1996, January). Technology and equity issues. *Technology and Learning,* 38–47.

Montana Early Care and Education Career Development. (1998). *Professionalism: Montana early child care and education knowledge base,* pp. 23–25. Bozeman: Montana State University.

Morris, S. (1992). Plato. In L. Williams & D. Fromberg (Eds.), *Encyclopedia of early childhood education* (p. 19). New York: Garland.

Murdock, G. P. (1949). *Social structure.* New York: Macmillan.

NAEYC. (1989). *Code of ethical conduct.* Washington, DC: NAEYC.

NAEYC. (1991). *Accreditation criteria and procedures of the National Academy of Early Childhood Programs.* Washington, DC: NAEYC.

NAEYC. (1996). *Guidelines for preparation of early childhood professionals.* Washington, DC: NAEYC.

NAEYC & NAECS/SDE (National Association of Early Childhood Specialists in State Departments of Education). (1992). Guidelines for appropriate curriculum content and assessment in programs serving children ages 3 through 8. In S. Bredekamp & T. Rosegrant (Eds.), *Reaching potentials: Appropriate curriculum and assessment for young children* (Vol.1) (pp. 9–27). Washington, DC: NAEYC.

NAEYC. (1993, July). Position statement: Violence in the lives of young children. *Young Children, 48* (6), 80–84.

NAEYC. (1996, September). Position statement: Technology and young children—ages 3 through 8. *Young Children, 51* (6), 11–16.

National Academy of Early Childhood Programs. (1991). *Guide to accreditation by the National Academy of Early Childhood Programs* (Rev. ed.). Washington, DC: NAEYC.

National Center for Early Development and Learning. (1997, Summer). *Early childhood research and policy briefs.* (Vol. 1, No. 1, CBH8185). Chapel Hill: Frank P. Graham Child Development Center, University of North Carolina.

Nunez, R., & Collignon, K. (1997, October). Creating a community of learning for homeless children. *Educational Leadership,* 56–60.

Opie, I., & Opie, P. (1992). *I saw Esau: The schoolchild's pocket book.* Cambridge, MA: Candlewick Press.

Osborn, K. (1991). *Early childhood education in historical perspective* (3rd ed.). Athens, GA: Daye Press.

Paley, V. (1981). *Wally's stories.* Cambridge, MA: Harvard University Press.

Papert, S. (1993). *The children's machine: Rethinking school in the age of the computer.* New York: Basic Books.

Parry, A. (1993). Children surviving in a violent world—"Choosing non-violence." *Young Children, 48* (6), 13–15.

Parten, M. (1932). Social play among preschool children. *Journal of Abnormal and Social Psychology, 27,* 243–269.

Pearce, J. (1977). *Magical child.* New York: Dutton.

Phillips, D. A. (Ed.). (1995). *Child care for low income families: Summary of two workshops.* Washington, DC: National Academy Press.

Piaget, J. (1932/1965). *The moral judgment of the child.* New York: Free Press.

Piaget, J. (1948/1974). *To understand is to invent.* New York: Viking.

Piaget, J. (1954/1981). *Intelligence and affectivity: Their relation during child development.* Palo Alto, CA: Annual Reviews.

Piaget, J. (1963). *The psychology of intelligence.* Totowa, NJ: Littlefield, Adams.

Piaget, J. (1981). Creativity. In J. Gallagher & K. Reid (Eds.), *The learning theory of Piaget and Inhelder* (pp. 221–229). Pacific Grove, CA: Brooks-Cole.

Piaget, J., & Inhelder, B. (1969). *The psychology of the child* (H. Weaver, trans.). New York: Basic Books.

Postman, N. (1982). *The disappearance of childhood.* New York: Delacorte.

Powell, D.R. (1998). Reweaving parents into the fabric of early childhood programs. *Young Children, 53* (5), 60–67.

Project Construct National Center (n.d.). Publicity flier. Columbia: Missouri Department of Elementary and Secondary Education.

Robinson, V. B. (1996, Spring). Cognitive development of children four through six years of age: Implications for the classroom. *Kindergarten Education: Theory, Research, and Practice, 1* (1), 11–27.

Rogers, F. (1994). That which is essential is invisible to the eye. *Young Children, 49* (5), 33.

Roorbach, G. (1997, February 2). Mommy, what's a classroom? *New York Times Magazine,* section 6.

Rose, D., & Smith, B. (1994, September). Providing public education services to preschoolers with disabilities in community-based programs: Who's responsible for what? *Young Children, 49* 64–66.

Ryan, K., & Cooper, J. M. (1995). *Those who* can, *teach* (7th ed.). Boston: Houghton Mifflin.

Schweinhart, L. (1994, January). *Lasting benefits of preschool programs.* (ERIC Document Reproduction Service No. EDO-PS-94-2.)

Schweinhart, L. J., Barnes, H. V., & Weikart, D. P. (1993). Significant benefits: The High/Scope Perry preschool study through age 27. *Monographs of the High/Scope Educational Research Foundation, 10.* Ypsilanti, MI: High/Scope Press, PS 021 998.

Schweinhart, L., & Weikart, D. (1997). The High/Scope preschool curriculum comparison study through age 23. *Early Childhood Research Quarterly, 12* (2), 117–143.

Sendak, M. (1963). *Where the wild things are.* New York: Harper and Row.

Seuling, B. (1978). *The teeny, tiny woman.* New York: Puffin Books.

Sinclair, H. (1995, March). *Piaget* [Videotaped lecture]. Auburn University College of Education, Auburn, AL.

Smith, D. C. (1991). Foundations of modern Chinese education and the Taiwan experience. In D. C. Smith (Ed.), *The Confucian continuum: Educational modernization in Taiwan,* pp. 1–61. New York: Pacific Cultural Foundation.

Snider, S. L., & Badgett, T. L. (1995). "I have this computer, what do I do now?" Using technology to enhance every child's learning. *Early Childhood Education Journal, 23* (2), 101–105.

Software Toolworks. (1992). *The San Diego zoo presents: The animals.* Novato, CA.

South Carolina's early care and education credentialing and professional development system. (1997). Center for Childcare Career Development, Greenville, SC.

Spodek, B., & Brown, P. (1993). Curriculum alternatives in early childhood education: A historical perspective. In B. Spodek (Ed.), *Handbook of research on the education of young children,* pp. 91–104. New York: Macmillan.

Stroud, M. (1993). *Reaching the children: In celebration of the rights of the child.* New York: United States Committee for UNICEF.

Surbeck, E. (1998). Challenges of preparing to work in collaborative early childhood settings. *Early Childhood Education Journal, 26* (1), 53–55.

Taylor, J. B. (1984). Shared writing experience. Paper presented at the Alabama Department of Education Early Childhood Workshop, Montgomery, AL.

Texas core knowledge and skills in early care and education. (1998). Application packet for trainer registration, Texas early care and education career development system initiative. Texas Head Start State Collaboration Office, Dana Center, University of Texas at Austin, Austin, Texas.

Thoreau, H. D. (1854/1995). *Walden.* Boston: Houghton Mifflin.

Toffler, A. (1990). *Powershift: Knowledge, wealth and violence at the edge of the 21st century.* New York: Bantam.

Trawick-Smith, J. (1997). *Early childhood development: A multicultural perspective.* Upper Saddle River, NJ: Prentice-Hall.

Van Allsburg, C. (1988). *Two bad ants.* Boston: Houghton Mifflin.

Van Horn, R. (1995, March). Power tools. *Phi Delta Kappan, 76* (7), 572–575.

Verstegen, D.A. (1994, November). The new wave of school finance litigation. *Phi Delta Kappan, 76* (3), 243–250.

von Glasersfeld, E. (1995). A constructivist approach to teaching. In L. Steffe & J. Gale (Eds.), *Constructivism in education.* Hillsdale, NJ: Erlbaum.

Wadsworth, B. J. (1996). *Piaget's theory of cognitive and affective development* (5th ed.). New York: Longman.

Weiser, M. G. (1991). *Infant/toddler care and education.* New York: Macmillan.

Whitin, D., & Wilde, S. (1992). *Read any good math lately?* Portsmouth, NH: Heinemann.

Whitin, P., & Whitin, D. J. (1997). *Inquiry at the window: Pursuing the wonders of learners.* Portsmouth, NH: Heinemann.

Williams, L. R., & Fromberg, D. P. (Eds.). (1992). *Encyclopedia of early childhood education.* New York: Garland.

Williams, M. (1922/1969). *The velveteen rabbit.* Garden City, NY: Doubleday.

Witherspoon, A., & Warnke, F. (1963). *Seventeenth-century prose and poetry* (2nd ed.). New York: Harcourt Brace.

Wolery, M., & Wilbers, J. (1994). Including children with special needs in early childhood programs. *Research Monograph of the National Association for the Education of Young Children.* Vol. 6. Washington, DC: NAEYC.

Wright, J. L. (1994). Listen to the children: Observing young children's discoveries with the microcomputer. In J. L. Wright & D. D. Shade (Eds.), *Young children: Active learners in a technological age* (pp. 3–17). Washington, DC: NAEYC.

Yang, H. (1992). Asian influences. In L. R. Williams & D. P. Fromberg (Eds.), *Encyclopedia of early childhood education* (pp. 13–14). New York: Garland.

Yates, J. (1905). Kindergarten and mother's clubs. *Colored American Magazine, 8* (6), 304–311.

Zigler, E., & Styfco, S. (Eds.). (1993). *Head Start and beyond: A national plan for early childhood intervention.* New Haven, CT: Yale University Press.

ACKNOWLEDGMENTS

Seri Azer, *Creating and Using Core Knowledge/Competencies,* 1997. Reprinted with permission.

Linda Bowen. Tornado web and list of tornado project activities. Reprinted by permission of Linda Bowen.

S. Bredekamp and C. Copple, "Developmentally Appropriate Practice in Early Childhood Programs," ©1997. Washington, D.C.: NAEYC. Reprinted by permission of the publisher

S. Bredekamp and B. Willer, "Of Ladders and Lattices, Cores and Cones: Conceptualizing an Early Childhood Professional Development System" *Young Children,* 47 (3), 1992, pp. 47-50. Reprinted with permission from the National Association for the Education of Young Children.

Kathryn Castle and Karen Rogers. "Rule-Creating in a Constructivist Classroom Community," *Childhood Education,* Winter, 1993-1994, pp. 77-80. Reprinted by permission of the Association for Childhood Education International.

Christine Chaille and Lory Britain, "Constructivist Teacher Roles" from *The Young Child as Scientist* by Christine Chaille and Lory Britain. Copyright 1991 by HarperCollins Publishers, Inc. Reprinted by permission of Addison Wesley Educational Publishers, Inc.

Carol Christine. Description of the history of a local center run by and for teachers. Reprinted by permission of Carol J. Christine.

Lloyd deMause, "Childhood and Cultural Evolution," *The Journal of Psychohistory,* 26 (3), 1999, pp. 642-723. Reprinted by permission of the author.

R. DeVries and B. Zan, "Setting Up a Sociomoral Classroom," excerpts reprinted by permission of the publisher from R. DeVries & B. Zan, *Moral Classroom, Moral Children: Creating a Constructivist Atmosphere in Early Education* (New York: Teachers College Press, ©1994 by Teachers College, Columbia University. All rights reserved.), pp. 58-62.

S. Feeney and K. Kipnis, "Code of Ethical Conduct" and "Statement of Commitment," ©1992. Washington, D.C.: NAEYC. Reprinted by permission of the publisher.

Laura Hines, "Multiple Perspectives: From the Field." Reprinted by permission of Laura Hines Wilhelm.

Joan Isenberg and Nancy Quisenberry, *Play: A Necessity for All Children.* Wheaton: MD: ACEI, 1988. Reprinted by permission of the Association for Childhood Education International.

Constance Kamii, illustration of war cards. Reprinted by permission of Constance Kamii.

Constance Kamii. Excerpt from Constance Kamii, "Toward Autonomy: The Importance of Critical Thinking and Choice Making," *School Psychology Review,* 20, 1991, pp. 382-399. Reprinted by permission of Constance Kamii.

Alfie Kohn. Excerpts from *Punished by Rewards.* Copyright ©1993 by Alfie Kohn. Reprinted by permission of Houghton Mifflin Company. All rights reserved.

Alfie Kohn, from "Benefits of Choice" and "Giving Choices," *Phi Delta Kappan,* 75 (1), September 1993, pp. 8-20. Reprinted by permission of Alfie Kohn.

NAEYC. "Reaching Potentials: Appropriate Curriculum and Assessment for Young Children." Position Statement on Violence," "Position Statement on Technology," "Child Abuse and Neglect: Prevention and Reporting," "Developmentally Appropriate Practice in Early Childhood Programs," "Children Surviving in a Violent World: Choosing Non-Violence." Reprinted by permission of the National Association for the Education of Young Children.

Iona and Peter Opie, extracts from *I Saw Esau* text ©1992 Iona Opie. Illustrations ©1992 Maurice Sendak. Reproduced by permission of Walker Books Ltd. Published in the U.S. and Canada by Candlewick Press Inc., Cambridge, MA.

Vivian Gussin Paley, excerpts from *Wally's Stories* reprinted by permission of the publisher from *Wally's Stories* by Vivian Gussin Paley. Cambridge, MA: Harvard University Press, Copyright 1981 by the President and Fellows of Harvard College.

M. Parten, from "Social Play among Preschool Children," *Journal of Abnormal and Social Psychology,* 27, pp. 243-269.

"Principles of Therapeutic Support for Children Exposed to Trauma." Reprinted by permission of the Child Witness to Violence Project.

Sarah Rother, "Infant Room Daily Report Form" designed by Marti White. Reprinted by permission of Sarah Rother.

"Self-Assessment Scale," "Personal Attributes/Characteristics," and "Professionalism" from Montana Early Care and Education Knowledge Base, 1998. Reprinted by permission.

Kimberly Waak, "Infant Room Daily Report Form" designed by Marti White. Reprinted by permission of Kimberly Waak.

Excerpts from "Pepys Diary," "Childhood," and "Of Parents and Children" from A. Witherspoon and F. Warnke, *Seventeenth Century Prose and Poetry.* Copyright ©1963.